MW01258453

Barton
S T O N E

Barton
STONE

A Spiritual Biography

D. Newell Williams

Chalice Press
St. Louis, Missouri

Cover Art: Bronze medallion of Barton Stone © Christian Church (Disciples of Christ)
Cover Design: Lynne Condellone
Art Director: Michael Domínguez
Interior Design: Wynn Younker

This book is printed on acid-free, recycled paper.

Visit Chalice Press on the World Wide Web at
www.chalicepress.com

10 9 8 7 6 5 4 3 2 1   00 01 02 03

Library of Congress Cataloging–in–Publication Data

(Pending)

Printed in the United States of America

For Mac, Coert, and Errett

Contents

Acknowledgments

During my second year as a student at Vanderbilt Divinity School, I became convinced that genuine Christian faith could only be the result of a miraculous or extraordinary experience of the Holy Spirit. This was a deeply troubling conclusion for me. Although I believed that I loved God and that I regularly enjoyed communion with God, I was quite sure that I had never had such an experience. That same year I discovered that Barton Warren Stone, host of one of the most famous revival meetings in American history and a "founder" of my own denomination, the Christian Church (Disciples of Christ), had once been troubled by a similar belief but had rejected it in favor of the view that genuine Christian faith comes through the Spirit's communication of the gospel of Jesus Christ. I accepted Stone's position and reclaimed my identity as a Christian. This was the beginning, now twenty-seven years ago, of my appreciation for the spirituality of Barton Warren Stone.

This book would not have been written without the encouragement, support, and help of many persons stretching back over many years. I remain grateful to Herman A. Norton and Richard C. Wolf, the Vanderbilt professors who introduced me to Stone, and to Daniel and Sandra Ellis-Killian, Nadia M. Lahutsky, Edward L. McMahon, John J. Turner, and Helen Lee Turner, Vanderbilt classmates and friends who encouraged my early study of Stone. As a teacher at Brite Divinity School of Texas Christian University and now at Christian Theological Seminary, I have benefited much from the responses of students to their encounters with Stone in courses that I have taught in American church history. One of those students, James P. Grimshaw, helped me to review the secondary literature on Stone at an early stage of my research for this book. Former student T. Wyatt Watkins, an American Baptist pastor and writer, read the manuscript as it emerged chapter by chapter, offering constructive comments and encouragement.

Much of the research and writing of this book were accomplished during research leaves that I completed in 1994 and in the fall of 1998. I am grateful to the Trustees of Christian Theological Seminary for the seminary's generous research leave policy and to the administration and faculty of the seminary for supporting my requests to work on this project. A CTS faculty writers group composed of Charles W. Allen, Ronald J. Allen, Frank Burch Brown, Brian W. Grant, Felicity B. Kelcourse, Dan P. Moseley, and Marti J. Steussy read and commented constructively on portions of the manuscript. CTS Dean

Clark M. Williamson honored my desire to complete the manuscript by the summer of 1999 by granting me an unusually light load of committee assignments for the spring of 1999.

Historians James O. Duke and Mark G. Toulouse of Brite Divinity School and Richard L. Harrison, Jr., of Lexington Theological Seminary read the entire manuscript and made helpful suggestions regarding the treatment of particular topics and matters of style and organization. I highly value their collegiality and good judgment. Secretary to the CTS faculty Joyce Krauser also reviewed the manuscript and made many valuable suggestions for improving the text. Jon L. Berquist of Chalice Press has been supportive at every stage of the project.

Finally, I express deep and abiding appreciation to my spouse, Sue McDougal, who read and critically commented on more than one draft of this book and supported my work on this manuscript in many other ways. The dedication is to our children, David McDougal Williams, Richard Coert Williams, and Lelia Errett Williams, who have demonstrated a surprising degree of respect for their father's commitment to writing this book. My hope is that it will enable them, and others, to appreciate Barton Warren Stone–in particular, Stone's integrity and his enjoyment and love of God.

Introduction:
A Spiritual Biography

Barton Warren Stone (1772–1844) was a leader of the remarkable growth of Christianity in the early American Republic. From 1800 to 1835 the number of Americans associated with churches increased from 40 to 75 percent of the United States population. Reared in Maryland and Virginia, Stone was host in August of 1801 to a six-day ecumenical camp meeting at Cane Ridge, Kentucky, that has been called America's Pentecost. Reports spread throughout America of thousands in attendance and persons "falling" under the influence of the Holy Spirit, triggering similar meetings in northern Georgia and the Carolinas. In 1803, Stone and four other promoters of the Great Revival in the West (1797–1805) separated from the Presbyterian Synod of Kentucky over their view of how God works in conversion. Stone also advanced interpretations of the significance of Christ's death and of Christ's divinity that challenged the traditional theology of most of his former Presbyterian colleagues. Influenced by millennial hopes born of the revival, Stone and the other ministers who separated from the synod disbanded their independent Springfield Presbytery in 1804, eschewing all names but "Christian." In 1805 two members of the former Springfield Presbytery joined the Shakers, who taught that the millennium had begun for all who would renounce their sins and adopt celibacy. Stone vigorously opposed the influence of the Shakers. A tireless advocate of Christian unity, Stone led many of the Christians to unite in 1832 with the followers of Alexander Campbell, known as Reformers or Disciples of Christ. By 1860 the movement, variously known as Christian Churches, Disciples of Christ, and Churches of Christ, was the fifth largest religious group in America, with a membership of nearly 200,000. Prior to the revival, Stone emancipated two slaves he inherited from his mother. He later supported the colonization scheme for ending slavery in America and ultimately endorsed the call for immediate abolition issued by the abolitionists of the 1830s. In order to allow for the liberation of slaves willed to his wife and their children, Stone moved his family from Kentucky to Illinois in 1834. In the 1840s, millennial hopes, coupled with growing disillusionment with the social and spiritual effects of the American political system, led Stone to recommend that Christians withdraw from civil government and to endorse pacifism.

Historians have recognized Stone as a significant figure in the religious history of the early American Republic. However, not all that has been published regarding Stone's background and religious leadership is accurate. In *The Democratization of American Christianity*, Nathan O. Hatch includes Stone in a list of leaders "without formal training…[who] went outside normal denominational frameworks to develop large followings by the democratic art of persuasion."[1] It is true that Stone traveled extensively to establish and nurture congregations in Kentucky, Ohio, and Tennessee and that he conducted much of his ministry through print. However, Stone did not lack formal training for the ministry. He completed a liberal education in North Carolina and received a standard Presbyterian theological education under the direction of North Carolina's Orange Presbytery. In addition to reading Latin and Greek, he later completed a course in Hebrew. Neither did Stone operate outside of a normal denominational framework. Although Stone and his colleagues dissolved their Springfield Presbytery, they established Christian Conferences that licensed and ordained candidates for the ministry and discussed issues pertaining to the life of the churches such as baptism, the ownership of slaves, and the acceptable limits of theological diversity.

Hatch also refers to Stone as one of several authors who emerged from "less-than-respectable ranks to produce forms of genuinely popular print."[2] According to nineteenth-century Presbyterian historian Robert Davidson, Stone's "simple, unambitious style, totally innocent of rhetorical embellishments, and plain occasionally to slovenliness" was "suited to the minds he sought to reach—the shrewd, though uneducated, mass of the people."[3] Nevertheless, Stone did not emerge from the lower ranks of society. Though Stone's mother was widowed when Stone was two years old and moved from Maryland to the western frontier of Virginia during the Revolutionary War, the family retained more than ten slaves and was clearly in the upper range of what Revolutionary War–era Americans called the "middling" rank of society.

Quoting Stone's confession that from his earliest recollection he "drank deeply into the spirit of liberty," Hatch argues that what set Stone and leaders of related groups apart from earlier revivalists was "the extent to which they wrestled self-consciously with the loss of traditional sources of authority and found in democratic political culture a cornerstone for new foundations." Hatch claims that, "taking seriously the mandate of liberty and equality," the Christians (1) placed laity and clergy on equal footing and exalted the conscience of the individual believer over the collective will of any congregation or church organization; (2) rejected the traditions of learned theology and called for a

---

[1]Nathan O. Hatch, *The Democratization of American Christianity* (New Haven, Conn.: Yale University Press, 1989), 13, 57.
[2]Ibid., 143.
[3]Robert Davidson, *History of the Presbyterian Church in the State of Kentucky: With a Preliminary Sketch of the Church in the Valley of Virginia* (New York: Robert Carter, 1847), 204.

new view of history that welcomed inquiry and innovation; and (3) called for a populist interpretation of the scriptures premised on the inalienable right of all persons to understand the Bible for themselves.[4] Stone clearly was willing to think for himself and frequently advised his readers to examine his views according to their own reading of the scriptures. Nevertheless, he maintained a Presbyterian view of ministerial authority, arguing that the ordaining of ministers and the trial of ministers charged with heresy was the responsibility of ordained ministers, rather than the laity. Moreover, Stone's disillusionment with the American political system began with his observation of the participation of ministers in the popular electioneering of the 1820s. Far from celebrating the rough and tumble of the emerging democratic order, Stone exclaimed, "My soul sickens" to see ministers "reviling the rulers of the people—speaking reproachfully of prominent men—and extolling their favorites to the skies."[5]

Stone receives attention, as well, in Paul Conkin's *Cane Ridge: America's Pentecost*. Conkin argues that, given Stone's ultimate rejection of the doctrine of predestination, he might have been a Methodist, except for his having been converted by Presbyterians.[6] According to the doctrine of predestination, God had chosen certain particular persons to believe the gospel and thus be saved and others to be damned. To be sure, Methodists rejected the doctrine of predestination, as ultimately did Stone. Conkin, however, fails to recognize Stone's *Presbyterian* spirituality. Presbyterians emphasized the transformation of the heart or will by a rational perception of the moral excellence of the God who saves helpless sinners, while eschewing the personal assurances of forgiveness and conversion received through visions and dreams so greatly prized by early American Methodists. Stone, who taught for a time in a Methodist academy and even traveled to a Methodist conference in the company of the leading Methodist preacher Hope Hull, had ample opportunity to become a Methodist prior to his ordination. Stone, who as Conkin notes never embraced visions and dreams, chose to seek ordination as a Presbyterian despite his questions regarding the doctrine of predestination.[7]

Conkin concludes that Stone eventually rejected the doctrine of predestination because (1) he could not accept that salvation "is never, in any possible sense, earned" and (2) he could not believe that human beings were "so helpless" in relation to their salvation. Stone's theology was influenced by the common-sense rationalism of the early American Republic. According to common sense, propositions that contradicted themselves could not be true. One such proposition was the Presbyterian teaching that God loved sinners but had determined from all eternity that some sinners would be eternally damned. According to common sense, God loved sinners and desired that they be saved; or, God did not love sinners—at least not all sinners. Stone did not reject Presbyterian teaching because he believed that human beings earned

---

[4]Hatch, 73–78.

[5]Barton W. Stone and J. T. Johnson, eds., *Christian Messenger* 6 (August 1832), 251–52.

[6]Paul Conkin, *Cane Ridge: America's Pentecost* (Madison, Wis.: University of Wisconsin Press, 1990), 73–74, 102.

[7]Ibid., 131.

their salvation as Conkin argues. Rather, he rejected the part of Presbyterian teaching that said that God had chosen some sinners to be damned because, when viewed according to common sense, this seemed to deny God's love for sinners and, hence, the glory of the God who saved helpless sinners. In other words, for Stone and other Presbyterians influenced by the common-sense rationalism of the early Republic, the doctrine of predestination threatened their *Presbyterian* spirituality by denying their belief in of God's love for sinners.

Neither did Stone believe that human beings had any power to save themselves, although statements of Stone can be quoted in isolation from a broader reading of his writings to suggest that he did.[8] For Stone, as for his former Presbyterian colleagues who defended the doctrine of predestination, the sinner's *will,* or desire, had to be changed by the sinner's perception or recognition of the glory of the God who saved helpless sinners before the sinner would *choose* to be forgiven and spiritually renewed by God. This perception or recognition was given by God through the message of God's love in Jesus Christ. In contrast to his former Presbyterian colleagues, Stone *did* assert that sinners could *resist* God's transformation of their wills by closing their eyes to the graciousness of God revealed in Jesus Christ. This placed the fault for their damnation clearly on their own heads and thus relieved God of the charge of duplicity in claiming to love sinners while having determined that some sinners would be damned. For Stone, sinners remained helpless in relation to their salvation until God revealed the glory of God's self to them through the gospel. As for their faithfulness to God following conversion, Stone taught that human beings were dependent on God for the gift of the Holy Spirit, by which human beings were enabled to love both God and neighbor.

Contemporary society displays a widespread interest in spirituality, whether Christian or other. But that interest only minimally influenced this biography's focus on Stone's spirituality. Historians of Christianity must pay attention to spirituality if they are to fully describe their subject. Studies of Christianity such as Nathan Hatch's *The Democratization of American Christianity* are immensely helpful in sketching the broader context of Christianity in America and identifying continuities between seemingly very different religious movements. But they are not enough. To understand Christianity in America, spirituality must also be studied. This is not an easy assignment. I define spirituality as one's fundamental orientation to God. Spirituality, though distinguished from theology and practice, is never separate from theology and practice and never occurs outside of a particular context. One perceives spirituality through the study of theology and practice in their context. Conkin's *Cane Ridge: America's Pentecost* focuses on spirituality without naming that focus. However, as already noted, I believe that Conkin has failed to see the continuities between Stone's spirituality and the spirituality of Stone's "fathers" in the ministry and thus has misunderstood Stone.

---

[8]Hatch, 172–73.

There are two earlier biographies of Stone. The first was written by Stone himself in the spring of 1843. Seventy-nine pages in length, it tells the story of his life from his childhood through the union of the Christians with the Reformers in 1832. Although Stone's chronology is unreliable, his interpretation of his spiritual development and ministry is a valuable source for writing his biography. Moreover, it is the only source we have for some periods of his life. Other sources for writing Stone's biography are the series of pamphlets and books that he published beginning in 1804, the *Christian Messenger*–the monthly journal that he published, with some lapses, from 1826 until his death in 1844–the published responses of contemporaries to those publications, and firsthand reports and memoirs written by critics and associates of Stone. In most of these sources, one encounters inconsistencies in spelling, capitalization, and punctuation. I have not used [*sic*] or corrected errors in quotations except where required for clarity.

Stone's autobiography was published in 1847, three years after his death, along with "additions and reflections" assembled by the Christian preacher John Rogers. Included among Rogers' additions and reflections, which swelled the total length of the volume to 404 pages, was the *Apology of Springfield Presbytery*, in which Stone and his colleagues explained why they had renounced the jurisdiction of the Synod of Kentucky; poems and hymns composed by Stone; excerpts from Stone's writings in the *Christian Messenger* regarding slavery and preparation for the ministry; notices of Stone's death; testimonials to Stone's character as a husband, father, neighbor, and minister of the gospel; and a discussion of the "physical exercises" that had characterized the meetings of the Great Revival. Rogers, who saw himself as "preparing materials" for later historians, declared that the biography of Stone would be "rewritten at a future day, when time shall have extinguished the prejudices that partyism has excited against him; and when the Christian world will be disposed to award to him that position as a Reformer, and Christian, to which he is so justly entitled."[9]

The second biography of Stone, written by Charles C. Ware, was published in 1932. Ware traces Stone's genealogy, establishes the chronology of his life, and provides a wealth of information regarding persons and places named in Stone's autobiography. Identifying Stone as a "Pathfinder of Christian Unity," Ware, a Disciples of Christ minister, wished that Stone's spirit would be "known and loved as it was in his day. A double portion of his spirit," wrote Ware, "will help mightily in our day to the climax of Christ's drama of union."[10]

---

[9] Barton W. Stone, *The Biography of Eld. Barton Warren Stone, Written by Himself, with additions and Reflections by Eld. John Rogers* (Cincinnati: Published for the author by J. S. and U. P. James, 1847); reprinted in *The Cane Ridge Reader*, ed. Hoke S. Dickinson (n.p., 1972), preface.

[10] Charles C. Ware, *Barton Warren Stone, Pathfinder of Chrisitian Union* (St. Louis: Bethany Press, 1932), 10. For an analysis of the renewed interest of Disciples in Stone beginnning in the 1930s, see Anthony L. Dunnavant, "From Precursor of the Movement to Icon of Christian Unity: Barton W. Stone in the Memory of the Christian Church (Disciples of Christ)," in *Cane Ridge in Context: Perspectives on Barton W, Stone and the Revival*, ed. Anthony L. Dunnavant (Nashville: Disciples of Christ Historical Society, 1992), 9–15.

In addition to the two biographies, there have been several studies of Stone's theology and practice. William G. West's *Barton Warren Stone: Early American Advocate of Christian Unity*, based on West's Yale doctoral dissertation, was published in 1954. West shows that Christian unity was the "dominant passion" of Stone's life.[11] Unpublished dissertations include a study of Stone's preaching techniques by Evan Ulrey,[12] a study of Stone's social thought by David C. Roos,[13] and my own doctoral dissertation, which examines the theology of the Great Revival through Stone's life and thought.[14]

There have been few studies that focus on Stone's spirituality, other than his autobiography. In addition to an early article of mine, C. Leonard Allen and Richard T. Hughes have argued that Stone had an "apocalyptic worldview." Hughes defines his use of the term "apocalyptic" in regard to Stone's worldview as referring not to millennial theories or speculation about the second coming of Christ, but to "an outlook" that led Stone "to act as though the final rule of the kingdom of God were present in the here and now."[15]

The thesis of this biography is that no influence was greater in the development of Stone's theology and religious and social practice than his Presbyterian spirituality. That spirituality worshiped a God of love and grace revealed in the gospel of Jesus Christ, maintained a chastened view of human nature, and identified the knowledge, enjoyment, and service of God as the purpose of life. By recognizing the influence of Stone's spirituality on his theology and practice, we will better understand this leader of the remarkable growth of Christianity in the early American Republic and the Christianity that he helped to foster.

[11]William Garrett West, *Barton Warren Stone: Early American Advocate of Christian Unity* (Nashville: Disciples of Christ Historical Society, 1954).

[12]Evan Ulrey, "The Preaching of Barton Warren Stone" (Ph.D. dissertation, Louisiana State University, 1955).

[13]David C. Roos, "The Social Thought of Barton Warren Stone and Its Significance Today for the Disciples of Christ in Western Kentucky" (D.Min. thesis, Vanderbilt University, 1973).

[14]David Newell Williams, "The Theology of the Great Revival in the West as Seen through the Life and Thought of Barton Warren Stone" (Ph.D. dissertation, Vanderbilt University, 1979).

[15]David Newell Williams, "Barton W. Stone's Calvinist Piety," *Encounter* 42/4 (Autumn 1981), 409–17; C. Leonard Allen, "The Stone That the Builders Rejected: Barton W. Stone in the Memory of Churches of Christ," in *Cane Ridge in Context*, 43–61; Richard T. Hughes, *Reviving the Ancient Faith: The Story of the Churches of Christ in America* (Grand Rapids: Eerdmans, 1996), 92–113.

PART 1

The Making
of a Presbyterian
Minister

1

Family and Religious Background

Barton Warren Stone was born December 24, 1772, to John and Mary Warren Stone near Port Tobacco, then the county seat of Charles County, Maryland. Charles County is on the peninsula between the Potomac River and Chesapeake Bay. One of the first trading places on the Potomac for English merchants, the wharf at Port Tobacco had been in use for more than a century when Stone was born.[1]

John and Mary Stone came from families long associated with public affairs and sizable holdings of land—the indisputable marks of Maryland's upper class. The first of Mary Warren's family to settle in Charles County was Colonel Humphrey Warren, who had served as justice of the quorum, coroner, and commander of the county's "Regiment of Foot." Colonel Warren's name also appeared on a remonstrance sent to the English throne in 1691 by the substantial Protestant families of Charles County, alleging intrigues of Roman Catholics and Indians against the welfare of Protestants. Included in the document was a call for Captain William Barton, another of Stone's maternal forebears, to be appointed to the Provincial Council. Mary's father, Barton Warren, inherited a portion of the family plantation and had a personal estate that placed him in the lower end of Maryland's upper class.[2]

John Stone was the great-great-grandson of Captain William Stone (1603–1695), who had received five thousand acres along the Potomac in reward for his services as the first Protestant governor of Maryland. Although the largest estates in Maryland ranged from twenty to forty thousand acres, estates of more than a thousand acres marked their owners as members of the upper class. Barton Stone's second cousin, Thomas Stone, was a signer of the Declaration of Independence and the owner of one of the largest estates in Charles County. Barton Stone's father owned land and sixteen slaves in addition to livestock and personal possessions. According to the standards of eighteenth-century Maryland, this identified him as upper middle class.[3]

---

[1]Ware, 5–6.

[2]Ibid., 1, 2, 4, 5; see also Charles A. Barker, *The Background of the Revolution in Maryland* (New Haven, Conn.: Yale University Press, 1950), 41; and Jackson Turner Main, *The Social Structure of Revolutionary America* (Princeton, N.J.: Princeton University Press, 1965), 67, 276.

[3]Ware, 1–2, 4, 8, 9; Barker, 36–37; "The Will of John Stone," State of Maryland, Department of General Services, Hall of Records; see also Main, *Social Structure,* 55, 276.

The Maryland society in which the Stones lived was characterized by a growing gap between rich and poor and an increasing consciousness of social class. The number of large estates was diminishing. Although a handful of southern Maryland planters grew quite rich, the source of wealth was shifting away from the production of tobacco toward trade and money lending.[4]

Consciousness of social class was increased in Maryland by the tendency of the moneyed class to display their wealth through fashionable dress and splendid residences, like the one that Barton Stone's cousin Thomas built in 1760. Amusements or "sports" were another way that Maryland's wealthy displayed their status. Card games, dances, horse races, and cockfights were popular among all classes in Maryland and Virginia. However, the kinds of dances danced, the types of races run, the dress of participants, and the cost of refreshments clearly displayed social rank. Only at dances sponsored by the wealthy did one dance a minuet. Under the patronage of the wealthy, the quarter race, a horse race on a straight quarter-mile track with owner-riders, was supplanted by course racing, with jockeys riding gentlemen-owned horses specially bred and trained to "stay the distance." In the case of cockfights sponsored by the wealthy, it came to be expected that ladies would attend in fashionable dress, and a formal ball was sometimes promised for the evening.[5]

Card games, horse races, and cockfights were contests. So were dances, and in southern Maryland the stakes at a dance could be high. The skillful young male dancer gained the approval not only of young women but also of the upper classes as a whole. To perform well at a dance could lead to a "good" marriage and advancement in social rank.[6]

The Church of England, to which the Stones belonged, had a building for worship in Port Tobacco at least as early as 1684 and was a strong institution in Charles County. In the 1750s residents of the county had successfully petitioned the legislature to impose a levy on the parish to replace the existing structure with a new brick church. From 1762–1777 the Port Tobacco parish employed Rev. Thomas Thornton, from whom it is likely that Stone received the "infant sprinkling" that he noted in his autobiography.[7]

In 1779, four years after Barton Stone's father's death, his mother moved "with a large family of children and servants" to Pittsylvania County, Virginia. Barton Stone was six years old. The reasons for Mary Stone's move are unknown. In the will that John Stone wrote in August 1775, he bequeathed his land to his two oldest sons, who appear to have been from an earlier marriage, specifying that it be divided equally between them. Although Mary legally owned one third of the Port Tobacco estate following her husband's death, Maryland and Tidewater Virginia planters alike had suffered economic

---

[4]Gloria L. Main, "Inequality in Early America: The Evidence From Probate Records of Massachusetts and Maryland," *Journal of Interdisciplinary History* (Spring 1977), 580. See also Barker, 30–31, 38–40.

[5]Rhys Isaac, *The Transformation of Virginia, 1740–1790* (Chapel Hill, N.C.: Institute of Early American History and Culture, 1982), 43–46, 80–87, 98–103. Isaac refers to southern Maryland and Tidewater Virginia as sharing a common "Chesapeake" culture.

[6]Ibid., 86–87.

[7]Ware, 6–8; Stone, *Biography*, 60.

hardships during much of the eighteenth century. The tobacco market, the principal income of the region, had fluctuated due to interruptions and losses caused by England's wars with Spain and France and later by the blockade of British commerce that followed the outbreak of the Revolutionary War. In the latter third of the eighteenth century, many Tidewater Virginia and southern Maryland planters, hoping to improve their lot, had joined the swelling throng of population moving to the West. In 1767 the Stones's neighbor from across the Potomac, George Washington, had urged John Posey to sell his Tidewater Virginia property and head to the frontier for a new start. Washington had encouraged Posey to believe that, given the price of land on the frontier, he would be worth five times his present wealth in twenty years.[8]

Exactly how many children and servants moved to western Virginia with Mary Stone cannot be determined. In his will, John Stone named six sons and one daughter. Barton Stone identified himself as his father's youngest child. It does not appear that John Stone's three oldest sons, two of whom had inherited land in Maryland, accompanied Mary Stone to Pittsylvania County. So the "children" in this family probably numbered four. The number of "servants" was probably larger. John Stone bequeathed seven slaves to his "beloved wife." To his daughter and three younger sons, all of whom appear to have been from his marriage to Mary Warren, he willed four slaves, including one who was "big with Child." Assuming that the baby lived and that none of the slaves willed to Mary and her children had died or been sold, the "servants" in this family would have numbered at least twelve.[9]

Pittsylvania County is located on the Virginia–North Carolina border. Fifty years before the arrival of Mary Stone and her family, William Byrd, who captained the commission that established the Carolina-Virginia boundary line, dubbed the region in which the Stones settled "The Land of Eden," noting the beauty of the Dan River, which runs through the region, and describing the river's valley as an "exceedingly rich land, full of large trees, with vines marry'd to them." Stone noted that Pittsylvania County was called the "back-woods" of Virginia.[10]

After the family had settled in Pittsylvania County, Stone was sent to school. He reported that his first teacher was a "tyrant" who "seemed to take pleasure in whipping and abusing his pupils for every trifling offense." It is possible that the teacher may simply have been a practitioner of the so-called evangelical philosophy of child rearing. According to this philosophy, the self-will of the child had to be "broken" before the moral development of the

---

[8] Stone, *Biography*, 1; John Stone, "Will"; Barker, 69–70; John R. Alden, *The South in the Revolution 1763–1789* (Baton Rouge: Louisiana State University Press, 1957; reprint, Gloucester, Mass.: Peter Smith, n.d.), 32 (page citation is to the reprint edition); Robert E. Brown and B. Katherine Brown, *Virginia, 1705–1786: Democracy or Aristocracy?* (East Lansing: Michigan State University Press, 1964), 16–31, 284.

[9] John Stone willed one slave each to his three older sons and another slave to his "beloved Grandson John Stone Gray," who appears to be the child of a deceased daughter ("Will"; Stone, *Biography*, 2, 6).

[10] William Byrd, *History of the Dividing Line*, ed. W. K. Boyd (n.p., 1929), quoted in Ware, 13; Stone, *Biography*, 1.

child could proceed. In any case, Stone indicated that he could not learn because of his "fear" of the teacher.[11]

Given Mary Stone's upper-class background, it is not surprising that Stone reported that after only a few days with this first teacher he was sent to another teacher of "a different temper." Rather than subscribing to the "break the will" philosophy of child rearing, the upper classes generally advocated either the "moderate" or the "genteel" methods that honored the will of the child. The moderate method sought to bend the will of the child, while the genteel philosophy tended to allow free expression of the child's will. As an adult, Stone advocated the moderate approach, admonishing teachers to use the rod "rarely" and advising that if teachers would gain the "respect and love" of their pupils they would "delight in obedience, and rarely fail to learn the lessons given to them."[12]

Stone indicated that he learned easily with Robert W. Somerhays, his second teacher, whom he identified as "an Englishman." He reported that after "four or five" years of study Somerhays pronounced him "a finished scholar" in his curriculum of reading, writing, and arithmetic.[13]

Social conditions in Pittsylvania County differed significantly from those the Stones had known in Maryland, despite the variety of primary school options available. Western Virginia for whites in the late eighteenth century was characterized by the absence of strictly defined social ranks and a remarkably equal distribution of wealth, due to the availability of cheap land. Stone remembered that "contentment appeared to be the lot of all, and happiness dwelt in every breast amidst the abundance of home stores, acquired by honest industry." He claimed that people in Pittsylvania County had "no aspirations for wealth or preferment," the latter term meaning advancement in social rank. While in southern Maryland sports or amusements could become quite elaborate under the patronage of the wealthy and, in the case of dances, might carry long-term social and economic consequences, Stone noted that in Pittsylvania County "Sports of the most simple kind were generally practiced," adding that "friendship and good feeling universally reigned."[14]

The Stones maintained their ties with the established church, which was a strong institution in Pittsylvania County, as it had been in their Maryland home. During the ten years prior to the Revolutionary War, the vestry of the Camden Parish, which included Pittsylvania County, had built seven churches and chapels. From Stone's comments concerning "our parson," it appears that the parish enjoyed the services of a pastor throughout the war, despite the fact that in June 1776 the state of Virginia had suspended the laws requiring tax support of the clergy. The Virginia law that all citizens must attend divine service at least once in four weeks had long been a dead letter. Nevertheless,

[11]Ibid., 3.
[12]Ibid., 3–4. For a discussion of styles of child rearing in colonial America, see Philip Greven, *The Protestant Temperament: Patterns of Child-Rearing, Religious Experience, and the Self in Early America* (New York: Alfred A. Knopf, 1977).
[13]Stone, *Biography*, 3–4.
[14]Main, *Social Structure*, 270; Stone, *Biography*, 2.

Stone indicated that throughout the war residents of the county did regularly attend the worship services of the parish.[15]

Certain types of eighteenth-century Christianity disdained desire for "things of this world," such as wealth and social standing, and frowned on sports and amusements. This was not the case with the Church of England in Maryland and Virginia. Most Church of England clergy did not question the lawful pursuit of wealth and social status. Moreover, the lives of the Church of England clergy would seem to have confirmed the high value generally placed on wealth and social standing. Many observers noted that regardless of their social origins, the clergy of the established church moved in the social circles of the wealthy. As regards amusements, Church of England clergy appear to have offered little reproach. Stone reported that the Pittsylvania parson participated in "all the sports and pastimes of the people, and was what may be termed a man of pleasure." Thus, despite his indication of support for the established church by the people of Pittsylvania County, Stone would assert that religion, by which he meant a type of religion that challenged the desire for wealth and preferment and opposed amusements, had "engaged the attention of but a few" in Pittsylvania County.[16]

Following the Revolutionary War, Stone encountered a type of religion that did challenge desire for wealth and social standing and discountenanced amusements–the religion of the Baptists and Methodists. According to them, wealth and preferment, even simple amusements, were "snares" or diversions that could distract one from pursuing life's true goal. This does not mean that there were no persons of wealth and social standing among the Baptists and the Methodists. Samuel Harris, one of the Baptist preachers whom Stone reported having heard after the Revolution, was both wealthy and socially prominent. Born in 1725 in Hanover County, Virginia, Harris had been one of the first settlers of Pittsylvania and had served the county as church warden, sheriff, justice of the peace, and colonel of the Militia. The Methodists also numbered wealthy and socially prominent persons among their membership, especially after the Revolutionary War. Nevertheless, Baptists and Methodists made it clear that the goal of life was not wealth or preferment or amusements, but right relationship with God.[17]

[15]George MacLaren Brydon, "New Light Upon the History of the Church in Colonial Virginia," *Historical Magazine of the Protestant Episcopal Church* 10 (June 1941), 76–77; Brydon, *Virginia's Mother Church* (Philadelphia: Church Historical Society, 1952), 43–44; Edwin Lewis Goodwin, *The Colonial Church in Virginia* (Milwaukee, Wis.: Morehouse, 1927), 106–7; Isaac, 59; Stone, *Biography*, 2, 4, 10.

[16]Hunter Dickinson Farish, ed., *Journal and Letters of Phillip Vickers Fithian, 1773–1774* (Williamsburg, Va.: Colonial Williamsburg, Inc., 1957), 167; Arthur Pierce Middleton, "The Colonial Virginia Parson," *William and Mary Quarterly*, 3d series, 26 (July 1969), 425–27; Stone, *Biography*, 2.

[17]Ibid., 4; John Taylor, *A History of the Baptist Churches of Which the Author Has Been Alternately a Member in More Than Fifty Years* (Frankfort, Ky.: J. H. Holeman, 1823), 117; Philip Doddridge, *The Rise and Progress of Religion in the Soul, Illustrated in a Course of Serious and Practical Addresses, Suited to Persons of Every Character and Circumstance* (Boston: Daniel Kneeland for Nicholas Bowers, 1771), 336–37; William L. Lumpkin, *Baptist Foundations in the South: Tracing Through the Separates the Influence of the Great Awakening, 1754–1787* (Nashville: Broadman Press, 1961), 48–50; John Atkinson, *Centennial History of American Methodism* (New York: Phillips and Hunt, 1884), 218–20.

Stone reported that he was for a time attracted to the Baptists and the Methodists, probably partly because of the novel character of their rituals. He commented that the Baptist preachers "had the art of affecting their hearers by a tuneful or singing voice in preaching" and that the preaching of the Methodists was "often electric on the congregation, and fixed their attention." He noted that he frequently attended the baptismal services of the Baptists and was particularly interested in hearing the candidates for baptism relate their experiences of conversion. He claimed that some spoke of visions, voices, and unusual appearances of light. Clearly, the participation of worshipers in both Baptist and Methodist services stood in bold contrast to the prayer book reading of the colonial Church of England, where even congregational singing appears to have been rare. Nevertheless, Stone implied that the most important factor in his attraction to the Baptists and the Methodists was his displeasure with the moral tone of post–Revolutionary War society.[18]

Stone reported that after the war, returning soldiers brought back vices such as "profane swearing, debauchery, drunkenness, gambling, quarreling and fighting" that had previously been "almost unknown" in Pittsylvania County. In Stone's mind, the postwar increase in vice was also a result of the declining strength of the Church of England. In 1786, when Stone was thirteen, the Virginia Legislature voted to sever all ties with the Church of England. During the war, many of the Anglican clergy had been sustained by the hope that as soon as the conflict was concluded the laws requiring citizens to pay the salaries of the clergy, which had been suspended with the outbreak of hostilities, would be reenacted. With these hopes dashed, the former established church entered a period of rapid decline characterized by an increasing shortage of qualified clergy and the consequent closing of churches. Stone reported that in Pittsylvania County, "Every man did what seemed right in his own eyes; wickedness abounded, the Lord's day was converted into a day of pleasure, and the house of worship deserted." In the religion of the Methodists and the Baptists, the adolescent Barton Stone appears to have seen hope for the moral renewal of the community. Of the work of the Baptists he wrote, "Great and good was the reformation in society." Of the Methodist preachers he commented, "Their very presence checked levity in all around them."[19]

Stone claimed that he attended the services of the Baptists and the Methodists for a time but at length became discouraged. He stated that the source of his discouragement was his failure to "obtain" religion. According to the Baptists and the Methodists, relationship with God was not something you learned, but something you "got." Moreover, one could not will oneself to be religious. Persons who desired to become religious were instructed to pray for conversion and to refrain from pastimes that were believed to distract one

---

[18]Stone, *Biography*, 4–5; Isaac, 166–67.
[19]Stone, *Biography*, 2–5; see also Ware, 16–17; Brydon, "New Light," 70–71. For a discussion of the forces leading to the decision of the Virginia Legislature to sever all ties with the church, see R. E. Brown and B. K. Brown, 249–60. For a different view of Virginia society *before* the Revolution, see Isaac, 100.

from seeking religion, such as card games, dancing, horse races, and cock-fights. Stone indicated that for a time he followed the advice of the preachers, "retiring in secret, morning and evening, for prayer, with an earnest desire for religion" and shunning amusements. He claimed that after some time, having not obtained religion, he "quit praying" and returned to "the youthful sports of the day."[20]

Stone reported that when he was "fifteen or sixteen" years of age his older brothers were ready to launch out into the world for themselves, and a division of inherited property was made to the satisfaction of all. He also stated that after his part of the inheritance had been assigned, his "mind" had been "absorbed day and night in devising some plan to improve it."[21]

Given Stone's family and religious background, his "absorption" in devising some way to improve his inheritance is not surprising. Although he had spent the later years of his childhood and youth in a society where, as he later remembered, the distribution of wealth was remarkably equal and where class lines were not sharply drawn, the earliest years of his life had deeply instilled in his mind class distinctions based on wealth. Furthermore, he was a descendant of families long associated with wealth and social standing. It seems likely that Stone would have known something of the social status of his maternal grandfather, Barton Warren, for whom he appears to have been named. It also seems likely that in an era that accorded great respect to leaders of the patriot cause, Stone would have known that he was related to a signer of the Declaration of Independence. It would hardly be surprising if Stone had desired to attain the level of status that Stones and Warrens had "always" possessed.

Stone's absorption in devising a plan to improve his inheritance would also have been encouraged by the books he had read. Stone claimed that from the time he was able to read he took great delight in books. He indicated that the only books available to him, other than the Bible he used at school, were contemporary English novels, such as Henry Fielding's *The History of Tom Jones* and Tobias Smollett's *The Adventures of Roderic Random* and *The Adventures of Peregrine Pickle*. In the world depicted by both Fielding and Smollett, wealth, though not to be prized above wisdom and virtue, was essential to human happiness. It would not be surprising, if having read this literature, Stone had wanted to avoid the mistake of Smollett's Peregrine Pickle, who in a state of deep remorse "compared his own conduct with that of some young gentlemen of his acquaintance, who, while he was squandering away the best part of his inheritance, had improved their fortune, strengthened their interests, and increased their reputation."[22]

---

[20]Stone, *Biography*, 4–5, 9; see also Taylor, 290–91, 293–95, and Isaac, 168–69. Stone's statement about returning to the "youthful sports of the day" should not be interpreted to mean that Stone engaged in "drunkenness and debauchery." See ibid., 3.

[21]Stone, *Biography*, 6.

[22]Ibid., 4; Tobias Smollett, *The Adventures of Peregrine Pickle* (London: Oxford University Press, 1964), 619.

Stone reported that as a result of intense deliberation, he had decided to invest his inheritance in a liberal education that would qualify him to pursue a career in law. Such an education included sciences, the classical languages, and moral philosophy. Stone's decision reflected sound judgment. In earlier times, the way to wealth and position in the South had been to secure some land and a few slaves, to farm until one had enough capital to buy more land and more slaves, and then to continue the process indefinitely. By the latter third of the eighteenth century, profits from agriculture were not great enough or reliable enough to fund this process very much beyond securing some land and a few slaves. In order to become wealthy in the late eighteenth-century South, one needed to enter commerce or one of the professions. The greatest wealth was to be found in trade, but trade involved risks and was not a sure road to wealth. Of the professions, the greatest wealth was to be found in the practice of law. Here one might expect to make ten times as much as the doctor or minister and as much as all but the wealthiest of merchants and planters. By acquiring a liberal education, he would stand in good position to pursue a career in law, a career that could be expected to assure him a place in what Revolutionary-era Americans called the "first rank" of society. [23]

---

[23]Stone, *Biography*, 6–8; Main, *Social Structure*, 101, 195–96. For a list of terms used by eighteenth-century Americans to denote "upper class," see ibid., 233.

2

Conversion and Call to Ministry

Options for obtaining a liberal education in the backwoods were limited. The state school at Chapel Hill, North Carolina, had not yet been established. Of the classical academies in the region, none had a better reputation than David Caldwell's academy. Caldwell, the sole teacher of the academy, was the sixty-five-year-old pastor of the Presbyterian churches at Buffalo and Alamance, North Carolina. Following an established Presbyterian pattern of combining teaching with pastoral ministry, Caldwell conducted the school in his home, a two-story log structure located on a gentle slope amid the streams and rolling hills of Guilford County, North Carolina, thirty miles southwest of Mary Stone's Pittsylvania County, Virginia, home. That five of Caldwell's graduates became governors of states is testimony to the quality of his instruction and the character of the students attracted by the school's reputation. Having decided on his future course, seventeen-year-old Barton Stone "bade farewell" to his family and friends and made his way to the Guilford County school in January 1790.[1]

Caldwell was a Presbyterian of the New Light tradition. The New Light Presbyterians had promoted the Great Awakening of the eighteenth century. They differed from Old Light Presbyterians, who had opposed the Awakening, by insisting that Christianity was a "sensible thing," an *experience* of the work of the Holy Spirit, not merely doctrine and morality. Caldwell had studied with the New Light preacher Robert Smith of Pequa, Pennsylvania, and Samuel Davies, the apostle of New Light Presbyterianism in the South. At Davies' death in 1761, Caldwell had been honored by being chosen to help bear the coffin of the esteemed New Light leader.[2]

---

[1] Stone, *Biography*, 6; Ware, 21–24; West, 3–4.

[2] E. W. Caruthers, *A Sketch of the Life and Character of the Rev. David Caldwell, D.D.* (Greensborough, N. C.: Swaim and Sherwood, 1842), 18–22. Jon Butler challenges the idea of the Great Awakening as an "event," noting that the term was not used by participants, nor was it known to historians of the revolutionary or early national periods, and that it is difficult to date, since it is linked to revivals that started in New England long before 1730 and did not appear with any force in Virginia until the 1760s (*Awash in a Sea of Faith: Christianizing the American People* [Cambridge, Mass.: Harvard University Press, 1990], 164–65). Butler does not deny that colonial Presbyterians divided over their responses to eighteenth-century revivals. The best account of this Presbyterian conflict remains Leonard J. Trinterud, *The Forming of an American Tradition: A Re-Examination of Colonial Presbyterianism* (Philadelphia: Westminster, 1949).

Stone entered the academy during "a great religious excitement" among the students. Of the probably no more than fifty students enrolled, thirty or more had recently "embraced religion" under the ministry of James McGready. McGready had received a grammar-school education from Caldwell and had studied in western Pennsylvania with New Light Presbyterian preachers John McMillan and Joseph Smith. During the winter of 1788, McGready had visited Hampden-Sydney College in Prince Edward County, Virginia, where he had witnessed firsthand a student awakening under the direction of college president John Blair Smith, another Presbyterian minister of New Light training and background. In the spring of 1789 McGready had accepted a Guilford County pastorate and frequently visited Caldwell's academy.[3]

Stone later wrote that his first response to the religious excitement at Caldwell's academy was to try to ignore it. A significant cost of studying at the Guilford academy was the expense of boarding in a nearby home. Thus, for financial reasons, it was desirable to complete the program as quickly as possible. Stone indicated that he saw the revival as a distraction from his studies. Moreover, Stone's family's religious ties were to the former Church of England. He stated that he believed that participation in the revival would not only impede his progress in learning but also expose him to the "frowns" of his relatives and companions.[4]

It was not easy, though, to ignore the religious excitement in Caldwell's academy. Stone was "not a little surprised" to find the recent converts assembled every morning before the hour of recitation, singing and praying in a private room. However, he reported that his greatest difficulty in trying to ignore the religious excitement in the academy was his observation of the "daily walk" of the recent converts, for it clearly showed him "their sincere piety and happiness." This, he declared, was a source of great uneasiness to him, frequently leading him to "serious reflection." At length, he accepted the invitation of his roommate to attend a preaching service conducted by McGready.[5]

---

[3]Stone, *Biography*, 7; William Henry Foote, *Sketches of North Carolina* (New York: Robert Carter, 1846), 367–99; Davidson, 259–60; Joseph Smith, *Old Redstone, or Historical Sketches of Western Presbyterianism, Its Early Ministers, Its Perilous Times, and Its First Records* (Philadelphia: Lippincott, Grambo and Co., 1854), 76, 78, 191, 359–64; Dwight Raymond Guthrie, *John McMillan: The Apostle of Presbyterianism in the West, 1752–1833* (Pittsburgh: University of Pittsburgh Press, 1952), 87. McMillan had grown up in a congregation pastored by Samuel Blair, one of the first graduates of Presbyterian revivalist William Tennent's famous Log College. For information on Blair, see George William Pilcher, *Samuel Davies: Apostle of Dissent in Colonial Virginia* (Knoxville: University of Tennessee Press, 1971), 9, 10; and William Henry Foote, *Sketches of Virginia: Historical and Biographical,* first series (Philadelphia: J. B. Lippincott and Co., 1850; reprint, Richmond, Va: John Knox Press, 1966), 144 (page citation is to the reprint edition). McMillan had received the bulk of his education under the direction of Robert Smith of Pequa (Guthrie, 10, 11, 17), who had professed conversion under the preaching of Whitefield and had been educated in an academy run by Samuel Blair (Foote, *Virginia,* first series, 408–9). Joseph Smith had studied at Princeton under the administration of Samuel Finley (Smith, 54–56). Finley was a graduate of the Blair Academy (Pilcher, 9–10). John Blair Smith was the son of Robert Smith of Pequa; see Foote, *Virginia,* first series, 391–92.

[4]Stone, *Biography*, 7.

[5]Ibid., 7–8.

McGready's message, judging from his published sermons, focused on the pursuit of happiness. In that respect, it was similar to the novels of Fielding and Smollett that Stone had read as a youth. For McGready, however, ultimate happiness was not to be found, as it was for Fielding and Smollett, in physical pleasure or through the possession of wealth or honor, but in the knowledge and enjoyment of the "infinite glory" and "adorable attributes" of God—that is, through relationship with God.[6]

According to McGready, human beings were originally endowed with a "spiritual principle." This spiritual principle, which he and other New Light Presbyterians described as a faculty, tendency, or source of life, enabled the first man and woman to know and enjoy God. As a consequence of humanity's first sin, human beings had lost this spiritual principle or faculty and thereby the ability to know and enjoy God. As a result, human beings sought happiness through the satisfaction of their "animal nature" and through the possession of "riches" and "honors," the very objects of desire so prominent in the popular novels that Stone read as a boy. McGready taught that human beings also sought happiness through a "religion of external duties" that they thought appeased God, who, in fact, remained unknown to them. However, he declared, no worldly enjoyment could take the place of the happiness that humanity was meant to enjoy in relationship with God.[7]

Failure in the pursuit of happiness was not, according to McGready, the only consequence of humanity's having lost the spiritual principle. Another consequence was that humanity stood under the judgment and wrath of God. The divine law required love of God with all of one's heart, soul, mind, and strength. Having lost the ability to know and enjoy God, human beings were unable to love God and thus continuously incurred God's displeasure. In this life the judgment and wrath of God are mitigated by God's favor. At death, McGready warned, sinners would be cut off from God's favor and would eternally suffer torments beyond human conception.[8]

---

[6] *The Posthumous Works of the Reverend and Pious James McGready, Late Minister of the Gospel in Henderson, Kentucky*, ed. James Smith, vol. 1, "On the Nature and Consequences of Sin" (Louisville, Ky.: W. W. Worlsley, 1831; and Nashville, Tenn.: Lowry and Smith, 1833), 53. Readers of the sermons in this collection claimed to have heard McGready preach several of them during his North Carolina ministry. See Foote, *North Carolina*, 372.

[7] McGready, "The Experience and Privileges of the True Believer," 1:144, 150–51; "On the Nature and Consequences of Sin." 1: 51, 53; "The Hindrance of the Work of God," 2: 363–64. In a famous sermon, Samuel Davies described the principles of the human mind, stating that in addition to the spiritual principle, which is the source of spiritual life, there is an animal principle, which is the source of animal life, and a rational principle, which is the source of intellectual life. See Samuel Davies, "Divine Life in the Soul Considered," *Sermons on Important Subjects*, 3 vols. (New York: R. Carter and Brothers, 1849), 2: 389–92.

[8] McGready acknowledged that it might seem unfair for God to judge humans by a law that they were no longer capable of obeying. However, he argued that when humans failed to delight in God as the source and essence of all happiness, they attacked the very being of God. "Sin," McGready asserted, "aims at nothing less than to extinguish the divine glory, to undeify the deity, to deprive him of his being, and, finally, to annihilate the source and essence of all happiness." Thus, God could not allow sin to go unchecked. McGready, "On the Nature and Consequences of Sin," 1:53–55, 58, 62–65.

The good news, according to McGready, was that God had chosen to save a portion of humanity, whom McGready referred to as "the elect." McGready proclaimed that the instrument of this salvation was Jesus Christ. By his life and death Christ had "paid down to the justice of God the whole infinite sum of the elect's ransom," thus saving the elect from suffering the judgment and wrath of God for their violation of the divine law.[9]

This was not all that Christ had done for the elect. According to McGready, Christ also saved them from "the very being of sin: from its dominion and enslaving power." McGready taught that this latter work was accomplished when the living Christ implanted into the hearts of the elect the spiritual principle that had been lost through humanity's first sin. Thus, salvation not only delivered the elect from future punishment, but enabled them to experience in this life the happiness for which they were created—the happiness of knowing and enjoying God.[10]

Heaven, for McGready, was but the continuation and fulfillment of the earthly happiness of the elect—the happiness of knowing and enjoying God. Thus, he warned sinners that even if they could be taken to heaven, they would not enjoy it: "Rather than spend an eternity in company so opposite to your nature, and be engaged in employments so unpleasant to your vitiated minds, you would leap o'er the high battlements of heaven down to the burning furnace of hell."[11]

McGready taught that God converts sinners by giving them a "view" of the "glory of God in the face of Christ Jesus." The glory of God in the face of Christ Jesus was the glory of One who sent the only begotten Son to save sinners by paying the penalty for their sins through his death and by implanting in their hearts the spiritual principle by which they were enabled to know and enjoy God. In accord with the New Light Presbyterian tradition, McGready argued that a view of the excellence or glory of God in the face of Christ Jesus caused sinners to fall in love with God and thus to grieve over the evil of sin and not merely its penalty. As a result of such love, and the genuine sorrow for sin produced by such love, the sinner was "willing" to "come to Christ" both for pardon from the penalty of sin and for release from the power of sin. This change of the will—a change of heart—was conversion.[12]

McGready's preaching had a powerful impact on Stone. "Such was my excitement," he wrote, "that had I been standing, I should have probably sunk to the floor under the impression." Surely Stone had heard a similar message from the Baptists and Methodists whose services he had attended in Pittsylvania County. Baptists and Methodists were spiritual and theological cousins of the New Light Presbyterians and shared with them an appreciation

[9]McGready, "On the Divine Authority of the Christian Religion," 1: 22.

[10]Ibid., 22–23.

[11]McGready, "The New Birth," 2: 108; "On the Nature and Consequences of Sin," 1: 53.

[12]McGready, "The Saving Sight," 2: 191–92; "Christ the Author and Finisher of the Life of Grace," 1: 93–95; "The Believer Embracing Christ," 1: 126–27, 132–33; "The Work of the Spirit Distinguished From that of the Devil," 2: 10; see also Doddridge, 313; Davies, "The Divine Perfection, Illustrated Through the Suffering of Christ," 2: 195–96. For a discussion of the New Light view that God works through "rational means," see Trinterud, 179–84.

for the writings of the English Puritans Joseph Alleine, Richard Baxter, and Philip Doddridge.[13] Stone noted McGready's remarkable "earnestness" and "zeal." Even so, Baptists and Methodists were also zealous preachers. No doubt Stone's unsettling observation of the sincere piety and happiness of the converts was also a factor in the powerful impact of McGready's preaching on Stone. Indeed, Stone seemed to suggest as much when he observed that from his experience at Caldwell's academy he had "learned that the most effectual way to conquer the depraved heart, is, the constant exhibition of piety and a godly life" in Christians.[14]

McGready concluded his sermon with a call to sinners to "flee the wrath to come without delay." For McGready, salvation–relationship with God–by which the judgment and wrath of God were avoided and true happiness was experienced, was a gift–it could not be earned. Nevertheless, in accord with the New Light Presbyterian tradition, McGready declared that only those persons who applied to Christ–who sought salvation–could have any assurance of receiving it. In response to the objection that since God had already chosen whom God would save, there was no reason to apply to Christ, McGready answered, in the tradition of his New Light teachers, that "it is the will of God" that sinners receive the gift of salvation by applying to Christ. For McGready, as for other New Light Presbyterians, God had determined both the salvation of the elect and that the elect would be saved by applying to Christ.[15]

How did one apply to Christ? One applied to Christ by using the "means of grace." Though McGready's lists of the means of grace varied slightly from one sermon to another, in one sermon he recommended the following eight: (1) Forsaking "vain companions, vain conversation, and every known sin"; (2) diligently performing "every known duty"; (3) reflecting on one's "dreadful condition while destitute of an interest in Christ"; (4) attending to the "voice of conscience" and "every motion of the Holy Spirit"; (5) crying out to God "to speak peace or pardon to your soul"; (6) resolving "never to rest" in one's

[13]Stone, *Biography*, 8. For a discussion of the influence of English Puritanism on the theology of the Great Awakening, from which both the New Light Presbyterians and Separate Baptists took their rise, see Trinterud, 160–70. For evidence of the popularity of the works of Doddridge and Baxter among Southern Presbyterians of the latter part of the eighteenth century, see "*Minutes* of the Synod of the Carolinas for 1790," quoted in Hubert William Morris, "The Background and Development of Cumberland Presbyterian Theology" (Ph.D. dissertation, Vanderbilt University, 1965), 67. See also Foote, *Virginia*, first series, 284. For evidence of the value placed on these works by Methodists, see Francis Asbury, "23 April, 1778," in *The Journal and Letters of Francis Asbury*, 3 vols., ed. Elmer T. Clark, et al. (Nashville: Abingdon Press, 1958), 1: 268; and *The Causes, Evils, and Cures of Heart and Church Divisions, extracted from the works of Mr. Jeremiah Burroughs and Mr. Richard Baxter* (Philadelphia: John Dickins, 1792), viii. It should also be noted that Baxter's *Call to the Unconverted* and *Saints Rest* and Alleine's *Alarm to the Unconverted* were among the first books published by the Methodist Church in America. This fact is noted in Leland H. Scott, "Methodist Theology in America in the Nineteenth Century" (Ph.D. dissertation, Yale University, 1954), Appendix 4, 553.
[14]Stone, *Biography*, 7.
[15]McGready, "Parable of the Dry Bones," 1: 73. For a similar response in the sermons of Samuel Davies see Davies, "Divine Life in the Soul Considered," 2: 396.

"reformations, duties, prayers, tears or melting frames" as a substitute for salvation; (7) meditating on "the fullness and freeness of the great salvation which is provided for miserable, lost, perishing sinners of every description"; and (8) trusting in God to grant pardon and implant the spiritual principle that makes possible the knowledge and love of God. McGready taught that only in using the means of grace could one hope to receive the spiritual principle that would make one willing to come to Christ both for pardon and release from the power of sin.[16]

Moreover, McGready admonished that if one hoped to be saved, one must flee the wrath to come without delay. Like other New Light Presbyterians, he advised that there was only a certain time in the sinner's life when the sinner might be saved: This was the time when the Spirit of God awakened the sinner to the sinner's dangerous situation apart from God and called the sinner to apply to Christ for salvation. This time was referred to by New Light Presbyterians as the sinner's "day of grace." McGready, like other New Light Presbyterians, warned that after the sinner's "day of grace" had passed, the sinner would no longer be "troubled" by the Spirit. And this, of course, would mean that there would no longer be any possibility of the sinner's being saved. Failure to use the means of grace without delay might well be to commit the "unpardonable sin," or, to use McGready's preferred terminology, to "sin away" one's "day of grace."[17]

Stone reported that after hearing McGready's sermon, he first returned to his room and then, as night began to fall, walked out into a field and seriously reasoned with himself on the subject of religion. He remembered that he put the matter to himself as follows: "If I embrace religion, I must incur the displeasure of my dear relatives, lose the favor and company of my companions—become the object of their scorn and ridicule—relinquish all my plans and schemes for worldly honor, wealth, and preferment, and bid a final adieu to all the pleasures in which I had lived, and hoped to live on earth." The answer of his heart to that scenario was "No, no." But the problem was the alternative: "Are you willing to be damned—to be banished from God—from heaven—from all good—and suffer the pains of eternal fire?" Again, the answer of his heart was "No, no." Stone recalled that after due consideration, he came to the decision for which McGready preached: "I resolved from that hour to seek religion at the sacrifice of every earthly good, and immediately prostrated myself before God in supplication for mercy."[18]

---

[16]McGready, "The Excellencies of Christ as Displayed in the Plan of Salvation," 1: 119–20; see also ibid., "Parable of the Dry Bones," 1: 73–74. For a similar list in the sermons of Samuel Davies, see Davies, "The Nature of Love to God and Christ Opened and Enforced," 2: 367; and "The Certainty of Death: A Funeral Sermon," 3: 331.

[17]McGready, "The Excellencies of Christ as Displayed in the Plan of Salvation," 1: 121, 123. For a reference to this notion in the sermons of Samuel Davies, see Davies, "The Danger of Lukewarmness in Religion," 1: 279. See also Davies, "The Guilt and Doom of Impenitent Hearers," 3: 471–74. See also Doddridge, 238–39.

[18]Stone, *Biography*, 8–9.

Stone did not believe, however, that he had been converted. From his exposure to the Baptists and Methodists in Pittsylvania County, he expected a "long and painful struggle" before he would be "willing" to "come to Christ" for both the pardon of his sins and for release from the power of sin. McGready taught that only when sinners had been convinced of their helplessness to save themselves did they *perceive* the "fullness, suitableness and preciousness" of the Christ who saved sinners both from the penalty and power of sin and thus the "excellence" or "glory" of the God who had sent him. The pain of seeking conversion was the anguish and grief born of the seeker's desire to be saved, coupled with the seeker's increasing discovery of the power of sin.[19] In the latter part of the eighteenth century, Baptists, Methodists, and Presbyterians alike assumed that the awakened sinner's period of seeking conversion prior to receiving it, which they commonly referred to as "distress," would typically last from several weeks to a year.[20]

The anguish and grief of applying to Christ was heightened for eighteenth-century seekers by the common belief that not all persons who sought conversion would obtain it. Baptists and Methodists, as well as Presbyterians, preached the doctrine of the "day of grace." Although preachers employed this doctrine to encourage sinners to "flee the wrath to come without delay," the doctrine had another effect as well. Coupled with the typical length of the period of seeking, the doctrine of the day of grace could, and did on occasion, lead seekers to conclude that they had "sinned away" their day of grace and would never be saved.[21]

The fear that one might never be saved was also supported by the Calvinist doctrine of predestination. This doctrine taught that before the beginning of time God had chosen particular individuals to be saved and particular individuals to be damned. Methodist preachers rejected the doctrine outright.

---

[19]Ibid., 9; McGready, "The Believer Embracing Christ," 1: 126–27, 132–33; "Christ the Author and Finisher of the Life of Grace," 1: 92–95; "Parable of the Dry Bones," 1: 75–76; and "The Hope of the Hypocrite," 2: 36. For a similar view of seeking in the writings of the New Light Presbyterians, see Davies, "The Method of Salvation Through Jesus Christ," 1: 50–51. For similar views among Baptists and Methodists, see Taylor, 290–91; William Hickman, "A Short Account of My Life and Travels, for More Than Fifty Years; A Professed Servant of Jesus Christ, to Which is Added a Narrative of the Rise and Progress of Religion in the Early Settlement of Kentucky; Giving an Account of the Difficulties We Had to Encounter, etc.," typescript, n.d., Dargin-Carvin Library, Southern Baptist Sunday School Board, Nashville, 3–4; Robert Paine, *Life and Times of William McKendree*, 2 vols. (Nashville: Publishing House of the Methodist Episcopal Church South, 1874), 1: 48–49; John M'Lean, *Sketch of Rev. Philip Gatch, 1751–1835* (Cincinnati: Swormstedt and Poe, 1854), 10–17; and Henry Smith, *Recollections and Reflections of An Old Itinerant* (New York: n.p., 1848), 237–41.

[20]Benjamin St. James Fry, *The Life of Rev. Richard Whatcoat* (New York: Carlton and Phillips, 1852), 62–63; Henry Smith, 237–41; M'Lean, 12–17; Paine, 1: 45–50, Hickman, 4; Taylor, 290–98; McGready, "Parable of the Dry Bones," 1: 75–76; and Foote, *Virginia*, first series, 427. For examples of the use of the term "distress" in the literature of Baptists, Methodists, and Presbyterians, see Taylor, 291; McGready, "Christ the Author and Finisher of the Life of Grace," 1: 92; and M'Lean, 6–12.

[21]For the preaching of this doctrine by Methodists, see Paine, 1: 47–48, and Asbury, "21 April 1793," *Journal and Letters*, 1: 756; for Baptists, see Taylor, 291. For examples of seekers pained by the thought that they might have sinned away their day of grace, see Taylor, 291; Paine, 1: 48; and M'Lean, 12–17.

Baptist and New Light Presbyterian preachers, while affirming the truth of the doctrine, did not emphasize it. The collected sermons of Samuel Davies included only two sermons on predestination.[22] Moreover, Davies had sought to calm the fears aroused by the doctrine by urging that "the number of holy and happy creatures in the universe will be incomparably greater than that of miserable criminals."[23] Nevertheless, eighteenth-century seekers could, and on occasion did, conclude that they had been chosen for damnation.[24]

Although there was a common core to the preaching of Baptists, Methodists, and Presbyterians reflected in their mutual appreciation of the writings of the English Puritans, there was a difference in the spirituality of Presbyterians from that of Baptists and Methodists. Baptists and Methodists put great stock in assurances of having been forgiven and converted that seekers professed to have received through dreams, visions, voices, seeing Christ with the eyes of the body, particular scriptures impressed upon the mind, and inexplicable feelings of having been forgiven and converted.[25] McGready, in the tradition of his New Light forebears, stressed that the only reliable assurance of having been forgiven and converted was the experience or feeling of a new heart or will toward God that made one willing to go to Christ for forgiveness and release from the power of sin. Moreover, in keeping with New Light Presbyterian tradition, McGready insisted that the love of God and consequent sorrow over sin born of a view of the glory of God in the face of Christ Jesus was not based on the sinner's assurance that God had forgiven his or her own sins. Rather, the love of God that made one "willing" to come to Christ both for pardon and release from the power of sin was based purely on one's perception of the "excellence" or "glory" of the moral character of the God who saves helpless sinners and not on anything that the seeker believed that God had done or would do for her or him in particular.[26]

Stone recalled that for one year he was "tossed on the waves of uncertainty–laboring, praying, and striving to obtain saving faith–sometimes desponding, and almost despairing of ever getting it."[27] Stone did not describe particular events from the first several months of his struggle for conversion. He did, however, describe the final period of his distress in some detail.

His account begins with a meeting that he attended on the Sandy River in Virginia along with several other students from Caldwell's academy in February 1791. This occasion was a "sacramental meeting" in the Scots tradition that had been widely adopted by eighteenth-century American

---

[22]See Davies, "God is Love," 1: 315–37; and "The Vessels of Mercy and the Vessels of Wrath Delineated," 2: 274–90.

[23]Davies, "God is Love," 1: 331–32.

[24]Taylor, 291–92.

[25]Stone, *Biography*, 5. See also John Wesley, *John Wesley's Fifty-Three Sermons*, ed. Edward H. Sugden (Nashville: Abingdon Press, 1984), 142–43, 146–54, 650–51, 658–59.

[26]McGready, "Christ the Author and Finisher of the Life of Grace," 1: 93–95; "The Work of the Spirit Distinguished From that of the Devil," 2: 10. For a discussion of the New Light Presbyterian view of "assurance," see Trinterud, 189–91.

[27]Stone, *Biography*, 9.

Presbyterians. Typically, several congregations and preachers shared in such observances of the Lord's supper. On Friday, Saturday, and Sunday the ministers preached sermons on general themes related to conversion and the Christian life. On Sunday the supper was observed. Oftentimes a thanksgiving service followed on Monday.[28]

Prior to the supper, one of the ministers delivered the "action" sermon, describing the characteristics of persons invited by Christ to share in the supper. If an earlier sermon had not done so, this sermon might also include a listing of characteristics of persons who were not to commune, lest they bring condemnation upon themselves. In the New Light tradition, the purpose of "fencing the table" was to encourage persons to examine their relationship with God. Though New Light preachers taught that the supper was "the peculiar privilege of such as are true Christians already; and is intended only to nourish and improve true religion where it is begun," they urged that if one had experienced even the slightest measure of love to God, one was invited, indeed commanded, by Christ to participate in the supper.[29]

Following the action sermon, individuals received tokens from the elders signifying that they fit the character of persons invited to the supper by Christ. Communicants were seated at long tables to celebrate the supper, one seating following another until all had been served.[30]

At the meeting Stone attended, the action sermon was delivered by Hampden-Sydney College president John Blair Smith. Smith preached from Psalm 51:17, "The sacrifices of God are a broken spirit; a broken and a contrite heart, O God, Thou wilt not despise."[31] Smith described a broken and contrite heart and urged all of that character to approach the Lord's table "on pain of his sore displeasure." In Smith's description of a broken and contrite heart, Stone recognized his own heart. To identify with a description of the character of persons invited to the Lord's table implied that one had been converted. Stone began to hope that he had been converted. At length, he responded to Smith's urgent invitations and partook of the Lord's supper.[32]

That evening, James McGready preached from Daniel 5:27, "Tekel, thou art weighed in the balances, and art found wanting." The purpose of McGready's sermon was to distinguish between true and false conversion, a purpose well honored by Presbyterians, Baptists, and Methodists alike. According to McGready, awakened sinners were often "deceived" about their relationship with God and thus "rested" in their pilgrimage toward conversion in something less than true religion. McGready taught that in every case of such "resting," deceived sinners believed that they had fulfilled the command

---

[28]Ibid. For an account of the Scots lineage of the American Presbyterian sacramental meeting, see Leigh Eric Schmidt, *Holy Fairs: Scottish Communions and American Revivals in the Early Modern Period* (Princeton, N.J.: Princeton University Press, 1989).

[29]Davies, "The Christian Feast," 2: 98–100, 171; Doddridge, 353–54. See also Trinterud, 181–82.

[30]For a description of such a meeting, see Foote, *Virginia*, 103–5.

[31] All biblical quotations are from the *King James Version*.

[32]Stone, *Biography*, 9.

to love God through the accomplishment of some "work." According to McGready, the "works" of the deceived varied greatly: Some were outward works, such as keeping the Sabbath and attending preaching services, while others were inward works, such as "a lively flow of affections" in response to preaching or "a more than common enlargement" in the act of prayer. However, all were alike "legal," motivated by a desire to fulfill God's law, rooted in love of self and fear of hell, rather than in true love for God. McGready allowed that deceived sinners were sincere in their profession. Nevertheless, they were "hypocrites," persons who professed to being something (in this case, Christians!) that they were not.[33]

Stone reported that before McGready had finished speaking, he had "lost all hope" of having been converted. Indeed, he claimed that he had lost "all feeling, and had sunk into an indescribable apathy." In other words, he had lost the "will" to continue striving for conversion. Relating a conversation between himself and McGready in which he reported that McGready "labored to arouse me from my torpor by the terrors of God and the horrors of hell," Stone stated, "I told him that his labors were lost upon me—that I was entirely callous." According to New Light tradition, to lose one's will to seek salvation was evidence of being damned. Although Stone did not use the term "eternal reprobation" or refer to having sinned away his day of grace, he appears to have believed that he was damned.[34]

Stone recounted that for several weeks following the meeting on the Sandy River, he remained in a state of deep depression: "I wandered alone, my strength failed me, and sighs and groans filled my days." He returned home at the request of his relatives, who had received word of his condition. As a consequence of his visit, his mother and several other relatives were awakened and led to seek religion. His mother eventually became a Methodist. These developments must have surprised him, given his earlier comment that he had feared that his relatives would oppose his decision to seek religion. However, he did not indicate that the interest of his relatives in religion did anything to lessen his despondency. Rather, he reported that he returned to Caldwell's academy from Virginia "in the same state of mind" as he had been when he left.[35]

---

[33]Ibid., 10. McGready, "The Hope of the Hypocrite," 2: 36–38; "The Work of the Spirit Distinguished From that of the Devil," 2: 10–13; and "The Experience and Privileges of the True Believer," 1: 145–48. See also Davies, "The Connection Between Holiness and Felicity," 1: 162; and "The Nature and Necessity of True Repentance," 2: 303. James Blair Smith was also concerned to distinguish between true and false religion. See Foote, *Virginia*, first series, 427, 444. For evidence of this concern in the teaching of Baptists, see Taylor, 288–90, 295–98. For evidence of the same concern in the teaching of Methodists, see Asbury, "10 August 1774," 1:127; see also Doddridge, 310–11. Asbury wrote that Doddridge's work had "pleased" and "instructed" him and "would be of great service to our societies." See Asbury, "23 April 1778," 1:268.

[34]Stone, *Biography*, 10; McGready, "The Excellencies of Christ as Displayed in the Plan of Salvation," 1: 121; "On the Nature and Consequence of Sin," 1: 60; Davies, "The Wonderful Compassion of Christ," 2:340–41; "The Danger of Lukewarmness in Religion," 1:279.

[35]Stone, *Biography*, 10.

Soon after his return, Stone attended a meeting at Alamance, one of the churches pastored by Caldwell. On Sunday evening, William Hodge, a preacher whom Stone claimed that he had not heard before, addressed the congregation. Hodge had earlier begun to prepare for the ministry but had become discouraged after the death of his mentor, Rev. John Debow, a Presbyterian of the New Light tradition who had pastored the Hawfield's Church in Guilford County. Under McGready's preaching, Hodge had once again felt the call to preach.[36]

Stone remembered that Hodge's text was "God is love" and that Hodge spoke "with much animation, and with many tears...of the love of God to sinners, and of what that love had done for sinners." Stone was deeply affected: "My heart warmed with love for that lovely *character* described...My *mind* was absorbed in the doctrine–to me it appeared new." According to Presbyterians, to find one's heart "warmed" with *love of God* and to find something "new" in the preaching of what God *had done for sinners* were signs of conversion or, to use McGready's term, the implantation of the spiritual principle. Stone reported that he began to hope anew that he had been converted, while at the same time seeking to repress his hope for fear that he was deceiving himself.[37]

Following the sermon, Stone retired to the woods with his Bible. "Here I read and prayed," he wrote, "with various feelings, between hope and fear." Judging by Stone's reference to the texts "Him that cometh unto me I will in no wise cast out" and "Jesus came to seek and save the lost" in his account of this event, it appears that Hodge may have concluded his sermon with a call to the "brokenhearted" or "helpless" sinner to come to Christ. Hodge's sermons were never published; however, McGready used these very passages of scripture in urging the sinner who felt "ruined and undone" to come to Christ for salvation. The purpose of such an appeal was not to convince the sinner that his or her own sins had been forgiven, but rather to convince the sinner who felt helpless to save him or herself and now loved the God who saved helpless sinners that he or she was welcome to "come to Christ" for forgiveness and release from the power of sin. Whether Hodge had used those texts or not, Stone appears to have been reading the Bible and praying in order to determine whether he now loved God and had a *will* to go to Christ for forgiveness and release from the power of sin. Stone indicated that he discovered his answer as he read and prayed: "...the truth I had just heard, 'God is love,' prevailed. 'Jesus came to seek and save the lost.' 'Him that cometh unto me, I will in no wise cast out.' I yielded and sunk at his feet a *willing* subject." [38]

Stone reported that after his conversion he experienced the happiness that he had earlier observed in the converts at Caldwell's academy. "Secret"

---

[36]Foote, *North Carolina*, 226; see also James Smith, *History of the Christian Church* (Nashville: Cumberland Presbyterian Office, 1835), 562, 668.

[37]Stone, *Biography*, 10–11. Italics mine.

[38]Ibid., italics mine; McGready, "The Lord Jesus Christ, A Mighty Conqueror," 1:48–49.

prayer and meditation became his special delight. Even the task of pursuing a classical education took on a new aspect: "The study of the dead languages and of the sciences were not irksome but pleasant, from the consideration that I was engaged in them for the glory of God, to whom I had unreservedly devoted my all."[39]

The happiness of eighteenth-century Presbyterians, however, was not all sunshine without clouds. The Christian faced challenges that "tried" the believer's relationship with God. Stone reported such trials. In particular, the cost of boarding, tuition, books, and clothes had been greater than Stone had anticipated. Not having sufficient funds to continue at the academy, he considered relinquishing his studies. Caldwell encouraged him to continue his studies and promised that he could pay him later. Thus, encouraged by Caldwell, he renewed his efforts and completed his liberal education in the winter of 1793. He was twenty years old, having studied with Caldwell for three years. [40]

Following his conversion, his earlier plan of studying law as a means to wealth and social advancement had given way to a desire to preach the gospel. He informed Caldwell of his desire to preach but indicated that he had no assurance of having been divinely called to preach. Stone may have heard Baptist and Methodist preachers tell of having been divinely called through dreams and visions. In keeping with New Light Presbyterian tradition, Caldwell assured him that he had no right to expect a miracle to convince him that he had been divinely called to preach; if he had a hearty desire to "glorify God and save sinners by preaching," and if his "fathers in the ministry" should encourage him, he should not hesitate to pursue ordination. Caldwell further stated that he was glad to hear of Stone's desire to preach and, in order to expedite his receiving a license to preach, assigned a biblical text to him on which he was to write a discourse to present to the spring meeting of the Orange Presbytery. [41]

---

[39]Stone, *Biography*, 11, 13.
[40]Ibid., 11, 12.
[41]Ibid., 12. See also Trinterud, 90, 300; Thompson, 194; James Finley, *Essay on the Gospel Ministry* (Wilmington, Del.: James Adams, 1763), 31, 55.

3

From Call to Ordination

Stone, like several of his former classmates, became a candidate for the ministry at the spring meeting of the Orange Presbytery in 1793. It was the responsibility of the presbytery to receive, educate, and try candidates for the ministry. At the spring meeting, the presbytery assigned Stone and the other candidates particular subjects in divinity to study as "parts of trial" on which they were to be examined at the fall meeting of the presbytery.[1]

The subjects given to Stone and former classmate Samuel Holmes included the being and attributes of God and the doctrine of the Trinity. Stone and Holmes were assigned a text from Herman Witsius, a seventeenth-century Dutch Reformed theologian whose writings had been highly valued by eighteenth-century revivalist Presbyterians.[2]

Stone found Witsius difficult to follow. There was nothing unusual, however, in Witsius' presentation of the doctrine of the Trinity. It was a standard statement of the doctrine as articulated by Augustine (354–430 C.E.) in *The Trinity* and reaffirmed in the seventeenth-century Westminster Confession. As Stone reported, "Witsius would first prove that there was but one God, and then that there were three persons in this one God, the Father, Son and Holy Ghost–that the Father was unbegotten–the Son eternally begotten, and the Holy Ghost eternally proceeding from the Father and the Son–that it was idolatry to worship more Gods than one, and yet equal worship must be given to the Father, the Son, and Holy Ghost."[3] Witsius concluded that one of the "practical" values of the doctrine of the Trinity is that it is an "incomprehensible mystery, which surpasses all sense and reason" and, as such, teaches "that we must renounce our own wisdom in divine matters, and reduce every thought into captivity to the obedience of faith."[4]

---

[1]Orange Presbytery had been organized in 1770, taking its name from the fact that two of the seven original ministers had lived in the Orange County, North Carolina of that day. Ware, 45. In addition to a desire to preach, Presbyterians required of ministers "good natural gifts," conversion or "saving grace," knowledge, and orthodoxy. Finley, 31. See also Trinterud, 90, 300.

[2]Stone, *Biography*, 12. The book that Stone and Holmes were given appears to have been Herman Witsius, *Sacred Dissertations on What is Commonly Called the Apostle's Creed*, 2 vols., trans. Donald Fraser (Edinburgh: A. Fullarton and Co., 1823), vol. 1, 121–43. For evidence of Witsius' popularity among New Light Presbyterians, see Trinterud, 53–56.

[3]Stone, *Biography*, 13.

[4]Witsius, 143.

Stone had previously prayed to both the Father and the Son without fear of idolatry or concern for according them equal worship. The result of his effort to follow Witsius' teaching on the doctrine of the Trinity was that he "knew not how to pray." Consequently, the enjoyment of God that he had known since his conversion was soon curtailed. "Till now," he wrote, "secret prayer and meditation had been my delightful employ. It was a heaven on earth to approach my God, and Saviour; but now this heavenly exercise was checked, and gloominess and fear filled my troubled mind." Upon discovering that Holmes had been similarly affected by Witsius, Stone and Holmes "laid the book aside," believing that it was "calculated" to involve their minds in "mystic darkness" and to "cool the ardor" of their devotion.[5]

Stone, like most citizens of the early American republic, had been influenced by the broad currents of the English Enlightenment. The Enlightenment identified propositions that were "inconsistent" with our clear and distinct ideas as "contrary to reason." To Stone the idea that there was more than one God, *implied* in Witsius' teaching that equal worship must be given to the Father, Son, and Holy Ghost, was inconsistent with the clear and distinct idea that there is but one God. Witsius, of course, had not taught that there is more than one God. Rather, he had countered the idea that there is more than one God, implied by the teaching that equal worship must be given to Father, Son, and Holy Ghost, by "proving" that there is but one God. Stone, who noted that Witsius was the first theological text that he had ever read other than the Bible, was not familiar with the method of doing theology that defined Christian truth by holding in tension seemingly contradictory propositions. Thus, for Stone, Witsius' treatment of the doctrine of the Trinity did not point to an "incomprehensible mystery, which surpasses all sense and reason," but was simply "unintelligible."[6]

Fortunately, from Stone's Enlightenment-influenced perspective, Witsius' work on the Trinity was not the only treatment of the doctrine available to North Carolina ministerial candidates. Henry Patillo, one of the oldest and most respected members of the Orange Presbytery, preferred and had done much to publicize Isaac Watts's treatment of the Trinity. Although remembered now primarily for his hymns, such as "Joy to the World" and "When I Survey the Wondrous Cross," Isaac Watts was also widely recognized in eighteenth-century England and America as a philosopher and theologian.[7]

Watts (1674–1748) wrote on the Trinity for persons who, like himself, had been influenced by the Enlightenment and had difficulty with classical

---

[5]Stone, *Biography*, 13.

[6]Ibid.

[7]For information on Patillo, see Foote, *North Carolina*, 213–17. See also Herbert Snipes Turner, *Church in the Old Fields: Hawfield Presbyterian Church and Community in North Carolina* (Chapel Hill, N.C.: University of North Carolina Press, 1962), 53–54. For evidence of Patillo's efforts to publicize Watts's view, see Henry Patillo, *Sermons* (Wilmington, N.C.: James Adams, 1788), 117. See also John Cree, et al., *Evils of the Work Now Prevailing in the United States of America, Under the Name of a Revival of Religion: Shown by a Comparison of That as It is Represented by Its Friends and Promoters with the Word of God* (Washington, Pa.,: n.p., 1804), 35. Samuel Davies praised Watts's philosophical writings; see Foote, *Virginia*, first series, 266, 292.

statements of doctrine such as that of Witsius. He argued that the biblical doctrine of the Trinity was not *contrary* to reason. To be sure, the doctrine that "three Gods are one God, or three persons are one person" was contrary to reason. Moreover, Watts asserted, in sharp contrast to Witsius' exalting of "incomprehensible mystery," that if the scriptures taught that three Gods are one God or that three persons are one person there would be "reason indeed to disbelieve" the scriptures, since "neither reason nor religion can require us to believe plain inconsistency." However, according to Watts, the scriptures did not teach that three Gods are one God. Rather, the scriptures taught that "the same true Godhead belongs to the Father, Son and Spirit, and...that the Father, Son and Spirit, are three distinct agents or principles of action, as may reasonably be called persons." Thus, according to Watts, to say that "the Father is God, the Son is God, and the Spirit is God" was not contrary to the proposition that there is one God. The mistake, according to Watts, was to confuse "opinions" or human explications of the revealed doctrine with the doctrine itself. Watts promised that the theologian who "well distinguishes between the plain Scriptural doctrine itself, and the particular explications of it" will hold "faith in the divine doctrine firm and unmoved, while several human forms of explication are attacked, and perhaps destroyed."[8]

As for human forms of explication of the doctrine of the Trinity, Watts argued that the primary problem with most explications of the doctrine was the identification of "the Son of God" as the second person of the Godhead. According to Watts, it was this identification of the Son of God that led to the idea that three Gods are one God, or three persons are one person. This problem would be solved, he suggested, by recognizing that the scriptures identified the Son of God not as the second person of the Godhead, but as the human *soul* of Christ–a human soul "formed" by God and "united to the divine nature" long before his human *body* was born of Mary. To be sure, the proposition that the human soul of Christ was a distinct agent or principle of action belonging to the one Godhead was *above* reason. That is, the truth or probability of this proposition could not be derived by reason. However, the proposition that the human soul of Christ was a distinct agent belonging to the one Godhead was not *contrary* to the idea that there was one God.[9]

In regard to the matter of the proper worship owed to the members of the Trinity, Watts asserted that the scriptures revealed all that was necessary for

---

[8]Isaac Watts, "The Christian Doctrine of the Trinity; or, Father, Son, and Spirit, Three Persons and One God, Asserted and Proved, With Their Divine Rights and Honors Vindicated, By Plain Evidence of Scripture, Without the Aid or Encumbrance of Human Schemes," in *The Works of The Late Reverend and Learned Isaac Watts*, 6 vols. (London: J. and T. Longman, 1757), 4: 417, 426, 461–65, 491.

[9]Watts, 468. If Watts's views of Christ were accepted, then all one would need to fully explicate Watts's scripture doctrine of the Trinity would be evidence that the Father and Spirit are distinct agents or persons united to the divine nature in the same sense as the human soul of Christ is a distinct agent or person united to the divine nature. In fact, further study seems to have convinced Watts that the Holy Spirit was not a person and that the one Godhead subsists in only two persons, the Father and the Son. See Watts, *A Faithful Inquiry After the Ancient and Original Doctrine of the Trinity, Taught by Christ and His Apostles* (London: n.p., 1745), quoted in Stone, ed., *Christian Messenger* 2 (6 April 1828), 128.

proper faith and practice. For Watts, it was not necessary to fully comprehend the doctrine of the Trinity in order to worship God aright. He argued that the Christian could be sure that it was proper to offer "divine worship and honors" to Father, Son, and Spirit because "their godhead, or communion in the divine nature" is clearly revealed in scripture. On the other hand, the Christian could be sure that it was wrong "to pay the same form of address and adoration to each of the sacred three" because the very content of revelation implied that one should worship and address the various members of the Trinity with an eye to the "special offices and character, which the Scripture assigns them."[10]

Having heard of Watts's "treatise" on the Trinity, Stone and Holmes obtained a copy, read it "with pleasure and understanding," and accepted Watts's views. As Henry Patillo administered the theological examination of the ministerial candidates at the fall 1793 meeting of the Orange Presbytery, Stone and Holmes had nothing to fear regarding their adoption of Watts's views. When Patillo "came to the subject of the Trinity, he was very short, and his interrogatories involved no peculiarities of the system." Stone remembered that Holmes's answers and his had been "honest and satisfactory."[11]

Stone's "trials," however, did not end with his discovery of Watts's treatise on the Trinity and his successful theological examination under Patillo. Before the spring 1794 meeting of the Orange Presbytery when he was scheduled to complete his theological trials and be licensed to preach, he became "much depressed" and decided to abandon the idea of preaching and to pursue some other calling. A major source of his depression was theological. "My mind," he wrote, "was embarrassed with many abstruse doctrines, which I admitted as true; yet could not satisfactorily reconcile with others which were plainly taught in the Bible." John Wesley, who had also been influenced by the Enlightenment, indicated having suffered similar intellectual embarrassment when, in 1740, he boldly rejected the doctrine that God chose certain persons to be saved and others to be damned before the foundation of the world, arguing that certain implications of the doctrine were inconsistent with the plain message of the Bible that God loves and desires the salvation of all persons.[12]

Two of the doctrines that "embarrassed" Stone's mind were the doctrines of "God's eternal decree" and "the secret will of God." Both of these doctrines, as taught in the Westminster Confession of the Presbyterian Church, combined what Stone viewed as a proposition "plainly" taught in scripture

---

[10]Watts, 417, 461–65, 472–84.

[11]Stone, *Biography*, 13, 14.

[12]Ibid., 14; John Wesley, "Free Grace," *The Works of John Wesley*, 14 vols. (London: Wesleyan Conference Office, 1872; reprint, Grand Rapids: Zondervan, 1955–1959), vol. 7, 373–86 (page citations are to the reprint edition). George Whitefield had responded that Calvinists did not teach the implications of the doctrine of predestination that Wesley had found inconsistent with the gospel. See George Whitefield to John Wesley, Bethesda, Georgia, December 24, 1740, in *Memoirs of Rev. George Whitefield*, rev., ed. John Gillies (Middletown, Conn.: Hunt and Noyes, 1837), 626–42.

with another proposition that appeared to him to have implications that were inconsistent with the proposition plainly taught in scripture. In the case of the doctrine of "God's eternal degree," the proposition plainly taught in scripture was that God is not "the author of sin." But the doctrine of "God's eternal degree," as taught in the Westminster Confession, also stated that "God from all eternity did by the most wise and holy counsel of his own will, freely and unchangeably ordain whatsoever comes to pass," which implied, to Stone, that God was the author of sin. In the case of "the secret will of God," the idea plainly taught in scripture was that God desired the salvation of all persons. This was the "revealed" will of God. But the doctrine also stated that God had a "secret will" by which God had determined that certain individuals would be damned, which implied, to Stone, that God did not desire the salvation of all persons. As earlier, when he had been confused by Witsius' treatment of the Trinity, Stone's intellectual embarrassment affected his devotion. "Having been so long engaged and confined to the study of systematic divinity from the Calvinistic mould," he wrote, "my zeal, comfort, and spiritual life became considerably abated."[13]

Having decided to abandon the idea of preaching and to seek some other calling, he traveled to the home of his brother, Matthew Stone, in Oglethorpe County, Georgia. Land adaptable to the cultivation of tobacco was ample and cheap in northeastern Georgia, and many Virginians had recently immigrated to the region. By the time Stone arrived at his brother's home, Matthew Stone had acquired plantations in Franklin, Green, Wilkes, and Oglethorpe counties totaling more than sixteen hundred acres.[14]

Through the influence of Matthew and Stone's half-brother Thomas, who had also immigrated to the region, Stone was chosen professor of languages at a newly established Methodist academy near Washington in Wilkes County. This appointment was fortuitous because the sources of Stone's depression in the spring of 1794 were not only theological, but also financial. His funds were exhausted, and none of his relatives had been willing to aid him.[15]

Stone exerted himself to fill his teaching appointment with honor to himself and profit to his students and had "the unspeakable satisfaction of receiving the approbation of the trustees of the institution, and of the *literati* of the country." He claimed, however, that the high esteem in which he was held in the community was another sort of trial—a spiritual trial that nearly caused him to "make shipwreck of faith and a good conscience." Educated persons were at a premium in the northeastern Georgia of the 1790s and, according to Stone, received marked attention from "the most respectable part of the community." Stone was frequently invited to "tea parties" and "social circles,"

---

[13]Stone, *Biography*, 14; *Christian Messenger* 13 (October 1843), 161–62; *The Constitution of the Presbyterian Church in the United States of America, containing The Confession of Faith, The Catechisms, and The Directory for the Worship of God: Together with the Plan of Government and Discipline* (Philadelphia: Presbyterian Board of Publication, 1842), *The Confession of Faith*, chap. 3, sec. 1, 21–22.

[14]Ware, 33.

[15]Stone, *Biography*, 14; Ware, 33.

which he attended for a time. These "fascinating pleasures" turned out to be what Baptists, Methodists, and Presbyterians referred to as a "snare." "Though I still maintained the profession of religion, and did not disgrace it by improper conduct," Stone wrote, "yet my devotion was cold, and communion with God much interrupted." Seeing his danger, he denied himself these fashionable social occasions in order to "live more devoted to God."[16]

The superintendent of the Methodist academy was Hope Hull (1763–1818), whom Stone rightly identified as "a very distinguished preacher of that denomination." Like other Methodist leaders of the era, Hull had come to the ministry out of a background in the trades. As an apprenticed carpenter in Baltimore, he had joined the Methodists in their first Episcopal Conference in America in June 1785. Having preached circuits in the Carolinas and Virginia, he had been assigned to Georgia in 1788. Stone recounted having accompanied Hull and several other Methodist preachers to a conference at Charleston, South Carolina, but made no comments regarding the conference.[17]

While in Georgia, and employed by the Methodists, Stone "constantly" attended the preaching of John Springer, whom he described as "a very zealous Presbyterian." Born near Wilmington, Delaware, Springer (1744–1798) was a graduate of Princeton who had pursued theological studies under the direction of James Hall, one of the leading members of the Orange Presbytery. His published works are remarkably similar in both style and content to those of James McGready. In short, Springer was a Georgia representative of the New Light Presbyterianism in which Stone had been converted and called to ministry.[18]

Under Springer's preaching, Stone "began to feel a very strong desire again to preach the Gospel." He tried to "resist" and "suppress" these "impressions," but as a result, his "comforts were destroyed." According to New Light tradition, such experience was evidence of a divine call to ministry.[19]

In the spring of 1796, after a year and a half of teaching in Georgia, Stone, now twenty-three years old, returned to North Carolina. On April 6, 1796, he successfully completed his remaining theological examinations and, along with two other candidates, was licensed by the Orange Presbytery to preach the gospel as a "probationer" for the ministry within the bounds of the Orange Presbytery or wherever he should be "orderly called." Henry Patillo addressed the candidates and presented a Bible to each of them with the solemn charge, "Go ye into all the world, and preach the gospel to every creature."[20]

---

[16]Stone, *Biography*, 15.

[17]Stone, *Biography*, 14, 15–16; George Gilman Smith, Jr., *The History of Methodism in Georgia and Florida from 1785–1865* (Macon, Ga.: Jno. W. Burke and Co., 1877), 41–43.

[18]Stone, *Biography*, 15; John Springer, *Solemn Truths Stated and Urged in a Lecture and Sermon to which is Prefixed a Short Sketch of the Author's Life* (Augusta, Ga.: Bobby and Bruce, 1805). For further information on Springer, see James Stacy, *A History of the Presbyterian Church in Georgia* (Elberton, Ga.: Press of the Star, 1912), 18–21.

[19]Stone, *Biography*, 15.

[20]Ibid., 16; Ware, 54.

At the same meeting, Stone adopted the Westminster Confession of Faith as containing the system of doctrine taught in the scriptures. This does not mean that he had overcome his earlier embarrassment with Calvinist theology. He claimed that during the first years of his ministry, he viewed the Calvinist doctrines of election, reprobation, and predestination as "true, yet unfathomable mysteries" and "confined" his preaching to "the practical part of religion." He may have adopted this stance on the advice of David Caldwell, who advised just such a course of action to another of his students who was troubled by the same questions.[21]

Whether Stone was advised by Caldwell or not, one might well ask why Stone adopted the Westminster Confession, especially given his exposure to the Methodists, who openly rejected the Calvinist doctrines of election and reprobation. One can only conclude that Stone felt more at home with the Presbyterians, intellectual embarrassment notwithstanding, than with the Methodists. He had been converted among Presbyterians. Moreover, he had been converted in the Presbyterian fashion. He had not heard a voice, seen a vision, or experienced unexplainable feelings of having been forgiven and accepted by God. Rather, his heart had "warmed" when he had beheld with his understanding the "lovely character" of the One who had acted for helpless sinners. Stone was a Presbyterian, as the members of the Orange Presbytery seem to have recognized.

Having been licensed, Stone and Robert Foster, another candidate of the Orange Presbytery, were appointed to itinerate in the "lower parts" of North Carolina until the fall meeting. The novels that Stone read as a youth depicted the adventures of young men whose travels introduced them to a variety of persons and challenges, interspersed by chance meetings with former acquaintances. Stone may have been influenced by this literature when he wrote his account of his travels during the two and a half years following his licensure by the Orange Presbytery.[22]

Following a brief visit to his mother's home in Virginia, Stone met Foster in North Carolina, and they set out on horseback for the lower parts of the state. The "lower parts" were the coastal counties of eastern North Carolina. There were few Presbyterians in that region, the overwhelming majority of the population having been affiliated with the former Church of England. After a few days' journey, they reached their destination and made appointments to preach the following Sunday. On Friday, however, Foster informed Stone that he had decided to leave the ministry, believing that he was not qualified for such a "solemn" task. Stone claimed that he "sunk" under this

---

[21]"*Minutes* of the Orange Presbytery (6 April 1796)," quoted in Thomas Cleland, *Letters to Barton W. Stone, Containing a Vindication Principally of the Doctrines of the Trinity, the Divinity and Atonement of the Saviour, Against His Recent Attack in a Second Edition of His "Address"* (Lexington, Ky.: Thomas T. Skillman, 1822), 171; Stone, *Biography*, 29. The other student was Samuel McAdow. See Richard Beard, *Brief Biographical Sketches of Some of the Early Ministers of the Cumberland Presbyterian Church*, second series (Nashville: Cumberland Presbyterian Board of Publication, 1874), 13–15.

[22]The following account is from Stone, *Biography*, 16–25.

disclosure, since he believed that Foster was more qualified for the task than he.

Secretly resolving to leave North Carolina and to travel to some "distant country" where he would be a total stranger, Stone mounted his horse on Saturday morning while Foster was absent and started for the thinly populated frontier of Florida. On Sunday morning, Stone attended worship in the neighborhood where he had lodged the night before. A "pious old lady" in the congregation, who knew him and suspected that he was "acting the part of Jonah," warned him "of the danger" and advised him that if he did not like the lower parts of North Carolina, he should go over the mountains to the West. While ignoring her warning not to play the part of Jonah, he did decide to go to the West, rather than to Florida. Later that day, he was surprised to see Foster at the evening service of the same congregation. Foster "gently upbraided" him for having left without him. He told Foster about his plan to travel to the West, and Foster decided to accompany him.

The following morning he and Foster started out together without naming their destination to anyone. They were "jogging leisurely along the way to Fort Chiswell" in Virginia and had just passed a small house near the road when Captain Sanders, a Presbyterian acquaintance from North Carolina, hailed them and caused them to halt. Sanders was moving from North Carolina to the Cumberland region in Tennessee and had stopped for a season in Wythe County, Virginia. As there were no Presbyterian preachers in the area, he insisted that Stone and Foster preach the next Sunday for the Presbyterians at Grimes's meetinghouse, located not far from there on Reed Creek. They both refused but at length agreed to worship with the congregation.

On Sunday Stone and Foster encountered a large congregation at Grimes's meetinghouse. With much effort, Stone was prevailed upon to ascend the pulpit. The result was different than he had expected. "While singing and praying," he remembered, "my mind was happily relieved, and I was enabled to speak with boldness and with profit to the people." Following the service, he was asked to make another appointment to preach. During the following week, he preached at several places in the area. He also accepted the "urgent and affectionate entreaties of the people" to remain in the region for a while. Thus, Foster continued west on his own. Stone remained in Wythe and Montgomery counties, preaching frequently, until July 1796. He then resumed his journey to the West.

Stone did not indicate why he continued his journey to the West in July 1796. Based on his experience in Wythe and Montgomery counties, he had surely overcome at least some of his doubts regarding his qualifications for the ministry. Given his subsequent willingness to preach, it does not appear that he was trying to run from the call to ministry. The lure of cheap land and the opportunity for a fresh start in the West may have captured his imagination as it had that of many North Carolina and Virginia Presbyterians. Or, as seems more likely, the attraction may simply have been the fact that large numbers of Presbyterians were moving to the West. In contrast to eastern

North Carolina, where there were few Presbyterians, Stone could expect to find in the West an increasing number of persons who shared his Presbyterian faith.

Stone described his journey from southwestern Virginia to the Cumberland settlements in Tennessee in great detail. The first night of his journey he stayed in the home of a Lutheran minister. He reported that he was "kindly received and entertained," but that he made the following notation in Latin in his journal: "At night fleas disturb me, and they drive away sleep. I am weary of life."

The second night of his journey he stayed in the home of a Thomas family. He had discovered in advance that the Thomases were pious Baptists, especially Mrs. Thomas and their daughter. Wanting to engage the family in theological conversation, he remarked that "if hell be worse than to be bedded with ten thousand fleas, it must be a dreadful place." In response, Mrs. Thomas stated that "there is a hell, and if you do not repent, and be converted, you will find it to your eternal sorrow." The daughter affirmed Mrs. Thomas' statements, and they both "affectionately exhorted" him to repent. He maintained the ruse by asking them whether they believed that a person must be "born again" in order to get to heaven. Calling him an "ignorant Nicodemus," Mrs. Thomas answered that she did. He then asked her what it meant to be born again. He reported that she "described it well" and seemed to be genuinely concerned for his supposed condition. He stated many "common cavils against the doctrine," which, he claimed, "she answered with intelligence" until, wearied with his "supposed infidelity," she ceased to talk.

Mr. Thomas offered to show him to his bed. He responded that first he wanted to hear Mr. Thomas pray, for he understood that Christians always prayed in their families morning and evening. He reported that Mr. Thomas was "thunder stricken" and paced the floor deeply groaning, while Mrs. Thomas laid the Bible on the table. He offered to try to pray, if Mr. Thomas would not. He then walked to the table, "read, sung and prayed, and immediately retired to bed." The next morning the mother and daughter "gently reproved" him for deceiving them, apologized for their conduct, and dismissed him "with their blessing."

Continuing his journey, he lodged Saturday night near the Holston River, close to the home of Presbyterian preacher Edward Crawford. On Sunday he attended a service conducted by Crawford, planning to keep his identity as a licensed probationer for the ministry a secret until after worship. Here, to his astonishment, he saw Robert Foster, who was teaching school in the area! Against Stone's protests, Foster introduced Stone to Crawford before the service, with the result that Stone preached.

After remaining in the Holston area for several days, he traveled to Knoxville to "the house of rendezvous" for persons wanting to journey through the wilderness to Nashville. Two men were there, waiting to form a company to make the trip. Stone agreed to join them and, after packing provisions for themselves and their horses, they left Knoxville on August 14, 1796.

About sunset they saw fifteen to twenty Indians about a hundred yards away from them. The Indians "sprang up," and Stone and his companions rode on at a quick pace. After several miles they slacked their gait for a council. They concluded that the Indians would pursue them, but that, unless the Indians had dogs, they could evade them. The Cumberland Mountain was only a few miles ahead. Knowing that they could not ascend it at night without danger to themselves and their horses, they determined to turn off the road near the foot of the mountain and lie concealed until morning. They rode to the mountain, turned aside into a thick brushwood, tied their horses, and lay down on their blankets to rest.

Being very tired, Stone slept so soundly that he did not perceive a shower of rain that awakened the other two and sent them off in search of shelter. At length, he awoke and noticed that his companions were missing. All was silent except for the sounds of wolves and foxes on the mountain. He noted that his feelings were "unpleasant," but that he consoled himself by remembering that the same God who had always protected him was present and could protect him still: "To him I humbly commended myself, laid down again, and securely slept till day." When he awoke, he saw his companions about a hundred yards off, sheltered by a large tree.

While climbing the mountain that morning, Stone's horse lost one of his front shoes and soon became lame. Stone asked one of his companions to put his pack on the lame horse and let him ride his pack horse. The companion refused. Thus, Stone trotted after his horse, driving him along after the others until he was overcome by weariness. His companions never slacked their pace and finally rode off, leaving him "vexed" at the their "baseness" in leaving him alone in the wilderness.

He continued his trip on foot, driving his horse before him, until he reached Major White's cabin on Bledsoe's Creek, where he was "kindly" received and rested for several days. From there he traveled to Shiloh, where he "joyfully" met several old friends who had recently moved there from North Carolina, including fellow Presbyterian ministers and former classmates William McGee and John Anderson. Anderson agreed to travel and preach with Stone through all the settlements of the Cumberland region.

The Cumberland settlements were in Davidson and Sumner counties, a few miles out from Nashville, which was then a village of fewer than four hundred people. Among the settlements that Stone and Anderson visited was Mansker's Creek, twelve miles northeast of Nashville, where they "often preached to respectable and large assemblies, from a stand erected by the people in a shady grove." Here he remembered engaging in two dramatic confrontations.

One of these confrontations was with a "dancing master," who was conducting a dancing school for the youth of the neighborhood. Baptists, Methodists, and Presbyterians opposed dancing, believing that, like other amusements, it distracted persons from seeking religion. Stone spoke "publicly and freely against the practice," with the result that some of the youth withdrew from the school. In response, the dancing teacher swore that he would "whip" Stone the next time he preached at Mansker's Creek. When Stone arrived for his next appointment at Mansker's Creek, he was met by the dancing master and a "band of ruffians, armed with clubs" who stood within "striking distance" of him as he preached. Undeterred, Stone proceeded with his sermon, not forgetting to oppose dancing. Noticing that the congregation was staring at them, the dancing master and his armed associates departed one by one.

The other confrontation was with a Deist. Deists relied on natural theology and approved only those portions of scripture that were in accord with reason. On one occasion, immediately after Stone had concluded his sermon and come down from the stand, he was approached by a man who said, "I suppose you know me, sir." When Stone replied that he did not, the man introduced himself as "Burns, the celebrated Deist of this neighborhood." Stone responded that he was sorry to hear him boast of his "infidelity" and asked him to define a Deist. Burns answered that a Deist "believes there is but one God." Stone replied, "But, sir, what is the character of your God?" Burns answered that he believed that God is "infinitely good, just, and merciful." Stone asked Burns where he had gotten this information. Burns answered, "From the book of nature," to which Stone replied, "show me the page in that book which declares that God is infinitely good." Burns answered, "We see the traces of goodness everywhere; hence I conclude that God, the great governor of the universe, is infinitely good." To which Stone replied, "Mr. Burns, please turn your eye on the opposite page of your book, and see the miseries, and attend to the groans of the millions who are suffering and dying every moment. You must conclude, from your own premises, that God, the great governor of the universe, is also infinitely evil and malevolent. Your God, Mr. Burns, is infinitely good, and infinitely evil–a perfect contradiction! You must be an atheist, Mr. Burns, not a Deist."

Pressing further, Stone asked Burns to show him the page in his book that teaches that God is infinitely just. Burns responded that "it is evident…that there is a principle of justice in every man: therefore I conclude that God, the Maker of all men, must be infinitely just." To which Stone replied, "Mr. Burns I can show you in your own book as many men of unjust principles, as you can men of just principles. Then it follows from your premises, that God, the Maker, is infinitely just, and infinitely unjust. Surely, Mr. Burns, atheism is your creed!" He continued, "Here is a good citizen, a good husband, a good father, acknowledged such by all; yet his whole life is full of suffering, pain, and want. Here also is a bad citizen, a bad husband, a bad father, acknowledged such by all; yet he is free from pain, and wallows in wealth. How can you reconcile this with the infinite justice of God, the great governor of the universe?" Burns responded that just rewards would be given in another world. To which Stone replied, "But Mr. Burns, your book nowhere teaches this doctrine; you have stolen it from our Bible." Stone claimed that Burns said that he would see him at another time and "retired in confusion, the congregation smiling approbation at his defeat."

Having "preached through" the Cumberland settlements, Stone and Anderson decided to visit Kentucky. Their route took them "through an extensive, uninhabited tract of barrens, or prairies" until they reached "a fine timbered country, densely settled by wealthy farmers." The center of this region was Lexington, the largest town west of the Alleghenies, with a population of about fifteen hundred. Stone and Anderson preached throughout the region until the winter became severe, at which time Anderson settled with the Presbyterian congregation at Ashridge and Stone with the Presbyterian congregations at Cane Ridge and Concord.

Stone did not offer any reason for his settling at Cane Ridge and Concord other than the coming of winter. There are two reasons, however, why this area may have been especially attractive to him. First, in 1797 the religious background of nearly the entire population of the Cane Ridge and Concord communities was Presbyterian. This was a significantly different religious context than that of the "lower parts" of North Carolina, where the majority of the population was former Church of England and where, less than two years earlier, Stone had concluded that he was not qualified for ministry. Second, as Stone indicated, the Cane Ridge and Concord communities were composed of "wealthy" farmers. Although Stone had relinquished his earlier dreams of wealth and preferment, he continued to travel in circles that included the middle and upper classes of society. Religiously and socially, then, Cane Ridge and Concord were communities seemingly made for Stone.[23]

Nevertheless, in an account of his theological development published in 1805, Stone indicated that it was after he had settled at Cane Ridge and Concord that he experienced the greatest challenge to his being ordained as a Presbyterian minister. Within a few months of his settlement with the Cane Ridge and Concord churches, several persons were added to the churches. In the midst of this "revival," his "soul was very happy in the enjoyment of God," and he "felt an ardent love for all the world and earnestly longed for their salvation." One evening it occurred to him that since God did not save all persons, God must not desire the salvation of all persons. Therefore, the spirit in him that loved all the world and earnestly desired the salvation of all must not be the Spirit of God, but a spirit of delusion. In deep distress he fell prostrate before God, to cry for mercy; but as soon as he began to pray, it occurred to him that as he was deluded, he must still be an unbeliever, and if so, his very prayers would be sin.[24]

For Presbyterians of the New Light tradition, to "believe" was to be willing to come to Christ for both pardon and release from the power of sin. It was a

[23]Fred J. Hood, "Kentucky," in *Religion in the Southern States: A Historical Study,* ed. Samuel S. Hill (Macon, Ga.: Mercer University Press, 1983), 102; Stone, *Biography,* 9.

[24]Barton W. Stone, *A Reply to John P. Campbell's Strictures on Atonement* (Lexington, Ky.: Joseph Charles, 1805), 3–5; for a slightly different account of this same event, see Stone, *Biography,* 30–32.

sign of election, evidence of Christ's implantation of the spiritual principle that enabled persons to know and enjoy God. Stone tried to use McGready's "means of grace" to receive a willingness to come to Christ for pardon and release from the power of sin but could not get past the notion that he might not be one of the elect. He asked himself the following questions:

> Do you believe that Christ died for you? No: for I know not whether I am one of the elect, and for these only he died. Do you believe that God will have mercy on you? No: for I know not whether I am one of the elect, and God can have mercy on none else. Do you believe he will hear your prayers? No: for he will hear none but the elect, and I know not whether I am one of that number.[25]

After "trying to believe" in this manner for some time, Stone concluded that it was impossible to receive a willingness to come to Christ in this manner, as God had provided no grounds on which one who did not have a willingness to come to Christ could "believe." "The fire of hell," he wrote, "got hold of my soul and was kindling to a flame against such a God. I could not believe. I dared not pray. I rolled in agony, not knowing what to do." For nearly three weeks he lived as a "creature bereaved of every enjoyment in the universe."[26]

Stone was relieved from his distress by reflecting on John 14:9: "Have I been so long time with you, and yet hast thou not known me, Philip? He that hath seen me hath seen the Father; and how sayest thou then, shew us the Father...I am in the Father, and the Father in me." Stone interpreted the passage to mean that there is no God but the One revealed in Jesus Christ, and thus God could be none other than the friend and lover of sinners. This conclusion allowed him to reject his image of the "dreadful God of vengeance, wrath and fury" that had seemed so contrary to the Christ who received sinners and came to "seek and save that which was lost." It was this image of God, of One who would *not* grant salvation to all who sought it, that he had been unable to get past when he had tried to believe. He concluded that if Jesus, the friend and lover of sinners, revealed the only true God, then God *was* love. "I cannot describe the transport of my soul," he wrote. "I sunk into God, and was fully relieved."[27]

Following this experience, he was convinced that his "love to all the world, and longing for their salvation" was the Spirit of God in him. "I now saw and could testify in the Spirit," he wrote, "that Jesus was sent to be the Saviour of the world; that he died for all, and that salvation was free for every creature." Consequently, Stone temporarily gave up the Calvinist or Presbyterian doctrine of election. Stone's rejection of the Calvinist view of election, however, raised for Stone another theological problem, rooted in the popular rationalism

---

[25]Stone, *Reply,* 4.
[26]Ibid.
[27]Ibid., 5.

that so influenced his thinking. "If Christ died for all, and God loves all, and is not willing that any should perish; and if he has almighty power, then if he does not save all," Stone reasoned, "will he not *contradict* his nature."[28]

Stone searched the scriptures for evidence in support of the doctrine of universal salvation, the teaching that God will save all persons. The disadvantage of this doctrine, from a revivalist perspective, was that it seemed to undercut the urgency of the preacher's call to "flee the wrath to come without delay." Stone's teacher, David Caldwell, had opposed the doctrine in a sermon titled "The Doctrine of Universal Salvation Unscriptural." Like his teacher, Stone found the doctrine of universal salvation "everywhere condemned in scripture."[29]

At length Stone concluded from Mark 16:16, "He that believeth...shall be saved, and he that believeth not shall be damned," that God had chosen to exercise the divine power in saving those who "believed" and in damning those who "believed not." This conclusion, however, raised another difficulty. According to Ephesians 2:8, faith is the gift of God. Thus, Stone inquired why God gave faith to one person and not to another. He knew that it could not be because some persons asked for it, since according to Romans 10:14, Hebrews 11:16, and James 1:6–8, one had to have faith before one could pray or receive anything from God. Stone further saw that God did not give faith to one and not to another because of "worthiness in one, and not in another." Therefore, he concluded that God simply gave faith to some persons and not to others, that God was a "respecter of persons," who gave faith in a "sovereign" manner. Consequently, he reaffirmed the doctrines of unconditional election and reprobation that he had temporarily rejected.[30]

Stone was helped in his reaffirmation of the Calvinist doctrines of election and reprobation by Jonathan Edwards' distinction between a natural and moral ability. According to Edwards, whose writings were highly valued by Presbyterians of the New Light tradition, natural ability was the freedom to act or choose without any physical constraint or compulsion. All persons had a natural ability to serve God. Thus, persons failed to serve God not because they lacked *natural* ability, but because they lacked *moral* ability; that is, because they did not *choose* to serve God. David Rice, widely recognized as the father of Presbyterianism in Kentucky, illustrated the distinction in a tract published in 1791. If an individual sees another person being physically attacked but lacks the strength or the weapon necessary to help that person, the failure to act may be credited to *natural* inability. If, on the other hand, the same individual observes another person being attacked and has the strength or weapon necessary to help the person being attacked but fails to do so, the failure to act must be credited to *moral* inability. Using this distinction, preachers proclaimed that God loved sinners, while affirming all the while the

[28]Ibid. Italics mine.
[29]David Caldwell, "The Doctrine of Universal Salvation Unscriptural," in Caruthers, 285–302; Stone, *Reply*, 5.
[30]Ibid., 5–6.

doctrines of election, reprobation, and predestination. Sinners were damned not because they lacked the natural ability to serve God, but because they lacked moral ability–they did not choose to serve God.[31]

In the fall of 1797 Stone set out on a trip to the Southeast with Cane Ridge neighbor Henry Wilson. The Transylvania Presbytery had recently established a school at Pisgah, ten miles from Lexington, and had appointed Stone to solicit funds for the school in Charleston, South Carolina.[32]

The route included a journey through the wilderness between Kentucky and Virginia. At the Crab Orchard house of rendezvous for travelers through the wilderness, Stone and Wilson learned that a party had just left two hours before their arrival, with the intention of encamping that night at "the Hazlepatch" in Lincoln County. Stone and Wilson followed at a quick pace, determined to overtake them. About 10:00 p.m. they arrived at the Hazelpatch but found no one there. Wilson, who was an early settler of Kentucky and had engaged in wars with the Indians, advised that they turn off the road and encamp until day. Catching up with the party of travelers toward the end of the following day, they learned that when the party had arrived at the Hazlepatch, they had found the recently slain bodies of an earlier party of travelers, "mangled in Indian style," and had pushed forward, traveling late into the night. Stone remarked that he and Wilson "clearly saw the kind hand of God" in delivering them.[33]

Having passed through the wilderness, the company parted, some, including Wilson, for Virginia, the rest, including Stone, for Georgia. Reaching Georgia, Stone visited his relatives and preached throughout the area for several weeks. Continuing his journey alone, he spent several days preaching on John's and Wadmelaw Islands before arriving in Charleston, where he had a "joyful" reunion with his former classmate Samuel Holmes.[34]

Having spent several weeks in Charleston and the surrounding area, he started with Holmes and two others toward Virginia. He arrived safely at his mother's home and found her well. However, many of his relatives were gone, either to the grave or to some other region. He claimed that when he had been in the West he had "often sighed at the remembrance of the home

[31]Ibid., 31; David Rice, *A Lecture on the Divine Decrees, To Which is Annexed a Few Observations on a Piece Lately Printed in Lexington, Entitled "The Principles of the Methodists, or the Scripture Doctrines of Predestination, Election and Reprobation."* (Lexington, Ky.: John Bradford, 1791), 22–23, 49; Robert Marshall, "A Sermon Preached at Bethel, June 1793, Prior to My Ordination, Text Appointed by Presbytery, John 15:5," Marshall Papers 1790–1808, Shane Collection, Presbyterian Historical Society, Philadelphia. For the origin of this distinction, see Jonathan Edwards, *The Works of President Edwards*, ed. Sereno E. Dwight, vol. 2: *A Careful and Strict Inquiry into the Modern Prevailing Notions of That Freedom of Will Which is Supposed to be Essential to Moral Agency, Virtue, and Vice, Reward and Punishment, Praise and Blame* (New York: S. Converse, 1829), 283. For a classic treatment of this distinction, see Joseph Bellamy, *The Works of Joseph Bellamy, D.D.*, vol. 1: *True Religion Delineated* (Boston: Doctrinal Tract and Book Society, 1853), 97–98.
[32]Stone, *Biography*, 25–26.
[33]Ibid., 26–27.
[34]Ibid., 27–28.

of my youth, and the former haunts of my boyish pleasures, and longed to revisit them." But he was disappointed at what he found: "the old school house in ruins—the old trees under whose shade we used to play, either destroyed or dwindling with age." He reported that he had more of a disposition to weep than to rejoice. "Those scenes," he wrote, "which had long ago passed away, never—ah! Never to return."[35]

After remaining some weeks with his mother, Stone returned to Kentucky. In the spring of 1798, he received a call through the Transylvania Presbytery to become pastor of the united congregations of Cane Ridge and Concord. The twenty-five-year-old probationer, who earlier had feared that he was not qualified for ministry, accepted the call. In the varied experiences of the ensuing two and a half years, his call to ministry had been confirmed.[36]

Stone's ordination was scheduled for October 4, 1798. He knew that he would be required to "sincerely receive and adopt" the Westminster Confession of Faith as "containing the system of doctrine taught in the Holy Scriptures." Therefore, he undertook a careful reexamination of the Confession. In his autobiography he wrote, "This was to me almost the beginning of sorrows. I stumbled at the doctrine of Trinity as taught in the Confession; I labored to believe it, but could not conscientiously subscribe to it. Doubts, too, arose in my mind on the doctrines of election, reprobation, and predestination, as there taught." In particular, the distinction between natural and moral inability seemed inadequate, "for," as he wrote, "by whatever name it be called, that inability was in the sinner, and therefore he could not believe, nor repent, but must be damned." Although Stone was spiritually a Presbyterian, his mind was also deeply influenced by the popular rationalism of the early American republic.[37]

On the day appointed for Stone's ordination, the eleven members of the Transylvania Presbytery assembled in the log meetinghouse at Cane Ridge along with a large congregation. Prior to the session of the presbytery in which he was to be examined and ordained, Stone took aside two of the "pillars" of the presbytery, James Blythe and Robert Marshall. He informed them of his difficulties and told them that he had determined to decline ordination at that time. Blythe and Marshall both sought to remove Stone's "difficulties and objections," but to no avail. The extent of the difficulties that Stone revealed at that time was later the subject of some controversy. In a letter written in 1822, James Blythe allowed that Stone "did at that time, make some objections

---

[35]Ibid., 28.

[36]"Extracts from the Minutes of the Transylvania Presbytery, 1786–1837," in William Warren Sweet, *Religion on the American Frontier, 1783–1840,* vol. 2: *The Presbyterians* (Chicago: University of Chicago Press, 1936), 172; Stone, *Biography,* 28–29. Stone's report that he received the call in the fall of 1798 is in conflict with the Minutes of the Presbytery, which report the call as having been issued and accepted on April 10, 1798.

[37] *The Constitution of the Presbyterian Church in the United States of America, containing The Confession of Faith, The Catechisms, and The Directory for the Worship of God: Together with the Plan of Government and Discipline* (Philadelphia: Presbyterian Board of Publication, 1842), *Form of Government,* chap. 11, sec. 12, 441; Stone, *Biography,* 29–31.

to the *terms* in which certain doctrines" were expressed in the Confession of Faith, but did not object "to any of the leading *doctrines* of the Confession." In a response to Blythe's letter, Stone stated that he had objected to the term "Eternal Son of God" in the doctrine of the Trinity and had been unsettled as to whether three "persons" in the doctrine of the Trinity meant three "intelligent beings" or three "appellations or relations." He did not share with Blythe and Marshall his "doubts" regarding the doctrines of election, reprobation, and predestination.[38]

According to the Adopting Act approved by the Presbyterian Synod of 1729, it was permissible to ordain a ministerial candidate who would only partially subscribe to the Confession of Faith if, in the view of the presbytery, the candidate's objections to the Confession concerned only "non-essentials." When the Presbyterians had divided over the revivals of the eighteenth century, one of the issues had been subscription to the Confession. Members of the Old Light, or antirevival party, had called for a policy of strict subscription, while supporters of the revivals had preferred the position of the Adopting Act of 1729. When the Presbyterians reunited in 1758, one of the terms of reunion was an agreement to encourage a policy of strict subscription. Nevertheless, Presbyterians of the New Light heritage, such as Samuel Davies, had continued to ordain candidates who were willing to adopt only the "substance of the Confession" even after the reunion. Having failed to relieve Stone of his stated difficulties with the Confession, Blythe and Marshall, both of whom had been nurtured in the New Light tradition, asked him "how far" he would be willing to adopt the Confession. Stone answered that he would be willing to adopt the Confession as far as he saw it consistent with the Word of God. Blythe and Marshall concluded that in Stone's case partial subscription would be sufficient.[39]

Stone entered the assembly with Blythe and Marshall. When asked if he received and adopted the Confession of Faith, he "answered aloud, so that the whole congregation might hear, 'I do, as far as I see it consistent with the word of God.'" No objection being offered, he was ordained to the ministry of the gospel by the Transylvania Presbytery.[40]

Of course, ordination did not solve the theological difficulties that Stone had identified in reviewing the Confession. In particular, he continued to wonder how God could condemn sinners for unbelief when it was impossible for them to believe until God gave them faith. Meanwhile, in Logan County, Kentucky, a revival had begun that would help to resolve Stone's theological difficulties.

---

[38]Stone, *Biography*, 29; Blythe to Cleland in Thomas Cleland, *Letters to Barton W. Stone,* 166; Stone, *Letters to James Blythe, D.D. Designed as a Reply to the Arguments of Thomas Cleland, D.D., Against My Address. Second Edition, on the Doctrines of Trinity, the Son of God, etc.* (Lexington, Ky.: Printed by W. Tanner, 1824), 157–59.

[39]Stone, *Biography*, 29–30. For the history of the Adopting Act, see Trinterud, 45–51, 66–67, 148–49.

[40]Stone, *Biography*, 29–30.

PART 2

The Great
Revival

4

"I Knew the Voice..."

Logan County, located forty miles north of Nashville, Tennessee, on the Tennessee-Kentucky border, was not settled by whites until after the Revolutionary War, when it was opened to land claims and settlement by Revolutionary War veterans. The decade of settlement that followed was chaotic, with numerous reports of lawlessness, earning for the county the epithet of "Rogue's Harbor." By 1795 the land was open to all, and a new generation of settlers moved in. Included in this second wave of settlement were Presbyterians from Virginia and North Carolina, who were soon establishing churches and calling for ministers to settle among them.[1]

In response to the pleas of Presbyterian settlers, James McGready, whose preaching had fired the revival in Caldwell's academy, became pastor in 1796 of three infant congregations named after Logan County rivers—Red, Muddy, and Gasper. By the spring of 1797 there was a brief awakening at Gasper River. In 1798 John Rankin, a former parishioner of David Caldwell's in North Carolina, relieved McGready as pastor of the Gasper River church. In a series of sacramental meetings during the summer and fall of 1798, first at Gasper River, then at Muddy and Red rivers, all three of the congregations seemed to have been awakened, and several young people professed to have been converted. These sacramental meetings were the three- to five-day communions of the sort that Stone had attended at Sandy River in Virginia in February 1791, while a student of Caldwell's academy. A similar pattern of heightened religious interest and reported conversions was repeated during the summer of 1799.

The hallmarks of what became known as the Great Revival in the West (1797–1805)—the unusually large crowds, the physical phenomena of persons "falling" and the practice of camping on the grounds for sacramental meetings—first appeared during the summer of 1800. In June 1800, hundreds, possibly a thousand, from all of the Presbyterian churches in the area, including those in nearby Tennessee, attended McGready's sacramental meeting at Red River. In addition to the host pastor, the leadership of the meeting included two other Presbyterian ministers with North Carolina roots, William Hodge, whose sermon "God is Love" had led to Stone's conversion, and William McGee, a former parishioner and student of Caldwell's whom Stone had

---

[1]The following account of the Logan County revival follows Conkin, 56–63.

encountered at Shiloh in Sumner County, Tennessee, in August 1796. McGee's brother, John McGee, another former parishioner and student of Caldwell's, who had become a Methodist and had formed a circuit in middle Tennessee, also shared in the preaching.

On the final day of the Red River meeting, after the Presbyterian ministers had already left the low-ceilinged log meetinghouse, which measured only twenty-eight by forty feet, John McGee suddenly arose and moved through the congregation exhorting the people with tears and shouts. As a result, several "fell" to the floor as if slain. The meeting was extended another day. McGready, who wrote a narrative of the revival, reported that several persons seemed to have been converted.[2]

In July the communion at Rankin's Gasper River meetinghouse also drew remarkable crowds, with some participants coming from as far as a hundred miles. Although participants in sacramental meetings had normally been housed with local families, some twenty to thirty families arrived at Gasper River with wagons and provisions and camped on the grounds of the meetinghouse (giving Gasper River a claim to having been the first "camp" meeting). In addition to Rankin, at least three other Presbyterian ministers, William McGee, McGready, and Hodge, and up to seven or eight congregations participated in the sacrament.

Before the summer was over, at least eight other sacramental meetings were conducted in Logan County and nearby Tennessee, scheduled so that no two occurred on the same weekend. The largest communion of the year may have been that hosted by the Shiloh church in Sumner County, Tennessee, and its new pastor, William Hodge. Anticipating large numbers, the meeting was held at nearby Deshas Creek to be near the water needed for horses and campers.

Stone was in Virginia and North Carolina during the summer and fall of 1800, attending to the affairs of his mother, who had died that year. He learned of the remarkable revival in Kentucky and Tennessee while returning in the fall from North Carolina in the company of fellow Presbyterian minister James Hall of Iredell County, North Carolina. Stone and Hall were met in the wilderness by a party returning from Tennessee who had letters addressed to Hall. The letters were accounts of the meeting at Shiloh, reporting that many had been "struck down as dead," that the saints were "all alive," that sinners had been "weeping and crying for mercy," and that "multitudes" had been "converted" and were "rejoicing in God."[3]

The excitement reported at Shiloh was a sharp contrast to the state of religion in central Kentucky. Following the growth in membership of the Cane Ridge and Concord churches that had accompanied Stone's settlement among them in the winter of 1796, things had "moved on quietly" in his congregations and in other central Kentucky congregations as well. The Methodists, who

---

[2]McGready, vol. 1, "Narrative of the Commencement and Progress of the Revival of 1800," IX-XVI.

[3]Barton W. Stone, *History of the Christian Church in the West* (Lexington, Ky.: College of the Bible, 1956), 1.

kept the best records of any of the frontier denominations, recorded a drop of sixty-seven in their Kentucky membership for the years 1792–1800, a period during which Kentucky's population nearly doubled.[4] As Stone put it, "Not only the power of religion had disappeared, but also the very form of it was waning fast away." Little wonder, then, that early in the spring of 1801, Stone traveled to Logan County to attend a camp meeting led by McGready and other North Carolina Presbyterians whom he considered to be his colleagues and fathers in the ministry.[5]

By the spring of 1801, "falling" by a large number of the participants was a standard feature of the Presbyterian communions in Logan County. In his autobiography, Stone described the phenomenon as he observed it early in the spring of 1801. "Many, very many fell down, as men slain in battle, and continued for hours together in an apparently breathless and motionless state— sometimes for a few moments reviving, and exhibiting symptoms of life by a deep groan, or piercing shriek, or by a prayer for mercy most fervently uttered." Gradually they would obtain release; the "gloomy cloud, which had covered their faces" giving way first to smiles of hope and then of joy, they would finally rise "shouting deliverance" and would address the surrounding crowd "in language truly eloquent and impressive." "With astonishment," Stone exclaimed, "did I hear men, women and children declaring the wonderful works of God, and the glorious mysteries of the gospel." He reported that their appeals to others were "solemn, heart-penetrating, bold and free." Noting that he was amazed at "the knowledge of gospel truth displayed" in their addresses, he observed that hearing their appeals, others would fall down "into the same state from which the speakers had just been delivered."[6]

Though Stone indicated that the phenomenon he observed in Logan County was new to him and "passing strange," it was not new in the history of British and American Christianity. While the number of persons falling was unusual, numerous accounts of individuals falling were associated with the eighteenth-century revivals of John Wesley in England and of Jonathan Edwards and George Whitefield in America. Moreover, American Methodists encouraged falling and "crying out" in worship. It was probably no coincidence that the first report of a person falling in the Great Revival occurred in response to the efforts of the Methodist John McGee, who exhorted the congregation at Red River after the Presbyterian ministers had left the meetinghouse.[7]

Stone carefully observed the behavior of persons who fell at the Logan County meeting. Some were acquaintances of his. "I sat patiently," he wrote, "by one of them, whom I knew to be a careless sinner, for hours, and observed

[4]Albert H. Redford, *The History of Methodism in Kentucky*, 3 vols. (Nashville: Southern Methodist Publishing House, 1868), 1:46–47, 249, quoted in Conkin, 57.

[5]Stone, *Biography*, 34.

[6]Ibid., 34–35.

[7]John H. Wigger, *Taking Heaven by Storm: Methodism and the Rise of Popular Christianity in America* (New York: Oxford University Press, 1998), 104–24. Stone's first biographer, John Rogers, included a history of the "exercises" in his additions and reflections. See Stone, *Biography*, 348–404. For a recent analysis of the "exercises" of the Great Revival, see Conkin, 103–14.

with critical attention everything that passed from the beginning to the end. I noticed the momentary revivings as from death–the humble confession of sins–the fervent prayer, and ultimate deliverance–then the solemn thanks and praise to God–the affectionate exhortation to companions and to the people around, to repent and come to Jesus." After attending to several such cases, Stone concluded that the Logan County "work" was "a good work–the work of God."[8]

Stone's observation of the Logan County revival also helped him to answer the question of how God could condemn persons for unbelief when it was impossible for them to believe until God gave them faith. This was the question that had continued to trouble Stone after his ordination. If God gave faith, how could God condemn a sinner for not having faith?

In a brief account of his theological development that was published in 1805, Stone reported that "all" his difficulties had been removed while observing "the work of God" in Logan County. "Many old and young, even little children," he wrote, "professed religion, and all declared the same simple gospel of Jesus. I knew the voice and felt the power." The "voice" that Stone *knew* was the voice of God. The "power" that he *felt* was the power of the gospel–the spiritual or "moral" power that made sinners willing to go to God for both forgiveness of sin and release from the power of sin. Stone reported, "I saw that faith was the sovereign gift of God to all sinners, not the act of faith, but the object or foundation of faith, which is the testimony of Jesus, or the gospel; that sinners had power to believe this gospel, and then come to God and obtain grace and salvation." That is, Stone saw that God gave faith–the spiritual or moral willingness to come to God–through the gospel and that sinners had the power to believe the gospel, which would make them willing to come to God. Thus, the gospel that made one willing to come to Christ was the gift of God; persons who ignored the gospel were responsible for their own condemnation.[9]

The notion that God spoke through the gospel to give sinners the power to "come to Christ" for release from the penalty and the power of sin was, of course, not new. New Light Presbyterians taught that God drew sinners to Christ for release from the penalty and the power of sin by giving them "a view of the glory of God in the face of Christ Jesus." This was the "glory" of the One who sent the Son to save helpless sinners. New Lights proclaimed that in response to a view of the glory of God in Jesus, sinners' hearts were filled with a love of God that made them willing to go to Christ for salvation. This is what New Light Presbyterians meant by "rational" religion–a spirituality or love of God rooted in one's "understanding" of what God had done for sinners through Jesus Christ, rather than in assurance of one's own forgiveness and conversion received through dreams and visions. What was new in Stone's understanding of how God gave faith was his belief that sinners

---

[8]Stone, *Biography*, 35.
[9]Stone, *Reply*, 6.

had the power to believe the gospel–to see the glory of God in the face of Christ Jesus that would fill them with love toward God without a previous work of the Spirit to convince them of the power of sin. Critics of Stone's position would charge that he denied the work of the Holy Spirit in preparing persons to believe.

Presbyterian minister John P. Campbell, who had been a member of the Transylvania Presbytery that ordained Stone in 1798, claimed that Stone learned his new doctrine of faith from Thomas P. Craighead, the first Presbyterian minister to locate in middle Tennessee. Craighead was a Princeton graduate with North Carolina roots who had settled in Spring Hill, five miles north of Nashville, in 1785. Craighead, like his brother-in-law David Caldwell, was a teacher as well as a preacher, having opened the Davidson Academy in the stone meetinghouse of the Spring Hill Church in 1786.[10]

Craighead participated in two of the sacramental meetings of 1800 but soon became a determined opponent of the revival. His opposition to the revival was related to his criticism of the practice of seeking conversion or "regeneration" by praying for the gift of faith that would enable one to come to Christ for salvation. You hear nothing from Christ, he wrote in a sermon published in 1809, "of the current cant–Pray to God to give you faith to believe–pray, pray, strive, agonize, wait until Christ comes and delivers you." For Craighead, faith was not the "moral" act of coming to Christ but an intellectual act. "No man," Craighead stated, "can resist the force of credible testimony if he suffers it to enter into the view of his understanding. Neither disposition, nor will, nor motives," he continued, "have the least effect." Thus, he advised sinners to attend to the "truth" that the Spirit of God teaches in the scriptures, not to pray for the Holy Spirit to give them faith.[11]

There is no reason to doubt that Stone was familiar with Craighead's views of faith and regeneration. In his autobiography, Stone reported that he and John Anderson often preached "in the neighborhood" of Craighead's church while making their tour of the Cumberland settlements in the summer of 1796 and that their final preaching appointment in the Cumberland settlements had been in "father Thomas Craighead's congregation." To support his charge that Craighead was the source of Stone's views, Campbell reproduced signed statements of persons who reported having been informed by Stone of Craighead's views of faith and regeneration as early as 1799, having heard from another as early as the summer of 1801 that Stone had received his new doctrine from Craighead or as having heard Stone espouse "virtually" the same views as Craighead's as early as 1800.[12]

---

[10] John P. Campbell, *The Pelagian Detected: Or a Review of Mr. Craighead's Letters Addressed to the Public and the Author* (Lexington, Ky.: Thomas T. Skillman, 1811). For information on Craighead, see Robert Davidson, *History of the Presbyterian Church in the State of Kentucky: With a Preliminary Sketch of the Churches in the Valley of Virginia* (New York: Robert Carter, 1847), 264.

[11] Thomas B. Craighead, *A Sermon on Regeneration with an Apology and an Address to the Synod of Kentucky Together with an Appendix* (Lexington, Ky.: William Worsley, 1809), 15, 26, 93.

[12] Stone, *Biography*, 24; Campbell, *The Pelagian Detected,* 56–60.

In his autobiography, Stone indicated that he had come to his new understanding of how God gives faith from a prayerful study of the scriptures prior to observing the revival, that objections to the doctrine had arisen in his mind, that these objections had been multiplied by a Presbyterian colleague to whom he had communicated his views, and that he had determined not to declare them publicly until he was able to defend them. Stone made no mention of the role of the revival in removing his objections. Hence, Stone's autobiography appears to contradict the account of his theological development that he published in 1805.[13]

It is possible that in describing in his autobiography events that had occurred more than forty years before, Stone simply forgot or failed to mention how his observation of the Logan County revival factored into removing his difficulties regarding how God gave faith.[14] Another explanation for the differences between Stone's autobiography and his 1805 account of his theological development is that Stone wrote, in both cases, with his audience in mind. Linking the development of his new doctrine of faith to the revival would have commended it to Stone's audience in 1805. Nearly forty years later, many of the younger members of Stone's religious movement identified the Great Revival with fanaticism.[15] Certainly, Stone would not be the first person to have told different parts of a story to different audiences.

A "harmonization" of Stone's two accounts that would also be consistent with Campbell's claim would read as follows: Stone was acquainted with Craighead's views and had developed his new doctrine of faith prior to observing the revival. Objections to the doctrine had arisen in his mind and had been multiplied by a Presbyterian colleague to whom he had communicated his views. His observation of the conversions in Logan County then "removed" his objections, leading him to believe that he could publicly declare and defend his views. The Presbyterian minister to whom he had communicated his views may have been Richard McNemar, who began preaching the new views in the winter of 1801.

It would be a mistake, however, to assume that Stone was simply a disciple of Thomas Craighead. Despite similarities in their views of faith, they held strikingly different views of the fundamental character of both conversion and the Christian life, making one an opponent and the other a promoter of the Great Revival. For Craighead, conversion or "regeneration" was a carefully reasoned decision to act in one's own best interest. Craighead taught that converts came to love the law of God only after they had lived by it long enough to discover "its tendency to personal and general happiness." Acknowledging that regeneration was often described by New Lights as "the implanting of a spiritual principle," Craighead argued, "Every moral, political or civil principle is formed by a fair examination of the objects of pursuit

---

[13]Stone, *Biography*, 33–34.
[14]Stone made chronological errors in his autobiography that appear to be simply the result of a failing memory. See Stone, *Biography*, 64.
[15]See Rogers' chapter on the history of the exercises in Stone, *Biography*, 374–76.

and aversion, with their several relations and consequences." Believing "in full confidence that God will accomplish what He has promised," the regenerated person knows "it to be infinitely best for him to keep God's law, and therefore, steadfastly resolves to keep that law as his greatest intent." "This choice or resolution built upon these promises," he continued, "is his moral or religious principle." For Stone, conversion was a change of heart born of a view of the glory of God that caused one to desire to be free from the power, as well as the penalty, of sin, rather than a carefully reasoned decision based on enlightened self-interest. For Craighead, the Christian life was a matter of keeping God's law as taught by God's Spirit in the scripture. According to Craighead, the Spirit, having written the scriptures, was no longer active in the world. For Stone, the Spirit was active in individual believers and in the church, as well as in and through the scriptures. In coming to Christ, one receives the Spirit, without which, for Stone, one could not be saved from the power of sin.[16]

In his autobiography, Stone reported that following the camp meeting he attended in Logan County early in the spring of 1801, he returned to his congregations in "ardent spirits." Arriving at Cane Ridge in time for his Sunday morning appointment, he met a crowd that had gathered to hear a report of the camp meeting. He ascended the high, boxed-in pulpit of the log meetinghouse, gave an account of what he had seen and heard, then preached from Mark 16:15–16: "Go ye into all the world and preach the gospel to every creature. He that believeth and is baptized shall be saved; and he that believeth not shall be damned." Confident of his new doctrine that God gave faith through hearing of the gospel, without any previous work of the Holy Spirit, he "urged the sinner to believe now, and be saved." The congregation was seriously engaged by the preaching, and many went home weeping.[17]

After making appointments to preach in the homes of members of the congregation, he made the ten-mile trip to Concord to preach that night. At the night meeting at Concord, two young girls "were struck down during the preaching of the word, and in every respect were exercised," as were the subjects of falling that he had observed in Logan County. Returning to Cane Ridge the next day, he learned that many persons were seeking salvation and that some "had found the Lord, and were rejoicing in him."[18]

Among the latter was Nathaniel Rogers, whom Stone described as his "particular friend." Rogers had served as one of Bourbon County's delegates to Kentucky's second constitutional convention in 1799 and was, as Stone observed, "a man of first respectability and influence in the neighborhood." As Stone approached the gate of William Maxwell's home for a preaching appointment, he encountered Rogers and his wife, who were also just arriving. Seeing Stone, Rogers "shouted aloud the praises of God." They hurried into each other's embrace, while Rogers continued praising the Lord aloud.

---

[16]Craighead, 23, 38, 43–44. Stone's view of the Spirit is developed in later chapters.
[17]Stone, *Biography*, 36. See also *Reply*, 6–7.
[18]Stone, *Biography*, 36.

The people who had gathered in the house quickly joined Stone and the couple outside the house, and in less than twenty minutes several had fallen.[19]

Others started to leave but either fell or returned to the crowd, as if unable to get away. An "intelligent deist" joined the crowd and remarked to Stone that he had previously thought him an honest man but was now convinced that he was deceiving the people. After Stone "mildly spoke a few words to him," he, too, fell and did not rise until he "confessed the Saviour." Others also "found peace in the Lord," and the "meeting" continued "in the open air" until late that night.[20]

There were reports of falling by an unspecified number of persons at the regularly scheduled sacramental meeting at Fleming Creek, northeast of Lexington, the first weekend in May. Falling, by perhaps as many as sixty participants, was reported at the sacrament at Richard McNemar's Cabin Creek congregation, six miles up the Ohio River from Maysville, Kentucky, two weeks later. McNemar was a former elder of the Cane Ridge congregation, and many people from Cane Ridge attended the Cabin Creek sacrament, despite the fact that Cabin Creek was a difficult, fifty-mile trip from Cane Ridge.[21]

The first Sunday in June, Stone conducted a sacramental meeting at Concord that was the largest religious meeting in central Kentucky to that date. In his autobiography, Stone noted, "The whole country appeared to be in motion to the place." Colonel Robert Patterson, a famed Indian fighter and militia captain and longtime patron of the Lexington Presbyterian Church, attended the sacrament at Concord and began a chronicle of the rising tide of revival in central Kentucky. Patterson judged the crowd at the Concord sacrament to have been four thousand. In an account of the revival written twenty-six years later, Stone estimated the attendance at Concord at between five and six thousand. Stone also indicated that Baptists and Methodists, as well as Presbyterians, participated. Both Patterson and Stone noted that the meeting went on continually day and night for five days and was conducted outdoors, since the Concord meetinghouse, erected in 1793, was not large enough to contain the crowd. Seven Presbyterian ministers were present. At least one Methodist, Benjamin Northcott, shared in the preaching. Patterson reported that 150 fell and that 250 communed. He also noted that twelve families brought provisions and camped on the grounds, "the neighborhood not being able to

---

[19]Ibid. For further information regarding Rogers, see Ellen T. Eslinger, "The Great Revival in Bourbon County, Kentucky" (University of Chicago, 1988), 334.

[20]Stone, *Biography*, 36–37. Eslinger suggested that the number of persons who fell at Maxwell's may have been exaggerated by Stone, noting the description of another participant, David Purviance, who wrote, "We found the people in the yard, mostly standing on their feet, but…found many persons under both physical and mental excitement." See Purviance, *The Biography of Elder David Purviance*, 299, quoted in Eslinger, 335.

[21]Stone, *History*, 2; Richard McNemar, *Kentucky Revival, or A Short History of the Late Extraordinary Outpouring of the Spirit of God, in the Western States of America, Agreeably to Scripture-Promises, and Prophecies Concerning the Latter Day: With A Brief Account of the Entrance and Progress of what the World Call Shakerism, Among the Subjects of the Late Revival in Ohio and Kentucky. Presented to the True Zion-Traveller, As a Memorial of the Wilderness Journey* (1808; reprint, Cincinnati: Art Guild Reprints, 1968), 23–24.

furnish strangers with accommodation; nor had they [the participants] a wish to separate."[22]

Well-attended communions marked by "falling" and the participation of Baptists and Methodists continued in central Kentucky throughout June. A sacrament was held at Salem on June 18. At least five Presbyterian ministers and two Methodist ministers were present. The Salem pastor, John Lyle, began a diary on this occasion. He noted that the first person to fall was a woman who breathed hard, "like a sheep down on a hot day." By the time the meeting ended on Wednesday, two days beyond the scheduled conclusion of the traditional sacramental meeting, Lyle believed that a total of three hundred had fallen. The following Sunday, Patterson attended the Stony Creek sacrament at the Point Pleasant meetinghouse in southern Bourbon County, noting forty wagons encamped, with eight thousand people in attendance, two hundred fifty who fell and three hundred fifty who communed. John Lyle, who also attended the Stony Creek communion, reported that "the people were engaged in singing and hearing and praying night and day from Friday morning to Tuesday evening."[23]

The next weekend there were sacraments at both Lexington and Indian Creek, thirty miles northeast of Lexington in southern Harrison County. John Lyle preached at Lexington. He reported that falling began late Sunday morning as preparations were being made for the Lord's supper. Patterson estimated six thousand people attended, with three hundred communicants and a total of seventy persons falling before the meeting concluded on Tuesday. Stone and Joseph P. Howe, of Point Pleasant, were among the preachers at Indian Creek. Patterson reported that ten thousand attended at Indian Creek, eight hundred fell, and five hundred communed.[24]

In July Lyle assisted with a sacramental meeting at Paris in Bourbon County. Indian Creek hosted a second sacrament the following week, in which McNemar participated. Although attendance figures are unavailable, one of the ministers at the Indian Creek meeting reported that "hundreds fell to the ground at once," suggesting, by comparison with reports of the number who fell at other meetings, that a sizable crowd attended.[25]

Meanwhile, during the last week in June, after publicizing a sacrament for Cane Ridge the first weekend in August, the twenty-eight-year-old Stone started a journey of six days or more by horseback over two hundred miles of pioneer trails to Greenville, in Muhlenberg County, Kentucky. Greenville, a village of twenty-six inhabitants, was the home of Elizabeth Campbell, who was eleven years his junior. On July 2 the two were married.[26]

[22]Stone, *Biography*, 37; Stone, *History*, 2; H. C. Northcott, *Biography of Rev. Benjamin Northcott a Pioneer Local Preacher of the Methodist Episcopal Church in Kentucky* (Cincinnati: Western Methodist Book Concern, 1875), 35. Patterson's report appeared in several publications. See Colonel James Paterson [sic] to Rev. John King, September 25, 1801, in *Increase of Piety, or The Revival of Religion in the United States of America* (Newburyport, Conn.: Angier March, 1802), 35–40.

[23]"Rev. John Lyle's Diary, 1801," Manuscripts Division, Kentucky Historical Society, Frankfort, Kentucky, 2–3.

[24]John Lyle, "Diary," 9–20.

[25]"Letter from Rev. John Evans Findley," 26–27, quoted in Eslinger, 340.

[26]Stone, *Biography,* 37.

There are no records of when or how the couple met. The Campbells were Presbyterians, and Stone noted that Elizabeth was "pious, and much engaged in religion."[27] It would not have been unusual for a pious Presbyterian to have traveled from Muhlenberg County to neighboring Logan County with her family or other members of her congregation to attend a camp meeting. Thus, they may have met at the Logan County camp meeting that Stone attended early in the spring of 1801.[28]

The Campbells also had ties to central Kentucky. Elizabeth's uncle, Colonel William Russell, lived at Russell's Cave, near Lexington. Her father, Colonel William Campbell, was a close friend of Colonel Robert Patterson and died in Patterson's home after traveling to Lexington for medical attention in the fall of 1800. Elizabeth, then, might have met Stone while visiting the Russells or tending her father. Colonel Patterson's report of the revival in central Kentucky includes no entries for July. It is possible that he accompanied Stone to Muhlenberg County to attend the wedding of his deceased friend's daughter and to help transport her dowry to the one-hundred-acre Bourbon County farm that Stone had purchased in May 1799.[29]

Following the wedding, presumably at Mrs. Campbell's home, Barton and Elizabeth "hurried" from Muhlenberg County to prepare for the August sacrament at Cane Ridge.[30] What was entailed in these preparations cannot be fully ascertained. Accounts of the meeting refer to the "tent"–a covered lecture platform or stage made of wood that was located about one hundred yards to the southwest of the meetinghouse. Whether this structure was built for the August meeting or had been used previously by the congregation is not known. One thing is certain: No one believed that the excellent log meetinghouse, thirty by fifty feet, even with its second-level gallery making it possible to accommodate up to four hundred people, would be adequate for the occasion. John Bradford, editor of the Lexington newspaper, believed the revival to be an exploitation of public credulity and refused to allow announcement of the meeting in his paper.[31] Nevertheless, word of the upcoming sacramental meeting had spread through a network of religious activities that Stone had made sure included the Methodists as well as the Presbyterians. Moreover, the religious excitement that had been building in central Kentucky since before May promised a crowd. One participant wrote in a letter dated Saturday, August 7, "I am on my way to one of the greatest meetings of its kind ever known." He noted that "religion has got to such a height here, that people attend from a great distance; on this occasion I doubt not but there will be 10,000 people, and perhaps 500 wagons. The people encamp on

---

[27]Ibid.

[28]Ibid.

[29]Information regarding the Campbells and the purchase of Stone's Bourbon County farm is from Ware, 91, 94–98. The surmise that Patterson may have accompanied Stone to Muhlenberg County is my own.

[30]Stone, *Biography*, 37.

[31]Eslinger, 344.

the ground, and continue praising God, day and night, for one whole week before they break up."[32]

During the day on Friday, August 6, 1801, people began arriving at Cane Ridge. The first scheduled service was in the evening. Stone undoubtedly gave a word of welcome, then a colleague, Matthew Houston, offered the opening sermon. The service was in the packed meetinghouse, where some lingered all night. Rain may have curtailed the numbers as yet on the grounds. John Lyle and others worshiped that evening in the home of Cane Ridge elder Andrew Irvine. No doubt worship was also conducted in the homes of other members of the congregation who, like Irvine, provided hospitality to visitors who had come to participate in the sacrament.[33]

On Saturday a growing crowd filled the grounds of the meetinghouse and spread into the adjoining grove owned by a Methodist, Ilai Nunn. The number of wagons encamped on the grounds, at least over Saturday and Sunday, was variously estimated at between 125 and 148, covering, as one observer reported, an area the equivalent of four city blocks. In addition, thousands of participants arrived for the day, including not only those who lived within horseback-riding range, but also people who found accommodations in neighboring communities. Stone noted that the roads to Cane Ridge were "literally crowded with wagons, carriages, horsemen, and footmen, moving to the solemn camp."[34]

Estimates of the number of people on the grounds on Saturday and Sunday ranged from ten thousand to twenty thousand and beyond. Since most daily visitors had to come by horse or wagon, logistical considerations, including space to accommodate horses and mules, suggest that no more than ten thousand persons could have been on the grounds at any one time. It is possible, of course, that twenty thousand different people were at Cane Ridge at some time during the week. In any case, the number who attended the meeting was remarkable in a state with a recorded total population in 1800 of 220,095.[35]

The first sermon on Saturday morning was delivered in the meetinghouse. In the afternoon, preaching was continuous both in the meetinghouse and from the tent. Lyle noted with disapproval that McNemar's preaching style that afternoon was "much like a Methodist." He also reported that the substance of McNemar's sermon was "what Mr. Stone and he call the true new gospel which they say none preach but ourselves." Lyle added, in the

---

[32]William W. Woodward, comp., "Extract 29 of a letter from a Gentleman, to his friend in Baltimore, Bourbon-county, August 7, 1801," *Surprising accounts of the revival of religion in the United States of America, in different parts of the world, and among different denominations of Christians. With a number of interesting occurrences of Divine Providence* (Philadelphia: William W. Woodward, 1802), quoted in Eslinger, 344.

[33]Lyle, "Diary," 21. Recent historians are agreed that of the firsthand descriptions of the Cane Ridge meeting, John Lyle's diary is the definitive account. The following day-by-day account of the meeting relies primarily on Lyle's diary as supplemented by contemporary reports published in evangelical magazines, quoted in Conkin, 83–97, and Eslinger, 345–52. There are also occasional references to memoirs written many years after the event.

[34]Eslinger, 345; Stone, *Biography*, 37.

[35]Conkin, 88.

first recorded hint of the controversy that was to follow, that "the conduct of these hot-headed men and the effect of their doctrine will separate the church of Christ."[36]

Before dark the grounds echoed with penitent cries and shouts. People crowded into the meetinghouse to hear Stone and others preach. Lyle reported that the sweltering heat, combined with the growing emotional pitch as people began falling, drove him outdoors. There he met McNemar, who expressed concern about the widespread distress and confusion. Part of the "confusion," according to McNemar, was related to the practice of removing persons who fell to some place where a smaller group would offer prayer in their behalf and engage in singing what Colonel Patterson called "some Psalm or Hymn suitable to the occasion." Lyle believed that this practice helped to maintain order. Stone, who according to Lyle did nothing to command order, agreed with McNemar, preferring to let the fallen remain where they fell. Lyle and McNemar joined Paint Lick pastor Matthew Houston at the tent, and the three decided to deliver unscheduled sermons from the tent. Whatever their intent, the outdoor sermons delivered by Lyle, McNemar, and Houston appear to have increased the religious excitement of the crowd.[37]

Sunday, the day reserved for the celebration of the sacrament, was marked by a steady, pouring rain. In the morning, exhorting and sermons were offered in the meetinghouse. The traditional action sermon was given from the stand by the Presbyterian minister Robert Marshall. The supper itself was served in the meetinghouse. Once inside, communicants were seated at long tables set up in the aisles, heard the scriptural words of institution joined with prayer, and received the elements of bread and wine. Estimates of the number of communicants ranged from eight hundred to eleven hundred. Since no more than one hundred could be seated in the meetinghouse at one time, at least eight table sittings, with the Presbyterian ministers administering the supper on a rotating basis, succeeded one another as the service continued late into the afternoon.[38]

Stone, along with leading local Methodist preacher William Burke, had promoted the meeting as a "united sacrament." Not all Presbyterians, however, were as enthusiastic as Stone about uniting in communion with the Methodists. According to a Methodist source, at the Concord sacrament in June when the Methodist Benjamin Northcott had preached, Stone had not disclosed his Methodist identity, fearing Presbyterian prejudice against Methodist preachers. Among the Presbyterians who had reservations about uniting in the sacrament with the Methodists were some of Stone's Cane Ridge elders. Early on Sunday morning, in response to their concerns, Stone asked Burke to make a statement from the stand regarding "how the Methodists held certain doctrines" before final arrangements were made regarding the administration of the sacrament. Taking Stone's request as an insult, Burke challenged him to do likewise for the Presbyterians, and Stone quickly

[36]Lyle, "Diary," 21–22
[37]Ibid., 22–23.
[38]Conkin, 89–90.

withdrew the request. Without further conversation, Burke mounted the trunk of a fallen tree that had lodged against another tree about a hundred feet east of the meetinghouse and began to pray, sing, and preach. Another Methodist held "an umbrella affixed to a long pole" over Burke's head. A large crowd quickly gathered and many fell. Lyle, who happened by the scene, judged from their behavior that many in the crowd were Methodists. [39]

Stone claimed that "four or five preachers were frequently speaking at the same time, in different parts of the encampment, without confusion." On Sunday, in addition to preaching from the tent and from Burke's fallen tree, there was also preaching by an unidentified African American preacher to a group composed largely of African Americans probably about 150 yards southeast of the meetinghouse. One participant counted "seven ministers, all preaching at one time" in different parts of the camp, some using stumps and wagons as makeshift platforms. [40]

By Sunday evening the rain had ended, and praying, preaching, exhorting, and falling continued throughout the camp. A Presbyterian minister wrote, "On Sabbath night, I saw above one hundred candles burning at once—and I suppose one hundred persons at once on the ground crying for mercy of all ages from 8 to 60 years." According to Lyle, "Many were falling and rising and rejoicing etc. etc....I turned to praying and exhorting among them, as did other ministers and continued I suppose near to one or two o'clock." [41]

Persons arriving on Saturday afternoon and Sunday encountered a remarkable scene. One minister reported

> Sinners dropping down on every hand, shrieking, groaning, crying for mercy, convoluted; professors [of religion] praying, agonizing, fainting, falling down in distress, for sinners, or in raptures of joy! some singing, some shouting, clapping their hands, hugging and even kissing, laughing; others talking to the distressed, to one another, or to opposers of the work, and all this at once...[42]

Another observed some people "crying for mercy; some shouting redeeming grace; and others collected in numberless small circles of twelve or twenty singing hymns; all serious; many walking to and fro, with anxiety pictured on their countenances."[43] Add to that several ministers preaching at once! One participant remarked that "the noise was like the roar of Niagara."[44]

By Monday many visitors had to leave, but the meeting continued. New arrivals kept coming until Wednesday or even, by some reports, Thursday,

[39]Northcott, 35; "Autobiography of Rev. William Burke," in J. B. Finley, *Sketches of Western Methodism*, 77–78; Lyle, "Diary," 24.
[40]Stone, *Biography*, 37; Lyle, "Diary," 27–28; Strickland, *Finley Autobiography*, 166, quoted in Eslinger, 355.
[41]Finley to Witherspoon, September 20, 1801, in Woodward, *Surprising Accounts*, 225, quoted in Eslinger, 350; Lyle, "Diary," 26–27.
[42]Extract 26. "Of a letter, from the Rev. Moses Hoge, of Shepherds Town, to the Rev. Ashbel Green, of this city, dated Sept. 10, 1801," in Woodward, *Surprising Account*, 53–54, quoted in Eslinger, 355.
[43]"Letter from Rev. John Evans Finley," 127, quoted in Eslinger, 355.
[44]Strickland, *Finley Autobiography*, 166–67, quoted in Eslinger, 355.

when organized activity came to an end. After breakfast on Monday, Lyle went to the meetinghouse, where the Presbyterian Isaac Tull was preaching. Lyle followed Tull's sermon with an exhortation. Tull and Lyle then alternated offering prayer and exhortation until Tull got the people to sing the hymn "Come Ye Sinners." At length, "One and another fell down and the work went on briskly." As the meetinghouse became "crowded and sultry," Lyle helped carry out the fallen. He then went to hear another sermon, but shortly returned to the meetinghouse to help "carry out and pray and exhort till the middle of the day or about one o'clock."[45]

Throughout the meeting, but especially after Sunday, the crowds were addressed by persons who fell. Lyle reported that "their orations consist of the plain and essential truths of the gospel that they themselves have been powerfully convinced of, but they speak them with all the feeling and pathos that human nature affected with the most important objects is capable of." He further noted, "They speak much of the fullness [of] Christ, his willingness to save etc."[46]

After the thanksgiving sermons on Monday, the normal communion schedule had been fulfilled. What followed was directed by the demand of the people for more singing, praying, and preaching and the willingness of preachers to minister to them. John Rankin from Gasper River and William Burke both preached on Tuesday, as did Lyle, who left at noon. Stone indicated that the meeting would have continued even longer had provisions in the neighborhood not been exhausted.[47]

Sixteen to eighteen Presbyterian ministers participated in the meeting. Most were from Bourbon County or adjoining counties. A few came from more distant neighborhoods, having to travel between thirty and fifty miles. John Rankin had traveled nearly three hundred miles from Logan County. In most cases, church members had accompanied their ministers, thus helping to account for the eight hundred to eleven hundred who received the sacrament. Methodist preachers included William Burke, Benjamin Lakin, Benjamin Northcott, and Samuel Hitt. Methodists also received the sacrament, though, given the total number who communed and the large number of Presbyterian congregations represented, probably no more than two hundred.[48]

Stone reported in his autobiography that both "Methodist and Baptist preachers aided in the work." Other accounts of the meeting refer occasionally to the presence of Baptists and Baptist preachers, though none are recorded as preaching in the meetinghouse or from the tent. The only Baptist minister named in an account was Governor James Garrard of Cooper's Run Church, located a few miles north. Garrard was hardly a representative member of the Baptist ministry, since he was already viewed by most Baptists as an apostate for having accepted Arian views of Christ. The unidentified African

[45]Lyle, "Diary," 28–29; Conkin, 96.
[46]Lyle, "Diary," 30.
[47]Ibid., 35; Stone, *Biography*, 38.
[48]Eslinger, 346; Conkin, 90.

American preacher may have been Old Captain, founding pastor of the first African American Baptist Church of Lexington. Cane Ridge coincided with the annual meeting of the Elkhorn Baptist Association, which convened at Higby's meetinghouse approximately six miles from Lexington. Baptist worship there attracted an estimated eight to ten thousand people, including, no doubt, a large number of the Baptist preachers in central Kentucky! Also, since Baptists viewed Presbyterians and Methodists as improperly baptized and would not join them in communion, Baptist preachers may have had reservations about participating in a "united" sacramental meeting.[49]

Some Baptist ministers may have served as exhorters. However, one did not have to be a preacher to exhort. Literally hundreds of persons exhorted at Cane Ridge; not only men, but women and even children. And, as had been the case with Stone in Logan County, observers especially marveled at the knowledge, eloquence, and depth of feeling communicated by persons not at all accustomed to preaching.[50]

The number who fell may have reached a thousand—estimates ranged from three hundred to three thousand! Given the size of the meeting and the high level of confusion, it was difficult to judge the number of converts. In an account of the revival published in 1827, Stone acknowledged that the number of converts could never be ascertained, but added that it was thought to have been between five hundred and a thousand. In his autobiography, he eschewed offering even an estimate of the number of converts, declaring instead that "the number converted will be known only in eternity."[51]

No matter how fully Stone had developed his new doctrine of faith prior to his observation of the Logan County revival in the spring of 1801, the notion that God transforms sinners' wills through the gospel, without a previous work of the Holy Spirit, would have seemed more convincing to Stone and to others in the midst of the Great Revival than it would have a decade earlier when lengthy periods of distress, such as the one that Stone himself had experienced, were the norm. As Stone sought to show in his 1805 account of his theological development, the view that God worked through the gospel to make sinners willing to come to Christ, without a previous work of the Holy Spirit to enable them to believe, was consistent with the remarkable conversions of the revival.

---

[49]Stone, *Biography*, 37; Eslinger, 346; Conkin, 91.
[50]Ibid., 94–95.
[51]Conkin, 92; Stone, *History*, 3; *Biography*, 38.

5

Conflict

Conflict regarding Stone and McNemar's view that God gave faith through the preaching of the gospel, without any previous work of the Holy Spirit, surfaced in McNemar's Cabin Creek congregation even before the Cane Ridge meeting. During the winter of 1801, Joseph Darlington, Robert Robb, and Robert Robinson, elders of the Cabin Creek congregation, noted that McNemar had begun to "deviate" in his preaching from the doctrines of the Confession of Faith. Individually and as a session–the official governing body of the congregation–they conversed with him regarding their concerns, but with no effect other than "to make him more zealous in propagating those sentiments" that they opposed. Although they sought to keep their differences regarding doctrine confidential, they claimed that McNemar "frequently made use of such language, when on those points, as naturally led the people to understand that there was a difference" between them and repeatedly "misconstrued" their conduct and principles, ridiculing them from the pulpit, though not by name. Because the next meeting of the presbytery was "far distant," they had sought the counsel of a neighboring minister and had conducted a public meeting to vindicate their cause and to show where McNemar's doctrine differed from that of the Presbyterian confession. Later, they proposed to McNemar, in the presence of neighboring minister John Dunlavy and two of his elders, that if McNemar would preach and defend the doctrines contained in the Confession of Faith, they would "bury all our former differences" and again support his ministry. But McNemar refused, responding that he would be bound by no system other than the Bible.[1]

In 1799 the Transylvania Presbytery that had ordained Stone in 1798 had been divided into three presbyteries. McNemar had been assigned to the Washington Presbytery, which included the northeastern part of Kentucky and southwestern Ohio.[2] On November 3, 1801, Darlington, Robb, and Robinson sent a statement of charges against McNemar's doctrine to the Washington Presbytery, along with a letter requesting the presbytery to "take such measures as in your judgment will best establish that faith, once delivered to the saints; and promote the interest and peace of Christ's kingdom

---

[1]"*An Apology for Renouncing the Jurisdiction of the Synod of Kentucky. To which is added a Compendious View of the Gospel, and a few remarks on the Confession of Faith,*" in Stone, *Biography*, 149–50.
[2]Ware, 124.

among us."[3] The presbytery met at Springfield, Ohio, on November 11, 1801. Darlington, Robb, and Robinson were not present. After reviewing their letter and statement of charges, the presbytery concluded that it would be "irregular to take any further notice of them," as no one at the meeting proposed to substantiate the charges. McNemar, however, requested and was granted liberty to make a few observations on the charges as "explanatory of his ideas."[4]

The first charge was that McNemar had opposed the idea of sinners attempting to pray, or being exhorted to pray, before they believed in Christ. McNemar responded that faith is the first thing that God requires of the sinner. He also noted that he did not understand how anyone could pray except in faith, quoting as his authority Romans 10:14, "For how then shall they call upon him in whom they have not believed."

The second charge was that McNemar had "condemned" persons who urged that "conviction" or distress was necessary to conversion. McNemar observed that the issue was whether any "convictions" were necessary to "authorize the soul to believe" other than those that arise from the testimony of God "in his word." McNemar believed not.

The third charge was that McNemar had expressly declared that "Christ has purchased salvation for all the human race, without distinction." This charge McNemar accepted as stated, adding that "Christ is by office the Saviour of all men."

The fourth charge was that McNemar had expressly declared that "a sinner has power to believe in Christ at any time." Not willing to accept this charge as stated, McNemar explained that "the sinner is capable of receiving the testimony of God at any time he heard it." He cited as his authority Romans 10:17, "faith cometh by hearing, and hearing by the word of God."

The fifth charge was that McNemar had taught that the sinner has "as much power to act faith, as to act unbelief." Again, not willing to accept the charge as stated, McNemar explained that "the sinner is as capable of believing as disbelieving, according to the evidence presented to the view of his mind." He turned to 1 John 5:9 for scriptural support: "If we receive the witness of men, the witness of God is greater."

The sixth charge had three parts. The first part was that McNemar had expressly stated that "faith consisted in the creature's persuading himself assuredly, that Christ died for him in particular." This accusation McNemar flatly denied. The second part was that McNemar had taught that doubting and examining the evidences of faith was inconsistent with and contrary to the nature of faith. To this accusation he responded that "doubting the veracity of God, and looking into ourselves for evidence, as the foundation of our faith, is contrary to Scripture; which represents the promises of the Gospel as the only sure foundation." He added that "self-examination has respect to the

---

[3]Quoted in "Apology," in Stone, *Biography*, 149–50.
[4]Springfield was located eleven miles north of Cincinnati. It was later named Springdale. The following account of McNemar's comments to the Washington Presbytery is from "Apology," in Stone, *Biography*, 151–53.

fruits, and not to the foundation of faith." The third part was that McNemar had "explained away these words—*Faith is the gift of God*, by saying it was Christ Jesus, the object of faith there meant, and not faith itself; and also, these words, 'No man can come to me, except the Father who hath sent me draw him,' by saying that the drawing there meant, was Christ offered in the Gospel; and that the Father knew no other drawing, or higher power, than holding up his Son in the Gospel." McNemar declared that if the interpretation of the texts cited in the charge "was explaining them away, he had done it."

The decision of the presbytery not to take further notice of the charges against McNemar's doctrine silenced opposition to his views at Cabin Creek. Although neither party changed its doctrinal position, on March 20, 1802, in the presence of neighboring minister John E. Finley, both parties signed a statement acknowledging that the difference between them had "threatened much evil" to the Cabin Creek congregation and promising to "pass over all past altercations, and cordially unite in communion for the future." Shortly thereafter, McNemar accepted a call through the Washington Presbytery to the Turtle Creek congregation in southern Ohio.[5]

Stone wrote that the "sticklers for orthodoxy" among the Presbyterian clergy "writhed" under the doctrines preached by him and McNemar but, seeing the "mighty effects" of these doctrines on the people, did not at first publicly oppose them for preaching their views. By the fall of 1802, the stance of the Presbyterian clergy had changed. The reason for the change, according to Stone, was the loss of members to the Methodists and Baptists. Although Stone did not identify the persons who became Baptists or Methodists, it may have been young persons raised in Presbyterian families who were the persons most likely to "profess religion" at a sacramental meeting. Stone reported that the "friends of the Confession" responded to the success of the Baptists and Methodists in "drawing away disciples" by boldly preaching the doctrines of the Confession of Faith and using "their most potent arguments in their defence." In response, the Methodist and Baptist preachers began to preach their distinctive doctrines. Stone claimed that in the ensuing confessional strife, the "friends of the Confession" were "indignant at us for preaching doctrines contrary to it" and "determined to arrest our progress and put us down."[6]

Growing tensions among the denominations are evident in Lyle's diary for the summer and fall of 1802. Lyle reported that he baptized the son of a popular Baptist preacher at the sacrament at Danville in the second week of August 1802. He confessed that he had been reluctant to do it, knowing that it would anger many of the Baptists and perhaps cause them to withdraw from the Presbyterian sacraments, which he added "has already taken place as I have been since informed." Lyle also reported an incident that occurred at the sacrament at Stonner Mouth, the last week in September 1802.

[5]"Apology," in Stone, *Biography*, 154.
[6]Stone, *Biography*, 45–46; see also Stone, *History*, 4–5.

Presbyterian Samuel Rannals said in introducing the supper "something like he did not choose to invite the Methodists to communion until a regular plan could be established for that purpose." In response, the two Methodist preachers present and most of the Methodist people went to the meetinghouse where one of the Methodist preachers, Mr. Hitt, preached in response to their having been excluded from the Presbyterian communion. Taking as his text 2 Corinthians 5:14, "For the love of Christ constraineth us, because we thus judge that if one died for all, then were all dead," Hitt first spoke of the love of God controlling "the true preacher" and also "a good deal about learning and *oratoraty* [*sic*] and College breeding etc.," declaring that without the love of God preachers were "as sounding brass and tynckling cymball," which was obviously a slam at the educated ministry of the Presbyterians. Hitt then argued that the scriptures teach that Christ died for *every* individual, in contrast, obviously, to the Presbyterian doctrine that Christ died only for the elect. Following Hitt's sermon, the Methodists left the meeting.[7]

At the October 6–9, 1802, meeting of the Washington Presbytery in Cincinnati, charges were brought against McNemar a second time, but with a different outcome than when the presbytery had met in Springfield the year before. Toward the end of the summer, an elder of the Turtle Creek congregation, a Mr. Tichner, had publicly expressed dissatisfaction with what he called McNemar's "free will" doctrine. Tichner had been advised by his fellow members of the session that if he had objections to McNemar's doctrine, he should submit them to the presbytery. Tichner indicated to the session that he had no intention of complaining to the presbytery, and the matter had appeared settled just days before the opening session of the presbytery.[8]

The second day of the presbytery meeting an elder from the Cincinnati congregation stated from the floor that he had heard that McNemar was a propagator of false doctrine and requested that the presbytery investigate the matter. He further stated that he had never heard McNemar preach, but that Mr. Tichner, an elder of the Turtle Creek congregation, who was also present, would be able to provide information regarding McNemar's preaching.

McNemar opposed the Cincinnati elder's request for an investigation of his doctrine, stating that charges could regularly come before presbytery only in writing. In contrast to the presbytery's scrupulous concern for due process just a year before, when they had refused to examine McNemar because no one was present to substantiate the written charges submitted by the former Cabin Creek elders, the presbytery proceeded, without written charges, to examine McNemar on the doctrines of particular election, human depravity, the atonement, the application of the atonement to sinners, the necessity of a divine agency in the application of the atonement to sinners, and the nature of faith. Following the examination, the presbytery adjourned until morning.

[7]Lyle, "Diary," 76, 87–89.

[8]"Apology" in Stone, *Biography*, 155. The following account of the actions of Washington Presbytery is from ibid., 155–60.

When the presbytery reconvened Saturday morning, the Cincinnati pastor James Kemper moved that the presbytery adjourn to the home of ministerial colleague Matthew Green Wallace, who was ill and had not attended the session the day before. The motion carried. When the presbytery convened at Wallace's, it was moved that McNemar be excluded from the meeting, which passed only with the vote of the moderator to break a tie.

After McNemar had withdrawn, the presbytery sent him a message to go to the meetinghouse and to preach to the congregation that was gathering there in preparation for the Lord's supper to be observed the following day. Kemper then brought forward a written statement declaring that upon examination the presbytery had found McNemar's views to be "strictly Arminian, though clothed in such expressions, and handed out in such manner, as to keep the body of the people in the dark, and lead them insensibly into Arminian principles; which are dangerous to the souls of men and hostile to the interests of all true religion." Jacob Arminius (1560–1609) was a Dutch theologian who had opposed the doctrine of predestination. Kemper's statement was adopted and ordered to be forwarded, as early as possible, to the congregations under the presbytery's care. Surprisingly, given their adoption of Kemper's statement, the presbytery also reappointed McNemar for one half of his time to the Turtle Creek congregation and for the other half to Orangedale, Clear Creek, Beulah, and Forks of Mad River.

Returning to Wallace's house, McNemar discovered that the presbytery was nearing adjournment. The minutes regarding his doctrine were read. He responded that it was not a fair statement of his views and requested that it be referred to the newly organized Synod of Kentucky that was to oversee the presbyteries carved out of the old Transylvania Presbytery and that was scheduled to meet for the first time the following week. No action was taken on McNemar's request.

Six months later, the Washington Presbytery meeting at Springfield received a petition from William Lamme and thirteen other persons from the congregations of Beulah, Turtle Creek, Clear Creek, Bethany, Hopewell, Duck Creek, and Cincinnati requesting a reexamination of McNemar on his "free will or Arminian doctrines" and also a like examination of John Thompson, minister of the Springfield church. This time supporters of McNemar were in the majority. The presbytery ruled that to engage in an examination of McNemar and Thompson in response to the petition would be "out of order," presumably because it contained no charges or names of witnesses. At the same meeting, McNemar received a call through the presbytery for the whole of his time at Turtle Creek. Disappointed by the actions taken, Kemper and Wallace, along with the two elders representing their churches, formally protested the presbytery's rejection of the request for examinations of McNemar and Thompson and also its presentation of a call to McNemar to Turtle Creek, citing the earlier minutes in the presbytery's records declaring his doctrine to be hostile to all true religion.

The division among Presbyterians regarding Stone and McNemar's preaching of how God gave faith was soon evident as well in the West Lexington Presbytery to which Stone had been assigned. According to John Lyle, on the Saturday evening of the sacrament at Bethel a month later, James Blythe preached a traditional Presbyterian sermon on examining oneself for evidences of having received saving faith by a work of the Holy Spirit. Having adopted Stone's and McNemar's view of faith, Robert Marshall, who with Blythe had counseled Stone on the day of his ordination, stated in the hearing of both Blythe and Lyle that Blythe's sermon contradicted Marshall's "new" doctrine of faith, which called for believing the gospel and coming to Christ, rather than seeking evidences of having received saving faith. Marshall confessed that formerly he, too, had misled his hearers on this point and "laughed at Blythe for sticking so close to the confession."[9]

On Sunday, Marshall preached the action sermon from Romans 3:25, "whom God hath set forth to be a propitiation through faith in his blood." Lyle reported that Marshall "told us to believe and come on our faith to Christ and act on our faith etc. etc." Lyle further noted that Marshall "seem'd totally to avoid speaking directly of divine Spirit and influence" in bringing persons to believe. "I must confess," Lyle penned, "this appear'd an odd way of talking about religion and that I did not understand what he meant." Lyle also stated that some of the congregation displayed "an unsolemn curiosity as tho waiting to hear some new thing." In administering the Lord's supper, Lyle offered a corrective to Marshall's sermon, commenting on the importance of examining oneself for evidences of saving faith wrought by the Holy Spirit.[10]

That evening Lyle, Blythe, and a licentiate of the West Lexington Presbytery, W. McPheeters, took Marshall aside from the crowd to talk with him about his doctrine. According to Lyle, Marshall "broke out in a rage" at him for having come to the sacrament and at Blythe for having brought Lyle, exclaiming that it was Blythe and not Lyle who had been appointed by the presbytery to administer the sacrament. Blythe, Lyle, and McPheeters responded that they meant to give him "a friendly hearing." Marshall declared that he would not say anything while they were together, but that he would talk with them one by one. Lyle replied that he did not want to talk with him privately, for he knew that he would try to proselytize him. Lyle also stated that Marshall had made a serious charge not only against himself but also against his ministerial brethren by indicating that he had previously misled the people. Marshall replied that he had not said that they were "all" wrong and added that Lyle's comments while administering the supper regarding the importance of examining oneself for evidences of saving faith had contradicted his doctrine of faith.[11]

---

[9]Lyle, "Diary," 107.
[10]Ibid., 108–9.
[11]Ibid., 109–10.

Blythe and McPheeters withdrew, leaving Lyle and Marshall in the private conference that Lyle had not wanted. According to Lyle, Marshall "profess'd to be more lively and more into the liberty of the gospel and to have assurance and to have left his former legal ground etc." Lyle responded that he had "felt liberty and Assurance long ago" and that "this was no new doctrine etc." Lyle added that his feelings were "much hurt" by Marshall's having upbraided him for coming to the sacrament, that Marshall's behavior seemed "unbrotherly," and that their "jangling" seemed more like the behavior of children of the devil than children of God. Lyle then "burst into tears and walk'd away." Lyle reported that later that evening he met Marshall in a crowd and that Marshall "loudly profess'd to love me, pray'd for love and friendship in a audible voice etc."[12]

Lyle preached Monday morning from 2 Corinthians 5:19, "God was in Christ, reconciling the world unto himself, not imputing their trespasses unto them, and hath committed unto us the word of reconciliation." According to his account, he treated the subject as he normally did. Lyle reported that Marshall stated that "this discourse was nearly correspondent to his doctrine" and that he "suppos'd we disagree'd only in the extent of the atonement etc." Lyle and Marshall "parted friends," though Lyle indicated that he remained "much wounded" by what Marshall had done "in turning the minds of the people to new Doctrines."[13]

Division among Presbyterian ministers regarding how God gave faith was also evident at the Walnut Hill sacrament the first week in June. Lyle reported that Stone preached that faith was simply believing the good news of God's love and grace and that all believers were authorized to "come to Christ" for the gifts of forgiveness of sins and newness of life. He added that Stone "studiously avoided saying anything of the work of the spirit in conviction and calls such descriptions legality." Following Stone's sermon, Lyle exhorted the congregation on the agency of the Spirit in convicting sinners of their sin as the necessary preparation for their believing the gospel to the salvation of their souls.[14]

The division in the West Lexington Presbytery, though focused primarily on the doctrine of faith, also extended to differences regarding order. From the beginning of the revival, some ministers, notably David Rice and James Blythe, had been more critical of the general disorder that characterized the sacramental meetings of the revival than were others. By the summer of 1803, the difference over order came to focus on what Lyle called "mingled exercises," the simultaneous offering aloud of individual prayers and exhortations. This practice, which had early been a feature of the revival in Logan County and the Cumberland district of Tennessee, appeared in central Kentucky late in the fall of 1801, following the Cane Ridge meeting.[15]

---

[12]Ibid., 110–11.
[13]Ibid., 112–13.
[14]Ibid., 118.
[15]Ibid., 58, 83–84, 100–101, 103–4, 107, 116, 117, 120, 121.

As the revival continued, mingled exercises were increasingly accompanied by "jerking" and "laughing." Lyle reported having observed one man "convulsed" at Cane Ridge and described another who had "laughed in a ha, ha, ha," at Silver Creek in May 1802. As with falling, the phenomena of jerking and laughing had been associated with the great revivals of the eighteenth century both in England and America.[16]

Stone described the jerking and laughing "exercises" in his autobiography. Of the jerks he wrote, "Sometimes the subject of the jerks would be affected in some one member of the body, and sometimes in the whole system. When the head alone was affected, it would be jerked backward and forward, or from side to side, so quickly that the features of the face could not be distinguished." He indicated that both "saints and sinners, the strong as well as the weak, were thus affected" and that no one who had experienced the jerks with whom he had spoken could account for them, though some had told him that "those were among the happiest seasons of their lives." The laughing exercise, he asserted, appeared only among the religious, and he described it as "a loud, hearty laughter" that "excited laughter in none else." He stated further that subjects of the laughing exercise appeared "rapturously solemn."[17]

Stone's descriptions of the jerking and laughing exercises make it appear that they were separate phenomena. However, as reported by Lyle, they were sometimes related, as at Salem in April 1803. Following a sermon by Blythe, during which the people had seemed quite attentive, the congregation had begun to sing. A Mrs. Bell fell to the floor and cried out for Christians to pray for sinners. Captain Bell, presumably her husband, joined her "for a considerable time one voice confounding the other." A Betsy Wing also fell to the floor and called for others to pray. Then Betsy Wing's brother fell and "was convuls'd insomuch that his hands struck the floor with inconceivable frequency and force." Lyle noted that "the noise was like quick drumming." He also stated that Wing's brother "seem'd to gasp for breath and look'd horribly wild out of his eyes." Nevertheless, "after sometime his countenance became more serene and he broke in convulsive laughter and a kind of *dizy* joy beam'd through his countenance. He essayed to utter a few words." Lyle continued, "All I heard him [say] was that he could not help laughing he was so happy."[18]

Stone and the other ministers who preached his new doctrine of how God gave faith generally supported simultaneous individual audible prayers and exhortations and did nothing to discourage the growing catalog of exercises. Presbyterians who opposed the new doctrine tended to view simultaneous audible prayers and exhortations as "irregular" and were wary of at least some of the "wilder" physical manifestations of religious excitement. Opponents of the new doctrine also tended to oppose conducting outdoor meetings after dark, believing that evening meetings conducted indoors were

---

[16]Ibid., 30, 68; Rogers, in Stone, *Biography*, 351–62.
[17]Ibid., 40, 41.
[18]Lyle, "Diary," 98–100.

less likely to become "disorderly." Attitudes regarding order among opponents of the new doctrine, however, were not uniform. In May 1802, Lyle had commented that "Stone's people were wild and disorderly more than needful." He added, "but as religion seems to be dull in my bounds I would probably rather wish them to be lively and wild and disorderly than cold and unanimated." Lyle did not "strongly" oppose conducting outdoor meetings after dark. Lyle also noted that when hundreds of people had offered individual audible prayers simultaneously for more than an hour at the Walnut Hill sacrament in early June 1803, it had appeared "that they pray'd in the spirit." However, on the whole he was against mingled exercises, noting that the religious understanding of the participants was "unfruitful as to the edification of others." James Blythe was opposed to the new doctrine and strongly opposed both mingled exercises and conducting outdoor meetings after dark. Isaac Tull opposed the new doctrine but favored conducting outdoor meetings after dark and changed his mind at least once regarding mingled exercises.[19]

At Paris, during the second week in June 1803, the mounting conflict in the West Lexington Presbytery regarding both doctrine and order reached a climax. On Saturday morning Tull preached on the distinguishing marks of Christian joy. Lyle believed that much of the sermon had been borrowed from Jonathan Edwards' *Treatise on Religious Affections*—and was quite pleased. However, toward the end of the sermon, to Lyle's dismay, Tull announced that although he had formerly been against "so many praying out at once and spoke against it," he now favored the practice.[20]

That afternoon Stone preached his understanding of faith from 2 Kings 5, the story of Naaman the Syrian, whose leprosy was cured when he believed the prophet Elisha and bathed as he had been instructed by the prophet. Lyle commented that Stone "told them not to wait to see their leprosy worse," intimating, Lyle thought, "that all by nature saw their spiritually leprous state so that they might come to Christ without seeing it worse." Lyle also commented that "he told them to believe and that he could tell them no more, but never mentioned the work of conviction or a discovery of our need of the Lord Jesus," which Lyle believed to be taught in the Bible and affirmed in the Westminster Confession.[21]

On Sunday morning Lyle preached from Psalm 51:17, "A broken and contrite heart, O God, thou wilt not despise." Assuming his usual role in the growing conflict regarding how God worked in conversion, he drew attention to "the conviction of sin by the law and the necessity of sinners feeling their need of Christ etc."[22]

The issue of outdoor night meetings was raised by the decision regarding the location of services. Morning and afternoon services were to be conducted

---

[19]Ibid., 66, 116, 125.
[20]Ibid., 125.
[21]Ibid., 125–26.
[22]Ibid., 126.

in a grove near Paris where the people had camped with their wagons and provisions. Evening services were to be held at the meetinghouse in Paris, nearly a mile away. Stone reported that this decision required that the people leave their tents and provisions exposed in order to attend the night meetings. Moreover, the meetinghouse, he noted, would not contain half the crowd. Thus, the participants in the meeting were divided, some choosing to remain at the camp during the evening service. In Stone's view, the result of this decision was that "the work [was] greatly impeded."[23]

The preacher on Sunday evening was Robert Stuart. Stone described Stuart as having always been "hostile to the work." He reported that "he lengthily addressed the people in iceberg style" and that the effect was "deathly." Stone was not alone in his judgment of Stuart's preaching style. Even Lyle, who was favorably disposed toward Stuart, noted that Stuart's trial sermon delivered before his ordination as pastor of the Salem church in April 1803, though "a tolerably good discourse," was "cold." Following the sermon, Stone arose and called the people to pray. At first only a few joined in. McPheeters, whom Stone stated was "of the same cast" as Stuart, took the opportunity to begin a second sermon. According to Lyle, Stone then "got down on his knees and begun [*sic*] to pray." Others, observing him, joined in, and within ten minutes the noise was so great that McPheeters gave up trying to preach. Stone reported that some of the preachers left by a window behind the pulpit! Lyle, though "hurt" by the conduct of Stone and others who had begun to pray, remained in the building and "silently pray'd for them and for myself." Meanwhile, Stone pushed through the crowd ministering to the distressed. At length, Lyle also moved out into the congregation and prayed and talked with one girl and one boy whom he found in distress.[24]

The following morning, Lyle was introduced to the "dancing" exercise. Like jerking and laughing, the dancing exercise became prominent at sacramental meetings during the summer of 1803. In his autobiography, Stone reported that subjects of the dancing exercise would "move forward and backward in the same track or alley," while offering prayer and praises to God. He noted a connection between dancing and the jerks, stating that dancing generally began with the jerks: "The subject, after jerking awhile, began to dance, and then the jerks would cease." "Sometimes," he noted, "the motion was quick and sometimes slow." This exercise, he asserted, affected only religious people.[25]

Lyle did not know how many people were engaged in the exercise. He restricted his gaze to three men whom he knew, a Mr. Ireland, David Purviance, who was a candidate for the ministry, and Malcolm Worley, an elder. After greeting these individuals, he convinced them to accompany him to the stand where another minister was exhorting. Arriving at the stand with Ireland, Purviance, and Worley, Lyle was prevailed upon to preach. Taking as his text

[23]Stone, *Biography*, 43.
[24]Ibid., 43; Lyle, "Diary," 98, 126–27.
[25]Ibid., 128–29; Stone, *Biography*, 40.

1 Peter 4:8, "Above all things have fervent charity among yourselves for charity shall cover the multitude of sins," he preached on "brotherly affection." Then, after taking many "cautions," he introduced the subject of order and "the impropriety of many praying at once etc."[26]

When Lyle finished speaking, a Colonel Smith "begun [*sic*] to pray and in his prayer to use his arguments in favor of all praying at once." In particular, Smith said that "there was one spirit but a diversity of operations." Lyle, who had sat down, arose and told the people that he "hoped they would not suppose that the spirit operated in any diversity not described in the word and beseech'd and charg'd them to attend to the divine word." From behind the stand two women "were agonized and pray'd out." A young man, whom Lyle thought was a Methodist, ran into the crowd and "with apparent rage" called on the people to pray aloud. Comparatively few responded. However, as if to make up in intensity for the small number who prayed aloud, one older man "pray'd out with clinched fists."[27]

Differences regarding order among Presbyterians in the West Lexington Presbytery should not, however, be overdrawn. After Lyle left the stand following his sermon on order, he was met by a Mr. McCune of Stonner Mouth, who thanked him for his sermon and remarked that "if ever he had like to pray out in his life it was today [in response to Lyle's sermon], but, (said he) I never have pray'd out in society because I thought it not agreeable to the word of God." A Mr. Patton, also of Stonner Mouth, told Lyle that he had been trying unsuccessfully to "regulate matters" for over a year, and that when he heard Lyle on the subject he was so overcome with joy, hoping that God had inspired Lyle to do what he had failed to do, that he had actually fallen! Lyle had spent Sunday night at Dr. Todd's, as did Barton and Elizabeth Stone. He reported that in the morning a group of people were singing in the hallway when "Mrs. Stone fell down and had a great manifestation of the divine glory insomuch as she intimated she could scarcely bear the view. Oh Lord, said she, no mortal can behold thy glory and live." A Mrs. Turner "got greatly affected, was much agitated in body and drew her breath short and hard with considerable noise." This led the doctor's wife and her three daughters to weep aloud till they were "greatly affected in body." A "negro woman of Doctor Todds" was also much affected. Despite Lyle's disapproval of Stone's behavior in the meetinghouse the night before, he joined the group in the hallway and all engaged in "talking, singing and praying till it was time to go to meeting."[28]

It may seem ironic that advocates of the new doctrine, who viewed God as giving faith through the hearing of the gospel, generally supported the simultaneous offering of prayers and exhortations, which made it difficult to hear individual prayers and exhortations, and could even drown out the preaching of the gospel. This irony may be explained by differences in openness to

---

[26]Lyle, "Diary," 129.
[27]Ibid., 130.
[28]Ibid., 127–28, 131.

change among the Presbyterian clergy. Stone, who had adopted a new doctrine of how God gave faith, was also open to new, or in this case Methodist, forms of worship. Lyle and other Presbyterians who saw no reason to adopt a new theology were also suspicious of new forms of practice. Lyle's complaint against Marshall was that he had turned the minds of the people to "new" doctrines. Colonel Smith, who "prayed" following Lyle's sermon against simultaneous prayers, asked Lyle how he accounted for the practice of "praying out" among participants in the revival in Logan County and the Cumberland district of Tennessee. Lyle replied that the practice had originated among the Methodists and that he would say more on the subject later. However, from Lyle's perspective, to say that a practice was Methodist was really all that one needed to say! "Praying out" was not Presbyterian.[29]

The division among Presbyterians in the West Lexington Presbytery also extended to the issue of slavery. In January 1801, Stone had filed a deed of manumission for two slaves, Ned and Lucy, whom he had received as a bequest from his mother after her death the year before. It is likely that they were traveling with Stone from Virginia when he first learned of the revival. Though he could have received money in lieu of the slaves, he had chosen to bring them to Kentucky and set them free.[30] Stone's provisions for manumitting Ned, whom he reported as about thirty, in two years and Lucy, whom he reported as about twelve, in ten years were in accord with the philosophy of gradual emancipation that required that slaves be prepared for freedom. Stone trained Ned in a skill before giving him his freedom. He reared Lucy in "the Bible and religion" as well as teaching her a skill before freeing her as a young woman.[31]

In his autobiography, Stone claimed that the "exciting cause" of his abandonment of slavery had been his observation of the institution in "more horrid forms than I had ever seen it before" while soliciting funds for a Presbyterian college in Kentucky on the John's and Wadmelaw Islands in 1797.[32] He may also have been influenced by antislavery sentiments in the Cane Ridge and Concord congregations. David Purviance, a Cane Ridge elder whom Lyle saw "dancing" at the Paris meeting, farmed without slaves and was elected to the Kentucky legislature as an antislavery representative the same year that Stone made his fundraising trip in behalf of the Transylvania Presbytery.[33] At the first meeting of the West Lexington Presbytery in 1800, Stone presented a resolution from the Cane Ridge and Concord churches declaring that slavery was "a subject likely to occasion much trouble and division in the churches" and that it was "a moral evil, very heinous, and consequently sufficient to exclude such as will continue in the practice of it from the privileges of the church." The presbytery referred the resolution to

---

[29]Ibid., 132.
[30]John R. Rogers, *The Cane Ridge Meeting-House*, 2d ed. (Cincinnati: Standard Publishing, 1910), 123.
[31]Roos, 81.
[32]Stone, *Biography*, 27–28.
[33]Rogers, *Cane Ridge*, 207, 212, 224.

the Synod of Virginia and the General Assembly, noting that although it was the opinion of the large majority of the presbytery that slaveholders should be excluded from church privileges, they hesitated to decide the matter until directed by higher judicatories.[34]

Not all Kentucky Presbyterians endorsed emancipation or believed it practicable. Among those who had reservations regarding emancipation was Samuel Rennels, pastor of the Paris church. Stone stated in a letter to Rennels eight reasons why he favored emancipation. The portion of the letter including the date and the first three reasons has been lost. The remaining five reasons focus on the cruelty of slavery and its incompatibility with the fulfillment of familial obligations. Stone concluded the letter by observing that it was often said by white Christians that it was not good policy to set the slaves free "amongst us." Many, he observed, thought otherwise. In any case, he continued, "christians ought not to let civil policy oppose the express will of God. If we know God's will, we are not to enquire whether it will be [in] our interest to do it."[35]

Lyle reported that before he left the stand at Paris after his sermon on order, a sister-in-law of a Dr. Seldon came forward, shook his hand, "and in a kind of agony told me to set my slaves free." Lyle responded that setting his slaves free depended on the will of another. He also stated that if his slaves were free, they could not support themselves. At that point a Colonel Fleming and his brother insisted that Lyle preach on the subject of emancipation. Lyle refused, but indicated that he would "talk with them about that subject at a proper time."[36]

Stone did not report the confrontation between Lyle and Dr. Seldon's sister-in-law regarding slavery. However, at the end of his account of the Paris meeting, he stated that he had emancipated his slaves "from a sense of right, choosing poverty with a good conscience, in preference to all the treasures of the world." Then he added, "This revival cut the bonds of many poor slaves; and this argument speaks volumes in favor of the work. For of what avail is a religion of decency and order, without righteousness?"[37]

Stone's claim that the revival resulted in the freeing of slaves is supported by the record of emancipations in Bourbon County, which shows an increase of emancipations during the course of the revival, largely as a result of deeds of manumission filed by members of the Cane Ridge congregation.[38] The

---

[34]Davidson, 337; "*Minutes* of West Lexington (Kentucky) Presbytery," ms. 41, quoted in Ware, 217.

[35]B. W. Stone to Samuel Rennels, Cane Ridge Preservation Project Museum, Cane Ridge, Bourbon County, Kentucky. Rennels' name was also spelled Rannells.

[36]Lyle, "Diary," 130–31.

[37]Stone, *Biography*, 44.

[38]Stone's deed of manumission of Ned and Lucy was one of thirteen filed by members of the Cane Ridge congregation between 1801 and the end of the Great Revival in 1805. Another sixteen deeds of manumission were executed during the fourteen years following the revival. If one adds the two slaves manumitted by members of the Cane Ridge congregation prior to 1801, a total of 46 of the 109 slaves freed in Bourbon County during the twenty-eight years between 1792 and 1819 were manumitted by members of the Cane Ridge church. See *Kentucky Citizens Newspaper*, June 28, 1957, quoted in Roos, 83.

freeing of slaves by participants in the revival may have been related to the popular rationalism of the early American Republic that had so influenced Stone's theological development. If one believed that slavery was against God's will, then not to emancipate one's slaves, for whatever reason, was a contradiction! In the deed of emancipation that Stone filed in January 1801, he declared, "I, Barton W. Stone...being fully convinced that involuntary unconditional slavery is *inconsistent* with the principles of Christianity as well as civil liberty, do emancipate my two negroes, Ned and Lucy..."[39] It follows that Presbyterians who were "embarrassed" by contradictions between their faith and theology would also have had difficulty with contradictions between their faith and practice.

The division in the West Lexington Presbytery had not surfaced in the actions of the presbytery as it had in the Washington Presbytery. However, Kemper and Wallace's formal protest of the actions of the Washington Presbytery regarding the request of Lamme and others for examinations of McNemar and Thompson and the call of McNemar to Turtle Creek ensured that the conflict would be addressed by the Synod of Kentucky, scheduled for Lexington the first week in September.

---

[39]Bourbon County Records, Paris, Kentucky, quoted in Roos, 80. Italics mine. The more common form of deeds of manumission made no reference to principles of Christianity or civil liberty. See Roos, 81.

6

Separation

The Synod of Kentucky opened Tuesday, September 6, 1803, at the two-story log meetinghouse of the First Presbyterian Church in Lexington with a sermon by the moderator, David Rice.[1] Rice advanced seven reasons for believing that "the present stir" was a genuine revival of the Christian religion. First, the revival had made its appearance in various places "without any extraordinary means to produce it." The preaching, singing, and praying had been the same to which people had been long accustomed. Second, there appeared to be in the subjects of the work "a deep...sense of the great unreasonableness, abominable nature, pernicious effects and deadly consequences of sin; and the absolute unworthiness of the sinful creature of the smallest crumb of mercy, from the hand of a holy God." Third, the subjects of the work appeared to have "a lively and very affecting view of the infinite condescension and love of God the Father, in giving his eternal and only begotten Son, for the redemption of mankind." Fourth, the subjects of the work seemed to have "a very deep and affecting sense of the worth of precious immortal souls, ardent love to them, and an agonizing concern for their conviction, conversion and complete salvation," regardless of the religious background, geographical location, nationality, or age of those souls. Fifth, a considerable number of individuals appeared to be "greatly reformed in their morals." Sixth, a number of families "who had lived apparently without the fear of God, in folly and in vice; without religious instruction, or any proper government," had taken up the practice of daily family worship. Seventh, the subjects of the work appeared to be "very sensible of the necessity of *Sanctification* as well as Justification."[2]

Turning to the "gathering clouds" that would darken the day of revival and at length bring on a dismal night of darkness, "unless it shall please God by some means or other to disperse them," Rice declared that "the important Scripture doctrine of divine influences in a work of conviction, conversion and sanctification, is, I believe, generally taught in our land." Nevertheless, if he understood them right, some preachers approached "too near" to representing the work of the Spirit in bringing persons to Christ as "a mere

---

[1]This structure was located at the corner of Short and Mill streets. See Ware, 64–65, 131.

[2]David Rice, *A Sermon on the Present Revival of Religion, etc. in this country; preached at the opening of the Kentucky Synod* (Lexington, Ky.: Joseph Charles, 1803), 25–28.

mechanical work, without considering the word of God as the means by which the Spirit works, in producing the excellent effect." Others, if he understood them correctly, "leave in this work, but very little for the divine spirit to do; after the inspiration of the holy Scriptures." Both of these positions he understood to be "departures from the principles of reformation, and, what is more, departures from the written word of God."[3]

Stating that the "the scheme of doctrines" that had produced the Reformation of the sixteenth century and every noted revival from the Reformation to their own day was "entitled to great respect," Rice warned of the danger of advancing "new" doctrines. He did not mean "that we should be confined to ancient systems and not inquire and judge for ourselves." We *should* inquire and judge for ourselves, he advised, but "with proper modesty, deliberation and diligence," never trying to distinguish ourselves by "advancing new notions, poorly digested, and but half understood." Especially, he admonished, "should innovations in doctrine be avoided, as much as possible in a time of revival; for they naturally tend to check a revival, by turning the spirit of it into a spirit of disputation." Persons' minds, he advised, are set in motion to find "arguments for and against the new opinions" and thereby turn away from the "one thing needful." As a consequence, the life and power of godliness is destroyed, or at least "that mutual love and confidence that should unite the hearts of christians, and especially christian ministers" is destroyed.[4]

Rice said scarcely a word regarding falling or the jerks, except that his confidence that the current excitement was a true revival of the Christian religion was not based on the fact that "many are thrown into great bodily agitations; sometimes into fainting or convulsive fits." Such bodily agitations, he asserted, "have been produced, and I suppose may again be produced, by the operations of imposture on the credulity and superstition of mankind; yea, by things which have no relation to religion."[5] As to the issue of order, Rice advised distinguishing "between the humble, solemn, fervent pleading of faith, and a bold, noisy kind of earnestness; at the same time making proper charitable allowances for difference of custom, in different places and societies."[6]

Rice mentioned slavery in relation to whether the millennium, the one-thousand-year earthly reign of Christ anticipated by nineteenth-century

[3]Rice, *Sermon*, 32–33.

[4]Ibid., 47, 49.

[5]Ibid., 23. In a footnote, Rice acknowledged that he had never experienced the exercises associated with the revival and that, therefore, it behooved him to "speak about them with modesty." He then observed that it appeared that if persons "have right notions of divine things, previous to their falling into these exercises, their ideas in the time are just, lively, and very impressive: and their exercises have a happy influence on their temper and conduct." The danger, he warned, was "enthusiasm," for persons with wrong notions of divine things, expressing those notions while engaged in such exercises, might assume that their "wrong" notions had been given to them by the Holy Spirit.

[6]Ibid., 41.

American Protestants, was at hand. While confessing that the question of when the reign of Christ on earth would begin was "too deep" for him, he ventured that the millennium was "not very near," given the "prevalence of arbitrary power in the world; and particularly that professors of christianity are not rightly disposed to 'break every yoke, and let the oppressed go free.'" Rice declared that he could have no hope that the reign of Christ was dawning while slavery "abounds and is practiced by christians."[7]

On the second day, the synod committee responsible for preparing business items presented Kemper and Wallace's protest of the actions of the Washington Presbytery regarding McNemar and Thompson. Rather than addressing the protest, the synod referred consideration of the matter to the synod committee appointed to examine the records of the Washington Presbytery and ordered that committee to be prepared to report to the synod the following morning.[8]

The synod spent all of Thursday and most of Friday considering the committee's report. All five of the synod's subsequent actions in response to the report supported Kemper and Wallace's position. (1) The synod approved the proceedings of the presbytery in examining McNemar at its October 1802 meeting in Cincinnati. (2) The synod approved the presbytery's publishing to the churches under their care the results of their examination of McNemar. (3) The synod censured the presbytery for having appointed McNemar to preach at the same session in which they declared against his doctrine. (4) The synod censured the presbytery for having rejected the petition of Lamme and others calling for examinations of McNemar and Thompson at its April 1803 meeting at Springfield. (5) The synod censured the presbytery for having presented a call to McNemar to Turtle Creek while he remained under the censure of the preceding session.[9]

Following the division of the original Translyvania Presbytery in 1799, the new Transylvania Presbytery had embraced the district south and west of the Kentucky River. At its first meeting in October 1802, the Synod of Kentucky had further reduced the bounds of the Transylvania Presbytery by constituting members of the presbytery located in Logan County and the Cumberland settlements in Tennessee as the Cumberland Presbytery.[10] None of the twenty members of the Cumberland Presbytery who—as will be noted—would have been likely to support McNemar and Thompson made the six-day journey from the Cumberland district to Lexington to attend the September 1803 meeting of the synod. Analysis of the voting pattern on the report of the committee that examined the records of the Washington Presbytery shows that seventeen of the twenty-four members of the Transylvania and West Lexington Presbyteries who voted generally supported Kemper and Wallace.

[7]Ibid., 40.

[8]"Minutes of the Synod of Kentucky," 1802–1811, in Sweet, *Religion on the American Frontier, 1783–1840,* vol. 2, *The Presbyterians,* 314–15.

[9]Ibid., 315–17.

[10]Ibid., 310–11.

Members of the Washington Presbytery were not allowed to vote on the review of their records.[11]

The Cumberland Presbytery included James McGready, William Hodge, William McGee, John Rankin, and others identified with the revival in the Cumberland district. While several of the members of this presbytery, and McGready in particular, affirmed the doctrines of the Confession without reservation, others did not. Moreover, the Cumberland Presbytery was unwilling to exclude ministers for holding "Arminian" sentiments and even welcomed one former Methodist. As a result, the Cumberland Presbytery was soon in a conflict of its own with the synod. This conflict would lead the synod to abolish the Cumberland Presbytery (returning its few "loyal" ministers to the Transylvania Presbytery) and would result in the formation in 1810 of the independent Cumberland Presbyterian Church. Had members of the Cumberland Presbytery attended the September 1803 meeting of the synod, the synod's actions regarding the proceedings of the Washington Presbytery, and later the Cumberland Presbytery itself, might have been different and, likewise, the history of American Presbyterianism.[12]

Marshall reported that by the close of the synod's session on Friday, September 9, it appeared to him, Stone, Thompson, and John Dunlavy, who had also accepted the new doctrine of faith, that the synod, by censuring the Washington Presbytery for appointing McNemar to preach and presenting him with the call to Turtle Creek, had implicitly declared that he was already suspended from the functions of ministry. It also appeared to them, according to Marshall, that the way was now open to censure any minister without written charge, witness, or prosecution by the short method of presbyterial examination. In his autobiography, Stone reported that there had been "much spirited altercation" in the discussion of McNemar's case and that it had been "plainly hinted to us," referring to himself, Marshall, Thompson, and Dunlavy, that they would be the next to be censured.[13]

During a short recess of the synod on Saturday, September 10, Stone, Marshall, Dunlavy, McNemar, and Thompson retired to a private garden to "ask counsel of the Lord, and consult one another." Since they were convinced that the examination of McNemar had been contrary to the constitution of the Presbyterian Church, it would have been appropriate for them to appeal to the General Assembly. However, they believed that as long as "human opinions" rather than the Bible were esteemed the standard of orthodoxy, they would have little hope of redress from any court of the Presbyterian Church. Therefore, they determined to withdraw from the jurisdiction of the synod and, in Marshall's words, "cast ourselves upon the care of that God who had led us hitherto in safety through many trials and difficulties;

---

[11]Ibid., 315–17.

[12]For the history of the Cumberland Presbyterian Church, see Ben Melton Barrus, Milton C. Baughn, and Thomas H. Campbell, *A People Called Cumberland Presbyterians* (Memphis: Frontier Press, 1972).

[13]"Apology," 168; Stone, *Biography*, 47.

and who, we believed, would lead us safely on to the end." The five ministers then drew up a protest against the proceedings of the synod and a declaration of their withdrawal and immediately returned to the meetinghouse.[14]

The synod was already in session when they appeared. Under discussion was a resolution to conduct "the examination or trial of Messrs. McNemar and Thompson, according to the prayer of the petitions [of Lamme and others], and the charges therein stated; and also, that this Synod resolve the questions of doctrines, seriously and reasonably proposed in their petitions." After each of the five ministers had stated his reasons for not having arrived earlier, Robert Marshall, who was stated clerk of the synod and whom Stone described as a "pillar" of the original Transylvania Presbytery that had ordained him in 1798, read the document that Stone and his colleagues had prepared.[15]

The document protested "the proceedings of Synod, in approbating that minute of the Washington Presbytery which condemned the sentiments of Mr. McNemar as dangerous to the souls of men, and hostile to the interests of all true religion" and stated the following reasons for the protesters' withdrawing from the jurisdiction of the synod. First, they believed that the resolution of the Washington Presbytery condemning the doctrine of McNemar gave "a distorted and false representation of Mr. McNemar's sentiments" and was "calculated to prevent the influence of truth of the most interesting nature." Second, they claimed the privilege of interpreting the scripture without reference to the Confession, affirming in the words of section 10 of chapter 1 of the Confession of Faith "that the Supreme Judge, by which all controversies of religion are to be determined, and all decrees of councils, opinions of ancient writers, doctrines of men and private spirits, are to be examined, and in whose sentence we are to rest, can be no other than the Holy Spirit speaking in the Scriptures." And third, that while remaining "inviolably attached to the doctrines of grace, which, through God, have been mighty in every revival of true religion since the reformation," they believed that those doctrines are "in a measure darkened by some expressions in the Confession of Faith, which are used as a means of strengthening sinners in their unbelief, and subjecting many of the pious to a spirit of bondage." When they attempted to obviate these difficulties they were accused of "departing from our Standard, viewed as disturbers of the peace of the Church, and threatened to be called to account." Therefore, they were withdrawing from the jurisdiction of the synod rather than be "prosecuted before a Judge [the Confession of Faith], whose authority to decide we cannot in Conscience acknowledge."[16]

They stated that they did not desire to separate from the communion of the members of the synod, nor to exclude members of the synod from their communion. On the contrary, they would "ever wish to bear, and forbear, in matters of human order, or opinion, and unite our joint supplications with

---

[14]"Apology," 169.

[15]"Minutes of the Synod of Kentucky," 317–18; "Apology," 169–70; Stone, *Biography,* 29.

[16]"Minutes of the Synod of Kentucky," 318–19. See also "Apology," 169–71.

yours, for the increasing effusions of that divine Spirit, which is the bond of peace." "With this disposition in mind," they concluded, "we bid you adieu, until, through the providence of God, it seem good to your reverend body to adopt a more liberal plan, respecting human Creeds and Confessions."[17]

Marshall's reading of their protest and declaration, which Stone thought was altogether unexpected by the synod, brought discussion of the resolution to enter into a trial of McNemar and Thompson to an abrupt halt. Stone and the other signers of the document left the meetinghouse and retired to the home of a friend.[18] Since Marshall had been the stated clerk of the synod, it was necessary to immediately hold an election to fill the vacancy created by his secession from the jurisdiction of the synod. Elected was James Welsh, one of the two ministers who had voted with Stone and Marshall against approving the proceedings of the Washington Presbytery in the examination of McNemar.

Returning to the petitions calling for an examination of McNemar and Thompson, the synod appointed Archibald Cameron, John P. Campbell, and Joseph P. Howe, all three of whom had voted approval of the examination of McNemar, to draft a letter to Lamme and the other petitioners assuring them that the synod did strictly adhere to the Confession and addressing any other matters that they deemed necessary.[19]

The next item of business was the appointment of David Rice, Matthew Houston, and James Welsh as a committee to meet with Marshall, Dunlavy, McNemar, Stone, and Thompson "to labor to bring them back to the Standard and doctrines of our Church." The composition of the committee suggests that at least some members of the synod really did want to bring them back. Rice, as moderator, had not voted on the resolution approving the action of the Washington Presbytery in examining McNemar. Houston, though he had voted approval of the Washington Presbytery's proceedings in the examination of McNemar, was sufficiently disposed toward the protesters as to soon accept their doctrine and join their group. Welsh, as already noted, had voted with Stone and Marshall opposing the proceedings of the Washington Presbytery in the examination of McNemar.[20]

The synod's next action was approval of a resolution calling for the printing of one thousand copies of the Confession of Faith to be distributed throughout the bounds of the synod. The final action of the day was the addition of Joseph P. Howe, who had voted approval of the Washington Presbytery's proceedings in the examination of McNemar, to the committee appointed to converse with Marshall, Dunlavy, McNemar, Stone, and Thompson.[21]

The committee met with Marshall, Dunlavy, McNemar, Stone, and Thompson the following night, and Stone reported that the conversation was friendly. He also remembered that Rice had tried to bring them back to

[17]"Minutes of the Synod of Kentucky," 319. See also "Apology," 171.
[18]Stone, *Biography*, 47; "Minutes of the Synod of Kentucky," 320.
[19]Ibid.
[20]Ibid.
[21]Ibid.

Calvinism by arguing that every departure from Calvinism was an advance toward atheism. The progress that Rice outlined was from Calvinism to Arminianism, from Arminianism to Pelagianism, from Pelagianism to deism, and from deism to atheism. Although Stone referred to Rice in his autobiography as "old father David Rice, of precious memory," he noted that this argument "could have no effect on minds ardent in search of truth."[22]

The seceding ministers agreed to confer with the synod on doctrine, provided that the questions were in written form and submitted to them at one time, and they indicated that they were ready to enter upon such a process immediately. The seceding ministers also stated that they would be willing to return to the care and jurisdiction of the synod on the condition that they be constituted as one presbytery, that any charges against them be brought forward in an orderly manner according to the Book of Discipline, and that their views be judged by the Word of God, rather than the Confession of Faith![23]

On Monday morning, September 15, the committee reported to the synod

> That the aforesaid gentlemen agree that as a body they will confer with Synod on points of Doctrine in the following manner, that is to say: they will answer any questions proposed to them by Synod which may be stated in writing…and that they are ready to enter upon the business as soon as they may receive notice for that purpose—The whole of the questions shall be given in at once.

No mention was made of their offer to return to the synod on condition that they be constituted as a presbytery. A resolution for synod to accept the proposal of Marshall, Dunlavy, McNemar, Stone, and Thompson for an examination of their doctrine met with a divided vote: seven yeas and twelve nays. The yeas were the members of the committee, Welsh, Houston, and Howe, along with William Robinson, who had voted with Stone, Marshall, and Welsh regarding the examination of McNemar, and three elders. The nays were Archibald Cameron and Samuel Findley of Transylvania Presbytery; Isaac Tull, James Blythe, John Lyle, Robert Stuart, and Samuel Rannells of West Lexington Presbytery; and James Kemper and John P. Campbell of Washington Presbytery; plus one elder each from the Transylvania, West Lexington, and Washington Presbyteries. Rice, as moderator, did not vote.[24]

The large number of elders who did not vote on the proposal, one from Transylvania Presbytery, five from Washington Presbytery, and four from West Lexington Presbytery, suggests that some elders had "withdrawn" from the synod with their pastors or simply had not stayed beyond the weekend. Had some of these elders been present, the vote might have been closer. Two of the four elders from the West Lexington Presbytery who did not vote on the proposal had earlier voted to disapprove the proceedings of the Washington Presbytery in the examination of McNemar and would have likely approved

---

[22]Stone, *Biography*, 47.
[23]"Apology," 172.
[24]"Minutes of the Synod of Kentucky," 320–21; "Apology," 172–73.

the proposal of the protesting ministers. Members of the Washington Presbytery had not voted on the review of their records. However, since elders in the synod seem to have generally followed the lead of their pastors, it seems likely that at least the three elders representing the churches of Dunlavy, McNemar, and Thompson would have voted in favor of the proposal.

Meanwhile, Marshall, Dunlavy, McNemar, Stone, and Thompson had formally united as the "Springfield Presbytery." The name Springfield was chosen because of positive associations with Springfield, Ohio, in the history of the Washington Presbytery. Friends of the new theology had been in the majority at Springfield in April 1803 when the Washington Presbytery deemed it improper to enter into an examination of McNemar and Thompson in response to the petition of Lamme and others. The sacrament also had been observed in conjunction with that meeting, and apparently Marshall and Stone, though members of the West Lexington Presbytery, had participated. "The evident displays of divine power, on that occasion," Marshall later wrote, "carried sufficient evidence that our ministrations in the gospel were not injurious to the souls of men."[25]

Having rejected Marshall, Dunlavy, McNemar, Stone, and Thompson's proposal, the synod appointed Samuel Rannells and James Kemper, both of whom had voted against the proposal, along with Matthew Houston, to be a committee to propose to the five that they submit in writing the following morning or before the synod adjourned, "what objection they have to our Confession of Faith, or, to any part of it, which they have in their remonstrance declared they cannot in Conscience submit to be judged by." Marshall reported that the Springfield Presbytery received the committee's proposal late Monday evening after they had adjourned. Since, according to Marshall, several of them were required to return to their homes that evening, they decided to meet in the morning to consider the resolution.[26]

Tuesday morning, September 16, the newly organized Springfield Presbytery met, considered the resolution from the synod, and drafted a letter addressed to the moderator of the synod, declaring their intention to comply with the request but stating that it would be impossible for them to do so as soon as the Synod had required. Rather, they promised to provide a statement to the next annual session of the synod. They also stated that a "party," or separate communion, was not their aim and that they were determined "to proceed no farther, than circumstances may require." They appealed to all to "unite our prayers to our common Lord and Father, that he would in his kind providence, heal our divisions, and unite us more closely in the bonds of love," and they concluded with a declaration that they remained united to the members of the synod "in heart and affection."[27]

[25]"Apology," 161.
[26]"Minutes of the Synod of Kentucky," 321; "Apology," 175.
[27]"Apology," 175–76.

Before their letter was delivered, the synod suspended Marshall, Dunlavy, McNemar, Stone, and Thompson "from the exercise of all the functions of the gospel ministry" and declared their congregations vacant. The resolution stated (1) that Marshall, Dunlavy, McNemar, Stone, and Thompson had withdrawn from the jurisdiction of the synod, (2) that Marshall, Dunlavy, McNemar, Stone, and Thompson had seceded from the Confession of Faith "and no more wish to be united with us until we adopt a more liberal plan, respecting human creeds and confessions," (3) that a committee charged with reclaiming them to the doctrines and standards of the Presbyterian Church had been "entirely unsuccessful," and (4) that Marshall, Dunlavy, McNemar, Stone, and Thompson had constituted themselves a separate presbytery and "persist in their schismatic disposition."[28]

The synod requested Blythe, Lyle, Welsh, and Stuart to draft a circular letter to the churches "relative to the unhappy division now existing," and appointed commissioners to go to the several congregations where the five had preached to announce their suspension from the ministry and to declare those congregations vacant. When the letter from the "Suspended Members" was received, it was read and ordered to be filed among the papers of the synod. The synod then adjourned to meet at Danville on the third Tuesday of October 1804.[29]

Stone wrote that after their separation from the synod, the members of the new presbytery returned to their communities with "sorrowful" hearts and " many tears." They were soon followed by the members of the synod who had been appointed to proclaim their suspension from the ministry and to declare their congregations "vacant." Stone claimed that "the great majority of our congregations cleaved to us and to the word we preached." Nevertheless, congregations, including Stone's congregations at Cane Ridge and Concord, were divided by the series of actions that had played out in Lexington. In his autobiography, Stone recounted that shortly after he returned from the synod he gathered his congregations together, informed them that henceforth he would preach "to advance the Redeemer's kingdom, irrespective of party," absolved them of their pecuniary obligations to him, and in their presence tore up the contract pledging their financial support. Noting that "never had a pastor and churches lived together more harmoniously than we had for about six years" and adding that "never have I found a more loving, kind, and orderly people in any country," he declared that "this was truly a day of sorrow, and the impressions of it are indelible."[30]

Different stances within the West Lexington Presbytery regarding order and slavery were not addressed in the proceedings of the synod. The heart of the conflict according to the synod was doctrine. To this issue was now added the charge of schism. To addressing the issue of doctrine and answering the charge of schism Stone and his colleagues now turned.

[28]"Minutes of the Synod of Kentucky," 322–33; "Apology," 176–77.
[29]"Minutes of the Synod of Kentucky," 323–24.
[30]Stone, *History*, 25–26; Stone, *Biography*, 48–49.

The new presbytery had promised to provide an account of the causes of their separation from the Synod of Kentucky and an exposition of their views of the gospel in a circular letter they had addressed to the congregations "formerly under our care" immediately after their constitution as the Springfield Presbytery. The promised account of the separation and doctrinal exposition, a pamphlet of one hundred pages, was published in January 1804–just four months after the protesters had withdrawn from the jurisdiction of the synod. The full title was *An Apology for Renouncing the Jurisdiction of the Synod of Kentucky. To which is added, a Compendious View of the Gospel, and a Few Remarks on the Confession of Faith.* The first section of the pamphlet, the "Apology," was written by Marshall. The two following sections were written respectively by Stone and Thompson.[31]

A major section of Marshall's "Apology" was his history of McNemar's conflict with the Washington Presbytery and the Synod of Kentucky, taken primarily from the minutes of the presbytery and the synod. Marshall's thesis was that both the presbytery and the synod had acted contrary to Presbyterian order by failing to require written charges against McNemar and witnesses to substantiate those charges.[32]

Marshall challenged the synod's claim that the suspended ministers were schismatics. Identifying a schismatic spirit with "partyism," Marshall allowed that the protesters' separation from the synod was the result of partyism. He argued that the protesters, however, were not the schismatics! Rehearsing the history of the revival, he asked if it had been "a party spirit" that induced preachers to lay aside their points of controversy when the revival had first begun? Was it not then, he asked, a party spirit that had "prompted some who were spectators only of this glorious work, to bring forward those speculative opinions, which at the time were neither publicly disputed, nor combated, and involve the church in a controversy?" The protesters, he insisted, had not wanted to leave the Presbyterian Church, but in the midst of the controversy created by those who had reintroduced the points of division they had not been allowed to remain in peace. Instead, he claimed, McNemar had been charged in 1801 with failing to preach the creed of a party–the Presbyterian party. And what, he asked, of the publication against McNemar issued by the Washington Presbytery in 1802? Did it not breathe a schismatic spirit? No doctrine was identified, or its dangerous tendency showed, but instead a "party" name, Arminian, had been "raised from the dead to set Christians at variance." And why, Marshall asked, had this action been taken? "Not for a deviation from the plain principles of Christianity, but because the suspected person would not be bound to fight under a party standard, and wound his fellow Christians around him with the arrows of disputation."[33]

[31]Robert Marshall and John Thompson, *A Brief Historical Account of Sundry Things in the Doctrines and State of the Christian, or as it is Commonly Called, The Newlight Church, Containing their Testimony Against Several Doctrines Held in that Church, and its Disorganized State; Together with Some Reasons Why those Two Brethren Purpose to Seek for a More Pure and Orderly Connection* (Cincinnati: J. Carpenter, 1811), 272.

[32]"Apology," 147–77.

[33]"Apology," 186–88.

Marshall asserted that the schismatic was Kemper. Division had been the aim of his actions in the controversy from the start. Indeed, he had actually begun the schism by attending, but publicly refusing to participate in, a sacrament at Beulah and encouraging others to do likewise. Marshall suggested that the synod would now have to decide whether to "join in the communion of Mr. Kemper" and shut the door against the suspended ministers. For their part, the suspended ministers would abide by the principles expressed in their protest–they would neither separate from the communion of the synod nor exclude the synod from theirs. Unfortunately, according to Marshall, the synod, in following Kemper thus far, had "again raised their standard, which for three happy years had been gathering dust." Marshall predicted that "the lines will probably now be cleared; the enemies of orthodoxy, however pious, be driven out of the pure church, drowsy bigots recalled to arms, and another bold push made to Calvinize the world." The protest of the seceding ministers, Marshall exclaimed, had been nothing more than their refusal to follow the synod in schism, concluding that it would now remain for the General Assembly, in its review of the proceedings of the synod, to determine whether the Springfield Presbytery or the Synod of Kentucky belonged to their body.[34]

Thompson's "Remarks on the Confession of Faith" was the new presbytery's response to the synod's request that they provide a statement of their objections to the Confession of Faith. It consisted of an introduction, followed by a discussion of "Creeds and Confessions in General," and a section on "The Confession of Faith."[35]

Thompson declared that the Christian Church had long been divided into sects and parties, each having a creed, confession of faith, or statement of doctrines that separated it from other bodies. The very existence of such doctrinal statements, he argued, implied "that the Scriptures are not sufficiently plain, and that men can remedy that defect;–that God will not give his holy Spirit [to enable believers to understand and practice the scriptures], or that it is easier to obtain help from man, than from God." This, he asserted, was a mistake: "Spiritual things can never be understood, until we submit to the teachings of God, by believing in Jesus." On the other hand, he declared that when one believed in Jesus, "the Spirit of Christ leads the soul, experimentally into those heavenly truths, and gives him ideas, which he could not obtain otherwise; even though he had all the creeds, and confessions in the world to help him." Thompson lamented that if one learned the words of a creed, one would be pronounced orthodox, even if one gave no evidence of "real, living religion," while one "confessedly pious" was rejected for not subscribing to the particular creed. Thus, he decried creeds' preventing the union of "the real lovers of religion" that would otherwise take place. Moreover, he continued, creeds, which were put forward as bonds of union, did not maintain

---

[34]"Apology," 188–89.
[35]John Thompson, "Remarks on the Confession of Faith," in *"Apology,"* 222–46; Stone, *History*, 38.

union even within a party: "For people soon begin to dispute as much about the meaning of their creeds, as about the Scriptures." And further, he insisted, "Any unity which they do preserve, is like its source, human, barren, unsavory; not like that sweet union of soul, which is produced by the Spirit of God, living in his people." Thus, Thompson proposed that Christians forget their creeds and confessions as they had in the revival. He prodded, "Say, ye that love the Lord, what is it that unites you together? Is it a creed, or the living Spirit of the crucified Jesus?" Thompson suggested that persons who thought that a church could not exist without a confession betrayed "their ignorance, of the uniting, cementing power of living religion."[36]

Thompson observed that it was evident from his forgoing remarks regarding creeds and confessions in general that if the Confession of Faith were as perfect as could be formed by human beings, it should nevertheless be rejected as a standard. But the protesters did not think that the Confession of Faith was as perfect as could be formed. On the contrary, they thought that it was "very defective, and ought not to be received, even if the practice of owning and subscribing human creeds, were right and Scriptural." Thompson identified five such "defects," each related in some way to the doctrine of predestination. [37]

Because Stone had developed the presbytery's new doctrine of faith, it was appropriate for him to author the presbytery's exposition of their views of the gospel, a statement titled, "A Compendious View of the Gospel." Stone declared that humanity was depraved. He defined depravity as being "carnally minded." To be carnally minded, he explained, was to be spiritually dead, to be estranged from God and in rebellion against God's law. Since humanity was created to find happiness in relation to God, the consequence of human depravity was vain striving for fulfillment. "All are in want," Stone declared, "of what they were made to enjoy, which is God; and have a propensity to satisfy that want with meaner things." "Hence arise," he continued, "the busy pursuits, the incessant labors, and the universal cry of a distracted, disappointed world, *Who will show us any good?*"[38]

Stone identified the remedy for depravity as nothing less than regeneration—the radical renewal or transformation of the person. He noted that regeneration was described in scripture as being "reconciled to God" (Romans 5:10), as being "made partakers of the divine nature" (2 Peter 1:4), and as having received "divine life" (1 John 1:2). However, he asserted, in keeping with his New Light Presbyterian heritage, that regeneration was more fully explained in 2 Corinthians 3:18, "But we all, with open face, beholding as in a glass, the glory of the Lord, are changed into the same image, from glory to glory, even as by the spirit of the Lord."[39]

[36]Thompson, 231–34.
[37]Ibid., 235–46.
[38]Barton W. Stone, "A Compendious View of the Gospel," in Robert Marshall, et al., *Apology of the Springfield Presbytery*, published with Stone, *Biography*, 191–92.
[39]Ibid., 192–93.

Stone defined "the gospel" by reference to Luke 2:10, as "good tidings of great joy which shall be to all people." He identified John 3:16 as a brief summary of the content of that good news: that "God so loved the world that he gave his only begotten Son, that whosoever believeth in him should not perish, but have everlasting life." Against the notion that God loved only an elect world, to whom alone God gave the Son, Stone argued (for four pages!) that "the world, the whole world of mankind, is the object of God's love" and that it was to all humanity that God had given the Son.[40]

But what had God given to humanity in the Son? Stone answered, "In him is fullness of salvation, pardon, eternal life, grace, wisdom, righteousness, sanctification, and redemption, the fullness of the spirit." All of these gifts, Stone declared, were "treasured up in Jesus, and with him are given to a lost world." Moreover, he argued, they were "freely and absolutely given, suspended on no condition whatever."[41]

The full salvation given in Christ, he asserted, was "represented by a feast, which was prepared for sinners," as in Proverbs 9:1–5, which tells of wisdom having built her house, set her table, sent out her servant girls, and called from the highest places in the town, "You that are simple...Come, eat of my bread and drink of the wine I have mixed." "The same truth," he continued, was "taught by our Lord himself" in Luke 14:16–25, in which a certain man prepared a great supper and invited many, sending his servant at the time for the supper to say to those who had been invited, "Come; for all things are now ready." "So it is a fact," Stone exclaimed, "that God has absolutely given his Son to the world, with all his fullness; whether we believe or disbelieve; whether we receive or reject the gift." Stone stressed that because the provisions of the gospel depended in no way on qualifications in the sinner, all were exhorted to believe the gospel now and to come to Christ immediately to receive the provisions of the gospel.[42]

This was the teaching that had so disturbed Lyle, for it seemed to ignore what for Lyle was the necessary work of the Spirit in convicting the sinner of sin and preparing the sinner to believe the gospel. For Stone, however, to teach that one must be convicted of sin in order to believe the gospel was to establish qualifications for coming to Christ. Stone argued that "these qualifications, by whatever name they may be called, are legal; and instead of preparing the soul to receive the gospel, they are turning it away from Jesus Christ." For Stone, the gospel invited "all to come *now*, and at no other time."[43]

Stone then proceeded to show from the scriptures that God renewed or transformed sinners through the gospel. Stone quoted 1 Corinthians 4:15, "In Christ Jesus I have begotten you through the gospel." Other texts quoted in support of his thesis that the gospel was the means of regeneration were James 1:18, Romans 8:2, John 15:3, John 17:17, 2 Corinthians 7:1, 2 Peter 1:4, 2 Corinthians 3:18, John 8:32, Psalm 119:130, and James 1:21. "From these

---

[40]Ibid., 193–97.
[41]Ibid., 197–99.
[42]Ibid., 199–201.
[43]Ibid., 201–2.

and similar passages," Stone asserted, "it is evident that the word of truth is the means of enlightening, quickening, regenerating and sanctifying the soul."[44]

But how did the gospel or word of truth effect regeneration? Stone answered that the gospel works through faith. Referring to John 6:63, 1 Peter 1:23, 25, and Hebrews 4:12, he declared that the gospel or word of God was "spirit" and "life," "living" and "enduring forever," "powerful" and "sharper than any two-edged sword." Nevertheless, "no means," he asserted, would "produce its effect without application." "Faith," he continued, was "applying the means or admitting the truth into the heart." Stone claimed that when sinners believed the gospel they were "quickened, renewed and sanctified." On the other hand, quoting Romans 1:16, that the gospel "is the power of God unto salvation, to every one that believeth," he argued that the word of God "cannot work in unbelievers, because of unbelief." Using the language of how God influenced human beings that he had learned from his New Light Presbyterian fathers in the ministry, he noted that "God does not operate upon us as upon dead matter," but as "rational" creatures. "The strongest motives," he continued, "are presented to our understanding; but they cannot move, excite, or influence us, unless we believe: in other words, they are not motives at all, without faith." Stone continued, "God has revealed himself to us in is his word; but he is invisible; he cannot be seen with mortal eyes; nor can we have any true knowledge of him, until by faith we receive the testimony he has given of himself in his Word."[45]

What is faith? Stone answered that faith was believing the gospel or testimony of God. Faith did not depend on a holy disposition, as Lyle had resolutely argued in his "correctives" that followed sermons by Marshall and Stone during the summer of 1803. Rather, faith depended "on the strength of the testimony"; that is, on its credibility. Stone acknowledged that faith had been defined as "coming to Christ" or "trusting in Him" but insisted that this was "not faith, but manifestly its fruits," as no one "will come to him or trust in him, till they believe in him, as able and willing to save them."[46]

Though Stone's new doctrine of faith was a departure from the teaching of his fathers in the ministry, the roots of the new doctrine were clearly in the New Light Presbyterian teaching that God used rational means to influence rational creatures. In a sermon titled "The Divine Authority and Sufficiency of the Christian Religion," Samuel Davies had declared that "it is certain that as God can accept no other worship than rational from reasonable creatures, he cannot require us to believe a revelation to be divine without sufficient reason; and therefore, when he gives us a revelation, he will attest it with such evidences as will be sufficient foundation of our belief." Among the evidences of the Christian revelation that Davies had cited were *intrinsic* evidences, such as the tendency of the gospel "to promote true piety and solid virtue in the world," which, Davies claimed, ruled out the possibility that it "could be the

---

[44]Ibid., 202–3.
[45]Ibid., 203–4.
[46]Ibid., 205–7.

contrivance of wicked infernal spirits, selfish, artful priests, or politicians, or a parcel of daring impostors, or wild enthusiasts" as some deists had claimed that it was. Another intrinsic evidence of the Christian revelation was "its glorious energy on the minds of men, in convincing them of sin, subduing their lusts, and transforming them into its own likeness." Davies had also identified *extrinsic* evidences of the truth of the Christian revelation, such as the healings that are reported to have accompanied Christ's ministry and the equally miraculous growth of the church in the face of a hostile world. Rooted in this New Light tradition of the "rational" evidences of the Christian revelation, as was his Presbyterian audience, Stone could confidently state that "No Christian will deny that there is sufficient evidence in the word to produce faith," adding that "if there is not, God cannot require us to believe it, nor condemn us for not believing," as it would be "impossible to believe."[47]

Since for Stone the word had sufficient evidence in itself to produce faith, sinners who heard the gospel but did not believe were without excuse. Stone illustrated his point with an analogy: "If a man be in a dungeon, and light be emitted, he must see, if he does not shut his eyes against the light." Stone argued that in like manner, "when the gospel is preached in the spirit, the light beams upon sinners in darkness, and were they not to resist the light, or shut their eyes against it, they would see, and believe without a previous mechanical operation, to enable them to believe."[48]

This did not mean that faith was any less the gift of God to Stone and his colleagues than it was for other Presbyterians. On the contrary, Stone insisted that "We hold faith to be the gift of God, in the same way." The difference, he declared, was as follows: "They say the mind must be enlightened by the spirit, in some secret, mysterious way, to see and *approve* the truth, before the sinner can believe it. We say, the truth which the spirit speaks, is that which enlightens the mind; and which cannot produce this effect until it is believed."[49]

At no point did Stone refer to the use of law in convicting sinners of their sin. Hence, in the introduction to his "Compendious View of the Gospel," he allowed that "by some we shall probably be considered as Antinomians," the literal meaning of the word *antinomian* being "against the law." Instead of using the law to convict sinners of their sin, Stone declared that the gospel or testimony that God "has given of himself in his Word" is the "discerner of the thoughts and intents of the heart." "The testimony of God being now admitted as true," Stone explained, "the sinner discovers how unlike he is to God; the more he sees of God, the more he abhors himself." "The sinner's fears," he asserted, "may be awakened by the thunders of Mount Sinai [a reference to the Ten Commandments]; but it is only a view of the holiness, goodness, love,–and the free, unmerited grace and mercy of God, which produces true

[47]Samuel Davies, "The Divine Authority and Sufficiency of the Christian Religion," *Sermons in Important Subjects*, 3 vols. (New York: R. Carter and Brothers, 1849), vol. 1, 10–14; Stone, "A Compendious View of the Gospel," 206.
[48]Stone, "Compendious View of the Gospel," 217–18.
[49]Ibid., 211.

conviction and true repentance, and which humbles the soul, slays the enmity of the heart, and makes him willing to depart from all iniquity." The sinner who receives God's word, Stone continued, "adores the riches of divine grace, which is extended to such a poor polluted worm of the dust. He hates sin, and laments over it, because he sees it is committed against a God of infinite holiness, condescension and love." For Stone, it was through God's self-disclosure in the gospel, and not the law, that the Spirit of God convicted sinners of their sin and made them willing to "come to Christ" for salvation from both the power and the penalty of sin.[50]

The new understanding of how God gave faith did not answer all the questions that friends and opponents alike might have asked. For example, it did not address the issue of God's relationship to persons who never heard the gospel. Neither did it address the question of the extent of God's power. What could it mean that sinners could "refuse" to hear the gospel? For Stone, it was enough to clear God of the charge of professing to love sinners while giving them impossible commands and then damning them for their failure to obey those commands.

Stone reported that the presbytery's pamphlet "had a happy effect on the public mind; not only to soften their prejudices against us, but also to convince many of the truth, of which they became zealous advocates." Before the end of 1804, there were congregations related to the new presbytery at Turtle Creek, Eagle Creek, Springfield, Orangedale, Salem, Beaver Creek, and Clear Creek in Ohio, and at Cabin Creek, Flemingsburg, Cane Ridge, Concord, Indian Creek, Bethel, Paint Lick, and Shawnee Run in Kentucky. Stone also noted, "The Methodists, thinking that we would all unite with them, were very friendly, and treated us with brotherly attention." However, the popularity of the presbytery was itself a problem, for, as Stone noted, it was hard not to think of themselves as "a party." At their June 1804 meeting, the presbytery would respond to this situation in a way that neither their opponents nor their most zealous supporters could have anticipated.[51]

---

[50]Ibid., 204–5.
[51]Stone, *History*, 26; McNemar, *Kentucky Revival*, 69.

PART 3

The Christian
Church

7

"We *Will*, That This Body Die..."

Richard McNemar proposed a solution to the problem of the Springfield Presbytery's perceiving themselves as a party at the June 1804 meeting of the presbytery at Cane Ridge. His solution was for the presbytery to sign a document that he had drafted titled "Last Will and Testament of Springfield Presbytery." The document declared, "We *will*, that this body die, be dissolved, and sink into union with the Body of Christ at large."[1] According to Marshall and Thompson, none of the other members of the presbytery had "the least thought" of dissolving their presbytery when they arrived at the June meeting and offered many objections to the proposal. Nevertheless, after several days together, all of the members had accepted McNemar's position and subscribed their names to the document, thus dissolving the Springfield Presbytery on June 28, 1804, less than a year after its constitution.[2]

Appended to the "Last Will and Testament," which the members of the former presbytery signed as "witnesses," was "The Witnesses' Address," which stated their reasons for dissolving the presbytery. They declared that they had viewed with deep concern "the divisions, and party spirit among professing Christians, principally owing to the adoption of human creeds and forms of government." Although they had "endeavored to cultivate a spirit of love and unity with all Christians," they had found it "extremely difficult to suppress the idea that they themselves were a party separate from others." This difficulty, they confessed, had "increased in proportion to their success in the ministry." Moreover, jealousies had been "excited in the minds of other denominations; and a temptation was laid before those who were connected with the various parties, to view them in the same light." Also, at their final meeting as a presbytery they had begun to prepare for publication an address titled "Observations on Church Government," in which the world would see "the beautiful simplicity of Christian church government, stript of human inventions and lordly traditions." As they had proceeded in their investigation of that subject, they had "soon found that there was neither precept nor example in the New Testament for such confederacies as modern Church Sessions, Presbyteries, Synods, General Assemblies, etc." They had realized

---

[1] "Last Will and Testament of Springfield Presbytery," in Stone, *Biography*, 53.
[2] Marshall and Thompson, 255–56.

that "however just…their views of church government might have been, they would have gone out under the name and sanction of a self-constituted body." Therefore, "from a principle of love to Christians of every name, the precious cause of Jesus, and dying sinners who are kept from the Lord by the existence of sects and parties in the church," they had "cheerfully consented to retire from the din and fury of conflicting parties—sink out of the view of fleshly minds, and die the death."[3]

Marshall and Thompson noted that the presbytery had also been influenced to adopt the "Last Will and Testament" by their belief that the millennium, the one-thousand-year rule of Christ that many Christians believed was prophesied in Revelation 20:1–6, was near. The association of the growth and increased influence of Christianity with the coming of the millennium can be traced through English Puritanism as far back as the sixteenth century. In the eighteenth century, Jonathan Edwards had referred to the worldwide evangelism and social transformation that he taught would usher in the millennium as "the glorious work of God," speculating that it would require two hundred and fifty years for God to complete this work, which Edwards hoped had begun in his lifetime. Other eighteenth-century Americans, more impressed than Edwards with the significance of the eighteenth-century awakenings in England and America, had believed that the reign of Christ was imminent.[4]

In his sermon opening the Synod of Kentucky in September 1803, David Rice had stated that, although the question of when the millennium would begin was "too deep" for him, he could not believe that it was "very near" given the prevalence of slave-holding by Christians. Rice had also mentioned other reasons for not believing that the millennium was near in September 1803. First, there was "too much of a spirit of party, and disposition for party debates" among Christians. He also noted that Christians had not yet disengaged themselves from "national attachments and political connexions, as to look upon themselves, and be looked upon by others, as citizens of the world at large, and equally friends to every nation under heaven."[5]

Included in the "Last Will and Testament" was the following "item." "We *will,* that preachers and people, cultivate a spirit of mutual forbearance; pray more and dispute less; and while they *behold the signs of the times,* look up, and *confidently expect that redemption draweth nigh.*" In their "Witnesses' Address" they called on all Christians to join them "in crying to God day and night, to remove the obstacles which stand in the way of his work, and give him no rest *till he make Jerusalem a praise in the earth.*" In conclusion, they declared, "We heartily unite with our Christian brethren of every name, in thanksgiving to

---

[3]"Last Will and Testament," in Stone, *Biography,* 53–54. *Observations on Church Government* was later published by Richard McNemar and is included in *The Cane Ridge Reader. Observations on Church Government, by the Presbytery of Springfield. To which is Added, The Last Will and Testament of that Reverend Body. With A Preface and Notes, By the Editor* (1808).

[4]See Gerald R. McDermott, *One Holy and Happy Society: The Public Theology of Jonathan Edwards* (University Park, Pa.: Pennsylvania State University Press, 1992), 50–60, 77–82.

[5]Rice, 37–40.

God for the display of his goodness in *the glorious work* he is carrying on in our Western country, which we *hope* will terminate in the *universal* spread of the gospel, and the *unity* of the church."[6] Thus, in dissolving their presbytery, the signers aimed at not only removing the perception that they were a party, but also hastening the coming of the millennium, which, in contrast to Rice, they believed to be near. Like Rice, they saw slavery, partyism, and nationalism in the church as obstacles to Christ's rule but were confident, in the words of Marshall and Thompson, that "a glorious church would soon be formed" and that they had "found the very plan for its formation and growth."[7]

Lest anyone think that in retiring from "the din and fury of conflicting parties" and sinking out of view of "fleshly minds," they intended to retire from public view, the signers of the "Last Will and Testament" wrote of themselves in their "Witnesses' Address," declaring that, though dead as a presbytery and "stript of their mortal frame," they "yet live and speak in the land of gospel liberty…blow the trumpet of jubilee, and willingly devote themselves to the help of the Lord against the mighty." Moreover, they published the "Last Will and Testament" as a tract, along with an announcement of a mass meeting for those holding like sentiments to be held at Bethel Church over the weekend of October 14, 1804. Far from putting their light under a bushel, they noted that Bethel, seven miles northwest of Lexington, was a central location for attendance from Kentucky, Ohio, and Tennessee.[8]

Neither did the signers intend to give up their ministerial prerogatives. The extent of what they intended to give up can be measured by a careful reading of the four "items" in the "Last Will and Testament" that bore directly on the calling and work of ministers.

"We *will,* that our power of making laws for the government of the church, and executing them by delegated authority, forever cease." The *Form of Government* of the Presbyterian Church stated that "all church power…is only ministerial and declarative; *that is to say* that the Holy Scriptures are the only rule of faith and manners; that no church judicatory ought to pretend to make laws, to bind the conscience in virtue of their own authority; and that all their decisions should be founded upon the revealed will of God." Rule in the Presbyterian tradition was explicitly defined as "the right of judgment upon laws already made," while the business of "making laws" for the church was explicitly forbidden.[9] Thus, for the presbytery to renounce their power of making laws was to affirm what Presbyterians had always taught! It did not mean that they were giving up their responsibility to rule. Rather, they were

---

[6]"Last Will and Testament," in Stone, *Biography*, 55. Italics mine.

[7]Marshall and Thompson, 255–56.

[8]"Last Will and Testament," in Stone, *Biography*, 54–55; Ware, 144.

[9]*The Constitution of the Presbyterian Church in the United States of America, containing The Confession of Faith, The Catechisms, and The Directory of Worship of God; Together with the Plan of Government and Discipline* (Philadelphia: Presbyterian Board of Publication, 1842); *Form of Government,* bk. 1, chap. 1, par. 7. This discussion of the "Last Will and Testament" follows my treatment of the same topic in *Ministry Among Disciples: Past, Present, and Future* (St. Louis: Council on Christian Unity, 1985), 8–10.

charging the Presbyterians with violating their own standards by what they saw as their "making laws" for the church.[10]

"We *will,* that candidates for the gospel ministry henceforth study the Holy Scriptures with fervent prayer, and obtain license from God to preach the simple Gospel, *with the Holy Ghost sent down from heaven,* without any mixture of philosophy, vain deceit, traditions of men, or the rudiments of the world." The subject of this item was not the licensing of candidates for the ministry (which the signers made the responsibility of congregations), but their studies. The signers willed that candidates for the ministry study the scriptures with fervent prayer, rather than the Presbyterian Confession, in order to preach the simple gospel with the unction of the Holy Spirit. The Presbyterian Confession being, in their view, a "mixture of philosophy, vain deceit, traditions of men, and rudiments of the world."[11]

"We *will,* that the Church of Christ resume her native right of internal government–try her candidates for the ministry, as to their soundness in faith, acquaintance with experimental religion, gravity, and aptness to teach; and to admit no other proof of their authority, but Christ speaking in them." The concern, again, was the Confession. Rather than trying ministerial candidates by their adherence to the Confession of Faith, the church should try ministerial candidates according to its own judgment of "Christ speaking" in them.[12]

"We *will,* that each particular church as a body, actuated by the same spirit, choose her own preacher…and never henceforth delegate her right of government to any man or set of men, whatever." Presbyterians taught that congregations were to elect their own officers, but that ordination was the work of the ministry. In the final section of the "Last Will and Testament," the signers indicated that, though they were dead as a presbytery, they would still "assist in ordaining elders, or pastors." The members of the former presbytery rejected interference by the synod in what they considered to be the responsibility of congregations and ministers.[13]

---

[10]Hence, in 1827, the year Stone began publishing the *Christian Messenger,* he could write in the same paragraph of the *Messenger* that conferences of ministers were "in no case to make laws for the rule and government of the churches" and that ministers who were charged with teaching false doctrine were to be tried by a conference of ministers. *CM* 1 (June 1827), 186; see also 1 (January 1827), 49–52.

[11]In February 1827, Stone stated in the *Messenger* that only licensed preachers and ordained elders should preach, declaring it improper "for a person impressed with the idea that he is divinely called to preach, to go abroad and travel from county to county preaching, without being sent by the church with letters of commendation." *CM* 1 (February 1827), 80. Seven months later he defended the content of the "Last Will and Testament," restating this item as follows: "We advised candidates for the gospel ministry to study the Holy Scriptures with fervent prayer, and to obtain license from God to preach the simple gospel without any mixture of philosophy, vain deceit, traditions of men, or rudiments of the world." *CM* 1 (September 1827), 240–45.

[12]The trying of candidates for ordination to the ministry was routinely the work of "conferences" of Christian ministers at least as early as 1819. John Rogers, "The Life and Times of John Rogers, 1800–1867, of Carlisle, Kentucky," transcr. Virginia M. Bell, abridg. Roscoe M. Pierson and Richard L. Harrison, Jr., with a Foreword by Virginia M. Bell. (*Lexington Theological Quarterly* 19 (January–April 1984), 19.

[13]*Constitution of the Presbyterian Church,* bk. 1, chaps. 13–14. In 1827, Stone stated the matter in the *Messenger* as follows: "Without the commendation of the church, the elders [or pastors] should ordain no man; without the satisfaction of the elders [or pastors], the church should not urge it to be done." *CM* 1 (June 1827), 26.

This "item "also called for congregations to support their preacher "by a free will offering, without a written *call* or *subscription.*"[14] Ministers were not to be bound by a written call and subscription to support a particular party, as Stone had believed that he had been prior to releasing his congregations from their salary obligations to him and literally tearing up their subscription papers in their presence after his withdrawal from the jurisdiction of the synod. As regards the material support of the ministry, the change in practice called for by the signers appears to have had little practical consequence, at least in the short run. The fact was that very few ministers in the Synod of Kentucky, Stone having been an exception, were able to live on the compensation subscribed by the members of their congregations. One of the members of the synod, John P. Campbell, with whom Stone would later engage in a written controversy, was so poor that he and his wife were required to subsist for a time exclusively on a diet of pumpkins. In his opening sermon at the meeting of the synod in September 1803, David Rice had addressed the issue of adequate support of the ministry, criticizing laity who withheld from their ministers needed support by suggesting that surely the laity were better able to support their minister than was the minister's wife, who usually also had to support their five or six children by her labor alone.[15]

Stone reported that in addition to signing the "Last Will and Testament," he and his colleagues determined at the June 1804 meeting to take "no other name than *christians,*" noting that *Christians* was "the name first given by divine authority to the disciples of Christ."[16] The idea of taking no other name than Christians, as the name given by God to the followers of Christ, had been recommended to the presbytery in a sermon by Rice Haggard at Marshall's Bethel Church in April 1804. Haggard's text was Acts 11:26, which he interpreted as meaning that God was the one who "appointed" that the disciples at Antioch be called "Christians."[17] Haggard had made a similar appeal nearly a decade earlier at a conference at Old Lebanon Church, near Surry, Virginia, which had resulted in the founding of the "Christian Church" movement in Virginia and North Carolina. The conference had been composed of thirty preachers who, along with Haggard and James O'Kelly, had recently seceded from the Methodist Episcopal Church in a dispute over the authority of Bishop Asbury to place ministers without their consent. On August 4, 1794, Rice had stood up, with New Testament in hand, and declared:

---

[14]"Last Will and Testament," in Stone, *Biography*, 52.

[15]Stone, *Biography*, 49; Ware, 152, 67; Rice, 19–22.

[16]Stone, *History*, 39. In his autobiography, Stone stated in connection with an account of the June 1804 meeting that "we published a pamphlet on this name [Christian], written by Elder Rice Haggard, who had lately united with us." See Stone, *Biography*, 50. This led at least one historian to conclude that Haggard had been present at the June 1804 meeting. See Joe Beckley Green, in J. Pressley Barrett, *The Centennial of Religious Journalism* (Dayton, Ohio: Christian Publication Association, 1908), 269, cited in Roberts, 70. However, Stone did not state that Haggard was present at the June 1804 meeting. There is also evidence that Haggard was in Cumberland County, Kentucky, at the time of the June meeting at Cane Ridge. See R. L. Roberts, "Rice Haggard (1769–1819) 'A Name Rever'd,'" *Discipliana* 54/3 (1994), 75–76.

[17]Joseph Thomas, *The Travels and Gospel Labors of Joseph Thomas* (Winchester, Va.: J. Foster, 1812), 80–81, cited in Roberts, 72.

"Brethren, this is a sufficient rule of faith and practice, and by it we are told that the disciples were called Christians, and I move that henceforth and forever the followers of Christ be known as Christians simply." Haggard's motion had been adopted unanimously, and the group, formerly known as Republican Methodists, had taken the name *Christian.*[18]

Having heard of the Springfield Presbytery, Haggard had traveled from Virginia to Kentucky to meet them, early in 1804.[19] It is likely, however, that Stone and his colleagues had heard of the Christian Church movement associated with Haggard and O'Kelley prior to Haggard's visit, especially given Stone's ties to Virginia and North Carolina. Moreover, they were surely familiar with the idea that the name *Christians* had been given to the disciples at Antioch by divine authority and should be the name of preference of all followers of Christ. This was the thesis of a popular sermon by Samuel Davies that had been widely circulated. A Christian Church movement had recently emerged in New England, led by former Baptists Elias Smith and Abner Jones. Thus, in taking the name *Christians,* Stone and his colleagues did not understand themselves to be doing something original, but joining a movement already underway, a movement associated, through Davies, with the New Light Presbyterianism that was the immediate background of the former presbytery.[20]

Meanwhile, efforts at reconciliation between the Synod of Kentucky and the members of the former Springfield Presbytery continued. The Presbyterian General Assembly meeting in the spring of 1804 had been duly advised of the rupture in Kentucky, and a committee of the General Assembly had been appointed to seek reconciliation between the two parties. The members of the General Assembly's committee were James Hall, Thomas Marquis, and Nash LeGrand. Hall was the North Carolina minister with whom Stone had been traveling when he had first learned of the revival at Shiloh. Marquis was on the executive board of missions of the Synod of Pittsburgh. LeGrand had been converted in the Hampden-Sydney revival that had influenced McGready and was described as "zealous" and "popular." In short, the committee was well chosen for its task.[21]

The Synod of Kentucky opened at Danville on Tuesday, October 16, just days after the mass meeting at Bethel advertised with the "Last Will and Testament," a gathering that Presbyterian historian Robert Davidson described as "sufficiently formidable to justify the apprehensions of the friends of

---

[18]W. E. MacClenney, *The Life of Rev. James O'Kelly,* reprint ed. (Indianapolis: Religious Book Service, 1950), 115–16.

[19]Thomas, 80–81, cited in Roberts, 72.

[20]For the history of the Christian Church movement in New England, see Michael G. Kenney, *The Perfect Law of Liberty: Elias Smith and the Providential History of America* (Washington, D.C.: Smithsonian Institution Press, 1994). For a comparison of the similarities and differences between the sermon by Davies and Haggard's pamphlet, see Colby D. Hall, *Rice Haggard: The American Frontier Evangelist Who Revived the Name Christian* (Fort Worth, Tex.: University Christian Church, 1957), 51–53.

[21]Ware, 144–45.

orthodoxy."[22] The members of the General Assembly committee were present, as were Stone and three of his colleagues, Marshall, Thompson, and Dunlavy. According to the minutes of the Synod of Kentucky, "as the Smiles of heaven in the business contemplated by the Committee, were most earnestly desired by Synod[,] it was unanimously resolved to spend some time in solemn prayer to Almighty God for his gracious Countenance and aid." Accordingly, Marshall and Thomas Marquis, of the General Assembly committee, were "called upon to lead the devotions of Synod."[23]

Worship concluded, the committee posed two questions to the members of the former Springfield Presbytery, which they answered in writing. The first question inquired of their reasons for renouncing the jurisdiction of the Presbyterian Church. Stone and colleagues provided two answers: (1) "Because we believed that those bodies, with which we stood connected, acted contrary to their own rules"; (2) "Because the confession of faith or standard of that church, contained several things which we viewed as contrary to the word of God, on which account we could not retain it as the standard of our faith, or submit to be judged, and condemned by its dictates." Stone and colleagues further stated, "While we were let alone, we were willing to let the confession of faith alone; but as soon as we found our sentiments were to be brought to that standard, we renounced its authority, and consequently had no alternative but to withdraw."[24]

The committee's second question was, "Can any method of accommodation be proposed, which may induce you to return to the jurisdiction of that church, and heal the division which has taken place in the Synod of Kentucky?" Stone and colleagues responded, "When we at first withdrew, we felt ourselves freed from all creeds but the Bible, and since that time by constant application of it, we are led farther from the idea of adopting creeds and confessions as standards, than we were at first; consequently, to come under the jurisdiction of that church now, is entirely out of the question." They further noted, in terms echoing Rice's view of the coming of the millennium, "We feel ourselves citizens of the world, God our common Father, all men our brethren by nature, and all christians our brethren in Christ." "This principle of universal love to christians," they continued, "gains ground in our hearts in proportion as we get clear of particular attachments to a party." "We therefore cannot," they declared, "put ourselves into a situation which would check the growth of so benign a temper and make us fight under a party standard." They could, however, "propose a method of accommodation, which, with the divine blessing, will heal the division." That method was:

1. Let us remember that all christians are one in Christ, members of his body, partakers of his nature and heirs of the kingdom: Therefore they have no power over one another to cut off, exclude, or unite.

[22]Davidson, 197.
[23]"Minutes of the Synod of Kentucky," 324–25.
[24]Stone, *History*, 41–42.

2. Let us pray for more of the uniting, cementing spirit.

3. Treat differences in lesser matters with christian charity and mutual forbearance, and bend our united force in the common cause.

4. Give up the care of the church to God by constant fervent prayer—counsel, advise, admonish, reprove, comfort and strengthen one another as necessity may require, in the spirit of love and meekness.[25]

The committee's response to this proposal was not recorded in the Minutes of the Synod. On Saturday, October 20, a joint committee composed of the General Assembly's committee and five members of the synod appointed by the synod on October 18 reported that reconciliation had not been achieved.[26] In a letter to the moderator of the Synod of Kentucky, dated October 18, 1804, Stone, Marshall, Dunlavy, and Thompson, confident that the millennium was near, had stated that "God has begun *a glorious work* in this western country, which calls aloud for the united exertions of all the friends of Jesus, *and of mankind.*" "Some," they observed, "are groaning for the wounds of the presbyterian cause; some for the Methodist; some for the Baptist, etc. each believing that it is the cause of Christ for which they are groaning—and some are as heartily groaning for the wounds of the Christian cause, without respect to names or parties." "If," they admonished, "we should unite our groans and cries to the Father of our mercies for the general release, and the *coming of the Lord's kingdom with power*, God would hear and answer us." In conclusion, they declared: "These things, dear brethren, are not vain imaginations, *for God is now about to take the earth.*"[27]

Stone reported that "about the time" of the October meeting of the synod, Haggard and two other ministers from the Christian Church in Virginia "united with us" and that Haggard's pamphlet was published "soon after."[28] In lieu of the author's name, Haggard's pamphlet, published in Lexington with a date of 1804, carried the following note: "Some may, perhaps, be anxious to know who the author of the following pages is, his name, and to what denomination he belongs. Let it suffice to say, that he considers himself connected with no party, nor wishes to be known by the name of any—he feels himself united to that *one body* of which *Christ is the head*, and all his people fellow members."[29]

The pamphlet itself, twenty pages in length, was a vigorous call for Christians to reclaim their family name and to unite on the scriptures alone, by the power of the spirit. The millennium would come, Haggard promised, when "the different denominations, which have long been at variance, shall join hands in an everlasting peace." Haggard asked, "Are you not all praying, brethren, Lord, hasten the approach of that day? The day has already begun

[25]Ibid., 42–43.

[26]"Minutes of the Synod of Kentucky," 326, 328.

[27]Stone, *Reply*, 63–64. Italics mine.

[28]Stone, *History*, 42.

[29]Rice Haggard, *An Address to the Different Religious Societies, on the Sacred Import of the Christian Name* (Lexington, Ky.: Joseph Charles, 1804), reprinted with a preface by John W. Neth, Jr., *Footnotes to Disciple History*, no. 4 (Nashville: Disciples of Christ Historical Society, 1954), 13.

to dawn among some. Let a spirit of union and love (which is the fruit of the spirit of God) prevail among you, and you will find, that this is day in the moral world."[30]

The influence of the former presbytery's confidence that the millennium was near was not limited to efforts specifically in behalf of Christian union. Jonathan Edwards, whose writings had been highly valued by Stone's New Light Presbyterian forebears, had declared that in the millennium theological problems that had long perplexed believers would be solved: "There shall then be a wonderful unraveling [of] the difficulties in the doctrines of religion, and clearing up of seeming inconsistencies...Difficulties in Scripture shall then be cleared up, and wonderful things shall be discovered in the word of God that were never discovered before."[31] Stone and his colleagues had been engaged in a study of the scriptures since the winter of 1804, which had shed what they believed to be new light on the doctrine of atonement. The revealing and defense of that new light would fall to Stone, who had written their "Compendious View of the Gospel" and had long been troubled by "seeming inconsistencies" in orthodox doctrine.

---

[30]Haggard, 31–32.
[31]*History of the Work of Redemption,* ed. John F. Wilson, vol. 9 of *The Works of Jonathan Edwards,* 480–81, quoted in McDermott, 63.

8

Atonement

During the winter of 1804, the members of the Springfield Presbytery had become "sorely pressed" by an objection to their preaching voiced by members of the Synod of Kentucky. Like other nineteenth-century Protestants, Stone and his colleagues preached the "substitutionary" theory of atonement that they had inherited from the Reformers of the sixteenth century. According to this view, Christ died as a substitute for humanity. Humanity had violated the covenant of the law that God had made with Adam and, through him, with all of Adam's posterity. Without Christ's death, humanity could only have looked forward to the wrath of a God who hated sin and punished violations of the law. With Christ's death, the elect of God could be assured that justice had been satisfied and that God had been propitiated toward them. The righteous Christ had taken the place of the guilty, suffering in their stead in order that his righteousness might be imputed to them. He was the "surety" or substitute of justified or forgiven sinners and had fulfilled the law on their behalf; he was their sacrificial lamb, the typological fulfillment to which the animal sacrifices under the Old Law looked forward.

The objection to the preaching of Stone and his colleagues stated by members of the Synod of Kentucky was that if Christ died to satisfy the claims of law and justice for *all* sinners, and not merely for a portion or part of humanity whom God had chosen to save before the foundation of the earth, as Stone and his colleagues proclaimed that he did, then *all* sinners would be saved. Members of the Synod of Kentucky argued that there was no way around it. If Christ had satisfied the claims of law and justice for all persons, then no one could be punished for his or her sins. Stone and his colleagues, they charged, were teaching universalism, the doctrine that God not only loved and desired the salvation of all persons, but that God would save all persons, whether converted in this life or not. Stone and his colleagues, like most Presbyterians, Baptists, and Methodists, believed that universalism undercut the call to "flee the wrath to come without delay" and was not taught in scripture. Thus, they had turned to the Bible, Stone wrote, "with prayerful attention to find the truth" regarding atonement.[1]

---

[1] Stone, *History*, 42–43. See also *Biography*, 56, and *Reply*, 7. David Purviance, who was ordained by the Springfield Presbytery, reported that this issue had been raised during his interview with the West Lexington Presbytery in the spring of 1803. See Purviance, 110.

Richard McNemar had been the first member of the presbytery to come up with a theory of atonement that would allow Christ to have died for all of humanity *without* implying that all persons would be saved. McNemar shared his theory with the other Ohio member of the presbytery, John Thompson, during the winter of 1804. In March 1804, McNemar presented his theory to a full meeting of the presbytery at Thompson's home. The fundamental principles of McNemar's doctrine of atonement were: (1) that the purpose of Christ's death was to restore humanity to union and fellowship with God; and (2) that it was not necessary for a substitute to satisfy the claims of law and justice for fallen humanity before God could save sinners.[2]

That the purpose of Christ's death was to restore humanity to union and fellowship with God was not, of course, a new idea to Presbyterians of the New Light tradition. Although Presbyterian preachers of the New Light tradition taught that Christ died as a substitute for sinners to satisfy the claims of law and justice, they maintained that God's ultimate purpose in Christ's death was to restore sinners to holiness. "That God," Samuel Davies had written, "intended from eternity to save all those who finally be [are] saved and that for this purpose he appointed his co-equal Son to sustain the character of mediator I freely grant. But, the objects of God's everlasting *benevolence*," he had continued, "cannot be the objects of his *delight* till they are conformed to Him in holiness. The blessed Jesus," he had asserted, "did not die to change the nature of God and render Him capable of loving deformity and sin."[3]

McNemar's second principle, that God could pardon and save sinners without requiring that a substitute satisfy the claims of law and justice, was a different matter. All the members of the presbytery, except McNemar's fellow Ohioan Thompson, raised objections to the principle that God could pardon and save without receiving payment or satisfaction for the violation of God's law. Moreover, according to Purviance, neither McNemar nor Thompson had "matured" the "scheme" so as "to exhibit it with clearness and obviate objections."[4]

Purviance, who was Stone's neighbor, claimed that after their return to Kentucky following the March meeting of the presbytery, Stone was "absorbed" in the subject. In his autobiography, Stone remembered, "My opportunity to read was very limited, being compelled to manual labor daily on my farm; but so intently engaged was my mind, on this and collateral subjects, that I always took with me in my corn-field my pen and ink, and as thoughts worthy of note occurred, I would cease from my labor, and commit them to paper." Although Purviance indicated that initially he was more open to

---

[2] Marshall and Thompson, 257–58; and Purviance, 150–51.

[3] See Samuel Davies' undated letter fragment (Princeton University Library, Princeton, N.J.).

[4] "Memoirs," in Purviance, 197. See also Marshall and Thompson, 5–6, note. The fundamental principles of McNemar's system are reconstructed from Purviance's accounts of the March meeting and Stone's first sermon on atonement; see 197–98.

McNemar's theory than was Stone, he reported that Stone soon "outwent" him.[5]

Stone claimed that he began his study of the atonement by seeking to find where Christ was said to be the surety or substitute for sinners. He reported that, to his surprise, he could not find the idea in a single scriptural text. He next sought to find where the "surety righteousness of Christ" was said to be "imputed" to sinners, with the same result. He then searched the scriptures to see where law and justice were said to be satisfied by the "vicarious obedience and suffering of Jesus." But, again, he could not find a single text. Finally, he inquired for what purpose Christ was said to have come into the world, lived, and died. He found the purpose of Jesus' life and death to be as McNemar had suggested, "to declare the Father–to bear witness to the truth–to confirm the promises–to reconcile sinners to God–to save sinners–to bring us to God."[6]

By the June 1804 meeting of the Springfield Presbytery, when the members of the presbytery signed their "Last Will and Testament," all the members of the presbytery had accepted the first principles of the theory of atonement that McNemar had presented in March. During the following winter of 1805, Stone addressed two letters on the subject to Presbyterian minister Matthew Houston, the substance of which he published in the spring of 1805 as a thirty-six-page pamphlet titled *Atonement: The Substance of Two Letters Written to a Friend*.[7]

In the first "letter" Stone argued that the doctrine of substitutionary atonement taught in the Presbyterian Confession and Larger Catechism could not be supported from scripture and, moreover, had a number of negative theological "consequences." Starting with the idea that God made a covenant based on the law with Adam and, through him, his posterity, Stone wrote, "I can find no mention of such a covenant in the bible." He added that "had there been one text to support it, certainly the general assemblies, synods and associations of Europe and America, would by this time have found it."[8]

Neither could he find a scriptural argument for the teaching of the Presbyterian Confession that there was "wrath" in God to which Adam and his posterity had been "bound over" as a consequence of their violation of the law. Moreover, Stone proposed that "if wrath be in God, it must be a perfection of his nature; for nothing imperfect can be attributed to him." "If it be a perfection," he continued, "it must be eternal, infinite and unchangeable; for if not infinite, it may be increased or diminished, therefore subject to change; if not eternal, it began to be, therefore God lacked a perfection before it did begin; if not unchangeable, it cannot be in God, for the scriptures every where

[5]"Memoirs," in Purviance, 197–98; Stone, *Biography*, 59.
[6]Stone, *Reply*, 7.
[7]Barton W. Stone, *Atonement, The Substance of Two Letters Written to a Friend* (Lexington, Ky.: Joseph Charles, 1805); Purviance, 150–51; On the dating of the pamphlet, see Marshall and Thompson, 257–58.
[8]Stone, *Atonement*, 6–7.

ascribe unchangeability to him." Stone observed that the scriptures declared that God is love, or "that which unites." Wrath was that which "disunites." "If wrath be in God," Stone suggested, "then there are two infinite, eternal and unchangeable principles in Him, contrary to one another, love and wrath." Stone also referred to Christian experience in support of his view that there is no wrath in God: "If wrath be in him, and believers be renewed after his image and partake of his nature, why is it that they feel wrath dying in them as they grow in grace?"[9]

Stone did not deny, of course, that "the scriptures every where attribute wrath to God." However, he asserted that they do so not in regard to God's "real" nature, but "relatively." Thus, he proposed that we are "to understand the wrath of God to be nothing else but his holy nature standing in opposition to sin." When sin is removed, he continued, so is God's opposition or wrath.[10]

As for the teaching that Christ was the surety or substitute of mankind, Stone reported that he could "find nothing in the Bible." Only in Hebrews 7:22 was the word "surety" used with reference to Christ: "By so much was Jesus made the surety of a better testament." The meaning of this passage, Stone averred, was not that Christ was made a substitute for sinners, but that "he gave assurance or certainty that the promises of this covenant or testament are faithful and true, and that they shall be fulfilled to all believers."[11]

Regarding the doctrine that Christ, as a substitute or surety for humankind, both satisfied the law and paid the penalty for the violation of the law on behalf of the justified, Stone first asked what it could mean to say that Christ had fulfilled or satisfied the law on behalf of the justified. Was the law, Stone asked, not the one stated in Matthew 22:37–40: "Thou shall love the Lord thy God with all thy heart, and with all thy soul, and with all thy mind,...[and] thy neighbour as thyself"? Had Christ, Stone exclaimed, freed the justified from the obligation of loving God and neighbor? If so, he asserted, then in contrast to Paul, "Christ is become the minister of sin," and "Faith has made void the law."[12]

As for texts that were said to teach that the righteousness of Christ is "imputed" to the justified, Stone offered alternative interpretations: (1) Romans 5:19, "By one man's disobedience many were made sinners, so by the obedience of one shall many be made righteous." Stone noted that there was no mention of imputation in the text. By Adam's disobedience, he declared, many were made sinners, "not by imputation, but in reality." So by the obedience of Christ, he continued, many were made righteous, "not by imputation, but in reality." (2) 1 Corinthians 1:30, "Who of God is made unto us wisdom, and righteousness, and sanctification and redemption." Stone proposed that if righteousness was imputed, then we must "also conclude that wisdom, sanctification and redemption are imputed; for he was made one as much as the

---

[9] *Confession,* chap. 6, sec. 6; Stone, *Atonement,* 5–6, 18.
[10] Ibid., 5–6
[11] Ibid., 6–7.
[12] Ibid., 7–8.

other." This, he declared, no one would affirm. How, he continued, was Christ "made unto us righteousness"? He answered, "By making us righteous." (3) Romans 10:4, "Christ is the end of the law for righteousness to everyone that believeth." Stone noted that 1 Timothy 1:5 taught that "the end of the commandment is charity out of a pure heart." "This end of the law," which he defined as "love to God and man," we get, he proposed, "not by imputation, but by faith in Jesus Christ."[13]

Turning to the notion that Christ, as surety for humankind, also paid for the justified the debt of suffering that was due for their violation of the law and so satisfied justice, Stone asked what debt of suffering Christ had paid. Was it the debt of temporal misery or death? "If so," Stone asked, "why have christians in every age suffered them again?" Stone asserted that the scriptures are "silent" regarding the debt that Christ had paid by his suffering.[14]

Stone further stated that there were a number of negative theological consequences of the doctrine of substitutionary atonement. One of those consequences was the destruction of the idea of grace and forgiveness. According to the notion that Christ was a substitute for sinners, God forgave sinners because Christ, as their substitute or surety, had perfectly obeyed the law on their behalf and suffered the penalty for their disobedience. Stone asked, "Is there any grace in this act of forgiveness?" "Or," he continued, "is it forgiveness at all?" "If I am in debt," he proposed, "and unable to pay, and my surety pays the debt, is it grace in my creditor to forgive me?" Stone noted that God was put forward in scripture as an example of how humans were to forgive. What were we to make of God's example in light of the doctrine of substitutionary atonement? Stone answered, "If God forgives not till our debts are paid by us or by our surety, and he is proposed as our example; then we must never forgive our debtors, till they or their surety have paid us their debts."[15]

Stone knew, of course, that it was declared that "the grace of God in forgiving us" appears in God's having given Christ "to make satisfaction to law and justice for us." In response, he proposed an analogy: Suppose someone to whom I am indebted one hundred pounds should say, "I cannot forgive you till law and justice are satisfied," but should then give me one hundred pounds to pay my debt. Stone asked, "Might he not as well have forgiven me at first?"[16]

Stone advised that another negative consequence of the doctrine of Christ as substitute for sinners was that it contradicted "the scripture doctrine of justification." The doctrine that Christ was a substitute for sinners taught that believers were "declared just" because the righteousness of Christ was *imputed* to them. Stone proposed that according to the scriptures, believers were declared just because they were *made* just or righteous by faith in Christ. Citing Romans 3:20 and Philippians 3:9, he argued that sinners were "engrafted"

---

[13]Ibid., 8–9.
[14]Ibid., 9–10.
[15]Ibid., 10–11.
[16]Ibid., 11.

into Christ by faith, and not through works of the law. The nature of Christ was "righteousness, or holiness." By union with Christ through faith, sinners became partakers of Christ's nature. Thus, believers were "justified, *made* just or righteous, and *declared* so because they are so indeed." This was also the meaning, he stated, of Paul's teaching in Romans 8:1 and 4: "There is no condemnation to them which are in Christ Jesus...who walk not after the flesh, but after the Spirit."[17]

Yet another negative consequence of the doctrine of substitutionary atonement mentioned by Stone was that it "lulls to supineness and slothfulness in religion." He asserted that persons who were not righteous or holy would give relationship with God little thought, hoping that they would be justified by the imputed righteousness of Christ. If the sinner's "conscience or heart condemn him," Stone asserted, "he appeases its clamor with this balmy doctrine. But O," Stone warned, "that all would consider, WITHOUT HOLINESS NO MAN SHALL SEE THE LORD."[18]

In the second "letter" Stone argued that the purpose of Christ's coming into the world, living, and dying was to restore humanity to relationship with God. Stone proposed that this was the meaning of Romans 5:11, where Christ is said to be the one by whom "we have received the atonement." The word atonement, Stone advised, was made up of the words "at" and "one" and the suffix "ment," which signified "to make" or the action of making or doing. Thus, "the word *atonement* signifies to *make one.*" Christ came as a mediator between God and humanity "in order to at-one them, or make them *one.*" Stone observed that since God was "holy, just and good" and humanity was "unholy, unjust and wicked," a change had to occur before God and humanity could be made one. That change, he asserted, occurred in humanity. "Hence," he continued, "it is plain that *atonement* differs not from regeneration."[19]

He proposed that atonement, or regeneration under yet another name, was also referred to in Romans 3:25, where Christ was identified as the one "whom God hath set forth to be a propitiation through faith in his blood." Noting that "to propitiate signifies *to appease,*" Stone argued that in Romans 3:25 propitiation takes place "through faith in the blood of Christ." Therefore, he stated, we must conclude that human beings, who believed in the blood of Christ, were propitiated or appeased by Christ. Thus, as in his interpretation of Romans 5:11, humanity, not God, was changed.[20]

Stone noted that in the scriptures Christ was also said to have come "to redeem, purchase, buy and ransom" sinners and that all four of these words, according to the Greek, had the same meaning. He suggested that to understand that meaning in reference to the life and death of Christ, it was necessary to "enquire into three particulars–[1] from whom, or from what did Christ

[17]Ibid., 14–15.
[18]Ibid., 17.
[19]Ibid., 20.
[20]Ibid., 21.

redeem, buy, purchase, or ransom us?–[2] for whom did he redeem us?–and [3] what was the price given?" Stone's answer to the first question was that Christ redeemed us from the power of the devil, from all iniquity, and from the curse of the law, which he defined as "the misery arising from the *want* of love to God and man, and all those actions which are the native fruits of this *want.*" Stone's answer to the second question was that Christ came to redeem us for God, taking as his text Revelation 5:9: "And they sung a new song, saying, 'Thou art worthy to take the book, and to open the seals thereof; for thou wast slain and hast redeemed us to God by thy blood.'" Stone's answer to the third question was that the price given for our redemption was the "blood or death of Christ." Stone explained that through the whole of his life, but especially in his death, Christ "displayed the love, the grace, and mercy of God, by which the believing soul is melted down and reconciled" to God. Thus, the death or blood of Christ was the "price" of redemption.[21]

Stone insisted that Christ did not come to redeem us from God or from "the hands of justice." God, he affirmed, was the redeemer and savior of sinners, thus "it follows, undeniably," he wrote, "that God did not redeem or save us from himself, but from *our enemies.*" Moreover, he observed that "the nature of God, as testified by John, is love." "Nothing but love," he continued, "can bind the universe together, therefore God, the life, the spring of all, must be love." Taking Psalm 84:11, "The LORD is a sun God," as his text, he declared that "the love of God flows in eternal, unchangeable streams upon all creation, to give light, life and happiness to all." Following New Light Presbyterian Samuel Davies' widely circulated sermon, "God is Love," Stone declared that God's justice is not opposed to God's love, but is an "emanation" or "modification" of God's love. "Can any christian understanding the truth," he exclaimed, "wish to be delivered out of the hands of justice?"[22]

Davies, of course, had *not* rejected the Presbyterian doctrine of atonement. When Davies had applied the notion that God's justice is an emanation or modification of God's love to the Presbyterian doctrine of atonement, the result had been a moral-government interpretation of that doctrine. Christ did not die, Davies had asserted, to appease a principle of wrath in God, but to maintain order in the universe. If God had chosen to forgive humanity without arranging for the payment of the penalty incurred through sin, he had suggested, it would have served to encourage license throughout the watching universe. Thus, in order for the mercy of God to function without causing disorder in the universe, the wisdom of God came up with a scheme by which humanity could be saved and yet the authority of God maintained. This scheme was the substitution of Christ in the place of sinners.[23]

Stone anticipated that it would be argued that "the honors of God's law, justice and government must be secured, or the sinner cannot be saved." In

---

[21]Ibid., 22–24, 27, 35.

[22]Ibid., 18–19, 24. See Davies, "God is Love," vol. 1, 315f.

[23]Davies, "The Method of Salvation Through Jesus Christ," vol. 1, 35–42, 49–51.

response, he offered an analogy from civil government. Suppose, he suggested, that the legislators of a state in which the majority of citizens were convicted murderers abolished the death penalty in favor of a law that reformed convicted murders and made them useful citizens. Would not, he asked, the honors of law, justice, and government have been secured? "Those men have now," he continued, "the very spirit of the law in their hearts, therefore law, justice and government are satisfied." "The application," he suggested, was "easy."[24]

Acknowledging that the sacrifices of the law were referred to in the New Testament as "types" of the death of Christ, Stone noted that, consequently, it had been concluded "that Christ was our substitute, and that our sins were imputed to him." Stone argued, however, that Hebrew sacrifices "were not designed to affect or change the mind of God, nor to be an equivalent or satisfaction for sin." Rather, they were designed, he proposed, to lead the offerer "to repentance and reconciliation to God" by demonstrating the true character of sin. He described the action of Hebrew sacrifice in connection with his interpretation of Hebrews 10:3 as follows:

> Here is a transgressor; He brings a lamb to the altar; he lays his hand upon his head and confesses his sin; he must then with his own arms slay it and have it burnt on the altar before his eyes. Lev. 1, etc. "By this a remembrance of sin was made," which leads to repentance. Heb. 10:3.

"The death of this lamb," Stone suggested, "was an ocular demonstration or outward visible sign of the evil and wages of sin" to the transgressor; the transgressor saw that "his sin was the cause why this lamb was slain." In this sense, Stone affirmed, "this lamb was a faint shadow of the great '*Lamb of God* which taketh away the sin of the world.' John 1, 29. For says the prophet," he continued, "'They shall look upon me whom they have pierced, and they shall mourn for him.' Zech. 12, 10." Christ died, Stone concluded, not because our sins had been imputed to him, but to show "the strength of the love of God, and the evil of sin, and by this to reconcile us to God."[25]

If Stone thought that *Atonement: The Substance of Two Letters to A Friend* would answer the objections to his teaching that Christ died for all, he was sorely mistaken. On the contrary, the publication of Stone's letters initiated a written controversy with former Presbyterian colleagues who viewed the letters not as a foretaste of the "wonderful unraveling [of] the difficulties in the doctrines of religion" that was to occur in the millennium, but as an attack on their doctrine and the fundamental truths of the Christian faith.

David Rice responded to Stone's letters in "An Epistle To The Citizens of Kentucky, Professing Christianity; Especially Those That Are Or Have Been, Denominated Presbyterians." Rice argued that Stone's new doctrine of atonement confirmed the danger of departing from Calvinism of which he

---

[24]Stone, *Atonement,* 34.
[25]Ibid., 29–31, 34.

had warned Stone and his colleagues when he had met with them on the Saturday evening following their withdrawal from the synod in September 1803. According to Rice, the distinguishing mark of the Calvinist doctrines was that they "consider man as totally ruined by his apostasy from God, and make his salvation wholly depend on the free grace of God, in Christ, and naturally lead true believers in Christ to say–'Not unto us, Lord, not unto us, but unto thy name be the glory.'" Rice charged that Stone's doctrine of atonement robbed Christ of the glory in humanity's salvation.[26]

Rice traced the "grades of error" from Calvinism through Arminianism, Pelagianism, Arianism, Socinianism, and Deism to atheism, which he had outlined to Stone and his colleagues as a warning not to depart from Calvinism. At the time he had viewed Stone and his colleagues as Arminians, Christians who had rejected the Calvinist doctrines of unconditional election, reprobation, and election in favor of the view that sinners can choose to accept or reject God's electing grace. Recognizing that not all of his readers would be familiar with the grades of error that he believed naturally followed Arminianism, Rice provided definitions of the terms Pelagianism, Arianism and Socinianism. *Pelagians* believed that the consequences of Adam's sin were confined to his own person, that infants are in the same relation to God as was Adam before his fall, and that the grace of God is given according to human merit. *Arians* maintained "that the Son of God was totally and essentially distinct from the Father; that he was first and noblest of those beings whom God had created, the instrument by whose subordinate operation he formed the universe, and therefore inferior to the Father both in nature and dignity; also that the Holy Ghost was not God, but created by the power of the Son." *Socinians* taught that Jesus Christ was a mere man who had no existence before he was conceived by the Virgin Mary, that he had been given "the name of God" as a "deputed title," vesting him with an absolute sovereignty over all created beings and rendering him an object of worship, that he had preached the truth to humanity, set before humanity an example of heroic virtue, and sealed his doctrines with his blood.[27]

Addressing "Christians who had been called Presbyterians," Rice asked, "Have you not been led on nearly in the steps I have pointed out, and which I imperfectly pointed out to some [of your] leaders near a year and a half ago?" Asserting, without providing any proof from Stone's letters, that they had reached the grade of Socinianism, of viewing Jesus as a mere man who had no existence before he was conceived by the Virgin Mary, he continued, "Are you not now standing on ground, which you would at that time have shuddered at the thought of approaching? And can you tell me," he inquired, "where you or your leaders will stop?"[28]

---

[26]Rice, "Epistle," in Robert H. Bishop, *An Outline of the History of the Church in the State of Kentucky, during a period of forty years: containing the memoirs of Rev. David Rice, and sketches of the origin and present state of particular churches and the lives and labours of a number of men who were eminent and useful in their day* (Lexington, Ky.: Thomas T. Skillman, 1824), 323.

[27]Ibid., 322–31.

[28]Ibid., 339.

Recognizing Stone's difficulty with propositions that were "contrary to reason" (though possibly mislabeling Stone's difficulty, since Stone did not reject propositions that were "above" reason), Rice asserted that behind the progression from Calvinism to atheism, and driving it at every point, was an unwillingness to accept mystery. He supposed that the advocates of the "new" views prided themselves on having "rid Christianity of all its frightful and unreasonable mysteries," believing that as a result "every deist may be rationally expected now to embrace Divine Revelation and become a Christian." Such hopes, Rice asserted, were mistaken, "for the greatest of all objections, the *Morals*, the Morals of the Bible," still remained. "Deists," Rice continued, "see that the Christian system, thus mutilated, is the same as their own; only it holds out the terrors of *certain* damnation to offenders, while their creed leaves this matter *doubtful.*" Moreover, Rice suggested, "Their system ascribes the honour of their discoveries to their strength, improvements, and exertion of their own minds; while the other humbles the pride of their understanding to the feet of Divine Revelation." Deists, Rice added, "have no relish for this humiliation of their understanding." Rather, he declared, suggesting that Stone lacked the humility of a real Christian, "They enjoy the same kind of pleasure in ascribing all their discoveries to the strength of their own minds, that our *illuminated* Christian finds in weeding out the mysteries, and removing the supposed absurdities of Christianity."[29]

Because the progression that Rice described began with opposition to the Calvinist doctrine of election, he declared that "the doctrine of Particular Eternal Election, when properly guarded against Antinomianism [the view that obedience to God's law is unnecessary] and Fatality [which ascribes human destiny to fate], when so explained as not to destroy free Moral Agency—to supersede the use of means, nor to prevent the natural operations of second causes—is the truth, according to the sacred Scriptures, and according to sound philosophy." He added that it was also "the only doctrine that can afford a truly convinced sinner any rational ground of encouragement to seek religion in the use of means, or that can save him from black despair, and the only doctrine that can support, in the mind of a real Christian, the hope of eternal life." A better example of the way of defining Christian truth that Stone had ultimately found unsatisfactory, by placing seemingly contradictory statements in tension with each other, could not have been found.[30]

John P. Campbell responded to Stone's letters with *Strictures, On Two Letters, Published by Barton W. Stone, Entitled Atonement.* Stone did not formally reply to Rice's *Epistle,* possibly out of deference to Rice, whom he considered to be "father" in the gospel. He did respond to Campbell in *A Reply to John P. Campbell's Strictures on Atonement.* Campbell, in turn, responded to Stone's reply with *Vindex: Or The Doctrines of the Strictures Vindicated Against the Reply of Mr. Stone.*

---

[29]Ibid., 323, 327. See also 337, note.
[30]Ibid., 323. See also 337, note.

Much of the exchange between Campbell and Stone was devoted to quoting and interpreting texts of scripture in support of the particular author's view of atonement, with Campbell defending the doctrine that Christ died as a substitute for sinners. In addition, each author sought to show how the other had misrepresented his position. Underlying the whole of the exchange was Campbell's charge that Stone's views were not merely incorrect, but denied the Christian faith. In his *Strictures,* Campbell demonstrated that Stone advocated views previously published by Deists.[31] Stone's response to that claim exhibited a different attitude toward Deists than that of Campbell or Rice, disclosing that Stone did, in fact, hope that his doctrines would make Christianity intellectually credible to persons who, like himself, could not accept Calvinism. Denying that he had learned his views from Deists, Stone nevertheless declared, "I have no doubt but these were men of discernment, and could easily see the inconsistencies and absurdities of Calvinism; and had they not considered this to be Christianity, they might not have been deists." As for the comparative moral character of Christians and Deists, the issue raised by Rice, Stone turned the tables on his Presbyterian opponents, pressing Campbell on the issue of slave-holding by Presbyterians:

> You think we are deists. You are at liberty to think. But show yourselves to be christians indeed, "Do justice, let the oppressed go free, break every yoke, love mercy and walk humbly with God." Till then the world will think the difference between a deist and a nominal or formal christian very little.[32]

Campbell responded in his *Vindex* to Stone's charge that Presbyterians morally denied the faith by accusing Stone of striking indiscriminately at the reputations of "all who hold slaves." "Can it be unknown to Mr. S.," Campbell asked, "that myself, most, if not all of my brethren in the ministry, and numbers of private Christians, belonging to our society, have emancipated our slaves, or are taking prudent measures to effectuate that object?" Campbell averred that "though we have the feelings of humanity and religion on this melancholy affair, yet we think it our duty as christians, to touch it with a delicate hand, and never to urge emancipation in other than a legal constitutional way." "We think it our duty," he continued, "to subject ourselves *to the powers that be;* to live peaceably; to 'exhort as many servants as are under the yoke, to count their own masters worthy of all honor; that the name of God and his doctrines be not blasphemed:' nay, more, to 'admonish them that have *believing masters,* not to despise them, but rather to do them service.'" Seeking to take the moral high ground from Stone, Campbell added, "But if in defiance of all authority, civil and divine, we attempt to disturb the public repose; if we whisper discontent in the ear of slavery, or rouse by declamation

---

[31]John P. Campbell, *Strictures, on Two Letters, Published By Barton W. Stone, Entitled Atonement* (Lexington, Ky.: Daniel Bradford, 1805), 24–25, 29, 33, 35–36, 43.
[32]Stone, *Reply,* 24. See also 66.

from the pulpit, the demon of insurrection; let the laws claim the penalty of our rashness, and visit upon our heads the full weight of our crimes."[33]

In his *Strictures,* Campbell also charged that Stone apparently believed that God might not fulfill God's promises, referring to Stone's claim that the Hebrews text in which Christ is identified as a "surety" should be understood as meaning that Christ gave certainty or assurance that the promises of God's testament would be fulfilled to all believers. Presumably, Campbell continued, Stone believed that Jesus became surety for God, "as a person of greater ability and credit" than God, in order to secure the fulfillment of God's promises. Campbell declared that such a doctrine should cause a Christian to "shudder." He then added, "and a reasoner" who denies Christ's "equality with the Father, should be ashamed to deliver such absurd doctrine." This latter comment was a reference to Stone's view of the Trinity, which he had adopted while studying for the ministry under the direction of the Orange Presbytery.[34]

Stone responded to Campbell's claim that he denied the "equality of Christ with the Father" in his *Reply* to Campbell. "Surely," he declared, "you have great confidence in the faith of the public, or you would not venture to state such weighty charges against me, without any show of proof." "I do absolutely deny the charge; and do believe that scripture which declares that Christ *thought it not robbery to be equal with God.* Phil. ii. 8." "But," he added,

I do not believe that the man Christ Jesus was equal to God; nor do I believe that the divinity in Christ was equal to God, for that divinity was God himself.—*In him dwelt all the fullness of Godhead bodily—The Father dwelt in him,* etc. Sameness and equality have a different meaning. Equality implies plurality, and one cannot be equal to itself. God is one, infinite, self-existent and independent being. Now if there is another equal to this one, then there are two equals in infinity, self-existence, power and independence. The very notion destroys itself; for two infinities is the greatest absurdity; as one infinity fills infinity, and leaves no room for another. But Christ is equal to the Father *in name. His name shall be called the mighty God, the Everlasting Father, the Prince of Peace.* Isai. ix. 6. By office he is equal to the Father. *For all power in heaven and earth is given to him—The father judgeth no man, but hath committed all judgment to the Son; That all men should honor the Son, even as they honour the Father. He that honoureth not the Son, honoureth not the Father who hath sent him.* John v. 22, 23.[35]

Campbell thanked Stone in his *Vindex* for having exonerated him of the charge of having misrepresented his views. It was obvious from Stone's

[33]John P. Campbell, *Vindex: Or The Doctrines of the Strictures Vindicated, Against the Reply of Mr. Stone* (Lexington, Ky.: Daniel Bradford, 1806), 45–46.
[34]Campbell, *Strictures,* 17.
[35]Stone, *Reply,* 19.

statement, Campbell declared, that "his idea of equality is that of Name and office only" and did "not extend to his essential divinity." Though Campbell would defer refuting the "Socinian hypothesis" until Stone "or some one of his party" had given a full explanation of their views on the Trinity, he believed that Stone had "made it plain enough, what lies behind the curtain, when he has stripped the divine Jesus of real, essential and personal divinity, and thinks him a God, only by a delegation of name and authority."[36]

Stone, of course, was not a Socinian, for whom Christ's death was primarily an example of heroic virtue, and certainly not a deist, for whom the revelation of scripture was to be accepted only so far as it was consistent with a religion that could be deduced from reason alone. In fact, there was nothing new or controversial in Stone's *positive* statements concerning the atonement. Stone's assertions were the common property of all Presbyterians of the New Light heritage: the notion that God was love, the conviction that the ultimate purpose of Christ's coming was to reconcile sinners to God, and the belief that sinners were reconciled to God by a view of the love, grace, and mercy of God displayed in the life and death of Jesus Christ. Purviance noted that when Stone first preached his new doctrine of atonement in a sermon at Concord, "few perceived that it would upset their scheme of vicarious atonement, for he said nothing directly on that point."[37] Even Stone's doctrine of justification, which stated that believers were declared just because they are just, was not as different from that of other Protestant revivalists as it might at first appear. Although Protestant revivalists maintained that believers were declared just only by virtue of the righteousness of Christ, they also taught that no one was justified who was not simultaneously regenerated. Indeed, the doctrine of "eternal justification," which taught that a sinner was justified prior to his regeneration or reconciliation with God, was anathema to Baptist, Methodist, and Presbyterian revivalists alike.[38] The difference in Stone's doctrine of atonement from that of other Protestant revivalists was not what he said, but what he refused to say: that Christ had died as a substitute for sinners in order to satisfy on their behalf the claims of law and justice.

Stone commented in his autobiography that he regretted that Campbell had accused him of being heterodox on the Trinity, as it required him to defend himself "and the doctrine I believed." He noted that he had never written on the Trinity and claimed that for years he had been "silent on that subject" in his public discourses. Campbell was a kinsman of Stone's wife, Elizabeth Campbell Stone, and they had been "intimate" friends. In April 1803, Stone had officiated at the wedding of Campbell and his third wife,

---

[36]Campbell, *Vindex*, 40–41.

[37]"Memoirs," in Purviance, 198–99.

[38]Rice, 30–34; Benjamin Latkin, "The Christian Hope," in *Sermons on Miscellaneous Subjects,* ed. Edward Thomson (Cincinnati: n.p., 1847), 360–61; and John Taylor, a "circular letter" in "Minutes of the Dover Baptists Association (Virginia) 1790–1902," Dargin-Carver Library, Baptist Sunday School Board, Nashville, Tennessee. For information on Taylor, see James B. Taylor, *Virginia Baptist Ministers,* series 1 (Philadelphia: J. P. Lippincott, 1859), 300–308. See also Stone, *Reply,* 51, 56.

Isabella McDowell. Stone claimed that he had disclosed his views to Campbell "as to a brother; not suspecting that I should be dragged before the public as I was."[39]

If Campbell's reference to Stone's views on the Trinity was meant to embarrass Stone and undermine his influence as a teacher of the Christian faith, it was unnecessary. Before Stone published his *Reply to Campbell* in September 1805, he had suffered a far greater embarrassment and threat to his authority as a teacher of the Christian faith.

---

[39]Stone, *Biography,* 59; Ware, 152. See also Campbell, *Vindex,* 38–39.

9

Dissension and Division

Shortly after publishing *Atonement*, Stone received Shaker missionaries from the East. Having heard reports of the remarkable revivals in Kentucky and Ohio, the Shaker leadership at New Lebanon, New York, had authorized a missionary expedition into the Ohio Valley. The missionaries, Issachar Bates, John Meacham, and Benjamin Seth Youngs, had set out from New Lebanon for Kentucky on January 1, 1805. Included in their provisions was a letter of introduction from the leadership at New Lebanon to "a people in Kentucky and the adjacent states." In this letter, the church at New Lebanon testified that Christ had made "his second appearing here on earth" in this "latter day" and that the witnesses to it, especially the "First Pillar"—an oblique reference to the movement's founder, Ann Lee—had been given "the same gifts of the Holy Spirit" as the apostles of the first century. The gospel, the New Lebanon leadership declared, demanded belief in the "manifestations of Christ," confession of all sins, and acceptance of the "cross against the flesh, the world, and all evil." Traveling most of the way on foot with only one horse to carry baggage, they reached Kentucky in March.[1]

The missionaries' first contact in Kentucky was with Matthew Houston, pastor of the Christian Church at Paint Lick, in Madison County. Houston, to whom Stone had addressed his letters on atonement during the winter of 1805, was a former member of the Synod of Kentucky who had united with Stone and his colleagues in response to Stone's letters. After a few days at Paint Lick, the missionaries went to Cane Ridge. According to Bates, who kept a journal of the mission, Stone and others at Cane Ridge "sucked in our light as greedily as ever an ox drank water, and all wondered where they had been that they had not seen these things before."[2]

On March 19, the missionaries crossed the Ohio River and traveled to Springfield, where they met with John Thompson. From Springfield they went to Turtle Creek, where Richard McNemar was pastor. McNemar granted the missionaries permission to address the Turtle Creek congregation. On Sunday,

---

[1]Stephen J. Stein, *The Shaker Experience in America: A History of the United Society of Believers* (New Haven, Conn.: Yale University Press, 1992), 57–58; David Meacham, Amos Hammond, and Ebenezer Cooley to People in Kentucky and Adjacent States, 30 Dec. 1804, cited in MacLean, *Shaker Community of Warren County*, 61-63, quoted in Stein, 59; Ware, 160.

[2]John Patterson MacLean, *Shakers of Ohio:Fugitive Papers Concerning the Shakers of Ohio, with Unpublished Manuscripts* (Columbus, Ohio:F. J. Heer, 1907), 41, quoted in Ware, 164.

March 23, Bates and Youngs made their first public presentation in the West to the Turtle Creek Church.[3]

McNemar reported that the message the missionaries delivered at Turtle Creek could have been "summed up" in the following saying of Jesus: "If any man come after me, let him deny himself and take up his cross, and follow me. For whosoever will save his life shall lose it; and whosoever will lose his life for my sake shall find it." McNemar related that after expressing on behalf of themselves and the church that had sent them "great union with the work of God that had been for years past among the people," they testified that "the time was now come for them to enter into actual possession of that salvation, of which they had received the promise–[and] That the way to attain it was by self denial, taking up a full cross against the world, the flesh and all evil in our knowledge, and following Christ, walking as he walked, and being in all things conformed to him, as our pattern and head." McNemar stated that the missionaries taught that the first step in the saving work "was to confess all our sins, and when we had confessed them, forsake them forever." The missionaries promised, McNemar continued, that in so doing they would "receive that measure of the holy spirit, which would be an overcoming power," not only sufficient to keep them "out of all actual sin and defilement, but to cleanse and purify both soul and body from the very nature of evil." McNemar observed that the missionaries delivered their testimony "not as matters of mere speculation, but as things that had for many years been reduced to practice, and established by the living experience of hundreds in the church of Christ, to be the way and only way of God; the one door of hope for a lost soul, and the sure entrance into the righteous, peaceful and holy kingdom of God's dear Son." McNemar reported that the missionaries also declared "that as Christ had now made his second and last appearance, for a final settlement with every soul of man," and as the Christians had been "illuminated in the great and marvelous light of the revival, to see the evil nature of sin, and stirred up to seek the way out of it," and as "the last and only way of God" had been "opened to them," should they reject that way, they would "fall under the power of the wicked one," gradually "lose the extraordinary effusions of the spirit they had been under, and leaven back into a more corrupt and deplorable state than ever."[4]

McNemar met privately with the missionaries, both before and after their public presentation on March 23. From their private conversations he learned "more particularly" the meaning of the Shaker testimony. "The first point of faith in relation to the testimony," McNemar reported, was "to believe that he who bears it is a *true messenger* and *witness* of Christ, in whom the spirit of truth continually abides; and that whatever instruction, reproof or counsel is ministered by such, it comes from Christ, who speaketh *in him*." All who are taught

---

[3]McNemar, *Kentucky Revival*, 75.
[4]McNemar, 75–77.

in this manner, McNemar noted, are thus "strictly and properly taught of God, and in obeying what they are taught they yield obedience *to Christ.*" He learned that the confession of sin of which the missionaries spoke was to be made in the presence of the Shaker leaders. He also learned that the forsaking of sin of which the Shakers spoke included marital relations and that the Shakers counted it "their distinguishing privilege to preserve their bodies in sanctification and honor," believing that the "lust of the flesh" was the source of every branch of evil, including pride, covetousness, anger, and hatred. In addition, he learned of the Shaker's positions on the Lord's supper, baptism, and the resurrection. Shakers did not practice the Lord's supper, having no occasion to call to memory "a departed Saviour, by signs and shadows of his dying love," as they believed that "the only Saviour that ever redeemed a lost soul" was formed and living in them. Neither did they practice baptism, as "water applied to the body appears a beggarly element, compared with the baptism of the spirit." Nor did they anticipate a resurrection of the body, believing that the natural body "belongs to the fall" and that the resurrection promised in scripture referred to "that spiritual body of which we are called to be members; which is already raised up by the power of God, and [is] ascending into the heaven of heavens, far out of sight from this lost world." The Shakers' rejection of baptism and the Lord's supper, which they held in common with Quakers, may have been a result of Ann Lee's association with a group known as the Shaking Quakers in Manchester, England, prior to her immigration to New York in 1774.[5]

The missionaries remained at Turtle Creek for several days, lodging at the home of Malcolm Worley. Worley had been a Presbyterian elder at Turtle Creek and later a licentiate of the Springfield Presbytery. On March 27, he became the first Shaker convert in the West.[6]

Following Worley's conversion, Bates returned from Ohio to Kentucky in time for a camp meeting at Cane Ridge the first Sabbath of April. Bates reported that Stone's attitude toward him and the Shaker testimony had changed. Arriving at Stone's house on Saturday night, Bates found many of the preachers there, along with a number of others. "I was received," he noted in his journal, "with outward kindness and a number of the people felt very friendly, but the preachers were struck with great fear and concluded that if I was permitted to preach that it would throw the people into confusion, and to prevent it they would counteract their former liberality and shut out all other sects from preaching at that meeting and that would shut me out." Bates indicated that the preachers made this decision without consulting any of the people.[7]

Bates went to the campground the following morning and heard sermons by Stone and Marshall. According to Bates, Stone and Marshall "preached

---

[5]McNemar, 82–84, 96–97, 99–100. For a critical account of the earliest history of the Shakers, see Stein, 3–25.

[6]Ware, 164.

[7]Bates, quoted in Ware, 166.

the people back to Egypt." Bates recorded that Stone told the people "to let no man deceive them about the coming of Christ, for they would all know when he came, for every eye would see him in the clouds and they would see the graves opening and the bones rising and the saints would rise and meet the Lord in the air, whose names are written in the Lamb's book of life (which is this little book that I hold in my hand), the Bible." He added that Marshall had continued in the same vein, warning his hearers not to "follow man," but to keep their Bibles in their homes and in their pockets, "for in them you have eternal life."[8]

Bates claimed that a large number of the participants paid little attention to the preaching of Stone and Marshall, but instead encircled him, asking questions, and responding to his answers with such expressions as "that is eternal truth" and "that is the everlasting gospel." He also claimed that Matthew Houston, who preached after Marshall, sounded a different note from that of Stone and Marshall. Bates recorded that, taking as his text "Let us go up and possess the land for we are fully able," Houston had the people "across the Red Sea in short order." According to his journal, many of the people interceded with the preachers to let Bates preach, but to no avail. He reported that he returned to Stone's that evening and engaged in conversation with many people. The following morning, he noted, the people again insisted on his preaching, eight men finally going to the stand to say that he should preach. He related that, at length, the preachers agreed that they would close the meeting at noon and that he might then preach. Bates indicated that as soon as the meeting was over, he "mounted a large log in front of the stand and began to speak, and although the preachers and many others went to their horses to get out of the way of hearing," when he began to speak "they all returned and all paid good attention."[9]

In a letter to McNemar dated April 2, 1805, delivered by Bates following the meeting at Cane Ridge, Stone wrote in Latin, which Bates could not read, "Certain men from afar whom you know inject terror and doubt into many; and now religion begins to lament in the dust among us. Some as I suppose will cast away the ordinances of baptism, the Lord's Supper, etc., but not many as yet. Most dear Brother, inform me what you think of these men among us and you from a distant region."[10]

Stone soon had his answer. Within less than a month, McNemar had confessed his sins and joined the Shakers. In a letter to the Ministry in New Lebanon dated April 27, the missionaries reported that a total of thirty persons had "opened their minds" to the testimony. On July 29, John Dunlavy, pastor at Eagle Creek, Ohio, followed suit. In February of the following year,

---

[8]Ibid., 166–67.
[9]Ibid., 167.
[10]Quoted in McNemar, 78.

Matthew Houston, who had been the missionaries' first contact in Kentucky, also became a Shaker.[11]

Stone observed that Meacham, Bates, and Youngs were well suited for their task. He reported that "their dress was plain and neat" and that their manner, at least at first, was "grave and unassuming." They were also, he noted, "very intelligent and ready in the Scriptures, and of great boldness in their faith." He related that they claimed to be able to work miracles, though they had not performed any in his presence.[12]

In addition, Stone stated that developments among the Christians had made them receptive to the Shaker testimony. As many of the Christians, he wrote, "were breathing after perfect holiness, they were disposed to listen to any proposition by which they might advance to that desirable state." He also indicated that prior to the arrival of the missionaries, "some of our leading preachers" had begun "to indulge in wild, enthusiastic speculations, and hesitated not to publish them abroad." "One," he continued, "proclaimed that the Millennium was come—another said that Christians would never die, but be made immortal by some extraordinary operation of the spirit; and plainly hinted at the denial of the resurrection of the body and of a future judgment."[13] In a letter dated June 1, 1805, the missionaries wrote to the New Lebanon Ministry that

> Many of the people here [in Ohio] have been in an expectation last fall [when the mass meeting was held at Bethel], & through the winter that Something extraordinary would take place this Summer— Some have thought it would be only the extending & spreading of the Same light they had already received—But others believed there would be Some new Revelation which would cause an entire new Revolution among those that had the light.[14]

Stone claimed that the success of the Shaker mission was "the first serious check" to the progress of the Christian Church in the West. "The opposition to our course before," he wrote, "had been so violent and ill-directed, that it rather increased, our influence in society, and inclined many to unite with us. But now the Shakers under the mask of friendship, were drawing the multitude after them and many for fear of them fled from us to the different sects for refuge." Our "sectarian opposers," he continued, concluded "that our doctrine was thus demonstrated to be false, because so many of its advocates had embraced Shakerism." The experience, he confessed, was "humiliating in the extreme."[15]

---

[11]Ware, 164; Meacham, Bates, and Youngs to New Lebanon Ministry, April 27, 1805, quoted in Stein, 59.

[12]Stone, *Biography*, 62. See also *History*, 45.

[13]Stone, *History*, 45. See also *Biography*, 64.

[14]John Meacham, Issachar Bates, and Benjamin S. Youngs to New Lebanon Ministry, June 1, 1805, in the manuscript collection of Western Reserve Historical Society, Cleveland, Ohio, collection number OCIWHi IV A 66, quoted in Stein, 455–56, note 57.

[15]Stone, *History*, 46.

In a postscript to his *Reply* to J. P. Campbell, dated September 4, 1805, Stone wrote, "You have heard, no doubt, before this time, of the lamentable departure of two of our preachers, and a few of their hearers, from the true gospel into wild enthusiasm, or shakerism. They have made shipwreck of faith, and turned aside to an old woman's fables, who broached them in New-England about twenty-five years ago." He insisted that this development represented nothing new: "Of the twelve who followed Christ, one proved a devil, and another denied him, and all the rest forsook him; but all repented, except Judas." He expressed the hope that his "deluded brethren" might yet repent. In any case, he asserted that the fact that two of their preachers had "revolted from the truth" was not "an argument that we are wrong." If it were, he advised, then the argument would be "equally strong against the truth of the christian religion, because many of its professors in every age have done the same; even too in the Synod of Kentucky." On the contrary, he boldly suggested that the success of the Shakers among the Christians was evidence "that we are right, because wolves always go among the sheep for prey." Identifying the Shaker missionaries as wolves "in sheep's clothing," he declared that they have "smelt us from far, and have come to tear, rend and devour."[16]

Though Stone did not mention it in writing, the success of the Shaker mission challenged the polity of the "Last Will and Testament" and tested the limits of the former presbytery's ecumenism. According to McNemar, John Thompson went to a camp meeting at Turtle Creek on April 27, raised an outcry against the Shakers, assumed the authority of leading the meeting, led a public investigation of the missionaries' doctrines, and pronounced in a loud voice that they were "liars!" McNemar reported that Stone, after inviting him to attend a general meeting at Concord the second Sabbath in August, forbade him to speak on the occasion or even to come to his house and "through a council of the *Christian clergy*" imposed upon Dunlavy, Youngs, and Worley an injunction of total silence through the whole of the meeting "on pain of being prosecuted as disturbers of the meeting." By his own account, Stone devoted himself to opposing the Shakers, laboring "night and day, far and near, among the churches where the Shakers went" with such intensity that "a profuse spitting of blood ensued."[17]

McNemar claimed that the impression of Shakerism that the world received from the Christians, presumably including Stone, could be summarized as follows: "that it went to disannul and cast away the Bible–to set up the word of man in room of it–to deny Jesus Christ–the resurrection and final judgment–to throw away the gospel and seek salvation by the works of the law…[and] to get people's land and property, by parting man and wife." In what appears to have been a personal letter to McNemar written in July 1806, Stone referred to the Shakers as "worldly-minded, cunning deceivers, whose religion is earthly, sensual and devilish," citing the "noisy report" that the

---

[16]Stone, *Reply*, 66–67.
[17]McNemar, 91–93; Stone, *Biography*, 63. For McNemar's view of the Christian ministers' understanding of their authority, see McNemar, 88.

Shakers had come to take people's land. In the same letter, he called them "liars," on the grounds that they had prophesied that persons who rejected their testimony would lose their former life and power, and yet "the work of God goes on in spite of all the Calvinists, Shakers, and devils in hell." The Barton Stone who opposed the Shakers was not, at least in private correspondence, the kinder, gentler Barton Stone of later hagiography.[18]

Stone claimed that through his efforts the Shakers' influence was "checked" in many places. McNemar concurred in his Shaker apology, *The Kentucky Revival*, published in 1808. "Too great a majority" of the subjects of the revival, he wrote, had "shut their eyes against the pure light of the Gospel" through the influence of the "prejudice and false reports" of Stone and other Christian preachers. Moreover, McNemar credited Stone and other Christian preachers for violence against the Shakers, such as assaulting their persons "with clubs and stones," breaking their windows, burning their place of worship, knocking down their fences, and cutting and tearing to pieces their apple trees. To be sure, McNemar did not charge that the Christian preachers had personally committed any of these particular acts of violence. Rather, he held them responsible for having encouraged a "spirit of persecution" by their "hard speeches," their refusal to allow Shakers to come to their homes, and their public representation of them as a people of the "most corrupt and mischievous principles."[19]

While McNemar criticized Stone's actions in opposing the Shakers in his 1808 apology for the Shakers, another former colleague turned Shaker, John Dunlavy, taunted him in a printed letter: "Dost thou not remember telling me…that thou wast never so completely swallowed up with any man as with Issachar Bates, while he opened the testimony? And that thou hadst never heard anything with which thou wast so well pleased…until they came on marriage?" According to Dunlavy, Stone had rejected the Shaker testimony because of his "opposition to the cross of Christ."[20]

There may have been some truth to Dunlavy's claim. When the missionaries visited Cane Ridge in March 1805, Stone had been married to Elizabeth Campbell, whom he affectionately called Eliza, for three and a half years. Two daughters, Amanda Warren and Tabitha Russell, had been born to their marriage. A third, Mary Anne, would be born within six months.[21] Stone's respect for the relations of husband and wife and parent and child is reflected in the arguments against slavery that he had addressed to Samuel Rennels. "Slavery," he had declared, "dissolves the ties of God and man; ties the most strong and indissoluble of all others. One of these ties is conjugal affection. The loving husband is torn from the weeping distracted embraces of the most affectionate wife[,] carried far off & sold like a beast…how must the happiness of this loving pair be forever destroyed! Perhaps they had children too ('dear

---

[18]McNemar, 94–95, 101–2.
[19]Ibid., 3. See also 93–94.
[20]Quoted in Davidson, 208; see also John Dunlavy, *The Manifesto: Or a Declaration of the Doctrines and Practices of the Church of Christ* (Pleasant Hill, Ky.: P. Bertrand, 1818), 468.
[21]Ware, 166.

to both' *crossed out)*…" "Say," he had asked Rennels, "can this be right? Can it be agreeable to a good God? Or that word which commands us to leave Father and mother and cleave to our wives?"[22]

Elizabeth had done much to support Stone's ministry. As is evident from Bates's journal, Stone's log home, located midway between Cane Ridge and Concord, had become by 1805 a center of hospitality for the Christian churches. An earlier biographer, Charles C. Ware, reported seeing a Wedgwood meat platter, with ladle of German silver, said to have been a remnant of Eliza's dowry. Eliza also owned land. These material contributions, in addition to her hospitality and homemaking, were surely appreciated by Stone, who had spent his inheritance from his father on a classical education, had emancipated the slaves he inherited from his mother, and then had given up what he termed an "abundant salary" in withdrawing from the synod.[23]

However, it was Elizabeth's contributions in the spiritual realm that Stone mentioned in his autobiography. He stated that she was "pious, intelligent, and cheerful," adding that "nothing could depress her." He noted that when he began "to think deeply on the subject of the Atonement," he was "entirely absorbed in it, yet dared not mention it to any, lest it might involve other minds in similar perplexities." Elizabeth sensed that he was "oppressed" by something, went to him while he was laboring in his field, and "affectionately besought" him "not to conceal, but [to] plainly declare the cause" of his oppression. They sat down, and he told her his thoughts on the atonement. When he had concluded, "she sprang up and praised God aloud most fervently for the truth." He noted that "from that day till her death, she never doubted of its truth." She was, he wrote, "truly a help-meet to me in all my troubles and difficulties."[24]

As McNemar noted in his account of the first Shaker preaching at Turtle Creek, the missionaries offered their testimony not as matters of mere speculation, but on the authority of the experience of "hundreds" who had found obedience to the testimony to be the only sure way to holiness. Surely Stone consulted his experience. On the basis of what is known of his marriage to Elizabeth, he could not have believed that he would have been a more perfect Christian were he not married to Elizabeth.

For Stone, the success of the Shaker missionaries had been a "great evil." Nevertheless, he stated in 1827 that he thought that it had "eventuated in good, great good to the Christian Church." This good result respected the doctrinal temperament of the Christians. "By it we are taught," he wrote, "to check our minds from indulging too freely in vain speculations, and to examine well by the Bible, every doctrine presented for our acceptance." The success of the Shaker mission had also been a practical lesson in Christian humility.

---

[22]B. W. Stone to Samuel Rennels. Letter fragment owned by the Cane Ridge Preservation Project. Cane Ridge, Ky. No date.
[23]Ware, 98; Stone, *Biography*, 68.
[24]Stone, *Biography*, 67.

"We are also taught," he observed, "our entire dependence upon the great Head of the Church for all good, and that he only can keep us from falling."[25]

The success of the Shaker mission did not cause Stone to question his renunciation of the jurisdiction of the Synod of Kentucky, the dissolution of the Springfield Presbytery, or his new light on the doctrine of atonement. This was not true for Marshall and Thompson. In 1811 they published a pamphlet declaring their "testimony" against "several doctrines" and the "disorganized state" of the Christian Church and announcing their intention to "seek for a more pure and orderly connexion." They suggested that a "look back" at the career they had run might be "salutary" to the Christians and "cautionary" to others. They had separated from the synod in September and formed the Springfield Presbytery. Their "Apology" had been published in January. In March they had begun to change their views on the atonement. In June they had signed the "Last Will and Testament" and dissolved their presbytery. About that time, McNemar and others had begun to deny the resurrection of the body and a future judgment. A few months later McNemar, Dunlavy, and many of the people had become Shakers. A year later, Matthew Houston, who had been converted to the Christians by reading Stone's letters on atonement, had also become a Shaker. "Are these things," they asked, "not worthy of notice?" They reported that as events had developed, they had reexamined the course they had taken and had rejected the "Last Will and Testament" and the views of atonement, Trinity, Son of God, and divine decrees commonly held in the Christian Church. They claimed that for more than a year they had been "labouring to effect a reformation" among the Christians, but having failed, they had at last concluded "to seek relief…in another manner, or from some other quarter."[26]

Stone believed that Marshall's and Thompson's dissatisfaction with the Christian Church had reached a new level in 1807 with the introduction of believers' immersion among the Christians. Prior to the revival, Robert Marshall had become convinced of the "truth" of the Baptist view that baptism was not the sprinkling of infants, but only the immersion of believers, and was about to unite with the Baptists. Fearing that Marshall would join the Baptists, Stone had written him "a lengthy letter" seeking to convince him of his error. Marshall had written a letter in reply in which he "so forcibly argued in favor of believers' immersion, and against pedobaptism" that Stone had stopped baptizing infants.[27]

The revival had soon begun, and discussion of baptism had subsided, as it was associated with the sectarian strife that was put aside during the early stages of the revival. After a few years, discussion of baptism revived. Many of the Christians became "dissatisfied with their infant sprinkling," including Stone. Meanwhile, Robert Marshall had reversed his earlier position, deciding

[25]Stone, *History,* 46.
[26]Marshall and Thompson, title page, 3, 20–21.
[27]Stone, *History,* 47; Stone, *Biography,* 60.

that infant-sprinkling *was* baptism. As the Christian ministers or elders had "agreed previously with one another to act in concert, and not to adventure on any thing new without advice from one another," a conference of elders and deacons came together to discuss the subject. "At this meeting," Stone reported, "we took up the matter in a brotherly spirit, and concluded that every brother and sister should act freely, and according to their conviction of right–and that we should cultivate the long-neglected grace of forbearance towards each other–they who should be immersed, should not despise those who were not, and *vice versa.*"[28]

The first person to be immersed by a minister who had attended the conference was a woman who made a profession of faith and specifically requested Stone to baptize her in this manner. Though none of the Christian preachers had been immersed, they had decided, according to Stone, that "if we were authorized to preach, we were also authorized to baptize." Stone held the baptismal service for the woman who had requested to be immersed at Stoner Creek at Paris, seven miles from Cane Ridge, in June 1807. Reuben Dooley preached. David Purviance was also present.[29]

Following the immersion of the woman for whom the service had been appointed, Stone immersed others, including a member of the church who made a short address to the congregation, the substance of which, according to Purviance, was that he hoped that other members of the church would not be "hurt" by his action, that though he was baptized in infancy, to be baptized was the command of God, and that he could not have a good conscience unless he obeyed the command. Purviance, who had already decided that infant-sprinkling was not baptism, reported that he was so affected by the man's speech that, after seeking the Lord's guidance in prayer, he called Stone and Reuben Dooley aside and requested Stone to immerse him, to which request Stone consented. Not long after this service, Stone himself was immersed.[30]

Stone claimed that despite the decision of the conference that "every brother and sister should act according to their faith" regarding believers' immersion, "some of our preaching brethren appeared rather uneasy and dissatisfied that their congregations were submitting to this ordinance, while they could not be convinced of its propriety." He further stated that though they "said but little" regarding the growing popularity of believers' immersion among members of their congregations, some of them began to recommend "that we should have some other bond beside the Bible and brotherly love; that these were insufficient to unite our growing churches, and keep them pure." They urged, he added, that "there was already a diversity of opinion among us on the doctrines of trinity, the son of God and atonement, and therefore it was necessary that some *formulary* should be made and adopted,

---

[28]Stone, *Biography*, 60. See also Stone, *History*, 47.

[29]"Memoirs," in Purviance, 151; Stone, *Biography*, 60–61; James R. Rogers, *The Cane Ridge Meeting-House*, 2d ed. (Cincinnati: Standard Publishing, 1910), 69–71.

[30]"Memoirs," in Purviance, 148–52.

by which uniformity might be promoted and preserved among us." Among the ministers calling for the adoption of a formulary were Marshall and Thompson, neither of whom, he noted, could see the propriety of members of the church being immersed. Stone further stated that "some of us saw plainly" that the arguments being used in support of a formulary were the same as those used for "the introduction of every human party Creed, which has ever been imposed on the world, and therefore opposed *formularies*, from a full conviction of their injury to the cause of Christ."[31]

The issue of baptism was discussed again at a camp meeting near Lexington in October 1808. There was a large attendance, including forty-seven ministers. According to a published account of the meeting, although all the ministers acknowledged believers' immersion to be a "gospel ordinance," they did not view it "precisely alike," but left everyone to be "fully persuaded in his own mind…"[32]

The major issue at the meeting in October 1808, however, appears to have been slavery. Some of the "brethren" from the free state of Ohio suggested that Christian fellowship should be withdrawn from members of the churches who held slaves. According to the published account of the meeting, Stone and Purviance made "some impressive arguments against such ideas, though they were great emancipators themselves." Stone was reported to have pointed out that

> so far as it had come, to his knowledge, he knew of no members among them that held slaves whose conduct and upright deportment, but what was worthy of example in every other particular, that numbers of them had borne the burden and heat of the day, and had suffered great persecutions for the Christian cause and name, and that to declare them out of fellowship would be ungenerous and cruel in the extreme."[33]

This was quite a change for both Stone and Purviance, who had earlier recommended to the West Lexington Presbytery that slaveholders be barred from communion, and may reflect their desire to hold together a communion that had suffered significant losses to the Shakers. They may have also concluded that the best way to influence others on both the issues of slavery and baptism was to remain in fellowship. This was a stance that Stone would later articulate regarding baptism.[34]

Though Marshall and Thompson made no mention of baptism in their pamphlet, their rejection of the "Last Will and Testament" and the views of the atonement, Trinity, Son of God, and divine decrees commonly held in the Christian Church, based on their dating in the pamphlet, *followed* the

---

[31]Stone, *History*, 47. See also Stone, *Biography*, 65. For references to Marshall's and Thompson's support of infant baptism, see Stone, *Biography*, 61; and, "Memoirs," in Purviance, 199–200.

[32]Letter from William Lamphier to the *Herald of Gospel Liberty*, May 12, 1809, 74–75, ed. Elias Smith, Portsmouth, N.H., quoted in Roos, 88.

[33]Letter from William Lamphier.

[34]*CM* 3 (December 1828), 34–37; Stone, *History*, 47.

introduction of immersion among the Christians in June 1807.[35] Whether, as Stone argued, discomfort with the growing popularity of believers' immersion in their congregations was the cause of Marshall's and Thompson's recommendations that the Christians adopt a formulary, it is clear that differences were emerging among the leaders of the Christians and that one of the differences was over baptism. On one side were those preachers who maintained the validity of infant-sprinkling as baptism, affirmed orthodox views of atonement, Trinity, and the Son of God, and advocated the adoption of a formulary that would promote uniformity among the Christians. On the other side were those preachers who supported the immersion of Christians who were not "satisfied" with their infant sprinkling, affirmed unorthodox views of the atonement, Trinity, and Son of God, and opposed formularies of any kind.

In the midst of the growing doctrinal and organizational tensions among the Christians, Stone suffered a personal blow in May 1810 with the death of Elizabeth after a year's illness. The cause of her death is unknown. Two more children had been born to the marriage: a fourth daughter, Eliza, and a son, Barton Warren. The bearing of five children within eight years before age twenty-six was not unusual. It may, however, have been a factor in her early death. Her fifth child, Barton Warren, who died in infancy, had been born July 26, 1809, two months after the onset of her illness.[36]

At a conference at Bethel three months after Elizabeth's death, in August 1810, a compromise was worked out by which the Christians would establish a "formal" union and publish a statement of their current views, but not adopt a formulary. On the recommendation of Marshall and Thompson, the following instrument was adopted:

> At a general meeting of ministers of the Christian church at Bethel, in the state of Kentucky, August 8th, 1810, the brethren taking into consideration their scattered local situation, their increasing numbers, and the difficulties arising in executing the duties of their office, agreed to unite themselves together *formally*, taking the word of God as their only rule and standard for doctrine, discipline and government, and promising subjection to each other in the Lord, have hereunto subscribed their names, according to their present standing in said connexion.

"Standing" referred to whether one was an ordained minister, a licensed candidate for ministry, or an exhorter. Exhorters "exhorted" congregations after the preaching of ordained ministers or licensed candidates for ministry.

---

[35]Marshall and Thompson, 4–10. Purviance reported that it was after his move to Ohio in 1807 that Thompson first informed him of his misgivings regarding Stone's doctrine of atonement. Purviance also stated that he and Thompson had "continued in the habits of intimacy and the most friendly intercourse" even though he had "deviated" from Thompson's course "respecting baptism" (Purviance, 199–200).

[36]Ware, 98. Stone expressed his grief over the loss of Elizabeth and extolled her faith in an elegy of nineteen stanzas that celebrated her victory over "the powers of death and hell," in Stone, *Biography,* 308–12.

Exhortations could become sermons in themselves but were meant to call the congregation to action on the basis of the sermon preached. Exhorters often became licensed candidates for ministry and, later, ordained ministers. The conference also approved, on the recommendation of Marshall and Thompson, that a committee be appointed "to write a piece for publication" expressing the Christians' "present and matured views on doctrine and church government," in the hope that it might "remove from the public mind those strong prepossessions" against them and thus open a door for them to have "some degree of communion with brethren and churches of other denominations." Marshall, Stone, Thompson, Purviance, and another minister, Hugh Andrews, were appointed as the committee and charged to report to a general meeting set for Mount Tabor, near Lexington, the second Monday of March, 1811.[37]

The committee agreed to meet in Ohio toward the end of September, 1810, to develop a plan for the proposed publication. Stone did not attend. Marshall, Thompson, Purviance, and Andrews met and, according to Marshall and Thompson, "appeared very cordial in their views, on all the subjects proposed, and particularly on the Atonement." David Purviance, writing after the publication of Marshall and Thompson's pamphlet, reported that although after moving to Ohio in 1807 he had been led by Thompson to question Stone's views on the atonement, he was, actually, "halting between two opinions" at the September meeting. After making assignments, the committee agreed to meet at Bethel, Kentucky, on December 26 to compare drafts and make further preparations for reporting to the conference.[38]

All the members of the committee attended the December 26 meeting, except Purviance, who was unable to attend due to his having been elected to the Ohio Legislature. According to Marshall and Thompson, Stone reported that he had written "none worth showing." Thompson read a paper on the atonement, which Stone took with him for further examination.[39]

The committee's next meeting was set for a few days prior to the meeting of the conference. Neither Stone nor Purviance attended. Marshall and Thompson reported that although the three members present were in agreement on the substance of all the points on which they were to write, they saw that the committee would not be prepared to present a document for publication as soon as was anticipated or desired.[40]

According to Marshall and Thompson, "a very general collection of the preachers" assembled on Monday, March 11, in the large stone meetinghouse of the Christians at Mount Tabor, four miles east of Lexington. After receiving leave of conference, the committee met privately to compare their writings. Four of the members had written on the doctrine of atonement. Marshall,

[37]Marshall and Thompson, 11–12. Stone may have depended on Marshall and Thompson's account in preparing his history of the August 8, 1810, Bethel conference. See Stone, *History,* 47–48.

[38]Marshall and Thompson, 12; Purviance, 200–202.

[39]Marshall and Thompson, 12. See also Stone, *Biography,* 65–66.

[40]Marshall and Thompson, 12.

Thompson, and Andrews had written in support of the traditional substitutionary view. Stone had written in defense of the view published in his *Atonement: The Substance of Two Letters Written to a Friend,* responding in particular to Thompson's arguments contained in the draft that he had borrowed from Thompson at the December 26 meeting at Bethel. After reading their writings on atonement, as well as some on the topic of church government, and discovering how much they differed, the committee decided to report to conference that they could not prepare the publication they had been appointed to write, since they were divided on their views of the topics on which they had read to one another, but that as individuals they would be willing to read what they had written to the conference.[41]

The committee made its report to conference on Tuesday morning. After considerable debate, the conference agreed to hear what the members of the committee had written as individuals. Reading their papers took the rest of the day. Purviance had devoted his "leisure hours" during the annual session of the General Assembly of Ohio to the study of atonement in the scriptures, and although he had written nothing for the Mount Tabor meeting, he had come down clearly in support of the view of atonement advocated by Stone. On Wednesday morning, Purviance stated his views on atonement orally, noting in his memoirs that the Lord being his "helper," he spoke "with ease and clearness" and that several of his hearers commented that what he said "was more satisfactory and had a greater effect than all that had been written and read."[42]

Marshall and Thompson reported that following Purviance's speech "some of us" requested further discussion of the doctrine of atonement, but that "the general voice was against it, supposing they had heard enough, and declaring that the difference in sentiment need not break fellowship." Thompson informed the conference that he had "written in connexion on all the subjects" and wished that the conference would hear what he had written, but the conference would not. Marshall and Thompson indicated that one of them had then asked whether the conference would appoint another committee, since the first had failed to complete its assignment, or whether the conference would publish anything. They reported that after considerable discussion the conference resolved to appoint no committee and to publish nothing, the "general voice" being "that they could easily bear with each other, and go on in love and union, notwithstanding the difference in doctrine."[43]

The conference then considered the instrument of union that had been approved at the conference at Bethel on August 8, 1810. Marshall and Thompson reported that "two long letters were read, sent from churches at a

[41]Ware, 179; Marshall and Thompson, 12–13. Stone, *History,* 48, appears to follow Marshall and Thompson's account.

[42]"Memoirs," in Purviance, 202–5. Stone commented that Purviance had spoken "forcibly" (*Biography,* 66). Marshall and Thompson supply the detail that Purviance spoke on Wednesday morning (13).

[43]Ibid., 13–14. See also Stone, *History,* 48. Stone, *Biography,* 65–66, indicates that it was Thompson who had "written considerably on the points or doctrines to be received." Marshall and Thompson identify the author merely as "One of us."

distance, warning, and cautioning us against that measure, lest it should be a yoke of bondage on the necks of the ministers and churches." They indicated that the authors of the letters had not been present at the previous meeting and that some of the members who had been present and had signed the instrument appeared "considerably uneasy, and wished to be clear" of it. "Finding," they continued, that "it could not be a general thing, and only served to excite the jealousy of such as were afraid to adopt it, it was declared, by a very general, we may say universal voice, to be null and void." "Thus," they concluded, "we quickly returned again to that disjointed, and disorganized state into which the Last Will and Testament had brought us; connected together by no tie, but a general profession of faith in the Bible, and of Christian love, which we professed to feel as strong for Christians of every denomination as for one another."[44]

Marshall and Thompson had been disappointed in the much boasted tolerance of the Christians. "It might have been expected," they wrote, "that we, as well as others, would be permitted to preach whatever we believe; and that ministers and people, would give us a patient hearing, without pointed controversy, or opposition, even though they differed from us in opinion." This, they reported, had not been the case, thus showing that the professions of forbearance offered at the conference were either "insincere, or that those who made them, had not counted the cost of forbearance in such circumstances." Some, they continued, "will not come to hear us, and some who do manifest great opposition to the doctrines which they have never fairly examined, yet show great unwillingness to understand; branding the preaching with ill names, as old stuff, darkness, leading to bondage, Calvinism, etc." They asserted that "though the body of the members in Conference, and our church in general profess to have no creed but the Bible, and to have adopted no system but the scriptures in general, yet facts show that profession to be unworthy of credit." "They have a system on certain points," they continued, "which they call the truth of the Bible, and unless every one holds and preaches these ideas, his doctrine is condemned positively as false, however full of scripture his statements may be."[45]

Having failed to reform the Christians, Marshall and Thompson began to investigate the possibility of returning to the ministry of the Presbyterian Church. Initial negotiations were conducted with John P. Campbell, who assured Marshall, in a letter dated just one month after the March 1811 conference at Mount Tabor, that there would be no obstacles to his and Thompson's returning to the ministry of the Presbyterian Church.[46] In November 1811 both Marshall and Thompson were received into the Presbyterian ministry by the presbyteries in which they resided.[47]

Stone did not believe that the church that had emerged from the dissolution of the Springfield Presbytery was without flaws. Presbyterian historian

[44]Marshall and Thompson, 14.
[45]Ibid., 15–16.
[46]Campbell to Marshall, April 13, 1811, cited in Davidson, 211, note.
[47]"Minutes of the Synod of Kentucky," quoted in Ware, 181–82. See also Davidson, 211.

Robert Davidson reported that when Stone discovered that Marshall and Thompson were considering a return to the Presbyterians, he had tried to dissuade Marshall in a letter in which he frankly confessed, "I see the Christian Churches wrong in many things—they are not careful to support preachers—they encourage too many trifling preachers—are led away too much by noise, etc."[48] Nevertheless, Stone remained firmly attached to the doctrines and polity that had emerged among the members of the former Springfield Presbytery in the course of the revival. Purviance reported that in private conversation Marshall and Thompson suggested "that we had become so diversified, we had better dissolve, and scatter to the different sects, as we could be best suited."[49] While Marshall and Thompson returned to the Presbyterians, and Andrews and another minister became Methodists, it is hard to imagine to which denomination Stone might have gone.[50] According to Marshall and Thompson, the publication of Stone's *Atonement: The Substance of Two Letters Written to a Friend* had caused whatever door of communion that had previously been open to them to be closed.[51] Moreover, Stone continued to believe, as was voiced by the conference at Mount Tabor, that Christians who were united by Christian love *could* tolerate doctrinal diversity of the sort that had been represented by the failed writing committee.

Stone claimed that Marshall and Thompson's pamphlet was viewed by the Christians as "a harmless production" and was therefore "scarcely noticed by us."[52] Be that as it may, Purviance responded to Marshall and Thompson's pamphlet with a pamphlet titled *Observations. Constitution, Unity, and Discipline of the Church of Christ, addressed to the brethren of the Christian Church.* Against Marshall and Thompson's criticisms of the "disorganized state" of the Christian Church, Purviance defended the Christians' commitment to be governed by the scriptures alone. Admitting that "evils do exist among us," he urged that the question was "whether this is occasioned by any defect or insufficiency in the rules prescribed in the word of God; or from a defect in our knowledge of those rules—and a want of faithfulness in the observance and execution of them." He offered for review and correction by others his own "ideas" regarding the teaching of the scriptures on the following topics: (1) receiving members, (2) church censures, or removing offenses, (3) sending out preachers of the gospel, and (4) the support of the ministry. In response to the claim that "there is such a diversity among christians, both as to doctrine and practice, that it is expedient they should be divided into separate societies, and each regulated according to their own views," he declared that though the reasoning appeared plausible, he dared not adopt the plan, since it contradicted the teaching in 1 Corinthians 1:10, "Now I beseech you brethren, by the name of our Lord Jesus Christ, that ye all speak the same thing, and that

---

[48]Stone to Marshall, Marshall mss. No. 8 quoted in Davidson, 210.

[49]"Memoirs," in Purviance, 206.

[50]Stone, *History,* 49.

[51]Marshall and Thompson, 6.

[52]Stone, *History,* 48.

there be no divisions among you." Moreover, he stated, it was "contrary to the spirit that every believer receives" when adopted into the church. "The spirit of Jesus," he continued, "the living head, binds the members of his body to each other in love." Thus, he could not advocate the adoption of standards of doctrine and discipline that would separate Christians from each other.[53]

Stone also responded to Marshall and Thompson's pamphlet. While Purviance had sought to defend and explain the *polity* of the Christian Church as rooted in their commitment not to divide Christians one from another, Stone sought to state their *doctrines* in such a way as to open a door to fellowship with other Christians who viewed them as heretics.

---

[53]"Observations," reprinted in Purviance, 70–72, 74–83.

10

An Address

Stone responded to Marshall and Thompson's pamphlet with a book titled *An Address to the Christian Churches in Kentucky, Tennessee and Ohio: On Several Important Doctrines of Religion.* Though Stone noted in his autobiography that the foundation of this book was the response he wrote to Thompson's connected statement of doctrines for the 1811 Mount Tabor conference, the book was not published until 1814.[1] The delay in Stone's publication of *An Address* was most likely due to a series of changes in his personal circumstances.

Following Elizabeth's death, Stone broke up housekeeping, boarded his four daughters with members of the church, and devoted all his time to preaching and establishing churches in Ohio, Kentucky, and Tennessee. The oldest of the girls was eight; the youngest was under three. Stone was joined in his evangelistic efforts by Reuben Dooley who, like Stone, had recently lost his wife and had boarded his children with members of the church.[2]

Stone enjoyed his evangelistic travels. He desired, however, to have a direct role in the nurture of his daughters. To have such a role required reestablishing a family home, and for Stone this entailed having a wife. Stone's commitment to his children does not rule out other reasons for his marriage on October 31, 1811, to Celia Wilson Bowen. Eight years younger than Elizabeth, Celia was 19; Stone was 39. Celia's mother, Mary Henley Russell, was Elizabeth's mother's sister. Thus, Celia was Elizabeth's cousin.[3]

It is not known how long Stone had known Celia. Her father, William Bowen, a captain of the Virginia militia during the Revolution, had been granted land in Tennessee for his military services. Having married Mary Russell in Virginia around 1777, he had moved with her to Mansker's Creek, twelve miles northeast of Nashville, in 1785 where, four years later, they had erected the first brick house in middle Tennessee. The house had two stories, an ell, and a basement, with nine rooms altogether. Stone had surely noticed the house when he itinerated in middle Tennessee with John Anderson fifteen years earlier, in the fall of 1796, and may well have met the Bowens at that time.[4]

---

[1] Stone, *Biography*, 65–66.
[2] Ibid., 67.
[3] Ibid., 72–75; Ware, 100–104.
[4] Stone, *Biography*, 72–75.

Stone reported that immediately following their wedding in Tennessee, he and Celia moved to his "old habitation in Bourbon county, Kentucky, and lived happily there for one year." At the end of that year, they were induced, according to Stone, "by advice and hard persuasion" to move to Tennessee, near Celia's widowed mother. Mrs. Bowen put them on a good farm, but without a comfortable house. The result, Stone noted, was that much of his time was devoted to building a house as well as to improving the farm. Stone may also have been distracted from his writing by the addition of another two children to the household, William Bowen, born in 1812, and John Henley, born the following year.[5]

Included in *An Address* were sections on the Trinity, the divinity of Jesus Christ, the atonement, the operations of the Spirit, and faith. Stone, of course, had previously published on all but the first two of these topics. The section on the atonement, though essentially affirming the position he had previously argued, also showed that Stone had been influenced by criticism of his views.

Stone, like other Christians, believed that the Old Testament sacrifices were "types," or prophecies, of the death or sacrifice of Jesus Christ. In his 1805 pamphlet, *Atonement: The Substance of Two Letters Written to a Friend,* he had argued that the sacrifices of the Law were not established to affect God, or designed to make satisfaction for sin, as was taught by proponents of the theory of substitutionary atonement. The Mosaic sacrifices, he had proposed, had been instituted to affect the spirit or conscience of the sinner–their demonstrating with a lamb the evil and consequences of sin led the sinner to repentance and reconciliation with God. He had argued that the death of Christ fulfilled the type of sacrifice by demonstrating to sinners the evil and consequences of sin, along with the strength of God's love, thereby leading sinners to repentance and reconciliation with God.[6]

While maintaining his view of the nature and purpose of Christ's sacrifice, Stone had become convinced that his earlier view of the purpose of Mosaic sacrifices could not be supported. In his *Address,* he offered a different view of the function of Mosaic sacrifices and their typological relation to the death or sacrifice of Christ. He developed this view under four headings: "Of Unpardonable Offences," "Of Pardonable Offences," "Of Bearing Iniquity Or Sin," and "Of One Bearing The Iniquity Of Another."

Stone identified unpardonable offenses as transgressions of the law for which no pardon was to be granted. Offenders were to be punished with death. Included in this category were idolatry, blasphemy, Sabbath-breaking, disobedience of children to parents, murder, adultery, and manstealing. By such offenses Israel was defiled. If Israel failed to put to death unpardonable offenders, the "political" union between Israel and God was broken, and Israel would suffer God's judgment and wrath. Only by putting to death

---

[5]Stone, *Biography*, 67–68; Ware, 103.
[6]Stone, *Atonement,* 34.

unpardonable offenders could Israel be cleansed and union with God as Israel's "temporal king" be restored.[7]

He identified pardonable offenses as offenses that were pardonable according to the law. These were sins of ignorance, error, and ceremonial uncleanness. Included in this category was the uncleanness of a woman after childbirth, the uncleanness of a leper, and the uncleanness of a person with a running issue.[8]

He showed that the transgressors of the law, regardless of the category of the offense, were said to "bear iniquity" or to "bear sin." The bearer of sin was to be cut off from the people, either by being put to death or by being excluded from the congregation and from the worship of the sanctuary for a limited time, according to the category of the offense. During the period of separation, the bearer of sin was unclean, and the "external union" between the offender and the people and the God of Israel was broken. In order to be cleansed, the law required the bearer of sin to make a sin offering, by which the priest would make an "atonement" for the bearer of sin with the blood of the sacrificial victim. Having been cleansed, the one who had made a sin offering was restored to the worshiping community.[9]

He noted that the priesthood was said to "bear the iniquity" of the congregation. The meaning of "bearing" in this case, he argued, was to "bear away" iniquity. That is, the function of the priesthood was to purify or sanctify the people and sometimes the sanctuary by prescribed rituals.[10]

He concluded that the effect of the sacrifices of the law was to "purge, cleanse, or sanctify the transgressor, and the unclean." "The consequence of this effect," he continued, "was that atonement or reconciliation took place between God and the purified offender." Stone noted that the whole effect of the sacrifices of the law "passed on man and things, and not on God; for they only were impure, and they only needed purging." God, he observed, was reconciled to the purified offender "without a change in himself."[11]

The difference between Stone's old and new views of Mosaic sacrifice was that according to his new views, Mosaic sacrifices had bearing only on Israel's "temporal" or outward relationship to God, since the law, he was now convinced, promised only temporal or outward blessings. That is, the Mosaic sacrifices, while relating to Israel's relationship to God as their "temporal king" or "political head," had no relation to Israel's spiritual relationship to God. This was a departure from *Atonement: The Substance of Two Letters Written to a Friend*, in which Stone had argued that the purpose of the sacrifices of the law was to bring sinners to spiritual repentance and reconciliation with God. Pointing to Hebrews 10, he stated that the sacrifices of the law "could not take

---

[7]Barton W. Stone, *An Address to the Christian Churches in Kentucky, Tennessee and Ohio, on Several Important Doctrines of Religion*, (Nashville: M. & J. Norvell, 1814), 26–28.

[8]Ibid., 28–31.

[9]Ibid., 31–35.

[10]Ibid., 35–43.

[11]Ibid., 43–45.

away sin—could not purge the conscience—and indeed did not pertain to the conscience; but to the purifying of the flesh." The pardon, granted through sacrifice, he maintained, "was only political, and did not deliver the offender from future judgment, and condemnation before God, the judge of all hearts."[12]

How, then, could an offender in ancient Israel be restored to spiritual union with God? Stone answered that although God, in his relation to Israel as their temporal king or political head, "granted no pardon to presumptuous offenders according to the law; yet as a spiritual Saviour and Redeemer, he did shew mercy and grant pardon to those offenders who repented, believed in, and plead his gracious promise or covenant." "In other words," he continued, "they were justified by faith in the gospel preached to Abraham four hundred and thirty years before the law, and which was continued to be preached to the Israelites; and by which alone, without the deeds of the law, all the children of Abraham, whether Jew or Gentile, have been in every age justified."[13]

If, then, Jews were justified by faith in the promises of God, apart from the sacrifices of the law, how was the sacrifice of Jesus Christ a fulfillment of the type of the Mosaic sacrifices? Stone answered that as with the Mosaic sacrifices, the sacrifice of Jesus Christ was instituted to cleanse sinners, not to change God. He argued that Christ is described in both Old and New Testaments as "bearing our sins," in the same sense that the Mosaic priesthood bore the iniquities of Israel; that is, by "bearing them away." The difference between Mosaic sacrifices, which affected only Israel's political or outward relation to God, and the sacrifice of Jesus was that the sacrifice of Christ was designed to effect humanity's spiritual cleansing and reconciliation with God.[14] How did the sacrifice of Jesus effect humanity's spiritual cleansing and reconciliation with God? Stone answered, "By faith in his blood." What did it mean to have faith in his blood? Stone responded that "we must know the designs of the death of Jesus before we can be rightly affected with it." In other words, humanity was spiritually cleansed and reconciled to God by faith in the God whose purposes in the death of Jesus Christ were revealed in scripture.[15] Stone identified five "designs" of the blood or death of Jesus revealed in the Bible.

First, Jesus' death abolished the law, "which was against us." Stone distinguished between the "moral law of love to God and man" and the "ceremonial laws." Stone did not believe that the obligation to love God and neighbor had been destroyed by Christ's death. However, there was, he stated, "an intimate connexion between his death and the ceremonial laws; for these were types and shadows of Christ." Stone asserted that by his death Christ fulfilled the predictions contained in the rites and ceremonies of the law, thus delivering humanity from its "curse," for where there is no law, there is no

---

[12]Ibid., 26–29.
[13]Ibid., 28.
[14]Ibid., 43–48.
[15]Ibid., 52–53.

transgression, and therefore no curse for violation of the law. Stone identified the "curse" of the law as condemnation to death in those cases for which the Mosaic covenant contained no sacrificial remedy, such as idolatry, blasphemy, Sabbath-breaking, and adultery. Thus, he continued, by fulfilling the types and becoming the substance of the shadows of the ceremonial laws, Christ abolished the condemnation to death required by the law. This, he suggested, was the significance of Jesus' response to the woman brought to him guilty of adultery: "He did not condemn [her] to death according to law; but preached to her mercy and forgiveness."[16]

Second, Jesus' death introduced the "everlasting Gospel with all of its blessings to Jew and Gentile–to all the world." For Stone, the "blessing of Abraham" referred to in chapter 3 of Paul's letter to the Galatians was "the gospel," which Stone believed Paul indicated was "preached" to Abraham four hundred and thirty years before the giving of the law. It was through Israel's faith in this gospel, Stone asserted, that God as spiritual Savior and Redeemer, as distinguished from temporal king, had justified transgressors of the law. By Jesus' death, Stone continued, this gospel was introduced to the Gentiles. Stone noted that the gospels reported that before Jesus' death and resurrection, he forbade his apostles to preach to the Gentiles. However, the gospels taught that after his death and resurrection, he commissioned the apostles to go into all the world and preach the gospel to every creature. Citing Hebrews 9:15 and 17, Stone explained that the beneficiaries of a testament have no right to the testator's estate until the testator has died: Jesus was the testator of a testament bequeathing the gospel to every member of the human family. Thus, by his death, Stone declared, all "have a right to all the blessings of the everlasting gospel."[17]

Third, Jesus' death destroyed death and procured and confirmed our resurrection. Stone read Hosea 13:14 as spoken by the Son before his appearance in the flesh: "I will ransom them from the power of the grave; I will redeem them from death. O death, I will be thy plagues; O grave, I will be thy destruction." Stone suggested that by his death and resurrection Jesus destroyed death, finding confirmation of this view in 2 Timothy 1:10, where Christ is said to have "abolished death and brought life and immortality to light through the gospel."[18]

Fourth, Jesus' death tore down the dark veil between earth and heaven. Drawing on Hebrews, chapters 4, 6, and 9, Stone pointed to the veil of the temple, which separated the "worldly sanctuary" and the "holiest of all" as a figure of the separation between earth and heaven. The worldly sanctuary, he suggested, represented this world, while the holiest of all represented heaven. Only the high priest was permitted to enter the holiest of all, and only with the blood of a victim. Alluding to the gospel accounts of the rending of the veil of the temple that accompanied the death of Christ, Stone stated, "So

---

[16]Ibid., 53–54.
[17]Ibid., 54–55.
[18]Ibid., 55–56.

Jesus our great high priest entered into heaven itself, by his own blood, having torn away the veil, and made the way into the holiest of all, into heaven
itself, manifest." "Before this," he continued, "the people were all their life
time in bondage through fear of death, not so clearly understanding the resurrection and entrance into heaven: but now, seeing Jesus pass through death
and the grave into heaven, they lose their fears, and like St. Stephen, they
look into heaven and rejoice."[19]

Fifth, Jesus' death displayed the love of God to sinners. For Stone, this
was the meaning of Romans 5:8, "But God commendeth his love toward us,
in that, while we were yet sinners, Christ died for us." He suggested that this
was also the meaning of 1 John 3:16: "Hereby perceive we the love of God,
because he laid down his life for us."[20]

Stone did not argue that one "must have a view of all of these designs of
his blood" before one could be a Christian. On the contrary, he argued that in
the death of Christ some may discover only the love of God for sinners and
may by this "be encouraged to trust in him." He illustrated his point by the
example of a father who provides plentifully for a large family of children.
Some of the children know the means by which the father got the provisions,
others may not know so well, while the youngest may scarcely know anything more than that the father's love supplied the provisions. Yet all of the
children eat and thrive, without quarreling about the means by which the
provisions were obtained. "O," he added, "that christians would do likewise!"[21]

While the section of his *Address* on the atonement showed that Stone had
been influenced by criticism of his earlier views, the sections on Trinity and
the divinity of Jesus Christ were his first published statements on these doctrines. Stone declared that it was a "plain doctrine of revelation" that "there is
but one living and true God." He further noted that both the Presbyterian and
Methodist creeds described God as "*an infinite spirit without parts.*" He asserted that no one who maintained the teaching of the scriptures and the
creed of either the Presbyterians or the Methodists would argue that "the
infinite spirit" was a "compound of two or three spirits, beings or Gods." He
acknowledged, however, that the scriptures taught "that 'There are three that
bear record in heaven, the Father, the Word, and the Holy Ghost, and these
three are one.' I John 5:7." He stated that the issue that had long troubled the
church was the question of what was meant by the terms Father, Word, and
Holy Ghost.[22]

He noted that some contended that the Father, Word, and Holy Ghost
were three "persons," while others argued that the Father, Word, and Holy
Ghost were three "distinctions" or three "relations." He argued that "they
who maintain the first proposition, do not–cannot believe that *these three persons,* are three distinct spirits, beings or Gods, each possessed of the personal

[19]Ibid., 56–57.
[20]Ibid., 57–58.
[21]Ibid., 58.
[22]Ibid., 8–9.

properties of intelligence, will and power; for this would contradict those sections of their Creeds…which declare that there is but one only living and true God, without parts." He further stated that "therefore they must understand the term *persons* in Godhead, not in the proper sense of the word person, but in such a qualified sense as to exclude the notion of three distinct spirits or beings." On the other hand, he asserted that "they who maintain that the one God is revealed to us in the three relations of Father, Word and Holy Ghost, do not deny three distinctions in Godhead." Thus, he was inclined to believe that the controversy was "a war of words," as it seemed to him that the combatants believed the same thing. Indicating that he preferred the term *distinction* to the term *person*, he declared that "they, who say *these three* are three persons, understanding the term *person* in such a sense as to exclude the notion of three Gods, just mean what I understand by *the three* distinctions in Godhead." Stating that he had "long wished to see this controversy end forever among christians of every order," he declared that he could not express the three in more appropriate terms than those "used by the inspired Apostle– Father, Word and Holy Ghost."[23]

Stone observed that some "more attached to the unintelligible language of their ancestors than to the simple expressions of scripture" might "retain notions or words contrary" to what he had stated. "They may," he continued, "so darken the doctrine by words without knowledge, as to bewilder and lose themselves, and then resolve it all into mystery; and lampoon and bite their fellow christians for not receiving their own inventions." He expressed his hope that the Christians had not "so learned Christ."[24]

Regarding the divinity of Jesus Christ, Stone argued that the scriptures taught that in Jesus "dwelleth, not a part, but *all* of the *fullness of Godhead* or divinity, bodily." Thus, he commented, "not only the Father dwelleth in Him, but also the Word and the Holy Ghost *without measure.*" For this reason, Stone continued, Jesus is called "the mighty God–the everlasting Father–the great God–the true God–He is even called Jehovah." Stone stated that *how* God could dwell in Christ in all of God's fullness was a "mystery" offered to faith in the scriptures. If asked how God could be seen in Christ, since 1 John 4:12 declared, "No man hath seen God at any time," he would answer that "we see not his being or essence, for that is invisible; but we see his 'glory shining in the face of Jesus.' 2 Cor. 4, 6." Though he did not state that Jesus Christ *was* God, he asserted that no charge could be "more unjust" than the accusation that he denied the divinity of Jesus Christ.[25]

He allowed that the "probable reason" that some had *thought* he denied the divinity of Christ was the way he had spoken of Christ's humanity. He noted that on this subject he would be "a little more particular," since for nearly twenty years his mind had "not wavered" respecting this topic. "That the humanity of Jesus consisted of a reasonable soul and true body," he asserted,

---

[23]Ibid., 9. See also Stone, *Letters to Blythe,* 159.
[24]Stone, *An Address,* 10.
[25]Ibid., 11–12.

"but few, if any deny." He further stated that all agreed that the part of Christ's humanity that is called his body "began to exist about eighteen hundred and thirteen years ago, when conceived and born of the Virgin Mary." The difference between his doctrine and that of other Christians was his belief that the *human* soul of Christ "existed before all worlds in the bosom of the Father, and was united with the body prepared for it eighteen hundred and thirteen years ago." While most Christians believed that both the human soul and human body of Christ had come into existence at the time of the incarnation, Stone noted that his view of the preexistence of the human soul of Christ had been maintained by "many divines of high respectability," including the "illustrious" Isaac Watts of England and the American Presbyterian Henry Pattillo.[26]

Stone further stated that the difference between him and other ministers regarding the humanity of Christ was "*substantially nothing,*" as all maintained "the proper humanity of Jesus Christ." Nevertheless, as it appeared to Stone that many persons had "misunderstood" his teaching, he discussed several texts of scripture that he reported had "induced" him to believe that the soul of Christ had existed "before all worlds in glory." The texts that Stone discussed were texts that most Christians interpreted as referring not to the *human* soul of Christ, but to the second person of the Trinity; that is, to the *divinity* of Christ.[27]

One of those texts was 2 Corinthians 8:9, "For ye know the grace of our Lord Jesus Christ, that though He was rich, yet for your sake He became poor, that ye through His poverty might be rich." Informed by the view that God is "immutable," as expressed in chapter 2, section 1 of the Westminster Confession, Stone asserted that "the person spoken of in the text" could not be God, for God was "unchangeable," and thus could not change from being rich to being poor. Nor, Stone continued, could the text refer to the life of Jesus Christ on earth, for in his earthly life he did not change from rich to poor in either "the goods of this world" or the "fullness and riches of grace." Thus, Stone reasoned that it was the preexistent human soul of Christ, and not the second person of the Trinity as the orthodox taught, who was rich before he came into the world and became poor for our sake.[28]

Stone also referred to John 17:5, "And now, O Father, glorify thou me with thine own self, with the glory which I had with thee before the world was." Stone commented that the person "prays for a glory which he once had, but has not now" and, therefore, "cannot be God, for God is unchangeable." He further noted that "this glory for which he prays he had with the Father before the world was," and therefore, "he must have existed before the world was." Hence, it was evident, he continued, "that a spirit or person, which was not God, existed with the Father before the world was" and that "this person or spirit" was later united with "a body prepared of the Father for him, and

---

[26]Ibid., 13.
[27]Ibid., 13–14.
[28]Ibid., 14–15.

was called Jesus." Stone concluded that this person was the *human* soul of Christ.[29]

Stone argued that the preexistence of the human soul of Christ was further evident from passages of scripture in which the Son was described as the instrument of creation, such as Hebrews 1:2, Ephesians 3:9, 1 Corinthians 8:6, and Colossians 1:15–17. He noted that in Colossians 1:15–17, the one by whom "all things were created" was also identified as "the first born of every creature." Though the orthodox interpreted these texts as referring to the second person in the Trinity, Stone suggested that they referred to the pre-existent *human* soul of Jesus, since the divinity in Christ, affirmed in the Presbyterian Confession to be eternal and therefore uncreated, would not be described as a "creature."[30]

Stone acknowledged that it could be inferred from his view of the preexistence of the human soul of Christ that he denied the teaching of the Presbyterian Confession that Jesus Christ was "eternally begotten of the Father." Operating from his Enlightenment view of propositions that are "contrary" to reason, he declared that "the notion of a being begotten from eternity appears absurd; because the agent begetting must precede the thing begotten." Noting that "we are told by some that it is an evidence of an humble heart to believe it," Stone asked how anyone could believe it, whether "humble or proud." To his mind, the notion was "incomprehensible." Nevertheless, if others received it as an article of their faith, he would not "blame them." Moreover, if the scriptures, and not merely a confession, had declared that Jesus Christ was eternally begotten of the Father, he would "humbly" receive it. "But," he asserted, "as no such declaration is made in the Bible," he could not admit it as an article of his faith.[31]

Stone further acknowledged that it could be inferred from his view of the preexistence of the human soul of Christ that he denied "the equality of the son with the Father." Referring to his earlier *Reply to John P. Campbell,* he stated that he had always thought the notion of the equality of the Son with the Father very obscure, "as equality implies plurality, and one is not equal to itself." "If God be one infinite spirit without parts," he continued, "and if there be but one infinite and true God, then there cannot be another equal to him." This, Stone declared, was "the language of consistent reason"; though if revelation spoke differently, he allowed, "reason must humbly bow." Stating that he had already "proved" the divinity of Christ, he allowed that "if this is what people mean by the equality of the Son with the Father," he was "satisfied with the idea, but not with the expression." "We have," he continued, "an abundance of scripture to establish the divinity of Jesus, without torturing such texts as those by which I have endeavored to prove the pre-existence of his spirit, or soul." Pressing such texts to prove Jesus' divinity, he advised,

---

[29]Ibid., 15.
[30]Ibid., 17–19.
[31]Ibid., 11, 19.

"has greatly darkened the truth, and added many to the number of its enemies."[32]

Finally, Stone observed that "the common prejudice of education may bear hard against some of these sentiments." Some might "make their own notions" the rule by which to judge them. Others who were afraid of thinking incorrectly and "never think for themselves at all" might rely on the "opinions of their party" as the standard of judgment. But the "honest enquirer" would "bring these things to the Bible, and judge according to this rule."[33]

In his *Vindex,* John P. Campbell had stated that he would defer refuting Stone's "Socinian hypothesis" of the equality of the Son with the Father until Stone "or some one of his party" gave a full explanation of their views on the Trinity.[34] As it turned out, Campbell, who was five years older than Stone, died in November 1814, the same year that Stone published his *Address,* as a result of exposure while preaching outdoors.[35] The task of refuting Stone's views of the Trinity and the Divinity of Jesus Christ, along with his revised understanding of the typological significance of the Mosaic sacrifices, was assumed by another Presbyterian minister, Thomas Cleland of Mercer County, Kentucky. In February 1815, Cleland, who was six years Stone's junior, published a one-hundred-page response to Stone's *Address.* Titling his book *The Socini-Arian Detected,* Cleland charged that Stone's views were Socinian and Arian, though "varnished and honeyed over in a manner calculated to deceive the ignorant and mislead the unsettled and wavering."[36]

[32]Ibid., 20–23.
[33]Ibid., 23.
[34]Campbell, *Vindex,* 41.
[35]Ware, 208.
[36]Thomas Cleland, *The Socini-Arian Detected: A Series of Letters to Barton W. Stone, on Some Important subjects of Theological Discussion. Referred to in his "Address" To the Christian Churches in Kentucky, Tennessee, and Ohio* (Lexington, Ky.: Thomas T. Skillman, 1815), 5.

11

Corrected and Enlarged

Stone had not written his last word on the Trinity and the divinity of Jesus Christ. However, he would not publish again on these topics or any others for another seven years, most likely because of another succession of changes in his personal circumstances.

That succession of changes began shortly after the publication of his *Address* in 1814. In his autobiography, he reported that he "labored hard at building a house and improving the farm" in Tennessee until he learned that his mother-in-law did not plan to give him the deed to the farm, but rather to deed it to her daughter and her children. He claimed that he did not blame her for this decision, as the lands of his first wife, by the laws of Kentucky, had become the property of her children at her death. Nevertheless, as soon as he learned of her decision, he decided to return to Kentucky. He reported that Celia approved of his resolve.[1]

Returning to Kentucky turned out to be more difficult than Stone could ever have imagined. He had sold his Bourbon County farm to Charles Wasson in 1812. The final papers on his conveyance of the Bourbon County farm had been executed in Tennessee on March 1, 1814. In the meantime, the building of turnpikes in Kentucky and the beginning of steamboat traffic on the Ohio and the Mississippi, along with the War of 1812, had boosted the price of farm products, significantly increasing the value of farmland in Kentucky. Stone reported that when he tried to purchase a farm in central Kentucky, he discovered that land of the sort that he had sold for $12 per acre could not be acquired for less than $30 per acre.[2]

Unable to purchase a farm in central Kentucky because of the increased price of land, Stone accepted the invitation of "the brethren in Lexington" to settle among them. He reported that they immediately sent a carriage for his family and a wagon for their possessions, rented a house for them in Lexington, and promised to supply their every need. The Lexington brethren, however, did not make good on their promises, and Stone, who had been well received as a teacher in Georgia, was required to open a high school in Lexington to support his family.[3]

---

[1] Stone, *Biography*, 68.
[2] Ware, 200–201.
[3] Stone, *Biography*, 68–69.

While teaching in Lexington, Stone took advantage of the opportunity to study Hebrew with a Prussian doctor whom he described as "a Jew of great learning." The class was composed of ministers, lawyers, and others interested in the study of the language. Stone reported that the doctor "taught by lectures; and in a very short time we understood the language so as with ease to read, and translate by the assistance of a Lexicon."[4]

In 1819 Stone was appointed principal of the Rittenhouse Academy in Georgetown, twelve miles north of Lexington. That fall, he bought a 123-acre farm near Georgetown, where he moved with his family. In addition to fulfilling his duties as principal of the academy during the fall and winter of 1819–1820, he preached in Georgetown, with the result that a Christian Church was constituted in Georgetown and soon grew to more than two hundred members.[5]

Without Stone's knowledge, the Christian churches in central Kentucky met, determined that he should devote all of his time to preaching the gospel, and in order to release him from the academy, agreed to support him and his family and to pay the debt he had incurred in purchasing the farm near Georgetown. The churches had made a substantial promise, since Stone's family had increased to eleven with the births of Mary Russell (also called "Polly") in 1815, Barton Warren in 1817, and Catherine in 1820. Stone agreed to the plan, resigned his charge of the academy, and devoted his full time to evangelizing among the churches. However, the United States had entered a major economic depression in 1819, and when the time came to pay the note on his farm, the promised funds were not forthcoming. Stone had to borrow funds to pay the debt on the farm and was required to open a school in Georgetown to repay the funds he had borrowed, the position at the Rittenhouse Academy having been filled. By this means, he was able to pay his debt. However, his health failed as a result, he believed, of "constant application to study." Consequently, he gave up teaching and, though nearly fifty years of age, "turned to hard labor" on his farm.[6]

In 1821 Stone published a second edition of *An Address*. In the introduction to the second edition, he stated that "being desirous to disseminate truth," he was sending to the Christian Churches a work that was "*corrected* and considerably enlarged."[7] Comparison of the second edition with the first shows that most sections of the book were, in fact, unchanged. Cleland had scoffed at Stone's criticism of the translation of certain texts in the King James Version of the Bible, declaring that Stone had "but a smattering of the Greek, and not even that much itself of the Hebrew." In the section on atonement, Stone added "a few remarks" from the Hebrew, "an imperfect knowledge of which,"

---

[4]Ibid., 69.

[5]Ibid.; Ware 204–5. The dating of Stone's period of service as principal of the Rittenhouse Academy is based on an autobiographical sketch by John Rogers, in W.C. Rogers, *Recollections of Men of Faith*, 173, quoted in Ware, 206.

[6]Stone, *Biography*, 70.

[7]Stone, *An Address to the Christian Churches in Kentucky, Tennessee, and Ohio, on Several Important Doctrines of Religion*, 2d ed., corrected and enlarged (Lexington, Ky.: I. T. Calvins and Co., 1821), iii. Italics mine.

he noted, "I have acquired since I published the first edition of my Address."[8] All of the corrections and most of the enlargements were in the sections dealing with the Trinity and the divinity of Jesus Christ.

In the section on the Trinity, Stone flatly stated that the word *Trinity* did not appear in scripture. He reiterated that Trinitarians "understand the term *persons* in God, not in the proper and common sense of the word *person;* but in such a qualified sense as to exclude the notion of three distinct spirits or beings." "What this qualified sense should be," he added, "has long puzzled divines" because "no idea of it is to be found in revelation, nor reason." Absent from the second edition of his *Address* was his earlier affirmation that there were "three distinctions in Godhead" by which the one God was revealed to humanity. He later wrote that in reconsidering this earlier affirmation he had become convinced that it was nothing other than "unitarianism, unhappily expressed." For Stone, Unitarianism denoted an unwillingness to worship the Son of God.[9]

He argued that attention to the context of 1 John 5:7, "There are three that bear record in heaven, the Father, the Word and the Holy Ghost, and these three are one," disclosed the meaning of the text. To "bear record" was to testify or to witness. "From reading the context," he continued, "it is plain, that the matter testified of, is that Jesus is the Son of God." The Father, he suggested, testified that Jesus was the Son of God at his baptism, the Word or Son testified that he was the Son of God "by the many wonders he performed when incarnate," and the Holy Ghost witnessed that Jesus was the Son of God by "the many miracles wrought thro' the apostles." He proposed that the statement that "these three are one" meant that they "agree in their testimony," since in the next verse the three who testify on earth, the Spirit, the water, and the blood are said to "agree" in their testimony. Stone also observed that this verse was viewed by many scholars as an interpolation, adding that it was "not found in Griesbach's Greek Testament, reckoned to be the most correct." Though he was personally "unwilling" to reject the "divine authority" of 1 John 5:7, he was "confident" that it could not "establish the notion of three persons in one God."[10]

Stone affirmed that "the scriptures speak of the Father, Son and Holy Spirit" and that "these three are *one* in some sense." In his view, this "oneness" was the unity expressed in 1 John 5:7. The Father, Son, and Holy Spirit were one in testifying that Jesus is the Son of God. While referring to the Father and the Son as persons or "beings" in both editions of his address, he had never referred to the Spirit as a being. In 1824 Stone clarified his position on the Spirit. "By the Spirit of God," he wrote, "I understand the Spirit of a person and not the person himself." He noted that "we often read in the Bible, that the Father loves the Son, and that the Son loves the Father; but we

[8]Cleland, *The Socini-Arian Detected,* 62–63; Stone, *An Address,* 2d ed. 49.
[9]Stone, *An Address,* 2d ed., 7; idem, *Letters to Blythe,* 159. For Stone's views on Unitarianism, see *CM* 2 (November 1827), 10–13, and (January 1828), 256.
[10]Stone, *An Address,* 2d ed., 8–9.

never read of either the Father or the Son loving the Spirit as a person, or of the Spirit loving the Father or the Son." He also noted that "we have examples and precepts to love and worship both the Father and the Son; but there is neither example nor precept for worshipping the Spirit in the Bible."[11]

The section on the divinity of Jesus Christ was replaced in the second edition by a section on "The Son of God." As in the first edition, Stone asserted that the Son of God did not begin to exist at the time of the incarnation, nor did he exist from eternity, but was the first begotten of the Father before time or creation began; that in the fullness of time he was sent by the Father into the world, and united with a body, prepared for him; and that "in him dwelt all the fullness of Godhead bodily." But who was this Son of God? In the first edition, Stone had clearly identified the Son of God as the *human* soul of Christ. Moreover, he had referred to him as having been begotten *or* created. In the second edition, Stone did not refer to the soul of Christ as human. Neither did he refer to the Son as having been "created." Rather, he proposed that Jesus was called "the only begotten of the Father, because the Father begat him *of* and *by* himself."[12]

If there was any question as to the significance for Stone of the changes in his references to the soul of Jesus Christ, it was answered by his response to the Presbyterian minister John R. Moreland, who, claiming to have read the second edition of Stone's *Address*, charged him with having taught that the Son was "a created being, a mutable, changeable creature." Stone asserted that the view that Moreland had charged him with teaching was the view of Arius, who had taught that the Son was created out of nothing, while his views were "high above those of Arius." He noted that the teaching of the church fathers, who had condemned Arius, was that "the Son is of the substance of the Father." If the Son was of the substance of the Father, he observed, "he was not a created being, but *derived* his being from the Father." "Against this," he declared, "I have no objection."[13]

Stone stated that his reason for differing from "the orthodox opinions" on the Son of God was that, to his mind, those opinions denied that the Son of God was a real being. He asked, "Did the Father from eternity beget a real, eternal being, or not?" "If the Son was a real, eternal being," he continued, "then there must have been two real, eternal beings, the Father who begat, and the Son who was begotten." Stone was confident that "the advocates for the doctrine...do not–cannot believe that a real, intelligent being was begotten from eternity; nor that a real, eternal, and intelligent being was sent into the world by the Father," as that would imply the existence of *two* real, eternal beings. "What then," he asked, "was begotten from eternity? What was sent by the Father into the world?" "Will it be answered," he asked, "that it was a

[11]Stone, *Letters to Blythe*, 25–29.

[12]Stone, *An Address*, 2d ed., 19–20, 25. Italics mine.

[13]John R. Moreland, *To the Members of the Mount-Pleasant Church* (n.p., 1821), 4; Stone, *A Letter to Mr. John R. Moreland, in Reply to His Pamphlet* (Lexington, Ky.: Office of the Public Advertiser, 1821), 10–11. Stone identified *Buck's Theological Dictionary* as his source on the views of Arius.

personal property–a divine perfection–a glorious effulgence?–that this was the Son of God?–that this was very God?" "To say this," he continued, "is certainly a denial of the Son, as a real, proper person; for no one can suppose that a property–a perfection–or effulgence, is a real intelligent being."[14]

Stone continued: "Let us turn to the cross, and ask, who is he that suffers, bleeds and dies?" Stone noted, on the authority of the Presbyterian Confession, that "all acknowledge that there is but one only *living* and true God; therefore we must conclude that the one that was dead was not the one only living and true God." Stone further stated, on the authority of the Presbyterian Confession, that "all acknowledge the one only living and true God is *without passions;* therefore he that suffered such exquisite passion on the cross, was not the only living and true God." Stone declared that the one who suffered on the cross "must be, according to these opinions, not the Son of God who came from heaven, but a mere man, born of Mary thirty-three years before."[15] This was indeed the position of Stone's Presbyterian opponents, who taught that it was the humanity of Christ, and not his divinity, that suffered and died, noting that according to their Confession the humanity and divinity of Christ were joined together in one person "without conversion, composition or confusion."[16] "How then," Stone asked, "is the love of God commended in his death?" Stone advised: "Let our brethren, who continually say that we deny Christ and the virtue of his blood–let them beware lest they be found, at least in words, doing it themselves."[17]

Stone noted that Socinians believed that the Son of God was a "man" in whom "dwelt all the fullness of Godhead bodily." As he saw it, the Socinians held the same view as the orthodox, "which is that the Son of God had no proper or real existence till born of the Virgin Mary." "Thus," he added, "Trinitarians and Socinians, though always contending, are in my view, the same on this doctrine."[18]

Though clearly Stone delighted in suggesting that the orthodox, rather than himself, were the real Socinians, the question of how Jesus Christ could be both God and a person sent from heaven appears to have been at the heart of Stone's struggle with the doctrine of the Trinity from the start. In his autobiography, he reported that as a student he had become so confused by Witsius' teaching that it was idolatry to worship more Gods than one, and yet equal

---

[14]Stone, *An Address*, 2d ed., 14–15. In his *Letter to John R. Moreland*, Stone asserted that he esteemed Jesus Christ "in a far more exalted sense" than did Moreland and other Trinitarians who, in his view, denied the proper person of Jesus Christ. Referring to a sermon in which a colleague of Moreland's had defined the three persons in Godhead as three "subsistences or modes," Stone exclaimed, "Now, sir, while you so unblushingly affirm that I deny the divinity of Christ, tremble at the idea of your denying his real existence, and frittering him down to a mere *mode.*" See *A Letter to John R. Moreland*, 4–6.

[15]Stone, *An Address*, 2d ed., 16. See Confession of Faith, chap. 2, sec. 1.

[16]John R. Moreland, *To the Members of Mount-Pleasant Church*, 4. See Confession of Faith, chap. 8, sec. 2. See also Cleland, *Letters to Stone*, 38, 64 and Cleland, *Unitarianism Unmasked*, 83, 105, 177.

[17]Stone, *An Address*, 2d ed., 16–17.

[18]Ibid., 18–19.

worship must be given to the Father, the Son, and the Holy Ghost, that he had not known how to pray. To approach his "God, and Savior" in prayer had been the joy of his new Christian life, and it was this exercise that had been "checked" by his efforts to make sense of the orthodox treatment of the doctrine. Watts's view of the Son of God as a human soul formed by God and united to the divine nature long before his human body was born of Mary had restored to Stone a "God, and Savior" to whom he could go in prayer. "Our brethren," Stone asserted, "worship the Son as the only true God; we worship the same only true God in and through the Son." "Our brethren," he continued, "do not believe that the Son is another eternal, distinct God from the Father; nor do we." He further stated that he felt free "to give praise and thanksgiving to Jesus for what he has done and suffered for me–to love Him for His perfections and goodness–to ask Him for the grace that is treasured in Him for sinners," but that the same Jesus had taught him that "the origin and foundation of all these things, is God." "Till it can be proved," Stone declared, "that God and the Lamb are one being, I will imitate heaven in worshipping the Lamb, without fear of being guilty of idolatry."[19]

In 1822 Thomas Cleland published a 172-page review of the second edition of Stone's *Address*, titled *Letters to Barton W. Stone Containing a Vindication Principally of the Doctrines of the Trinity, the Divinity and Atonement of the Saviour, Against His Recent Attack in a Second Edition of His "Address."* Having found the style of both *The Socini-Arian Detected* and Cleland's *Letters* abusive, Stone responded to Cleland's *Letters* in 1824 with a book titled *Letters to James Blythe, D.D. Designed as a Reply to the Arguments of Thomas Cleland, D.D.* Blythe, along with Robert Marshall, had been one of the members of the presbytery to whom Stone had confided his difficulties with the Presbyterian confession on the day of his ordination in October 1798. In the introduction to his reply to Cleland's arguments, Stone informed Blythe that he had written to him, rather than Cleland, because Blythe's "long experience and acquaintance with mankind" had, it was hoped, "checked and restrained" the "fire of youth" in him from "bursting forth into passionate effusions of invective against a fellow creature, for honestly thinking and speaking differently from you."[20] Cleland responded to Stone's *Letters to Blythe* in 1825 with *Unitarianism Unmasked: Its Anti-Christian Features Displayed: And its Foundation Shewn to be Untenable; in a Reply to Mr. Barton W. Stone's Letters to the Rev. Dr. Blythe.*

For Stone, doctrinal disputes ultimately related to the terms of Christian fellowship. In the introduction to both editions of his *Address*, Stone wrote, "Believing mankind to be fallible creatures, we therefore feel a spirit of toleration, and union for all those christians, who maintain the divinity of the Bible, and walk humbly in all the commandments and ordinances of the Lord Jesus Christ, and who live by faith in his name, though they may hold opinions contrary to ours." He further stated, "We wish others to exercise the same

---

[19]Stone, *Biography*, 13; Stone, *An Address*, 2d ed., 31.
[20]Stone, *Letters to Blythe*, 4.

spirit towards us, that we might be mutually edified–that the interests of our Redeemer's kingdom might be advanced–and that foul blot on christianity, *the division of christians*, might be wiped away, and thus a powerful weapon against revelation be wrested from the hand of infidelity."[21] Noting in both editions of his *Address* that he would not "blame" someone for receiving the doctrine that the Son is eternally begotten of the Father, he added: "But to make it a term of christian fellowship I think unwarrantable from the word of God."[22]

Stone's concern for the terms of Christian fellowship was also evident in his *Letters to Blythe*. Of the eleven letters, one was devoted entirely to discrediting Cleland's casual remark that the "ancient fathers" had believed the doctrine of Trinity as "Trinitarians now do." Relying on Unitarian collections of writings of the fathers, Stone argued that many of the fathers, up to and including the Nicene fathers, did not suppose that the nature or essence of the persons in trinity was the same *individual* substance, as did Cleland, but merely a "specific" nature common to the persons in trinity, as human nature is common to all human beings. He also argued that the Nicene Council of 325, which opposed Arius' view that the Son was *created* out of nothing, represented God not as three persons, as did Cleland, but as *one person only* and the Son as begotten or *derived* from God. Stone noted that it was not until the Council of Constantinople in 381 that the doctrine of *three persons in one God* received its full and classic expression.[23] Stone also quoted extensively from Trinitarian Moses Stuart's *Letters to Doctor Miller* to show that in the first three centuries the great body of Christian fathers believed that the Son of God was begotten at a period not long before the creation of the world and, hence, did not believe, as did Cleland and most Trinitarians, that the Son was *eternally* begotten.[24] Stone advised Blythe that he would leave it to him to decide whether the fathers had believed as did modern Trinitarians.[25]

For Stone, the terms of Christian fellowship could not be stated once and for all. The Bible was the only standard for determining the terms of Christian fellowship, and there was still "light to break forth" from the Bible. In the introduction to the second edition of his *Address* he declared, "We do not believe that all the seals of the Book are yet opened; therefore we wish not to bind our own hands, nor the hands of our brethren with the fatal cords of authoritative creeds and confessions of men."[26]

---

[21]Stone, *An Address*, 6–7. See also 2d ed., 4.

[22]Stone, *An Address*, 10–11. See also 2d ed., 12.

[23]Stone, *Letters to Blythe*, 30–32, 39–46. For the documents of the Arian controversy, along with a helpful introduction, see *The Trinitarian Controversy*, trans. and ed. William G. Rusch, Sources of Early Christian Thought (Philadelphia: Fortress Press, 1980).

[24]Stone, *Letters to Blythe*, 32–38.

[25]Ibid., 46. In later years, Stone frequently mentioned that his views were in complete accord with the ruling of the Nicene Council. See Barton W. Stone, ed., *CM* 2 (December 1827), 30; 7 (May, 1833), 138; 12 (November 1842), 12–13.

[26]Stone, *An Address*, 2d ed., 5.

Stone's two editions of his *Address* and his *Letters to Blythe* did little to improve relations between Christians and Presbyterians, and they may have injured relations between Christians and Methodists. In 1821 the Methodist William Thompson published a comparison of the doctrines of the Christians and the Methodists, in order to advise Methodists of the differences in the teaching of the two groups. "From their common preaching," Thompson allowed, there had appeared "but little difference" between the doctrines of the two communions.[27] Though at least a handful of Methodist preachers adopted Stone's views of atonement and the Son of God, the majority of Methodists maintained the views of the Methodist Confession and remained wary, well into the 1820s, of communion with the Christians. In contrast, Stone's views of atonement and the Son of God, or at least his view of the terms of Christian fellowship, proved quite attractive to certain Baptists. Stone's achievements in Christian union would be with Baptists.

[27]William J. Thompson, *A Sketch of the Differences between the People Commonly Called Newlights and the Methodists* (Cincinnati: James A. Mason, 1821), 3.

PART 4

Union and
Growth

12

The Bible Alone

Within two decades of the return of Marshall and Thompson to the Presbyterians in 1811, the Christian Church in the West numbered more than sixteen thousand members in Kentucky, Tennessee, Alabama, Ohio, and Indiana. Many had joined the Christian Church through profession of faith and baptism. Others had been identified with the Christian Church movement associated with former Methodists Rice Haggard and James O'Kelley in Virginia and North Carolina. A sizable number, however, had been added when Baptist congregations, and sometimes whole associations of Baptist congregations, had united with the Christians in response to their call to Christian union on the Bible alone.[1]

The lineage of most of these congregations and associations was Separate Baptist. The Separate Baptists had emerged out of the Great Awakening in New England. Known as *Separates* because of their separation from anti-Awakening Congregational Churches, the term *Baptist* was added to distinguish those Separates who adopted believers' baptism. Starting with one congregation in North Carolina, the Separate Baptists had grown dramatically in North Carolina and Virginia in the latter half of the eighteenth century. In the course of westward migration, Separate Baptist congregations were established in Kentucky, Tennessee, and Ohio. Although initially the Separates had no confession of faith other than the Bible, there had been unions of Separate Baptists with Regular Baptists in 1787 and 1801, which had entailed upon Separate Baptists the Philadelphia Confession of the more Calvinist Regular Baptists.[2]

An early accession of Separate Baptist churches to the Christian Church were the "Mulkey" churches, located on both sides of the Kentucky-Tennessee border, on the eastern edge of the Barrens near Tompkinsville, Kentucky. In 1809 John Mulkey, who was serving the Mill Creek Baptist Church, renounced the doctrine of predestination. Cited for heresy by the Mill Creek Church, Mulkey organized a church "on the Bible alone" from former members of the Mill Creek congregation. He was joined by his brother and fellow preacher,

---

[1]J. W. Roberts and R. L. Roberts, Jr., "Like Fire in Dry Stubble–The Stone Movement 1804–1832," *Restoration Quarterly* 7/3 (1963), 148–54; 8/1 (1965), 32–35.

[2]William L. Lumpkin, *Baptist Foundations in the South: Tracing Through the Separates the Influence of the Great Awakening, 1754–1787* (Nashville: Broadman Press, 1961).

Philip Mulkey. Approximately one half of the membership and churches of the Stockton's Valley Baptist Association chose to follow the Mulkeys. In 1810 the O'Kelleyite Christian preacher Joseph Thomas visited the Mulkey churches. In his journal, he noted that Reuben Dooley "met" him at a two-day meeting at John Mulkey's Mill Creek Church. Not long after this meeting, John Mulkey united with the Christians, later making at least one visit to the Christians in central Kentucky.[3] As a result of additional unions, nearly a sixth of the Kentucky Baptist churches of Separate lineage had become Christian Churches by 1827.[4]

Stone described the process of uniting the Christians and an association of Separate Baptists in Meigs County, Ohio. Stone, joined by Reuben Dooley, had gone to Meigs County to fulfill a preaching appointment and to baptize a former Presbyterian preacher by the name of William Caldwell. The Separate Baptists were conducting the annual meeting of their association at the same time, and the two parties agreed to worship together. Stone noted that early in the meeting he baptized Caldwell in the Ohio River, which "drew the cords of friendship more closely between us and the Baptists." The association met daily to conduct its business in a house near the preaching stand, while worship was conducted from the stand. Stone was invited to join the deliberations of the association and was frequently requested to give his opinion. In response to one particularly difficult case, he suggested that they had no right to become involved, as it was "a party measure." He reported that he exerted himself "with meekness against sectarianism, formularies, and creeds, and labored to establish the scriptural union of Christians, and their scriptural name." He noted that he further advised them that "till Christians were united in spirit on the Bible...there would be no end to such difficult cases as now agitated them." Having completed his speech, he retired to the worshiping ground. The association considered what he had said, agreed to "take the Bible alone for their rule of faith and practice—to throw away their name Baptist, and take the name Christian," and thus to "become one" with the Christians "in the great work of Christian union." The members of the "former" association then "marched up in a band to the stand, shouting the praise of God, and proclaiming aloud what they had done." Stone reported, "We met them, and embraced each other with Christian love, by which the union was cemented."[5]

In 1826 Stone began the publication of a monthly journal, *The Christian Messenger*. He was fifty-three years old in a century when the average American life expectancy was less than fifty years. Two years earlier a tenth child had been added to his and Celia's family with the birth of Samuel Matthew. The marriage date of Stone's oldest child, Amanda Warren, to Captain Samuel Adams Bowen is not known. His second oldest, Tabitha Russell, did not marry

[3]Roberts and Roberts, 154–55.
[4]See Frank M. Masters, *A History of the Baptists in Kentucky* (Louisville: Kentucky Baptist Historical Society, 1953), 171–72.
[5]Stone, *Biography*, 71–72.

until 1828. Stone's health had been restored after he had given up teaching and turned to farming to support his family, which now numbered at least nine children still at home. By publishing the *Messenger*, he was able to increase his influence among the Christian Churches without traveling as extensively as he had at earlier periods in his ministry.

In the first issue of the *Messenger*, Stone called for Christian union in an essay titled "Of the Family of God on Earth." Under the heading of "The character of this family," he argued that each member of the family had trusted in Christ for their present and eternal interests. He added that this implied that they were "convinced of their own ignorance and weakness—of their own inability to save themselves" and also that the "revealed truth of God in the scriptures" had led them to believe that Christ is "able and willing to save them, wise to guard and guide them, benevolent and merciful to receive and bless them." He stated further that they who had believed and trusted in Christ had received "the spirit of promise." Other terms for this spirit of promise were "the spirit of God—the spirit of Christ, or Christ dwelling in us." He defined this spirit as "the spirit of holiness, which, when received, hungers and thirsts for righteousness, pants for God and a perfect conformity to his lovely character." He defined it also as the "spirit of adoption, *whereby we cry Abba, Father.*" He asserted that every person who has this spirit, "whether bond or free, black or white, rich or poor, prince or slave, is a child of God, the favorite of heaven." He asked, shall anyone who has "believed in the Lord Jesus, and trusted in him, and is sealed with the Holy Spirit of promise, be denounced, because he has not received a party name and mark? because he cannot receive the creed and dogmas of human invention? or because he cannot pronounce the Shibboleth of reputed *orthodoxy*?"[6]

Stone declared that the privileges of the family of God were "high, above all comparison." Pointing to Romans 8:17, he noted that members of the family were acknowledged by God "as *his children; and if children, then heirs, heirs of God, and joint-heirs with Christ.*" Referring to 1 Corinthians 3:22, he advised that "*all things are theirs, whether Paul or Apollos, or Cephas, or the world, or life or death, or things present or things to come; all are theirs; and they are Christ's and Christ is God's.*" Stone asked, "Who then can dare to debar any of God's children from the enjoyment of what God has provided?" He suggested that it would be as if an earthly father threw a feast for his children and some of them said to others of his children that they were not welcome. "What," he asked, "must be the feelings of the wounded father?"[7]

The rules of the family, Stone asserted, were not to be invented by the various sects or denominations, but to be received, and they were none other than the New Testament. "Will any plead," Stone asked, "that God has given uninspired men authority to make and give rules for the regulation of his family?" "If he has," he continued, "to whom is the authority given?" Echoing Purviance's *Observations on Church Government*, Stone promised that the New

[6]Stone, *CM* 1 (November 1826), 5–7.
[7]Ibid., 8–9.

Testament "will promote union, peace and love in the whole family, if they obey it."[8]

As for the name, Stone argued that it was "evident that the name given by divine authority to this family, is Christian." Calling on biblical authorities Doddridge, Benson, and Clark, Stone declared that this was clearly the meaning of Acts 11:26, which he proposed, following Doddridge, should be translated, "And the Disciples were by divine appointment first named Christians at Antioch." He noted that this was also the view of Samuel Davies. "Who," Stone asked, "will deny the name given by divine appointment, and assume another?"[9]

In conclusion, he noted that it was frequently asked, "Why so much zeal in the present day, against authoritative creeds, party names, and party spirits?" He answered: "Because I am assured, they stand in the way of Christian union, and are contrary to the will of God." He noted that it was further asked, "Why so zealous for Christian union?" He answered: "Because I firmly believe that Jesus fervently prayed to his Father, that believers might all be one—that the world might believe in him as sent by the Father." Stone suggested that the "obedient believers" in every party "who are persuaded that division is an evil, and that union is the will of God and their duty" should not expect God to "work miracles" to effect union, but should simply act upon their convictions: "Let them all agree *to walk by the same rule,* the New Testament." He continued, "Again: Let the believers in each party adopt the name *Christian,* as that given by divine appointment, and let them give up the party name, by which they have been distinguished from others."[10]

In the fourth issue of *The Christian Messenger,* Stone began a "History of the Christian Church in the West." The inclusion of the words "in the West" in the title of the series recognized that there were also Christian Churches in Virginia and North Carolina that had been led by former Methodists Rice Haggard and James O'Kelley and in New England that were associated with the former Baptists Abner Smith and Elias Jones. Stone was confident that his churches were part of a larger movement. The series continued through nine issues, running from February through October 1827.[11]

Stone began his account of the Christian Church in the West with a report of prayers for revival at the beginning of the century, which, he declared, God had answered by pouring out his spirit "in a way almost miraculous" in Tennessee and Kentucky. The final event in his *History* was the return of Marshall and Thompson to the Presbyterians in 1811. For Stone, the response of the Christians to Marshall and Thompson's proposal of a formulary had established their identity as a Christian unity movement. He reported that since the departure of Marshall and Thompson, they had "lived in peace and

---

[8]Stone, *CM* 1 (November 1826), 10–11.
[9]Stone, *CM* 1 (November 1826), 12–15.
[10]Ibid., 15–16.
[11]The phrase "in the West" in the title of the series first appeared in the third installment. The series was reprinted as *History of the Christian Church in the West* (Lexington, Ky.: The College of the Bible, 1956). It also appears in the *Cane Ridge Reader.*

harmony" among themselves and that their number had swelled from a handful to several thousand, with several churches doubling their numbers "every year for some time past." Noting that "we are yet warmly opposed and spoken against every where," he declared, "we trust in the living God, and labor to be accepted of him *not doubting but that on the ground we now occupy, the whole church of God on earth will ultimately settle.*"[12]

As if to confirm Stone's confidence in the coming union of the church on the Bible alone, a correspondent to the *Christian Messenger*, writing on July 25, 1828, reported a union of former Baptist churches and "six or eight Elders" at a conference in Bartholomew County, Indiana. As with the union of the Mulkey churches more than a decade before, the Baptist group had previously determined to be ruled by the Bible alone. Stone's correspondent, the Christian preacher Joseph Hatchitt, wrote, "When we met in conference together, we could find nothing to separate us asunder." Hatchitt continued, "In fine, we saw as nearly eye to eye as any company of Elders who have assembled in modern times—and then there was such a sweet spirit of love." Stating that he would never forget the meeting, he added that "we were almost as cautious of wounding one another's feelings as if we had been in our Father's own country." The minutes of the conference, published in the *Christian Messenger*, made no mention of a union, but simply listed the former Baptist elders among elders present and reported their assignments along with those of other elders, including participation in the ordination of a candidate approved by the conference for ordination.[13]

Meanwhile, a movement had emerged among Baptists in Virginia, Pennsylvania, Ohio, and Kentucky known as "Reformers" or "New Testament Baptists," which, though distinctive in some respects, had much in common with Stone's Christians. The leader of the Reformers or New Testament Baptists was Alexander Campbell (1788–1866). Alexander's father, Thomas Campbell, had been a minister of the Anti-Burgher Seceder Presbyterian Church in Northern Ireland. Coming to the United States in 1807, Thomas Campbell affiliated with the Anti-Burgher Associate Synod of North America, which assigned him to the Chartiers Presbytery, west of Pittsburgh. Conflict stemming from Thomas Campbell's having served communion to Presbyterians not affiliated with the Associate Synod soon led to his separation from the Associate Synod. Nevertheless, he continued to preach in the area around Washington, Pennsylvania. In the summer of 1809, two years after the Christians had begun baptizing believers by immersion, he organized the Christian Association of Washington to support the preaching of the gospel without regard to human creeds and confessions.[14]

---

[12]Stone, *History*, 49. Italics mine.

[13]Stone, *CM* 2 (September 1828), 259–60. For a full discussion of this meeting and the parties involved, see Henry K. Shaw, *Hoosier Disciples: A Comprehensive History of the Christian Churches (Disciples of Christ) in Indiana* (St. Louis: Bethany Press for the Association of Christian Churches in Indiana, 1966), 45–51, 76–82.

[14]William E. Tucker and Lester G. McAllister, *Journey in Faith: A History of the Christian Church (Disciples of Christ)* (St. Louis: Bethany Press, 1975), 96–114.

In 1811 the Christian Association constituted itself as a church and built a meetinghouse in the valley of Brush Run, two miles above the junction of that stream with Buffalo Creek, near the Virginia (now West Virginia) border. Thomas Campbell, a graduate of the Anti-Burgher seminary at Whitburn, Scotland, was elected elder, and Alexander, who was preparing for the ministry under the instruction of his father, was licensed to preach. In 1812 Alexander Campbell was ordained by the Brush Run Church. Later that year, the Brush Run Church adopted believers' immersion as baptism, following the lead of the younger Campbell.[15]

The adoption of believers' immersion by the Brush Run Church led to closer ties with local Baptists. In 1815 the Brush Run Church was admitted to the Redstone Baptist Association. There were a number of differences, however, between the Brush Run Church and most Baptists churches. The "reformers," as they were soon called, practiced weekly observance of the Lord's supper, as advocated by the Scottish Independents, and they baptized believers on a simple confession that Jesus is the Christ, the Son of the Living God (Mt. 16:16), rather than an account of the believer's conversion. Moreover, in affiliating with the Redstone Association, they not only refused to subscribe to the Baptist Philadelphia Confession of Faith, but also expressly reserved the right to preach whatever they "learned from the Holy Scriptures, regardless of any creed or formula in Christendom."[16]

In June 1820, at the urging of Baptist minister John Birch, Alexander Campbell accepted a challenge that Seceder Presbyterian minister John Walker had issued to Birch or any Baptist preacher in good standing whom Birch might choose to debate the "subject" and "means" of baptism. The debate, held over two days, took place at Mount Pleasant, Ohio, twenty-three miles from the farm that Alexander Campbell's father-in-law had deeded to him in Brooke County, Virginia (now West Virginia). Upon returning to his farm, Campbell and his father edited and published the debate as taken from Alexander's notes. The sale of the first edition of one thousand copies, quickly followed by the printing of a second edition of three thousand copies, convinced the Campbells of the possibilities for extending their influence through publication. In October 1823, Campbell debated the Presbyterian W. L. Maccalla for eight days at Washington, just south of Maysville, Kentucky on the subject and means of baptism. Though the debate was to have been conducted in a church, crowds were so large that some sessions were moved to a grove where the Methodists had just completed a camp meeting. Campbell published the Maccalla debate the following spring.[17]

In response to invitations from Baptist ministers who attended the Maccalla debate, Campbell made a two-month preaching tour of Kentucky in the fall

---

[15]Tucker and McAllister, 117–19.

[16]"Minutes of the Redstone Baptist Association" (Pittsburgh: S. Engles, 1815), 5, quoted in Tucker and McAllister, 120.

[17]Tucker and McAllister, 123–25, 127; Robert Richardson, *Memoirs of Alexander Campbell*, 2 vols. (Philadelphia: J. P. Lippincott, 1868, 1870), 2: 71–73.

of 1824, the same year that Stone published his *Letters to Blythe.* Campbell's itinerary included Lexington, Versailles, Louisville, and smaller communities and rural churches in between. Stone noted that when Campbell came to Kentucky he "heard him often in public and in private" and that he was "pleased with his manner and matter." At Stone's invitation, issued to Campbell while he was at Paris, Kentucky, Campbell spoke at the Christian Church in Georgetown and lodged in Stone's home.[18]

Two months prior to the Maccalla debate, Campbell had published the first issue of an eighteen-page monthly journal that he called the *Christian Baptist.* At an informal gathering of Baptist ministers in the home where Campbell was staying during the Maccalla debate, he had distributed copies of the first issues, helping to create interest in the journal in Kentucky. Through the *Christian Baptist,* Campbell called for a "restoration of the ancient order of things," while attacking the clergy, confessions of faith, church judicatories, and "modern missionary schemes," often with biting sarcasm.[19]

Campbell argued that the ancient faith was not the metaphysical dogmas of the creeds, but the gospel or good news of what God had *done* through Jesus Christ, as testified by the apostles. To be a Christian, he asserted, was to believe that Jesus was the Messiah, upon the testimony of the apostles, and to be baptized, in accord with apostolic practice, into the name of the Father, and of the Son, and of the Holy Spirit. He declared that confession that Jesus was the Christ, followed by baptism, was *all* that was necessary for the union of Christians.[20] He further stated that only when the church was united through faith in the gospel, or "testimony of the apostles," would the world believe that Jesus was the Christ. Hence, he argued the futility of missionary "schemes" prior to the restoration of the unity of the church.[21]

Campbell maintained that all attempts to found the unity of the church upon the adoption of a "human" creed were "incompatible with the nature and circumstances of mankind." "Human creeds," he argued, "are composed of the inferences of the human understanding speculating upon the revelation of God." Inferences drawn by human understanding, he asserted, partake of all the "defects" of human understanding. For this reason, he continued, we "often observe two men sincerely exercising their mental powers, upon the same words of inspiration, drawing inferences or conclusions, not only diverse but flatly contradictory." This, he suggested, was the result of many factors: "the prejudices of education, habits of thinking, modes of reasoning, different degrees of information, the influences of a variety of passions and interests, and above all, the different degrees of strength of human intellect."

[18]Stone, *Biography,* 75; *CM* 4 (December 1829), 7. For a recent account of the development of Campbell's influence in Kentucky, see Richard L. Harrison, Jr., *From Camp Meeting to Church: A History of the Christian Church (Disciples of Christ) in Kentucky* (St. Louis: Published for the Christian Church (Disciples of Christ) in Kentucky by the Christian Board of Publication, 1992), 41–48.
[19]Richardson, 2: 88–89.
[20]*Christian Baptist* 1 (April 1824), 220–23; 3 (April 1826), 204–5; 3 (May 1826), 225–31; 4 (September 1826), 34–37.
[21]*CB* 2 (March 1825), 183–84.

He noted that "the persons themselves are very often unconscious of the operation of all these circumstances, and are, therefore, honestly and sincerely zealous in believing and in maintaining the truth of their respective conclusions." Therefore, unity, he observed, would never be established on the basis of human speculations.[22]

He further stated that attempts to establish the unity of the church on a human creed were contrary to "the prayer and plan of the Lord Messiah." The prayer and plan of the Messiah to which he referred was Jesus' prayer in John 17:20–21, which he read as: "I do not pray for these only (for the unity and success of the apostles) but for those also who shall believe on me through, or by means of their word–that they all may be one,–that the world may believe that you have sent me." "Who does not see in this petition," he asked, "that the words or testimony of the apostles, the unity of the disciples, and the conviction of the world are bound together." "The words of the apostles," he continued, "are laid as the basis" of the unity of the disciples, which is requested as "the only successful means of converting the world to the acknowledgment, that Jesus of Nazareth is the Messiah or the Son of the Blessed, the only Saviour of men." Thus, he maintained, to attempt to found the unity of church "upon any creed, other than the apostles' testimony" was not merely doomed to failure, but was to oppose the Messiah's method of uniting the church and converting the world.[23]

Campbell's "ancient order" included weekly observance of the Lord's supper, weekly contributions for the poor, a ministry of bishops (Campbell's preferred term for local church pastors) who would teach and shepherd congregations (as distinguished from clergy who simply delivered sermons), and a ministry of deacons or servants who would attend to the temporal needs of the congregation, the bishops, and the poor (as distinguished from officers who merely carried a "plate" so many times a year).[24] Campbell also called for a return to "pure speech." He defined pure speech as the language of the Bible, as distinguished from what he called the "dialect" or "phraseology of Ashdod," a typological reference to the language of the children of the Jews who had married the women of Ashdod in the time of Nehemiah (Neh. 13:24). Campbell included as examples of the "modern" language of Ashdod: "Trinity," "First, second, and third person in the adorable Trinity," "God the Son," "God the Holy Ghost," "The divinity of Jesus Christ," "the humanity of Jesus Christ," "the incarnation of Jesus Christ," "Original sin," "Spiritual death," "Covenant of works," "Total depravity," "General and particular atonement," and "Moral, ceremonial, and judicial law." Such language, Campbell asserted, interfered with understanding the scriptures and divided Christians.[25]

---

[22]Ibid., 179–80.

[23]Ibid., 181–82.

[24]See Campbell's series on "A Restoration of the Ancient Order of Things" in *CB*, especially 3 (August 1825), 11–15; (September 1825), 30–36; (October 1825), 55–59; (November 1825), 83–86; (January 1826), 136–40; (April 1826), 208–15; (June 1826), 241–45; 4 (August 1826), 5–8; (May 1827), 234–36.

[25]*CB* 2 (June 1825), 256–59; 4 (March 1827), 169–75.

A division of Kentucky Baptists was foreshadowed in 1825, when a Baptist church in Louisville rejected the Baptist Philadelphia Confession of Faith and took the Bible alone as its guide for faith and practice, becoming the first church in Kentucky to formally identify with Campbell's reformation. Vigorous opposition to Campbell's reforms soon emerged among the leadership of Kentucky Baptists. In the spring of 1826 Baptist Spencer Clack of Bloomfield, Kentucky, charged Campbell in the pages of the *Christian Baptist* with setting up his own creed in his series on "A Restoration of the Ancient Order of Things," while attacking confessions of faith. Within a year, Campbell's opponents were using their own magazine, the *Baptist Recorder*, to oppose Campbell's reforms, and associations had begun suspending preachers who advocated Campbell's views.[26]

Stone addressed Campbell in a July 1827 article titled "To The Christian Baptist." He professed high respect for Campbell's talents and learning and "general" approval of the course that Campbell had followed. "Your religious views, in many points," he noted, "accord with our own–and to one point we have hoped we both were directing our efforts, which point is to unite the flock of Christ." He continued, "We have seen you, with the arm of a Samson, and the courage of a David, tearing away the long established foundations of partyism." He observed that it was "not as unconcerned spectators" that the Christians had followed "the mighty war" between Campbell and his opposers–a war in which he asserted that many of the Christians had been engaged for many years before Campbell "entered the field."[27]

Stone had not written, however, to praise Campbell, to encourage him in the good fight, or to sympathize with him as one well acquainted with religious controversy. Claiming to have learned from Campbell "more fully the evil of speculating on religion," Stone expressed surprise and sorrow to have discovered that Campbell had "speculated and theorised on *the most important point in theology*," and in a manner "more mysterious and metaphysical" than his predecessors. Stone was referring to an article on the Trinity in the May issue of the *Christian Baptist.*[28]

Campbell had stated that he objected to the Calvinist or orthodox doctrine of the Trinity for the same reason that the Calvinists objected to the views of the Arians–that, in his judgment, the Calvinist views derogated "the eternal glory of the Founder of the christian religion." To call the Founder of the Christian religion an "Eternal Son," he suggested, was to give him "very little, if any more glory" than the Arians gave him. The fundamental problem, he argued, was an error common to both Calvinists and Arians, the error of assuming that the terms "Christ," "Messiah," "Only Begotten Son," and "Son of God" expressed a relation existing before the Christian era. He asserted that there was "no Messiah, no Christ, no Son of God, no Only Begotten, before the reign of Augustus Cesar."[29]

---

[26]Harrison, 43–45.

[27]*CM* 1 (July 1827), 204.

[28]Ibid. Italics mine.

[29]Ibid., 231–32.

The relation that existed before the Christian era, he suggested, was not that of a son and a father, terms that he declared "always imply disparity," but that which was expressed in John 1:1: "In the beginning was the Word, and the Word was with God, and the Word was God." He declared, "As a word is an exact image of an idea, so is 'The Word' an exact image of the invisible God." He continued, "As a word cannot exist without an idea, nor an idea without a word, so God never was without 'The Word,' nor 'The Word' without God." He further opined that "as an idea does not create its word, nor a word its idea; so God did not create 'The Word,' nor the 'Word' God." He declared, "As God was always with 'The Word,' so when 'The Word' becomes flesh, he is Emanuel, God with us." He proposed, "As God was never manifest but by 'The Word,' so the heavens and the earth, and all things were created by 'The Word'." And, finally, Campbell asserted, "as 'The Word' ever was the effulgence or representation of the invisible God," so he would always be known and adored as "The Word of God."[30]

Campbell suggested that the Calvinist view of the Savior, with its concept of the "eternal" generation of the Son, could be described as on "a mountain." By comparison, the Arian view of the Savior as an exalted being was "on a hill," while the Socinian view of the Savior as a mere man could be seen "moving upon a hillock." He maintained that his view of the meaning of John 1:1 was so high above those views that from its "lofty eminence," the Calvinist, Arian, and Socinian views lost their "disproportion to each other." He also declared that he would not "dispute or contend" for his views "as a theory or speculation" with anyone and that he would not have been willing even to publish his views, so much was he opposed to being understood as introducing a new theory on the subject, were it not for "a few prating bodies" who were always striving to destroy his influence by charging him with "Unitarianism, or Socinianism, or some other obnoxious *ism*."[31]

Stone agreed that Campbell had assumed "very high grounds"; so high, he warned, that one should fear to venture there, lest "giddiness should be the consequence." He advised Campbell "not to soar too high on fancy's wings above the humble grounds of the gospel, lest others adventuring may be precipitated to ruin." Stone inquired, "Shall we think," echoing his earlier controversies with Cleland and Moreland, "that the word, which was God, and by which all things were made, and which was made flesh, was nothing but an unintelligent name, relation or sign of the only true God?" He demanded, "Can this be the saviour of sinners?" Giving Campbell the benefit of the doubt, he declared, "We dare not impute this absurdity to you, but we fear your unguarded speculations may cause the less informed to err."[32]

Campbell's response to Stone's letter was cordial, if somewhat condescending. Addressing Stone as "Brother," he wrote, "I will call you *brother* because you once told me that you could conscientiously and devoutly pray

---

[30]Ibid., 232–33.
[31]*CB* 4 (May 1827), 233–34.
[32]*CM* 1 (July 1827), 204–9.

to the Lord Jesus Christ as though there was no other God in the universe than he." Reporting that some "weak heads" among the Baptists were scandalized that he would refer to Stone, whom they viewed as an "Arian heretic," as brother, Campbell informed Stone that he had told them that he knew nothing of Stone's Arianism, that he had never "seriously read one entire pamphlet of the whole controversy," and that he fraternized with him as he did Calvinists. He had also told them, he advised Stone, that neither Arianism nor Calvinism "are worth one hour," whereas they "who tell me they supremely venerate, and unequivocally worship the King my Lord and Master, and are willing to obey him in all things, I call my brethren." Campbell added that Stone's enemies, who were "not a few," had "to a man" spoken highly of his "christian character."[33]

Nevertheless, Campbell expressed his regret that Stone had written so much on two topics, neither of which he, nor Campbell, nor anyone else living could fully understand. One of those topics had been the subject of Stone's recent letter to him. The other was atonement. If Stone did not like his comment on John 1:1, he should have just said so and "let it alone." He reminded Stone that he had stated that he had no intention of contending for his comment on John 1:1 or for *any* theory on the subject. Nevertheless, he noted that he had observed that "the strongest objections urged against the Trinitarians by their opponents are derived from what is called the unreasonableness or the absurdity of *three* persons being but *one* God, and that each of these three is the Supreme God." To his mind, the doctrine could neither be opposed nor established on the basis of reason, as reason related to human knowledge of things that occupied both time and space. He suggested that because we know "nothing about the mode of existence of spirits, we cannot say that it would be incompatible with their nature, or modes of existence, that three might be one, and that one being might exist in three beings." He observed that it was equally *unreasonable* that there could "be a God at all, or an *Eternal First Cause;* because in all the dominions of reason" there was nothing to "suggest the idea," and because it was "contrary to all the facts before us in the whole world that any cause can be the cause of itself, or not the effect of some other cause."[34]

The Christian's knowledge of God, he asserted, came from biblical revelation. Referring to one of his articles in an earlier issue of the *Christian Baptist* advocating "pure speech," he asked Stone, "Why not, then, abide in the use of Bible terms alone?" Though he would fight for no system, he would affirm "that God so loved the world that he sent his only begotten Son; that Jesus was the Son of God, in the true, full and import of these words; that the Holy Spirit is the Spirit of God, the Spirit of Christ, which was sent by the concurrence of the Father and the Son to attest and establish the truth, and remain a comforter, an advocate on earth, when Jesus entered the heavens."[35]

[33] *CM* 2 (November 1827), 6–7.
[34] Ibid., 7–9.
[35] Ibid., 9.

Campbell also advised Stone that he was "truly sorry" to find that "certain opinions, called Arian or Unitarian, or something else," along with "particular views of atonement," were about to become the "sectarian badge" of a people who had "assumed the sacred name *Christian.*" "I do not say that such is yet the fact," he warned, "but things are, in my opinion, looking that way; and if not suppressed in the bud, the name *Christian* will be as much a sectarian name as *Lutheran, Methodist,* or *Presbyterian.*" As for the particular concern that had occasioned Stone's letter, Campbell assured Stone that he believed that an "intelligent person, the Word, existed long before he was called Jesus Christ or Messiah."[36]

Stone's reply to Campbell was equally cordial. He stated that he would call Campbell brother, but not for the reason that Campbell had assigned for calling him brother. Personal integrity required him to inform Campbell that if Campbell recognized as brethren only those who could "conscientiously pray to the Lord Jesus as though there were no other God in the universe than he, and who supremely venerate him," then Stone was excluded from his brethren. Stone asked Campbell if he had misunderstood him, or if Campbell had changed his mind regarding the basis of Christian fellowship. "From all your public exhibitions from the press and from the pulpit, as well as from your private communications," Stone wrote, "we have been induced to believe that you fraternized with all who believe that Jesus Christ was the Son of God, and who were willingly obedient to his commands." "This," he continued, "we have thought was the only term of fellowship on which you insisted."[37]

As for Campbell's observation that the strongest objections urged against Trinitarianism were derived from what was called the unreasonableness or absurdity of three persons being but one God, and each of them the supreme God, Stone thought Campbell should know that the unreasonableness of the doctrine was "by no means" his "strongest objection" to it. His strongest objection to the doctrine of the Trinity was that it was "not a doctrine of revelation." Repeating Campbell's question back to him, Stone asked, "Why not abide in the use of Bible terms alone?" Stone declared that he "unequivocally" subscribed to every item of Campbell's biblical statement of his faith. "On the Bible," he added, "we agree."[38]

Regarding Campbell's fears that the name *Christian* might become as sectarian a name as any other, Stone remarked that the Christians could not prevent their opposers from "attaching what names they please" to the Christians and their opinions. Stone denied that their opinions were Unitarian, if Unitarian were understood as denoting an unwillingness to worship the Son of God. He acknowledged that the Christians in the East had accepted the name Unitarian, which, he allowed, had "caused much sorrow to some of us in the West." However, he expressed confidence that the Christians in the

[36]Ibid., 10.
[37]Ibid., 10–11.
[38]Ibid., 12–13.

East had "admitted the term without due consideration of the consequence," and that they would "retract it on mature reflection."[39]

Following this exchange with Campbell in 1827, Stone wrote in the *Messenger* opposing Campbell's views on ordination and communion with the unimmersed, but without mentioning Campbell's name. Like other Baptists, Campbell believed that congregations had the right to ordain their own ministers. In a letter from Joshua Irvin dated November 30, 1827, Stone learned that the Antioch Christian Church in Clinton County, Ohio, had recently come to the same conclusion. Stone asked the Antioch Church from what part of the New Testament they had drawn the conclusion that each church had the right to ordain its own ministers. As Stone read the New Testament, ministers were to be ordained by the ministry, who stood in a succession reaching back to the apostles. Churches, as distinguished from the ministry, he argued, were not authorized to ordain ministers.[40]

Stone again took up the topic of ordination in "A Friendly Dialogue," published in the April 1828 issue of the *Messenger*. The two fictional participants, James and John, were identified as Elders of the Church of Christ. James acknowledged himself to be "an advocate for the ancient order of things." In response to James's questions, John argued that it was evident from the scriptures that the apostles were "divinely authorized to ordain others" to preach, baptize, and teach and that those so ordained were likewise divinely authorized to ordain their successors. John's question to James, which James did not answer, was where in the scriptures the church, as distinguished from the ministry, was authorized to commission persons to preach, baptize, and teach.[41]

Like other Baptists, Campbell made believers' immersion a qualification for participation in the Lord's supper. Though the Christians had generally adopted believers' immersion, they had refused to make believers' immersion a qualification for receiving the Lord's supper. In May 1828 Stone published an extract from a letter from a Rushville, Indiana, correspondent who feared that Stone would make baptism a term of communion. Stone responded that baptism should be a term of communion only if it were a term of salvation. To Stone, it was evident that God had converted persons who had not been immersed. If God granted to the unimmersed "salvation and the gift of the Holy Spirit," Stone asked, "what are we that we should withstand God? If God communes with them, let us be followers (imitators) of God, as dear children."[42]

Stone's position on the terms of communion was more fully developed in the final section of a three-part series on "The Communion of Christians at the Lord's Table" that appeared in the *Christian Messenger* in the fall of 1828. The author of the series was "Timothy," who from the content and style of the

[39]Ibid., 13. See also *CM 2* (January 1828), 256.
[40]*CM 2* (January 1828), 61–64. For Campbell's position, see *CB 2* (October 1824), 49–50.
[41]*CM 2* (April 1828), 135–140.
[42]*CM 2* (May 1828), 151–55. For Campbell's position, see *CB 6* (March 1829), 183–85.

essays appears to have been Stone himself. Timothy stated that pious infant baptizers, whom he referred to as "Paido-baptists," differed from pious Baptists only in their interpretation of what constituted baptism. He argued that "the general devotion of the Paido-baptist to the cause of Christ fully evinces that if he errs in this case, it is an error of the judgment, and not of the will." Since all Christians were guilty of errors of judgment, who, Timothy asked, would "cast the first stone at the Paido-baptists?" Timothy further argued that both scripture and the "reason and fitness of things" taught "that God requires more or less of his creatures, in exact proportion to their capacities and circumstances." He exclaimed,

> When it is considered that the version of the Bible now in common use, was translated by the authority of King James, who forbade the translators to translate certain old ecclesiastical words, among which was the word baptize [which Campbell had translated as immerse]; –that many learned divines of different ages, have made learned, labored, and ingenious defences of infant baptism; that many thousands of the present day, are taught this doctrine from their cradles,

it was no "marvel" that many were Paido-baptists! Timothy further stated that one must recognize that "our circumstances are vastly different from those of primitive Christians" who, he suggested, were not presented, as were modern Christians, with a confusing variety of baptismal practices. Combining references to Revelation 9:2, 18:10 and 21, and Ezekiel 34:12 with Campbell's use of the Babylonian captivity of the Jews as a biblical "type" of the nineteenth-century captivity of the church, Timothy declared that "the Church has been carried away into Babylon; has been scattered in the dark and cloudy day;– her language has been mingled and confounded with the language of Babylon; –the smoke of the bottomless pit has darkened the sun of her hemisphere: and she is lost in the almost numberless streets and lanes of the *Great City.*" Although thousands, he asserted, were seeking the way to "Jerusalem," it was "contrary to the fixed laws of the natural and moral worlds, and therefore, morally impossible, that they should, at once, throw off all the shackles of error, and superstition which attach to them, and come into the full blaze of gospel light."[43]

Timothy knew, of course, that Baptists claimed to exclude Paido-baptists from communion in order to impress upon them the "truth" that believers' immersion alone was baptism; hence, the exclusion was from a "principle of love." Though Timothy would not deny that "some" Baptists acted from love in excluding Paido-baptists from the Lord's table, he declared that their action was "perfectly adapted to defeat their own avowed object." By excluding pious Paido-baptists from the Lord's table, they lost access to them and

---

[43] *CM* 3 (December 1828), 34–37. For the earlier installments in the series by "Timothy," see *CM* 3 (November 1828), 11–14; and *CM* 2 (October 1828), 271–75.

confirmed them in their error. By receiving pious Paido-baptists at the Lord's table, he advised, they would pave the way to their "conversion to the truth."[44] This, of course, had been the experience of the Christian Church, which, as Stone related in his "History of the Christian Church in the West," had refused to make immersion a term of communion and had gone from being a Paido-baptist church to being a church in which there was not "one in 500" who had not been immersed.[45]

Despite his reprimand of Campbell for "speculating" on the relationship of the Father and the Son, and his disagreements with Campbell regarding ordination and the terms of communion, Stone was convinced by the spring of 1828 that the Reformers, like the Christians, were committed to the union of the church on the Bible alone. In the May 1828 issue of the *Messenger*, "Timothy" stated that the Christians could "heartily adopt the language of A. Campbell," who had recently declared, "I do attribute to creeds, in the proper acceptation of the term, all the divisions and strifes, partyism and sectarian feeling, of the present day."[46] "Timothy" could have also reported that over the past two years a number of Christian preachers had applied Campbell's view of the design or purpose of baptism, which, along with the rejection of creeds and weekly observance of the Lord's supper, would soon distinguish the Reformers from other Baptists.

---

[44] *CM* 3 (December 1828), 37.
[45] Stone, *History,* 47.
[46] *CM* 2 (May 1828), 147.

13

Remission of Sins

Baptists taught that the design or purpose of baptism was to set apart or "seal" believers as members of the church. Prior to baptism, candidates were required to demonstrate that they were believers, typically by describing their conversion. On the second day of the Campbell-Maccalla debate in October 1823, Campbell introduced an argument against infant baptism based on a distinctive view of the "design or import of baptism." Campbell stated that he would be as "full as possible" on the topic because "of its great importance, and because perhaps neither Baptists nor Paedobaptists" sufficiently appreciated the design or import of baptism. After quoting a handful of New Testament texts that Campbell suggested pointed to the importance of baptism in the New Testament, he declared that the design of baptism was to give believers an assurance or "formal token" of their "cleansing" from all sins. Campbell argued that baptism, "being ordained to be to a believer a formal and personal remission of all his sins, cannot be administered unto an infant without the greatest perversion and abuse of the nature or import of this ordinance."[1]

Campbell's biographer, Robert Richardson, stated that Campbell did not "make a direct and practical application" of the doctrine of baptism for remission of sins. By a direct and practical application of the doctrine, Richardson meant recommending baptism to penitent believers who desired an assurance of the forgiveness of their sins and the indwelling of the Holy Spirit. Richardson claimed that the first person to make a direct and practical application of Campbell's view of the purpose of baptism was Campbell's colleague, Walter Scott. Scott was appointed evangelist of the Mahoning Baptist Association in August 1827 and began recommending baptism to penitent believers in November.[2]

Apparently unknown to Richardson, Christian Church preachers had been recommending baptism for remission of sins to penitent believers for more than a year before Scott began preaching the doctrine. By his own report, the first minister to make a direct and practical application of Campbell's view of the design of baptism was Benjamin Franklin Hall. Hall, who was twenty-two

---

[1]Campbell-Maccalla debate, quoted in Richardson, 2: 80–83.

[2]Richardson, 2: 84. See also Dwight E. Stevenson, *Walter Scott: Voice of the Golden Oracle* (St. Louis: Christian Board of Publication, 1946), which chronicles Scott's development of his plan of salvation.

years old when ordained in 1825, recounted that he was troubled in the first year of his ministry by observing that some persons who "mourned" their alienation from God did not experience "pardon." The goal of much of the preaching of the Christians, of course, was to awaken sinners to their situation apart from God and to encourage them to "go" to Christ for salvation. At the close of a sermon, the preachers would often invite the "mourners" to come to the front of the stand or pulpit where the ministers would kneel among them and pray for them to receive salvation. Hall claimed that he had "spent whole nights singing, praying and trying to instruct weeping, broken-hearted sinners how to 'get religion,' and, now and then rejoicing with one who had just 'got through.'" He related having attended a camp meeting in middle Tennessee in the fall of 1825, at which more than fifty mourners came forward to be prayed for by the ministers. Hall stayed up with those mourners the whole night and reported that though some "professed religion," many did not. As the meeting came to a close, one of the preachers proposed that a song be sung and that first the "brethren and sisters" and then the "mourners" who were "resolved to strive" to meet the "preachers in heaven" be invited to "take leave of the preachers." The preachers stood in a row in front of the stand, and a long line of "saints" gave them the parting hand. Then came the mourners, reaching out their hands to the preachers, "weeping as if their hearts would break." It had been too much for Hall to endure: "I cried aloud, and wept like a child."[3]

Following the meeting in middle Tennessee, Hall began to ask himself why some who seemed to be deeply penitent did not receive an assurance of forgiveness. He claimed that he found the answer to his question in the spring of 1826 by reading Campbell's speech on the design of baptism in the Campbell-Maccalla debate. He had stopped for the night at the cabin of a Brother and Sister Gess on Line Creek on the border between Tennessee and Kentucky while traveling to his brother's home in Kentucky. Entering the cabin on his own, while Brother Gess tended to Hall's horse, he found a copy of the Campbell-Maccalla debate on a corner bookshelf and began reading Campbell's speech on the design of baptism. He indicated that even before he finished Campbell's speech, "the light began to dawn," and he saw that the reason that some mourners did not receive pardon was not the fault of the penitents, nor of God, but of the preachers who advised penitents to pray for pardon rather than instructing them to be baptized for the remission of their sins. Hall sprang to his feet in ecstasy, crying aloud, "Eureka! Eureka! I have found it! I have found it!!"[4]

---

[3]Benjamin Franklin Hall, *The Autobiography of B. F. Hall*, typescript in the library of Christian Theological Seminary, 51–52, 69. For further information on Hall, see R. L. Roberts, "B. F. Hall: Pioneer Evangelist and Herald of Hope," *Restoration Quarterly* 8 (1965), 251–54; and D. Newell Williams, "The Autobiography of B. F. Hall: Window on the 19th Century Stone-Campbell Movement," *Discipliana* 50 (Spring 1990), 9–13. Richard T. Hughes argues that the Christian preachers convinced Campbell of the practical value of the doctrine of baptism for remission of sins. See *Reviving the Ancient Faith: The Story of the Churches of Christ in America* (Grand Rapids: Eerdmans, 1996), 102.

[4]Hall, 54–55.

Hall told other Christians of his discovery as he continued his journey to his brother's home. One of those Christians was the preacher S. E. Jones. Hall noted that although Jones initially rejected the doctrine, he agreed to study it, and the next time he saw him, Jones was preaching baptism for the remission of sins![5]

Hall also shared his discovery with his sister-in-law. He reported that she had been brought up as a Baptist and had often tried to "get religion," but could never "get through." After they had discussed the doctrine, she requested to be baptized. As she came up out of the water she "clasped her hands together, and said: 'Thank the Lord!'" Hall remarked that because she was the first person that he baptized for remission of sins, her joy increased his "confidence in the truth."[6]

Hall shared his discovery with Stone at Georgetown early in July 1826. According to Hall, Stone strongly advised him against preaching the doctrine, claiming he had preached it early in the century and "it was like throwing ice water on the people;…it froze all their warmth out, and came well nigh driving vital religion out of the country." Hall asked Stone why he had preached the doctrine. Stone replied he had found it in the scriptures. Hall noted that, though he was respectful of Stone as a father in the faith who had been preaching the Great Revival when Hall was born, he "ventured" to tell him that if the doctrine was in the Bible, as Stone admitted it was, it was certainly right to preach it. Hall indicated that after further conversation, he advised Stone he was resolved to preach the doctrine, and if anyone objected, he would tell them "brother Stone says it is taught in the Scriptures." Hall noted that, Stone laughed and "pleasantly remarked" that Hall was "so hardheaded" he could do nothing with him![7]

Not many days later, Hall and Stone traveled with others to a two-day meeting near the Sulphur Well, eight miles from Georgetown. At Stone's request, Hall agreed to refrain from preaching what he claimed Stone called his "chilling and religion-killing doctrine" until an evening service after Stone had left the meeting. As events unfolded, someone else preached the evening service, but a downpour prevented the people from leaving the meetinghouse until after midnight. Hall reported that he used the additional time in the meetinghouse to persuade several of the mourners to be baptized for remission of sins and baptized them the following morning upon the confession of their faith. Hall noted that another preacher present that evening, Samuel Rogers, had not avowed his belief in baptism for remission of sins, but was soon a "warm advocate of the sentiment."[8]

Soon after the meeting at the Sulphur Well, Hall attended a camp meeting at Mill Creek, in Monroe County, Kentucky, near the home of John Mulkey. On Saturday night, Hall exhorted the congregation, and some fifty persons

---

[5]Ibid., 55–56.
[6]Ibid., 56.
[7]Ibid., 56–58.
[8]Ibid., 59–60.

came forward. Some knelt down and began to pray. There was some weeping and sobbing aloud, but after the mourners became somewhat composed, Hall preached to them baptism for the remission of sins. He reported that "four or five" made their confession of faith and asked to be baptized that evening. Although it was near midnight, the congregation prepared lamps and torches and, as Hall remembered, a long procession moved off, with scarcely a word spoken above a whisper, down a slope and through a dense forest to a "gurgling" stream. After the penitents had been baptized and received "the congratulations" of their friends, "a sweet, melodious song arose" as the procession slowly made its way back up the hill and the participants dispersed to their tents for the night. Hall added that the next time he saw John Mulkey, Mulkey was preaching baptism for the remission of sins.[9]

Despite his initial objections to the doctrine, as reported by Hall, Stone was advocating baptism for the remission of sins within six months of Hall's visit to Georgetown. In the January 1827 issue of the *Christian Messenger*, he declared that "faith and baptism are the divinely instituted means of salvation." This, he argued, was the obvious meaning of Mark 16:16, "He that believeth and is baptized, shall be saved." Stone also referred to Peter's instructions in Acts 2:38: "Repent and be baptized, every one of you, in the name of the Lord Jesus Christ, for the remission of sins, and ye shall receive the gift of the Holy Ghost." Stone also cited Saul's conversion, as reported in Acts 9:1–19 and 22:6–16. Conflating the Acts 9:1–19 account of Saul's conversion (in which Ananias is instructed that Saul is "praying") with the Acts 22:6–16 account of Saul's conversion (in which Ananias says to Saul, "Why tarriest thou? Arise and be baptized, and wash away thy sins"), Stone noted that Saul had believed and was *praying* when the Lord sent Ananias to him saying, "Why tarriest thou? Arise and be baptized, and *wash away thy sins.*" Stone observed that a "*modern* doctor" acting in this case would have said something like the following: "Poor Saul, you are in a pitiable condition; I cannot help you; pray on; it may be you shall be heard, and God in his *own time* will send his spirit to cleanse you from your sins, and save you; after you have experienced this, I advise you to be baptized." In response to the objection that water cannot wash away sins, Stone asked, "Did the waters of the Jordan, into which Naaman dipt himself at the command of Elisha,–Did these waters literally wash away his leprosy? or was it not the power of God through this act of obedience? [2 Kings 5:10–14]." Stone concluded that in like manner, "baptism saves us, and washes away our sins; not the water, but the grace and power of God through this act of obedience."[10]

The *application* of baptism for the remission of sins had a significant impact on the worship of the Christians. Well into the 1820s, the worship of the Christians had continued to resemble the worship of the Great Revival. Describing the preaching of the Christians prior to their adoption of baptism for remission of sins, Hall wrote that "we would clap and rub our hands, stamp

---

[9] Ibid., 60–61.
[10] *CM* 1 (January 1827), 59–61.

with our feet, slam down and tear up the Bible, speak as loud as possible and scream at the top of our voice, to get up an excitement."[11] When the itinerant Joseph Thomas, called "The White Pilgrim" because he dressed in white, visited the Christians in 1811, he reported frequently observing the "exercises" that had been associated with the Great Revival, noting in particular dancing, laughing, and the "jirks."[12] Though the exercises had disappeared before Hall's introduction of baptism for remission of sins, "crying out" and simultaneous "praying aloud" had continued to mark the worship of the Christians, especially when praying for mourners. "Sometimes," Hall wrote, "the excitement would be so great, so many brethren all praying aloud at once, and mourners screaming and begging for mercy, that no single voice could be distinguished from the rest."[13]

The substitution of baptism for the mourners' bench reduced the number of occasions for crying out and simultaneous praying aloud. It also changed the expectations of congregations regarding how the Spirit would be received and, correspondingly, their behavior in seeking the Spirit. In June 1832, six years after Hall baptized his sister-in-law for the remission of sins, John Longley reported to Stone on "the success of Gospel truth" in Rush County, Indiana, noting that "there is no particular excitement among the people as we have seen in great revivals; but there appears to be an inquiring for truth." Longley, who was fifty years old and had been a Christian preacher since 1805, continued, "In general, the congregations are large, and more attentive than I have ever seen before; and the converts seem more like they were convinced from the force of testimony under a sense of duty, believing the facts recorded in the word of God, than from the impulse of the moment, under the influence of heated passions." Longley concluded, "They expect to receive the spirit as promised, in obedience, and not obedience as the fruit of the spirit."[14]

Less than two years later, in March 1834, Stone responded to an article describing the Christians as having about them "a kind of noise or fuss, which they call religion" in imitation of "the Methodists." Stone stated that "for a number of years back we have neither heard, nor seen" anything like "noise or fuss" among the Christians. He remarked, "When we were in the Presbyterian church, and for some years after, it is true, we saw and heard a great deal of what was called by many, 'noise and fuss,' but these things have passed away from us, and are by no means characteristic of our religion."[15] Though Stone did not credit baptism for the remission of sins for the change, Z. M. Landsdown, a Christian from Locust Creek, Kentucky, who opposed the doctrine, did. "The Christians before embracing this doctrine," he wrote in 1841,

[11]Hall, 50–51.

[12]Joseph Thomas, *The Life of the Pilgrim Joseph Thomas* (Winchester, Va.: J. Foster, 1817), quoted in Ware, 184–87.

[13]Hall, 51.

[14]*CM* 6 (August 1832), 246.

[15]*CM* 8 (March 1834), 74.

"enjoyed religion, attended the house of worship, and you might hear the shouts of praise, and praying for more heartfelt religion." But now, Landsdown claimed, "their worship is nothing but a form."[16]

In April 1829, Stone began a series in the *Messenger* by the Christian preacher James E. Matthews advocating baptism for the remission of sins. The series was titled "The Gospel Plan of Saving Sinners."[17] According to Hall, Matthews had been convinced of baptism for the remission of sins by a sermon that Hall preached at a camp meeting in Alabama in September 1826 and later wrote the articles at Hall's request and with Hall's assistance. Hall claimed that he personally delivered the articles to Stone, adding that he had "no little difficulty" inducing Stone to publish them in the *Messenger*. Assuming that Hall's report is reliable, it is likely that Stone was trying to avoid controversy regarding the doctrine. He had concluded his January 1827 article advocating baptism for the remission of sins by admonishing, "Let the free spirit of the meekness and wisdom of Christ be ever exercised in all our attempts to restore the primitive order of Christ in his church." He may have been especially concerned to check the exuberance of Hall, who was known as "the proud preacher" and had frequently been charged with "introducing new-fangled notions."[18]

Hall indicated that it was the publication of Matthews' articles in the spring of 1829 that led to the first full discussion of baptism for the remission of sins among the Christians. Nevertheless, a significant number of Kentucky Christians had adopted baptism for the remission of sins nearly a year before Stone's publication of Matthews' series. In July 1828, Ohio correspondent J. E. Church informed Stone that Elder Walter Scott (whose name Stone would have recognized from his contributions to Campbell's *Christian Baptist*) had "made an unusual number of disciples the past year." Church reported that Scott's "method and manner are somewhat novel to me." He related that Scott seemed "to suppose the Apostolical Gospel to consist of the five following particulars, viz.: faith, repentance, baptism for the remission of sins, the gift of the Holy Ghost, and eternal life." "Thus you see," Church underscored, "he baptizes the subject previous to the remission of his sins, or the receiving of the Holy Spirit." Stone responded that he was sorry that he did not have back issues of the *Christian Messenger* in which he had treated the subject of baptism for remission of sins to send to his correspondent, stating "We have for some time since practiced in this way throughout our country."[19]

By 1830 the division of Kentucky Baptists was nearly complete, as individuals and congregations in association after association were excluded for advocating Campbell's reforms. Perhaps as many as one fourth to one third

---

[16] *Christian Palladium* (1841), 47, quoted in Ware, 276–77.
[17] *CM* 3 (April 1829), 125–29; *CM* 3 (May 1829), 150–54; *CM* 3 (July 1829), 211–13. B. F. Hall claimed to have convinced Matthews of the doctrine.
[18] Hall, 45, 47, 68; *CM* 1 (January 1827), 63.
[19] Hall, 68–69; *CM* 2 (September 1828), 261–62.

of Kentucky Baptists (possibly as many as ten thousand persons) had sided with Campbell. But if the Reformers were no longer accepted as Baptists, who were they? Stone believed that the Reformers were Christians and that his churches and the Reformers should become one people. In September 1829, Stone reported in the *Christian Messenger* that "a worthy Baptist brother" had recently asked him why the Christians and the "New Testament Baptists" did not become one people. Stone responded that "the New Testament reformers among the Baptists have generally acted the part which we approve." They had "rejected all party names" and had taken the name Christian, they allowed each other "to read the Bible, and judge of its meaning for themselves," and they did not "bind each other to believe certain dogmas as terms of fellowship." If there was a "difference" between the two groups, he knew it not. "We have nothing in us to prevent a union," he declared, "and if they have nothing in them in opposition to it, we are in spirit one." "May God," he added, "strengthen the cords of Christian union."[20]

---

[20] *CM* 3 (September 1829), 261–62; Harrison, 45–47.

14

Formal Union

Campbell did not respond to Stone's September 1829 statement that if there was nothing in the Reformers opposed to union with the Christians, they were in spirit one. Rather, he allowed others to state his reservations regarding union with the Christians. In the January 1830 issue of the *Christian Baptist*, an Irish correspondent identified Stone as an Arian and took Campbell to task for having called Stone "brother."[1] Having published nearly seven volumes of the *Christian Baptist* by the end of 1829, Campbell began a new publication in January 1830, which he boldly titled the *Millennial Harbinger*. In the May issue of the *Harbinger*, Campbell published the letter of a "traveller" who reported having been told about a Christian church in New England that was "Unitarian in sentiment" and "very ignorant and enthusiastic." The "Christian Churches" in New England were associated with former Baptists Abner Jones and Elias Smith. The writer observed that were it not for the "abuse" of the name Christian, he "would be called by no other," but that as things were, he thought that he would keep the name "Baptist."[2]

Despite Campbell's reticence regarding union with the Christians, Stone raised the issue of a union of Reformers and Christians in the *Christian Messenger* a second time in August 1830. Declaring that the millennium would be ushered in by a "flood" of truth that would sweep away sectarianism, he commented on the progress of "reform" among the Baptists. He asserted that "the doctrine preached" by the Reformers, and "the object they profess to have in view, which is to unite all christians in the spirit and truth of the New Testament, are, as far as we can judge, the very same that we have constantly preached and defended for nearly thirty years." Stone added that even baptism for the remission of sins and the gift of the Holy Spirit had "long been advocated, by some of us, as the truth." At the same time, he warned that certain attitudes among the Reformers could subvert their efforts to "unite the children of God in one body." "Should they," he advised, "make their own peculiar views of immersion a term of fellowship, it will be impossible for them to repel, successfully, the imputation of being sectarians, and of having an authoritative creed (though not written) of one article," which, he declared, "would exclude more christians from union than any creed" with which he

---

[1] *CB* 7 (January 1830), 139.
[2] *Millennial Harbinger* 1(May 1830), 199–200.

was acquainted. Stone also warned against the attitude of the "traveller" who had rejected the name Christian because he believed it to be "abused" by its association with Unitarianism. Stone asked whether this "traveller" would refuse "every thing abused by men." If so, Stone remarked, he would have to reject Christianity itself! And certainly, Stone ventured, he would have to reject the Reformed Baptists, for were he to travel in the West, he "would be informed, by their enemies, that they were Unitarian in their sentiments, and enthusiastic too, and that many of them were ignorant as well."[3]

Campbell responded in the *Millennial Harbinger* to Stone's warning to the Reformers not to make their "peculiar views of immersion" a term of fellowship nor to reject the name "Christian" because of its associations with Unitarianism. He expressed his hope that Stone's examination of his "Extra" to the *Millennial Harbinger* on "Remission of Sins" would convince him that "there is no immersion instituted by Jesus Christ, save that *for the remission of sins.*" If Stone were to call "the plain, literal proclamation of Peter and the Apostles" on immersion "a *peculiar* view," Campbell continued, he would have to "call every act of obedience to the word of Jesus, a *peculiar* view." Repelling the charge of sectarianism, Campbell declared, was "impossible" if "obedience to Jesus Christ" was called "*sectarianism.*" "No opinion, creed, or dogma of human invention," he continued, "shall be with us a term of communion; but *obedience* to the commands of Jesus will always be, unless we should unhappily renounce the Lord Jesus as our Lord, King, and Lawgiver." On the other hand, Campbell agreed with Stone that more "Christians" would be "excluded by insisting on this command—'Be immersed every one of you, in the name of the Lord Jesus, for the remission of your sin'—than by any creed in christendom." In Campbell's view that was simply because there were incomparably more "nominal than real christians—more who say, 'Lord, Lord,' and yet do not the things which he says, than there are who obey the will of the Heavenly Father." Campbell added, however, that he had "no liking for a church after the similitude of Noah's Ark." "In such a church," he observed, "the vermin and ravenous beasts, their noise and clamor, (to say nothing of their filth and uncleanness,) are less to be endured than the tempest which beats upon the outside."[4]

Regarding the name Christian, Campbell claimed that he had always given it the "approbation" of his heart. The problem, he asserted, was that some had "assumed it as a *name* only." "Suppose," he suggested, "that these reforming Baptists who contend for the ancient gospel and the ancient order of things, should assume to be called *Christians,* how would they be distinguished from those who call themselves *Christians,* who neither immerse for the remission of sins, show forth the Lord's death weekly, nor keep the institutions, manners, and customs of those called 'Christians first at Antioch?'" "If," Campbell continued, "our friends who assume this good name, never

---

[3] *CM* 4 (August 1830), 199–202.
[4] *MH* 1 (August 1830), 372.

had gone into a crusade in favor of opinions, nor had laid so much stress upon them; fighting for years about their *peculiar views* of the Deity, and other abstractions which I need not name; and if they had given to their churches the institutions of christians," the name would "not now designate a *sect*, instead of the body of Christ." Nevertheless, Campbell stated, he *had* chosen the name Christian, "with all its abuses," and had not for many years referred to the particular congregation to which he belonged by a name other than *the Church of Christ*. However, if any should suppose that the term Christian denoted "a Unitarian, or Trinitarian, in its appropriated sense," he would "choose the *older* name, 'disciple'; and recommend to all the brotherhood to be called not 'Christians,' but 'the disciples of Christ.'"[5]

Stone did not immediately reply to Campbell's response. He did, however, come out in the September 1830 issue of the *Messenger* in support of weekly observance of the Lord's supper, which, along with immersion for the remission of sins, Campbell had identified as one of the distinguishing practices of the Reformers. Citing Acts 20:7 and 1 Corinthians 11:20, Stone argued that it was the practice of the disciples to come together on the first day of the week to "break bread." Stone also stated that "every Lord's day" observance of the Lord's supper had been practiced by the church for the first three centuries after Christ and that "whenever the church shall be restored to her former glory, she will again receive the Lord's supper on every first day of the week."[6]

Campbell commended Stone's endorsement of weekly celebration of the Lord's supper in the October 1830 issue of the *Harbinger*, referring to Stone as "the zealous and intelligent Editor of the *Christian Messenger*," who, he was "pleased to see," was "directing his readers to the ancient order of things." He added, however, that he had thought "some time ago" that Stone had also "come out for immersion for the remission of sins," though he could not see how Stone could teach immersion for remission of sins and continue to commune with the unimmersed. Drawing attention to a statement by Stone in the September issue of the *Messenger* that he had "found nothing in scripture" to "forbid" him from communing with "unbaptized persons at the Lord's table," Campbell remarked that "this might be said of a hundred things which the Christian Messenger would tremble to do." The question, Campbell suggested, was "by what authority, command or precept, does he commune at the Lord's table with unbaptized persons?" Campbell declared that whatever was "not commanded by the Lord" in religion was "will-worship," and, as such, was forbidden. In Campbell's view, for Stone to commune with the unimmersed was "inconsistent" with his teaching of baptism for remission of sins. [7]

In November, Stone met with Campbell and other Reformers and Christians at the home of B. A. Hicks near Lexington. Stone disclosed to Campbell

---

[5]Ibid., 372–73.

[6]*CM* 4 (September 1830), 228–29.

[7]*MH* 1 (October 1830), 474–75. Campbell's reference was to *CM* 4 (September 1830), 235–36.

his fears that "should a union not take place" between them, the argument they both had long used against authoritative creeds and sectarian establishments "would be nullified," and they would put into the hands of their opponents a "weapon" that they would "successfully" wield against them. He pointed out that their opponents "would say that the Bible alone was insufficient to unite christians," and their failure to unite "would be adduced as proof." Campbell responded that when he first began to preach the reformation, it was "considerably checked" by reports of the Christians in the West who were said to have advocated "the same cause" and "run into the wildest extravagancies in doctrine and practice." He "plainly intimated his fears" that should a union occur, the existing prejudices against the Christians "would impede the progress of the reformation." Stone replied that the Christians would have "as much to lose" as the Reformers, since the Christians were "equally, if not more respected by the orthodox."[8]

Following an editorial silence of several months on the union of Christians and Reformers, Stone raised the issue a third time in the *Christian Messenger* in August 1831. He observed, "The question is going the round of society, and is often proposed to us, Why are not you and the Reformed Baptists, one people? or, Why are you not united?" Stone reported that he had "uniformly answered, In spirit we are united, and that no reason existed on our side to prevent the union in form." It was well known, he continued, "that we have always, from the beginning, declared our willingness, and desire to be united with the whole family of God on earth, irrespective of the diversity of opinion among them." Stone claimed that the Reformed Baptists had "received" the doctrine that the Christians had taught for many years regarding the importance of Christian unity, the divisiveness of authoritative creeds and confessions, and the work of the Spirit in conversion. He repeated his claim that even "baptism as a means, in connexion with faith and repentance, for the remission of sins, and the gift of the Holy Spirit," had been preached by some of the Christians "many years ago." He acknowledged a difference of opinion from the Reformers on points he did not specify but declared that those differences would not prevent his uniting with the Reformers. On the other hand, he asserted that the Reformers' objections to some of the Christians' opinions were the reasons they would not unite with the Christians. He stated he would name those objections and "let all duly consider their weight."[9]

Stone claimed that the first objection of the Reformers to union with the Christians was that the Christians communed with the unimmersed. Stone

---

[8] *CM* 5 (November 1831), 251; *MH* 2 (January 1831), 27. Among the persons whom Campbell noted as present were the "Creaths," Baptist preachers who supported Campbell, and "Fleming," who appears to be L. I. Fleming, whom Richardson identified as a Christian. See Richardson, 2: 335–36.

[9] *CM* 5 (August 1831), 180. Stone had earlier responded to Campbell's charge that the name Christian designated a sect by stating that they had known no other way of renouncing their sectarianism than to "take the name *Christian*, and endeavor to adorn it by a holy life." See *CM* 4 (December 1830), 274–75.

noted, "They contend, (so we understand them) that according to the New Institution [Campbell's term for Christianity], none but the immersed have their sins remitted; and therefore they cannot commune with the unimmersed." Stone stated that the Christians could not affirm "this sentiment" since it would in their view "exclude millions of the fairest characters, for many centuries back, from heaven" for nothing more than their "ignorance" of the meaning of the command to be baptized. "What," Stone asked, "should we think of an earthly king, if a province of loving subjects, being ignorant of the meaning of a certain law, and yet endeavoring to obey it according to their understanding of it, should by his order be cut off by an excruciating death?" "Surely," Stone answered, "we should reprobate his conduct, and should see in his character that which is less amiable than otherwise." He asked, "Is it possible to divest ourselves of the same thoughts and conclusion respecting the lovely King of saints?" "Should we not, by presenting his character in this view," he declared, "expose it to the contempt of a scoffing world?" Stone allowed that the Reformers did not declare that the unimmersed were excluded from heaven, but only from the kingdom on earth. Nevertheless, he did not believe immersion could be made the "sine qua non" of Christian fellowship without leading to the conclusion that the unimmersed were excluded from heaven. "We therefore," he declared, "teach the doctrine, believe, repent, and be immersed for the remission of sins; and we endeavor to convince our hearers of its truth; but we exercise patience and forbearance towards such pious persons, as cannot be convinced."[10]

Stone noted, "Our brethren, the Disciples, ask us, How can you grant the privileges of the kingdom to such as have not been immersed, when it is plain that by immersion only they are born or made members of the kingdom?" Stone answered that "prayer, praise, thanksgiving, teaching, preaching, and even the Lord's supper, were divinely instituted, before Jesus died, and was buried and rose again"; consequently, before the gospel was preached with its command to be baptized. In other words, the Lord's supper had been instituted *prior* to baptism. By what authority, Stone asked, was the Lord's supper to be "taken" from the unimmersed? Stone further questioned, "What authority have we for inviting or debarring any pious, holy believer from the Lord's table?" "The King's will," he continued, "is, that his friends do this in remembrance of him—and all that his law [1 Corinthians 11:28] expressed on the subject is, 'Let a man examine himself, and so let him eat and drink.'" Stone declared that Christ "has no where established a court of inquisition to fence his table, nor to prevent any from praying, praising, or worshipping him, unless they have been immersed."[11]

Stone claimed that the second objection of the Reformers to union with the Christians was the Christians' attachment to the name Christian. Stone noted that the Reformers "acknowledge the name *Christian* most appropriate;

---

[10] *CM* 5 (August 1831), 180–81.
[11] Ibid., 184–85.

but because they think this name is disgraced by us who wear it, and to it may be attached the idea of Unitarian or Trinitarian, they reject it, and have taken the older name, *Disciple.*" Although Stone had no objection to the "scriptural name, Disciple," he argued that the Reformers' taking of the name Disciple, to distinguish themselves from the Christians, would require that the Christians give up the name Christian in order to unite with the Reformers. This, Stone explained, the Christians could not do, believing that Christian was the name given to the church "by divine appointment" and believing that because "there are none who deny that Christian is the most appropriate name for the followers of Christ," it "will supersede all other names, and be a means of uniting the scattered flock."[12]

Campbell replied immediately in the *Millennial Harbinger*, asking Stone what he meant by "union in form." Did he mean, Campbell asked, a "formal confederation" of all the preachers and people called Christians and Disciples? If so, Campbell inquired, what were to be the "articles of confederation," and how would they be adopted? Should there, Campbell further inquired, be a "general convention" of messengers from all the societies of Christians and Disciples, or one general assembly of the "whole aggregate" of both groups? Campbell asked if there had ever been "an incident in ecclesiastical history of a whole people formally and in good faith uniting with another whole people without such a formal confederation?" He noted that Stone had tendered no proposal for a formal union, nor had he heard of any general meeting among the Christians to "deliberate upon the terms and conditions." Did Stone think, he asked, "that one or two individuals, of and from themselves, should propose and effect a formal union among the hundreds of congregations scattered over this continent, called christians or disciples, without calling upon the different congregations to express an opinion or a wish upon the subject?"[13]

Campbell also raised a question regarding the meaning of Stone's claim that the Reformed Baptists had "received" the doctrine taught by the Christians many years before. In Campbell's view this was not true, and it was precisely the identification of his "reformation" with earlier anticreedal movements that he was most concerned to prevent. "Many persons," he asserted, "both in Europe and America, have inveighed against sects, creeds, confessions, councils, and human dogmas, during the last two centuries, and some even before Luther's time; but what have these to do with the present proposed reformation?" "This," he continued, "is only the work of a pioneer: it is clearing the forests, girdling the trees, and burning the brush." Campbell claimed that "both friends and foes of the cause which we now plead, seem to be agreed that not the anti-creed, and anti-council, and anti-sectarian questions, but what may be denominated the questions of 'the ancient gospel and ancient order of things,' distinguish it most easily from every other cause plead on this continent or in Europe since the great apostasy."[14]

---

[12]Ibid., 181–84.
[13]*MH* 2 (August 1831), 389–90.
[14]Ibid., 390.

As if to demonstrate the difference between the proposed reformation and simple anticreedalism, Campbell noted that Stone's "opinion" regarding the terms of communion that he had put forward as a "reason" why the Reformers would not unite in form with the Christians was not an *opinion*, but a *practice.* What the reformers opposed was the Christians' practice of making immersion "of non-effect by receiving persons into the kingdom of Jesus, so called, irrespective of their being legitimately born; or in brief, regardless of the command, '*Be baptized every one of you.*'"[15] Campbell had earlier criticized Stone's use of the word *opinion* in response to an article Stone had published in January. Stone had stated that it was his opinion that "immersion is the only baptism." If, Stone had asked, he were to make his opinion in this case a term of fellowship, where would he stop making his opinions terms of fellowship? Campbell had stated that "opinions are always, in strict propriety of speech, doubtful matters, because speculative." If, he had continued, the word were "applied to matters of testimony, to laws, institutions, or religious worship," the church would have no way of determining its faith and practice.[16]

As for the name Christian, Campbell stated he was not prepared "to say *Amen* to all the criticism offered to prove that we must, by divine authority, be called Christians, whether we deserve it or not." He noted that the name disciple was not only older than the name Christian, but also "a much more *humble* name than the name Christian." To be a Christian, he explained, was to be a follower of Christ, while a disciple was merely a learner. He stated he had "no objection to the name Christian if we only deserve it; nor predilection for the name disciple, except for its antiquity and modesty." However, when the name Christian was "plead for as of divine authority, and as the only or most fitting name which can be adopted," he would lift up his voice "against the imposition, and contend for our liberty, where the Lord has left us free."[17]

Campbell added that he had "high respect" for Stone and "the brethren who are with him." "Many of them with whom we are acquainted," he continued, "we love as brethren; and we can, in all good conscience, unite with them in spirit and form, in public or in private, in all acts of social worship." "We should like," he added, "to have a very free, familiar, and affectionate correspondence with brother Stone on these subjects which he has introduced through the medium of the press."[18]

Stone's reply to Campbell was free and familiar, if not exactly affectionate. Expressing his long-held view that union depended on the Holy Spirit, Stone suggested that pride (he did not say whose!) was standing in the way of a union of Christians and Reformers. "I am aware," he stated, "of the deceptibility of the human mind, and of its strong propensity to make for ourselves a *great name.*" "Until," he advised, "this proud spirit sink at the feet of Jesus, and we become cordially and joyfully willing to decrease, that Christ

[15]Ibid., 390–92.
[16]*MH* 2 (February 1831), 102–3.
[17]*MH* 2 (August 1831), 393–95.
[18]Ibid., 395–96.

may increase, I cannot anticipate as near that happy period of the church [the millennium], so much talked of and prayed for at this time." "So long," he added, "have the clergy stood in the way of truth's advancement—so long has the deleterious shade of sectarianism, like the shadow of death, chilled the life's blood of christianity—so long and so often have the preachers divided those whom God had joined together by the spirit of truth, that I am afraid of myself, and jealous [suspicious] of others."[19]

Regarding the form of union he would propose, he thought brother Campbell knew well that he had long since rejected "a confederation of churches, and such unscriptural associations, as practiced by the different sects." Knowing of "neighborhoods" where there were small numbers of both Christians and Reformers, neither of which was large enough to form a "respectable church," he had thought it desirable for them to "*formally* unite, and worship together as a congregation of brethren." To "effect this union," he had "endeavored to remove the objections made against it."[20]

Stone observed that as to his claim that the Reformers had "received" the faith and practice that the Christians had taught for many years, he had not stated that Campbell had received those views from the Christians. He hoped Campbell had received them from the Bible! As for "distinguishing traits" between the ancient gospel pled by the reformers and that which the Christians had taught for many years, all he could see was that "they attach more importance to baptism, than we have generally done, and that they may not attach so much virtue to the direct operations of the Spirit in obedient believers as we do." In regard to the ancient order, he stated that both groups had rejected sectarianism, authoritative creeds, and ecclesiastical councils; in addition, both groups immersed penitent believers and some, though not all, of both groups contended for and practiced weekly communion. The Reformers, he continued, differed from the Christians in "rejecting from communion the unimmersed, and in the ordination of elders or bishops." If there was more than that to Campbell's ancient order, he would be glad to know it and, if convinced it was the ancient order, nothing would prevent him from observing it.[21]

Stone was not impressed with Campbell's distinction between Christians as followers of Christ and disciples as mere learners or scholars of Christ. Pointing to Luke 14:27, "Whosoever doth not bear his cross and come after me, cannot be my disciple," Stone asked if *disciple* was not here defined as *follower*. In Stone's view, the distinction between Christian and disciple that Campbell had proposed could not be found in scripture.[22]

Despite, or possibly because of, what could be interpreted as a breakdown in his relationship with Campbell, Stone continued to seek a union of Christians and Reformers. Earlier in the year he had established a cordial relationship with the Reformer John T. Johnson. Johnson, a lawyer and former

---

[19] *CM* 5 (November 1831), 248–49.
[20] Ibid., 249.
[21] Ibid., 250–51.
[22] Ibid., 253–57.

member of Congress, had been a member of the Baptist church in Great Crossings, just west of Georgetown. Having failed to lead the Great Crossings Baptist Church into Campbell's reformation, Johnson and two others had withdrawn their memberships and formed a Disciples congregation at Great Crossings in February 1831. Two or three others had been added by baptism at their first meeting. At the same time, Johnson had given up the practice of law to devote full time to preaching the gospel. In October the Disciples and Christians in the vicinity of Georgetown and Great Crossings had begun meeting and worshiping together. The prospectus for the 1832 volume of the *Christian Messenger*, published in December 1831, announced that Johnson would join Stone as coeditor of the *Messenger*.[23]

Late in November, there was an informal and private conference in Georgetown regarding the union of the Reformers and Christians. Among those present were the Christian John Rogers and the Reformer John Smith. Earlier in November, Smith had assisted Johnson in a meeting at Great Crossings that had increased the number of Disciples at Great Crossings to around forty. Smith and Rogers expressed their willingness to travel together throughout Kentucky to conciliate and unite congregations of Christians and Reformers. It was agreed, however, that before launching this effort, they would hold a four-day meeting at Georgetown over Christmas Day and a similar meeting at Lexington over New Year's Day and would invite Christians and Reformers from across the state to be present. In the November issue of the *Messenger*, Stone made the following proposal without any reference to a union of Christians and Reformers: "Would it not greatly conduce to the advancement of truth, if the churches (say in the North of Ky.) were to engage two preachers to ride steadily, and preach among them day and night?" Stone reported that two highly qualified preachers, whose names he did not disclose, had been consulted, and each was "anxious to serve his master and the churches in this way." As each had a dependent family, it had been determined that "$300 to each, paid quarterly" would be needed for their support. Stone requested that each church meet "immediately" to act on this proposal and that their deacons inform him how much each member was willing to give so it could be determined whether the proposed plan could be adopted.[24]

The four-day Christmas and New Year's meetings planned by the Georgetown conference were well attended by both Christians and Reformers, and, according to John Smith's biographer, John Augustus Williams, the participants "worshipped and counseled together with one spirit and one accord."[25] Though there are no official records of either meeting, Williams provided an account of the Lexington meeting.

The Lexington meeting was conducted in the modest facilities of the Christian Church on Hill (later named High) Street, a former cotton factory

[23]*CM 5* (January 1831), 6; *CM 5* (December 1831), 286. For the life of John T. Johnson, see John Rogers, *The Biography of Elder J. T. Johnson* (Cincinnati: Privately printed, 1861).

[24]John Augustus Williams, *Life of Elder John Smith* (St. Louis: Christian Publishing Company, 1870), 449; *CM 5* (November 1831), 257–58.

[25]Williams, *Smith*, 449–50.

that had been dedicated by the Lexington Christians just two months be-fore.[26] It was agreed that one speaker from each "party" would deliver an address plainly stating, according to the speaker's perspective, the scriptural ground of Christian union. Smith was selected to represent the Disciples and Stone to represent the Christians. When the selection was announced, Smith and Stone withdrew from the meeting and conferred in private. At length, Stone asked Smith if he preferred to speak first or last. Since Smith stated no preference, Stone stated that he wished Smith would speak first and he would speak last.[27]

Smith stated in his address that the union God enjoins "must be based on the Word of God, as the only rule of faith and practice." He noted that there were "certain abstruse or speculative matters–such as the mode of the *Divine Existence*, and the *Ground and Nature of the Atonement*" that had been the subject of "intemperate discussion" for centuries. He claimed that for several years he had "tried to speak on such subjects only in the language of inspiration," since he believed that it could "offend no one to say about those things just what the Lord himself has said." He further observed that "while there is but one faith, there may be ten thousand opinions; and hence, if Christians are ever to be one, they must be one in faith, and not in opinion." He concluded, "Let us, then, my brethren, be no longer Campbellites or Stoneites, New Lights or Old Lights, or any other kind of *lights*, but let us all come to the Bible and to the Bible alone, and the only book in the world that can give us all the Light we need."[28]

Stone responded in his address that he would not attempt "to introduce any new topic," but would say a few things "on the same subjects already presented by my beloved brother." Stone confirmed that "the controversies of the Church sufficiently prove that Christians never can be one in their speculations upon those mysterious and sublime subjects which, while they interest the Christian philosopher, can not edify the church." He reported that after the Christians had given up all creeds and taken the Bible alone as their rule of faith and practice, he had been led to deliver some "speculative" discourses. Those discourses, he stated, had never "feasted" his heart. He was in perfect accord with Brother Smith "that those speculations should never be taken into the pulpit; but that when compelled to speak of them at all, we should do so in the words of inspiration." He concluded, "I have not one objection to the ground laid down by him as the true scriptural basis of union among the people of God; and I am willing to give him, now and here, my hand."[29]

Williams noted that Stone "turned as he spoke, and offered to Smith a hand trembling with rapture and brotherly love, and it was grasped by a hand full of the honest pledges of fellowship." He reported, "It was now proposed

---

[26]Ware, 242–43.
[27]Williams, *Smith,* 451.
[28]Ibid., 452–54.
[29]Ibid., 454–55

that all who felt willing to unite on these principles, should express that willingness by giving one another the hand of fellowship; and elders and teachers hastened forward, and joined their hand and hearts in joyful accord." "A song arose," he continued, "and brethren and sisters, with many tearful greetings, ratified and confirmed the union." Williams added that "on Lord's day, they broke the loaf together, and in that sweet and solemn communion, again pledged to each other their brotherly love."[30]

The *Messenger* for January 1832 announced "the union of Christians in fact in our country." It also announced that "to increase and consolidate this union," John Smith and John Rogers, "the first known *formerly*, by the name of Reformer, the latter by the name Christian," had been set apart "to ride together through all the churches, and to be equally supported by the united contributions of the churches of both descriptions." In response to the question, "Will the Christians and Reformers thus unite in other States and sections of our country?" Stone and his new coeditor answered: "If they are sincere in their profession, and destitute of a party spirit, they will undoubtedly unite." The coeditors rejoiced to have received information of unions in Rush County, Indiana, and Maury County, Tennessee, noting, "It appears that the spirit of union has simultaneously acted in the three states, and in a very similar way." They encouraged the brethren to give them "intelligence of the progress and triumph of truth, in their different sections of the country," noting, possibly in reference to the previous exchange between Stone and Campbell, "such intelligence is worth more than volumes of dull theology, and vain speculations."[31]

Despite Campbell's reservations, Christians and Reformers had initiated a formal union of the two communions. There were no "articles of confederation." There had been no "general convention" of messengers from all the societies of Christians and Disciples to deliberate on terms and conditions. Though the meetings in Georgetown and especially Lexington had consisted of members and preachers from many churches, neither meeting could have been described as a general assembly of the "whole aggregate" of both parties. Two individuals, Stone, a Christian, and Smith, formerly known as a Reformer, had proposed a formal union among the hundreds of congregations called Christians or Disciples scattered over the continent, without calling upon the different congregations to express an opinion or a wish upon the subject. In short, the union had been initiated in a way not unlike that of the earlier union of the Christians with the Mulkey churches, the Separate Baptist Association in Meigs County, Ohio, and the former Baptists in Indiana. The union, however, had *only* been initiated. It could continue and grow only as embraced by individual congregations and leaders. To increase and consolidate the union, Stone, now fifty-nine years of age, turned his attention.

---

[30]Ibid., 455.
[31]*CM* 6 (January 1832), 6–7, 30.

15

Union with Christ

Stone's efforts to increase and consolidate the union of Christians and Reformers focused on winning Christians to union with the Reformers. Responsibility for winning Reformers to union with the Christians was assumed by John T. Johnson. Stone's efforts included convincing Christians that union with the Reformers did not require giving up their distinctive views of the Son of God and atonement, responding to objections of Christians to views and practices of the Reformers, reassuring the Christians that he had not rejected prayer and the Holy Spirit, no matter what they might infer from the comments and actions of others, and reminding them, all the while, of their commitment to Christian unity.

In an early effort to head off objections to the union from both Christians and Reformers, Stone and Johnson published a joint editorial in April 1832 stating that neither side had "joined" the other. They noted, "One will say, the Christians have given up all their former opinions of many doctrines, and have received ours–another will say, the Reformers have relinquished their views on many points, and embraced ours." Such statements, they observed, were "doing mischief to the cause of Christian union" and were "well calculated to excite jealously, and to give offence." Moreover, they declared, such statements were not true: "We have met, together on the Bible, being drawn together there by the cords of truth–we agreed to walk together according to this rule, and to be united by the spirit of truth." "Neither the Christians nor Reformers," they remarked, "professed to give up any sentiments or opinions previous to our union, nor were any required to be given up in order to effect it." Rather, "We all determined to learn of Jesus, and to speak and do whatsoever he says to us in his word."[1]

In the same issue of the *Messenger*, Stone reported that he was often asked if he had relinquished his former views on the Trinity and the Son of God. He observed, "Should we say we have relinquished them, many who yet honestly believe them would be wounded; and should we say that we have not, then many who honestly reject them, would be offended." Therefore, Stone stated, he was determined to speak and write in the language of the Bible, confident that in so doing he would "speak and write what all Trinitarians and Unitarians believe." "They may," he observed, "entertain different notions or opinions of what we speak and write; to these opinions they are welcome" as

---

[1] *CM* 6 (April 1832), 110.

long as they believe that "the Father sent the Son to be the Savior of the world; that the Son of God lived, died and rose again for our justification and salvation; that the Holy Spirit is given to them that obey him."[2]

A year later, Stone responded in the *Messenger* to a query regarding whether the Son of God was "created" or "derived." He began with a discussion of the history of the question, drawing on sources that he had quoted in his *Letters to James Blythe.* He acknowledged that in years past he had "indulged in specula-tion" on this issue and indicated that "in common with others, who think at all," he had his own opinion on the subject. He stated that he was now "disposed to use scriptural terms alone, when speaking on this subject" and, therefore, called Jesus the "Son of God, the only begotten." He continued, however, that he could see "nothing in scripture to justify the idea of the Son of God being created" and commented on two texts that had been used to argue that the Son was created. As for the derivation of the Son from the Father, he understood that the Son "proceeded from the Father, or was begotten of the Father—or that he was the Son of God." "But," he added, "of the manner of his proceeding from the Father, or of his being begotten, we know nothing by revelation and therefore to speculate on the subject is unwarrantable folly, and has produced incalculable mischiefs."[3]

Stone never considered his views on the atonement to be "speculation." As if to clarify that point following the New Year's meeting in Lexington in January 1832, Stone published in the June 1832 issue of the *Messenger* a three-page summation of his views of atonement, declaring that "as multitudes are now inquiring after the truth…I beg leave to bring to their view the doctrine of atonement as taught in the Holy Scriptures, and as written and proclaimed by some of us many years ago."[4] A year later he entered into a published correspondence on the topic with Thomas Campbell. The correspondence began with Stone's response to Campbell's criticisms of a recently published work on the atonement by Noah Worcester, who had presented a view of the atonement similar to Stone's. Stone continued the correspondence, bringing it to an end in September 1833 only, he stated, because some were "afraid that the passing remarks of Bro. Thomas Campbell and myself will ultimate in a controversy, and injury to the cause in which we profess to be engaged." Stone continued, however, to publish his views of the atonement.[5]

In August 1834, Stone noted a report that he had publicly "relinquished" his "former views of the atonement and many other contested doctrines" at the Lexington meeting in January 1832. "This," he declared, "is not true." "In my address there," he continued, "I did state that in former years I had in-dulged in speculations on some doctrines; but observed, that for some time

---

[2] Ibid., 118–21.

[3] *CM* 7 (May 1833), 138–39.

[4] *CM* 6 (June 1832), 210.

[5] *CM* 7 (July 1833), 204–10. Campbell's article had appeared in *MH* 4 (June 1833), 256–62. Futher installments were in *CM* 7 (August 1833), 225–30; and (October 1833), 293–94. Campbell had responded to Stone in *MH* 4 (August 1833), 421–25; and (September 1833), 439–45. Stone continued with another three installments: (October 1833), 503–9; (November 1833), 548–53; and (December 1833), 594–98. For Stone's later treatments of the doctrine, see *CM* 8 (January 1834), 11–16; (April 1834), 120–23; (October 1834), 288-94.

back these things were viewed by me as useless and injurious, and that I had relinquished them, being determined to speak in the language of revelation." He was astonished to learn that he had been "accused of speculating *again* on the doctrine of atonement" in his letters to Thomas Campbell. "I must be blind," he declared, "if speculation be found there."[6]

Meanwhile, Stone sought to answer objections of Christians to baptism for the remission of sins, receiving into church membership *only* the immersed, and the refusal of the Reformers to commune with the unimmersed. In the February 1832 issue of the *Messenger,* he responded to a correspondent from Bloomington, Indiana, who had written that his ears were "astounded" by the teaching that "immersion makes a part of regeneration; and that none are in the kingdom of Jesus Christ but those who have been inducted by immersion, and none others have a divine right to the Lord's table." Stone acknowledged he believed immersion to be "a divinely instituted means, in connexion with faith and repentance, of salvation, remission of sins and the gift of the Holy Spirit." The significance of immersion, he suggested, was similar to that of an immigrant taking the oath of allegiance to the United States: Prior to taking the oath of allegiance, an immigrant might well love America but was not entitled to the privileges and immunities of citizenship. Immersion, he continued, did not change the heart, but one's "state." He observed that when the Reformers referred to immersion as part of regeneration, they were not using regeneration "in the general acceptation of the term," which meant a change of heart. For the Reformers, he explained, the term "regeneration" meant "a change of state." As for the teaching that none are in the kingdom of Jesus Christ except those who have been inducted by immersion and that no others have a right to the Lord's table, Stone observed that Presbyterians and Methodists excluded from church membership Quakers and others who rejected water baptism. The only difference between excluding the unimmersed from church membership and the practice of the Presbyterians and Methodists, he observed, was the definition of baptism. He noted, "The Presbyterians and Methodists acknowledge many of the Quakers pious and godly people." "Thus," he continued, "we think of many of the pedo-baptists."[7] As for the

---

[6] *CM* 8 (August 1834), 239. Italics mine.

[7] *CM* 6 (February 1832), 60–62. See also *CM* 6 (November 1832), 343. Reformer John Smith claimed in the statement of the beliefs and practices of the Christians that he prepared for his congregation at Mount Sterling, Kentucky, that the Christians "had not for several years past, received any as members of their body without immersion." See *CM* 6 (March 1832), 88–89. In January 1833, Stone responded to a correspondent who charged that he had "forsaken" the Christian Church by adopting the Reformers' views of church membership. "The Christian Church," Stone observed, "was constituted upon the New Testament alone, and not human opinions, as the only rule of her faith and practice—and did formally reject all human Creeds and Confessions as authoritative." Stone acknowledged that he would now "admit no unimmersed person into the church." This was, of course, a departure from the earlier practice of the Christian Church, which had allowed individual members to decide for themselves whether or not they had fulfilled the command to be baptized. Stone repeated that Pedobaptists and Baptists alike required baptism for admission to the church, as did his correspondent. The difference, he observed, was that he "understood immersion alone to be baptism." Stone stated that he could not "see any way according to the law of Christ of entering into his Church but by baptism or immersion." "If my brother," he declared, "or any other bro. shall inform me of any other way in the New Testament[,] I shall rejoice to know it." See *CM* 7 (January 1833), 4–6.

Lord's table, he stated that his practice was to "neither invite nor debar" the unimmersed or the immersed, but simply to quote 1 Corinthians 11:28–29: "Let a man examine himself, and so let him eat of that bread and drink of that cup, for he that eateth and drinketh unworthily, eateth and drinketh damnation to himself not discerning the Lord's body."[8]

Stone concluded his response to his Indiana correspondent with a statement of his hopes regarding the union. "My dear brother," he wrote, "I never saw higher prospects for the spread of truth and true religion than at the present time." "The prayer of the Saviour," he continued, "is in part answered—union of christians is effected among us, and the smiles and approbation of our Lord are evidenced by the faith, obedience and love of many who were lately of the world." "Fear not," he admonished, "be strong in the faith and hope of the Gospel—and obey it too."[9]

In September 1832, Stone issued "An Address to the Churches of Christ" regarding the growing controversy among the Christians over the Reformers' view of baptism. He declared, "There are some amongst us very clamorous against written or printed creeds, who yet have a creed of their own, of which they are as tenacious, as any other sectarian is of his written creed; and they are equally intollerant against those who dissent from their doctrines or opinions." The persons to whom Stone referred were Christians whom he declared had "received it as an article of their unwritten creed that none should be baptized, but such as are saved, and have their sins forgiven, and who have in themselves the evidence of that forgiveness and salvation." Asserting that there were both advocates and opponents of baptism for the remission of sins who did not understand the doctrine, Stone sought to clarify the teaching in order to meet the objections of its opponents. "Does," Stone asked, "the advocate for remission of sins by baptism, plead that by baptism the heart of a sinner is changed and that he is saved from the love and reign of sin?" "If he does," Stone answered, "he is entirely ignorant of the doctrine for this change must take place before he is a fit subject for baptism." The sinner, he continued, "must believe and repent or reform, before he should be baptized." "And what is reformation," he asked, "but change of heart?" Baptism, Stone asserted, did not change the heart of the sinner, but was "a confirmation and seal of his pardon." "But, you may still say," Stone continued, "can God forgive none but the immersed?" Stone answered, "We are far from saying, that God has so bound himself by his plan, that he cannot pardon an humble penitent without immersion!" On the other hand, Stone remarked, "We are assured" that God *will* "forgive the immersed penitent, because his word has assured us he will."[10]

Noting that some had said they would oppose "Campbellism," Stone responded, "In this we wish you success." "But," he added, "beware lest you are either beating the air, not understanding what it is; or lest you oppose the

---

[8] *CM* 6 (February 1832), 62. See also *CM* 8 (February 1834), 51–52.
[9] *CM* 6 (February 1832), 63.
[10] Ibid., 263–65. See also 250–51; *CM* 7 (April 1833), 101–2; and *CM* 8 (May 1834), 135–36.

truth of God, because Bro. Campbell has advocated it." Drawing a comparison, he observed, "But says another, I am determined to oppose Stone's
Arianism, and Socinianism, with all my might." To which he indicated he
would respond, "Amen! But be sure, you fight not an image made by yourself
or by others, and call it Stone's doctrine; and beware lest in your opposition
you lift your arm against the truth of God and do great injury to yourself."
Stating that the refusal to impose opinions as tests of Christian fellowship was
"the principle on which we as christians commenced our course many years
ago," he declared he could not "but view those as departed from this principle, who will not bear with their brethren, because they believe in baptism
for the remission of sins, and because they meet every Lord's day to worship
the Lord in praying, singing, exhorting, and breaking bread." All of the dis-
putants, he added, "believe that immersion is baptism—why should they who
submit to the one baptism contend and separate because they do not exactly
view every design of it alike?" Stone advised: "If you think your brother in
error, labor in the spirit of love and meekness to convince him; but imposing
zeal against him will only harden him against any good impression you would
make." The latter approach, he suggested, would "probably stir up strife, and
ultimately destroy love, which is the bond of union." He admonished, "Let
the unity of christians be our polar star. To this let our eyes be continually
turned, and to this let our united efforts be directed—that the world may believe, and be saved."[11]

In January 1833, Stone responded in the *Messenger* to a letter from his old
friend and colleague David Purviance, who raised several concerns regarding
the place of prayer and the Holy Spirit in the united church. Purviance stated
that some advocates of baptism for the remission of sins objected to praying
for penitent souls, urging that penitents should be directed to be baptized,
and also made light "of a sinner obtaining pardon, or getting religion in the
woods, or behind an old log, in answer to secret prayer." To Purviance such
advocacy of baptism was "a great extreme." Seeking to conciliate both sides,
Stone remarked that he could see no great "extreme" in directing penitent
souls to be baptized. "We have," he declared, "taken the New Testament for
our directory; do we find any precept or example for inviting penitent souls
to come up to the anxious seats, or altars, or before the stand or pulpit to be
prayed for?" "Have we not," he continued, "express examples in that book
for urging such to be baptized straightway?" On the other hand, Stone affirmed that individuals who made light of secret prayer were "undoubtedly"
wrong and "should be boldly reproved by the righteous."[12]

---

[11] *CM* 6 (September 1832), 265–66.
[12] *CM* 7 (January 1833), 18. See also *CM* 6 (December 1832), 364. Stone argued a more
positive view of the practice of inviting penitents to come forward for prayer in March 1832: "I
am very far from thinking that the practice alluded to, is contrary to the letter and spirit of the
gospel; for if it were we cannot conceive how God should have blessed so many in the practice of
it," while insisting, at the same time, that "every well instructed teacher will instantly urge [upon
mourners] the duty of reformation and baptism." See *CM* 6 (March 1832), 86–87. See also *CM* 7
(April 1833), 103.

According to Purviance, another "extreme" in the teaching of baptism was to place "undue reliance on the act of the creature" by making baptism an "indispensable evidence [or assurance] of forgiveness." As a result, Purviance suggested, the creature would look to "his own act," rather than to "what God has done," as the evidence of forgiveness. This scheme, Purviance continued, "excludes or neutralizes any divine communication, any internal witness, or work of the Spirit in the heart as evidence." Stone agreed that placing undue reliance on the act of the creature was an extreme, observing, "How foolishly would Naaman, the Syrian leper, have acted, had he boasted that he had healed himself by dipping himself seven times in the Jourdan!" "Equally foolish and wicked," he declared, "are they who say they saved themselves by being baptized." In the case of Naaman, so with the baptized, Stone asked, "did not the power of God manifest itself?" At the same time, Stone observed, if Naaman had not obeyed God, he would have remained unhealed. As for excluding any divine communication or internal witness of the spirit in the heart as evidence of pardon by making baptism the "only assured evidence" of the remission of sins, Stone could not have agreed with Purviance more emphatically: "Exclude love, joy, peace, etc. as evidences of our acceptance, and salvation, and there is nothing in religion desirable."[13]

Purviance added that he had recently heard a Reformer introduce his sermon by denouncing as "delusion" the practice of preachers praying "that they may be directed to a text, that the word may be brought to their remembrance, and that they may be enabled to preach in the spirit," declaring, instead, that preachers ought to use the judgment and understanding God had given them and choose a text adapted to their audience. Purviance commented that before the sermon was finished he thought the preacher "might have preached better, and his discourse might have been better adapted to his audience if he had pursued the plan he called delusion." Six months later Stone published an article on prayer in which he declared, "Whatever checks the spirit of prayer, must be anti-christian, and destructive to our soul's best interests." He further observed that no one can pray who believes God will not respond to prayer. He explicitly stated that God "will give the Holy Spirit to them that ask him," asserting that without this spirit "a Doctor of Divinity knows nothing as he ought to know, and with it children are wiser than their teachers are." Lest he be misunderstood, Stone added, "I speak not with regard to the FORM OF KNOWLEDGE; but to the spirituality and power of it."[14]

In September 1833, Stone asserted that the sects had recognized the way to "put down" the combined forces of the Christians and those *formerly* known as Reformers was to break up their union. "The device now employed to divide us," he observed, "and which we should dread as the most formidable" was to persuade each side that by uniting with the other side they had "done

---

[13] *CM* 7 (January 1833), 18–19. See also *CM* 6 (December 1832), 364–65.
[14] *CM* 7 (July 1833), 202–3; *CM* 6 (December 1832), 365.

wrong and injured the cause." He indicated that the sects well knew that "The *Reformers* (so called) view with horror the odium attached to the old exploded heresy of Unitarianism or Arianism; and cannot brook the idea of being considered in union with such." The Christians, he observed, "hear our ingenious opponents describe the horrors of Campbellism, of water regeneration; denying the operations of the spirit, establishing a new party, etc." He suggested that in order to clear themselves of "heresy," each side felt compelled to "publicly protest" the views of the other side. While some, he claimed, were "stumbling" on both sides, there was a "middle class" that refused to take the bait. "We," he declared, "have nothing to do with Arminianism, nor Campbellism, nor Calvinism: we renounce all." "The Bible, the Bible," he asserted, "is our religion." Those, he continued, "who believe in, and obey the Saviour; who walk in the spirit, and bear the fruits of the spirit we love, and acknowledge [as] our brethren, altho' they be stigmatized as Campbellites, Arians, Calvinists, Wesleyans, or Baptists."[15]

Stone reminded his readers that "sects" were divided from the body of Christ by "glorying in their different leaders, doctrines, and names." Though he would not "judge" the "multitudes" who cleaved to sectarian "establishments," nor deny that the Lord had blessed them "with his presence and favor for a long time," he argued that "another seal" had been opened a few years before, and "floods of light" had issued upon the "partially benighted world." Buoyed by the numerical increase that accompanied the union of the Christians and the Reformers, he boldly asked, "Can Sectarians boast of God's blessing upon them; and a great increase to their party now, where the truth shines?" He asserted it was "impossible for sects to unite on any human creed." Aware of divisions that were occuring in the Presbyterian and Baptist denominations over theology and missionary organizations, he declared, "The parties are crumbling; and can never more be established but on the one foundation laid by God in Zion."[16]

In October 1833, Stone reminded his readers it was the unity that Christ alone could establish to which the Christians had long been committed. He reported having seen himself in a "late retrospect" of his life, more than a quarter century earlier, addressing "a large, attentive congregation" on the subject of Christian union. He remembered having remarked that there were four different kinds of union. Book union was founded on a creed or confession of faith. Head union was the same as book union, except that the articles of the confession were not written in a book. Water union was founded on immersion into water. Fire union was "the unity of the spirit—a union founded on the spirit of truth."[17]

Fire or spirit union, he argued, alone would "stand," and no other union was "worth the name." "This spirit," he observed, was "obtained through faith, not in a human form or set of opinions, whether written or not written,

---

[15] *CM* 7 (September 1833), 257–58.
[16] Ibid., 258–59.
[17] *CM* 7 (October 1833), 314–15.

but in the Lord Jesus Christ, the Savior of sinners; and by a cheerful obedience to all his known commands." "This spirit," he continued, "leads us to love God and his children—to love and pray for all mankind." He stated that it was fire union "for which Jesus prayed, and by which the world will believe that he is the Christ of God." Employing another image, he observed, "How vain are all human attempts to unite a bundle of twigs together, so as to make them grow together, and bear fruit!" To grow together, he continued, twigs "must first be united with the living stock, and receive its sap, and spirit, before they can ever be united with each other." "So," he asserted, "must we be first united with Christ, and receive his spirit, before we can ever be in spirit united with one another." "Men," he observed, "have devised many plans to unite christians—all are vain." "There is," he admonished, "but one effectual plan, which is, that all be united with Christ, and walk in him."[18]

Despite Stone's efforts, many Christians in Ohio and some in Indiana refused to unite with the Reformers. In their view, the union of the Christians and Reformers was not the spirit or "fire" union that Stone hailed, but a "head" union based on acceptance of the doctrine of baptism for remission of sins. Matthew Gardner, an opponent of the union in Ohio, reported that the Christian-Reformer union consisted of the Christian churches' "receiving the system of doctrine, and adopting the new practice, modes, and forms of the Disciples." "Nor," he continued, "was there one case of union on any other ground."[19] In his November 7, 1832, letter to Stone, Purviance noted that he had hoped for some time "that the brethren would fall into the plan of simply preaching the word; teaching the people to observe all things the Lord has commanded, without manifesting such a partiality for their peculiar and favorite notions [regarding baptism]." This, of course, had been the practice of the Christian preachers when Stone and Purviance had embraced believers' immersion. The difference between the two situations was that when Stone and Purviance accepted believers' immersion as the apostolic form of baptism, they did not view it as a means of salvation. Once one became convinced, as did Stone, that "repent and be baptized for the remission of your sins" was the apostolic answer to the penitent believer's question, "What must I do to be saved," it was difficult *not* to preach one's "peculiar" notion of baptism. Purviance reported that it was said of a colleague whom he loved and esteemed, "Let him take what text he will, and he will soon be in the water."[20]

Stone worked for union in the spirit the rest of his life. By 1834, however, much of his attention was directed toward moving his family from Kentucky to Illinois. This move was occasioned by his concern over slavery, an issue to which he had devoted much attention during the same years he had worked to unite Christians and Reformers.

---

[18]Ibid., 315–16.
[19]Matthew Gardner, *Autobiography*, 74, quoted in Ware, 269.
[20]*CM* 6 (December 1832), 366; *CM* 7 (April 1833), 101.

PART 5

Church and Society

16

"Congress...Will Aid
in the Laudable Work"

Although Stone had emancipated his own slaves "from a sense of right," he had continued to live in a slave-holding society. Moreover, he was a minister in a slave-holding church. The Christian Church had appealed to the whole spectrum of classes in Kentucky society. Whereas the Presbyterians largely represented Kentucky's small middle class, the political and economic leadership of the state was clearly reflected in the leadership of the Christian congregations. The decision at the camp meeting near Lexington in 1808 not to disfellowship slaveholders had not been without consequences. By the 1820s there were a sizable number of slaveholders among both the members and ministers of the Christian Church.[1]

Stone had advised Samuel Rennels that concern for "civil policy" was no argument against manumitting one's slaves. However, John Rogers noted that "subsequent observation" had convinced Stone that in general "something called freedom" which the free blacks had, was "a curse both to them and the whites." Thus, during the 1820s, Stone became a vigorous advocate of the American Colonization Society, whose purpose was "to ameliorate the condition of the Free People of Colour now in the United States, by providing a colonial retreat either on this continent or that of Africa." The founders of the society also believed that slaveholders *would* manumit their slaves if assured of their removal. Though established in 1816 as a voluntary organization, the society sought public funding. In 1821 it purchased a tract of land in Western Africa and established the colony of Liberia to demonstrate to the federal and state governments the feasibility of colonizing free Blacks in Africa.[2]

Stone stated in the third issue of the *Christian Messenger* his intention to "awaken the attention of the West" to the Colonization Society. He followed up on that intention by publishing the society's appeal "to the Clergy of the United States" to take an offering for the society on the Sunday either immediately preceding or following the fourth of July. The appeal also called on the clergy to obtain signatures on the society's petition urging Congress to

---

[1]Stone, *Biography*, 44; Hood, 106.

[2]Rogers in Stone, *Biography*, 292; *National Intelligencer*, January 4, 1817, quoted in Roos, 96; George M. Frederickson, *The Black Image in the White Mind* (New York: Harper & Row, 1971), 11.

fund the colonization of "free People of Colour" who desired to immigrate to the coast of Africa.[3]

In December 1827 Stone stated in the *Messenger* his reasons for supporting the Colonization Society in response to the question, "Is slavery right or wrong according to the New Testament?" Stone replied that "with all Christians," he was assured that slavery as practiced in the United States was wrong. The question, he asserted, was how to "remedy" the evil. Noting that he had demonstrated his hostility to slavery by emancipating the slaves under his authority, he declared he would "be the first to leave the land, in which this should become universal." Thus, in his view, the "only effective remedy" for the evil of slavery was the colonization plan. He confidently observed, "It is believed that our Congress can, and will aid in the laudable work," and that slavery would be removed from America. "The experiment," he reported, "is made, and hundreds have been taken there, and are happy in the enjoyment of liberty." "Their children," he added, "are all at school, and peace, health and plenty smile upon the colony." He also expressed the expectation, shared by other supporters of the society, that the immigrants to Liberia, having become Christians in America, would play a central role in the evangelization of Africa.[4]

Stone continued through the 1820s to promote the society through the *Messenger*. In July 1828 he published a letter from the Colonization Society calling on the clergy to aid in establishing state colonization societies, with subordinate auxiliary associations in the counties or towns of each state.[5] Less than a year later he published "An Oration" delivered in Indianapolis, Indiana, by Dr. S. G. Mitchell calling for the organization of an Indianapolis auxiliary to the national organization. Mitchell, the first physician to locate in Indianapolis, was a Christian who had left Kentucky because of his opposition to slavery. Acknowledging that Indiana was a free state, Mitchell admonished, "Though we in this happy state of the union have none to emancipate, we can assist in making happy those, emancipated by the good and benevolent in our sister states." In "Remarks" appended to the oration, Stone declared, "With the apostle of the Gentiles I speak to all whom I can influence to right: 'Be imitators of me,' in this respect—Unite, as I have done, with this benevolent society and unite speedily."[6] The following month, Stone published an address of his own, inquiring whether Christians would be "idle spectators" while "the greatest and most influential statesmen and politicians of our nation" were "attempting to do justice to our long oppressed brethren of color by removing the free ones to the land of their forefathers." Introducing the image of increasing light, Stone observed that "the question is no

---

[3] *CM* 1 (January 1827), 95–96; (June 1827), 180–81.
[4] *CM* 1 (December 1827), 37.
[5] *CM* 2 (July 1828), 196–98.
[6] *CM* 3 (May 1829), 163–65. For information on Mitchell, see David Edwin Harrell, Jr., *Quest for a Christian America* (Nashville: Disciples of Christ Historical Society, 1966), 100. See also "S. G. Mitchell," in *Encyclopedia of Indianapolis,* ed. David J. Bodenhamer and Robert G. Barrows (Indianapolis: Indiana University Press, 1994), 1012.

longer now, as thirty years ago–Is the slavery of the Africans right or wrong?" In Stone's view, the nation had answered that it was wrong, "both politically and morally." As evidence of his conclusion, he pointed to the federal government's use of armed vessels to suppress the slave trade. "Shall we as a nation–shall we as Christians," he asked, "approve this course of protecting...the liberty of Africa, and not regard her children among us at home?"[7]

Stone also used regional gatherings of the Christians to promote the society. In September 1829, Stone's Georgetown church raised the colonization concern in its letter to the annual meeting of the North Kentucky Conference of the Christians at Berea, in Fayette County. "Brethren," the letter asked, "can we do nothing to aid the good cause of colonizing the free blacks? We wish you not to legislate as a Conference, but can you not, among other matters, converse on this subject, and agree to aid the good cause?"[8]

In February 1830, not long after Stone had raised in the *Messenger* the issue of a possible union of Christians and Reformers, he published an address advocating the organization of a colonization society by Carlisle, Kentucky, pastor John Rogers. After quoting from a circular composed of the reports of colonists who described the general health, climate, and fertility of the colony in the most favorable terms, Rogers noted there were two "classes of the community" who opposed the society. One class consisted of citizens who supported slavery and saw the society as attempting to interfere with the institution. To that class of opponents, Rogers declared that the society "has nothing to do with slavery–it cannot touch it–it has no such power–it can do no more than mourn its existence–than lament that they are forced to witness the unnatural sight of men holding the Constitution of the United States in one hand, which declares that all men are born free and equal, and at the same time with the other, brandishing whips over their slaves!" The other class of opponents of the society "would have all slaves turned loose upon society, in their present unprepared state," and viewed colonization as "a scheme got up by slaveholders, to remove the free blacks, that their slaves may be more valuable; and that they may rivet, more effectually, the chains of slavery upon them!" Defending the aims of the society to those opponents, Rogers argued, "Great as are the evils of slavery, and much as this society deplores them, yet it is well aware, that an immediate, and indiscriminate emancipation of all slaves, would produce evils much greater."[9]

The June issue of the *Messenger* carried news of the organization, on April 21, 1830, of a Colonization Society at Georgetown, with Stone as president.[10] Succeeding issues of the *Messenger* carried firsthand reports from Liberia, including one from John Russwurm, a recent immigrant to the colony, who seemed impressed with both the humanitarian and missionary potential of the colony. "Ah!" Russwurm wrote, "it is so pleasing to behold men who

[7] *CM* 3 (June 1829), 198–99.
[8] *CM* 3 (October 1829), 285.
[9] *CM* 4 (February 1830), 57–62.
[10] *CM* 4 (June 1830), 163–64.

formerly groaned under oppression, walking in all the dignity of human nature, feeling and acting like men who had some great interest at stake; but still
more pleasant to behold them assembled in the house of worship, rendering
thanksgiving and prayer to him who ruleth the nations."[11] The report of a
Captain Sherman of Philadelphia, who had recently returned from the colony,
described the capital of the colony, Monrovia, as consisting of "90 dwelling
houses and stores, two houses of public worship, and a court house." Sherman
noted, "Many of the dwellings are handsome and convenient, and all of them
comfortable."[12]

In the first issue of the *Messenger* for 1831, Stone appealed to Christians to
manumit their slaves and deliver them to the Colonization Society. "Now,"
he wrote, "is the time to try men's souls, and to discern by what spirit they are
actuated." "To see a man zealous in religion," he declared, "and yet retaining
in vassalage his fellow creatures, having by nature an equal right to liberty
with himself, is a lamentable sight to one who loves justice, mercy and fidel-
ity." In response to the objection that the Colonization Society would not be
able to receive all of the free people of color, he replied, "Then let us endeavor to enable them, by becoming members of the society, and by pecuniary assistance." Moreover, he asserted, "The general and state governments
will doubtless aid the good work in freeing America from this foul blot on the
escutcheon of the nation. The state and federal governments smile on the
mighty project, and wink approbation." "Let us," he encouraged, "make the
glorious offer; none have yet been rejected."[13]

In August 1831 the news that bondsman Nat Turner had staged an insurrection in Southhampton County, Virginia, killing some sixty whites in a
twenty-four-hour period, spread terror among whites throughout the South.
Stone published two articles related to slavery as his response to the Turner
uprising in the October issue of the *Messenger*. First, he noted there were thirty
free people of color in his own Scott County who were "willing and anxious"
to go to Liberia. They had applied to the Georgetown Colonization Society
for counsel and assistance. Therefore, the Society had called a meeting for
October 30 at the Scott County Courthouse. "Never," Stone noted, "did justice
and mercy more cordially unite their pleas for our aid in any cause–never
were louder calls addressed to our long slumbering country." The second
article was an account of an antislavery meeting in London that concluded
with the prediction that measures for either gradual or immediate abolition of
slavery throughout the British Empire would soon be proposed and approved
by Parliament. In "Remarks" following the second article, Stone asked, "Shall
England be awake to the evil of slavery?…and shall America, the land of
boasted liberty, lie supinely inactive?" Stone admonished, "Let the freemen
of America blush to be last in the great cause of removing oppression and
bonds from the poor Africans, and of restoring them to that liberty which has

[11] *CM* 4 (July 1830), 178.
[12] *CM* 4 (September 1830), 248.
[13] *CM* 5 (January 1831), 10–11.

been unjustly wrested from them by superior power." Stone recommended that Americans, and in particular "Christians of every order," look to the Colonization Society, which he predicted would "ultimately sweep the black population of America across the Atlantic to the shores of Africa."[14]

In April 1832, Stone published a specific proposal for government support of the colonization effort. The author of the proposal was none other than Alexander Campbell, who had included the proposal in the February issue of the *Millennial Harbinger*. Noting that the national debt was "as good as paid," Campbell recommended that the ten million dollars of federal revenue formerly needed annually to amortize the national debt be applied to the colonization of people of color. Three groups were covered in his plan: "those already free, slaves whom their masters might be induced to emancipate," and "female slaves of certain ages" who would be *purchased* "at certain prices" from slaveholders who would not emancipate. Campbell projected that an appropriation of ten million dollars a year for fifteen or twenty years would rid America of slavery and "bind the union more firmly than all the rail-roads, canals and highways which the treasury of the union could make in half a century."[15]

Southern white reaction to the Turner uprising resulted in the passage of a host of laws in Southern states aimed at protecting the white population from slave insurrections. In the July issue of the *Messenger* for 1832, Stone and coeditor Johnson reported that a friend had informed them that Louisiana had passed a law against encouraging any publication in opposition to slavery and that their Louisiana subscribers were "violent against the Messenger and will not read it" because of their publication of Campbell's proposal. The editors professed to "indulge the hope that no professors of Christianity have rejected the Messenger on this ground—at least, that no friend of reformation has done it." Such, they declared, "would be a burlesque on the profession." They also stated that they had read the law and were conscious that they had published nothing in opposition to the spirit or letter of that law.[16]

Despite the reaction of the Louisiana subscribers to the publication of Campbell's proposal, Stone continued to express hope in the ultimate success of the colonization effort. In February 1833 he published a letter from Captain Seth Crowell, commander of the *James Perkins*, which had conveyed more than three hundred immigrants to Liberia the previous year. Crowell commented that Liberia "has a climate uniformly warm, but by no means so hot or uncomfortable" as he had imagined, noting that the thermometer never rose above 83 degrees during the twelve days of his stay. Crowell also commented that the colony's trade was rapidly increasing and that it was "deemed a rare occurrence" when the flag of a trading vessel of the Americans, the

---

[14] *CM* 5 (October 1831), 236–37, 238.
[15] *CM* 6 (April 1832), 114. See *MH* 3 (February 1832), 86–88. For Campbell's views on slavery, see Harold L. Lunger, *The Political Ethics of Alexander Campbell* (St. Louis: The Bethany Press, 1954), 193–232.
[16] *CM* 6 (July 1832), 222–23.

English, or the French "does not wave in the Bay." Stone noted that he had seen extracts of letters from persons in Virginia, Tennessee, Mississippi, and North Carolina wishing to know how and when arrangements could be made for transporting to Liberia "a great number of emancipated coloured persons" who desired to emigrate. In Stone's view, the supporters of the society had "great reason for encouragement and perseverance in this great and glorious cause."[17]

Turning to his frequently used image of increasing light, Stone declared, "It is evident to all, that as Christianity progresses, and as its light and savor increases, so in the same ratio, do the horrors and injustice of slavery appear, and its asperities and oppressions diminish." Alluding to the union of Christians and Reformers, Stone noted, "The most of those who have lately *reformed*, look at slavery in the light of truth, and turn from the sight with sighs and tears." He observed, alluding to the title of Campbell's journal, the *Millennial Harbinger*, "They are well persuaded that this state of things cannot exist in *Melenial* [*sic*] glory." Stone expressed confidence that "more light and piety will utterly remove the evil." Referring to his own "Christians," in particular, he proclaimed, "Christians in deed will do right, if they have to make great sacrifices in doing it—they will forsake father and mother, brothers and sisters, husbands and wives, houses and lands, and slaves too when convinced of the evil, for the kingdom of heaven's sake."[18]

The facts, however, were that increased demand for slave labor in Mississippi and Louisiana after 1820 had made Lexington a center of the slave trade, tempting Kentuckians to "free" themselves of slavery by selling their slaves. Aware of this temptation, Stone concluded his remarks with a denunciation of the slave trade.

> Let all christians, indignantly frown upon the practice of men buying up droves of negroes for market, and chaining them together, and driving them like brutes, regardless of their tears, which flow at the constant recollection of being torn forever from the loving embraces of parents, or children, or wives, or husbands. Can a christian do this? In the former days of ignorance and darkness, it is possible—but in this day of light, we must doubt.[19]

In the June issue of the *Messenger*, Stone published a report of the departure from New Orleans on April 23, 1833, of an expedition to Liberia that included 102 emigrants from Kentucky. Among the passengers listed in the article were four emigrants "liberated" by the heirs of Stone's former physician, Dr. A. Todd. Stone referred to the work of the society again in September 1833. Responding to the objection that the society did not have funds sufficient to remove all the slaves who might be manumitted, he recommended that every Christian should "hire his slaves for one or two years, and let their

[17] *CM* 7 (February 1833), 62–63.

[18] *CM* 7 (February 1833), 63–64. Italics mine.

[19] Roos, 64–65; *CM* 7 (February 1833), 64. Stone had concluded the address he published four years earlier with a similar denunciation of the slave trade. See *CM* 3 (June 1829), 199–200.

hire be given for their removal." This is what Stone himself had done three years earlier, in the case of a twenty-five-year-old man whom he had inherited and reared from the age of "6 or 8." Acknowledging that many slaves did not want to go to Africa, Stone advised, "Let the offer be made, and the advantages taught them, and then they will be persuaded." If the slaves remained unpersuaded, Stone recommended making "their condition as comfortable as possible" and endeavoring "to prepare their offspring by education to emigrate at a future day." Stone added, "The spirit of emigration is evidently increasing among the blacks" and hailed "in anticipation" the day "when our general government shall take up the subject."[20]

Nevertheless, there was an edge to Stone's comments in September 1833. He was clearly disappointed in the failure of Christians to manumit their slaves. "Who," he asked, "has moral courage enough to do right?" Stone printed no further reports of the work of the Colonization Society. His only reference to the society after 1833 was in response to a letter from Daniel Travis of Illinois, dated January 16, 1834. Travis reported to Stone that among the immigrants to Illinois were individuals "well recommended as christians by churches in the slaves states" who had "sold all their slaves, and now buy farms, and live on the gains of their oppressed fellow creatures." Stone replied that "the conduct of such professors cannot be too highly censured, and reprobated." Acknowledging that he knew Kentuckians who had gone to Illinois after selling their slaves, he stated he did not know how they could be happy when they thought of their former slaves "groaning, and writhing under the burden, and lash of a cruel master—children born for generations and years to come, doomed to perpetual and hard bondage—and this done on account of one dreadful deed—they were sold." "The reflection," he suggested, "must be like a gnawing worm on their conscience." "Some excuse," he noted, "might be plead, if there were not a Colonization Society in our land, which would gladly receive the slaves, and send them to Liberia where they can be happy and free." As before, he suggested that if the slaves were unwilling to go to Liberia, "other ways could be devised, by which their situation might be meliorated." He advised Travis to "endeavor to suffer patiently this affliction," adding, "I know of no present remedy."[21] Neither the federal or state governments nor his own Christians had lived up to his high expectations of their support of the Colonization Society.

The *Messenger* for September 1834 carried a notice of Stone's intention to move to Jacksonville, Illinois, that fall. The notice advised that it was Stone's intention to continue publication of the *Messenger* from Jacksonville after the completion of the current volume and that John T. Johnson would begin a new publication in Kentucky. Although Stone offered no explanation for his decision to relocate, longtime readers of the *Messenger* knew it was related to his opposition to slavery.[22]

---

[20] *CM* 7 (June 1833), 167–68; 7 (September 1833), 274; 4 (December 1830), 276–77.
[21] *CM* 7 (September 1833), 274–75; 8 (March 1834), 94–95.
[22] *CM* 8 (September 1834), 288.

In December 1830 Stone had responded to the rumor that he had become a slaveholder. The basis of the rumor was the fact that Stone had one
African man, two African women, and four African children on his farm in
Georgetown. Stone explained that these persons had been bequeathed to his
wife and her children forever by the will of his wife's deceased mother, which
placed them under the authority of trustees. He stated that because he could
not emancipate them, he was seriously disposed to emancipate himself and
his family from them. Such an emancipation could be effected by moving his
family to a free state, in which case the slaves willed to his wife and children
might be considered free. "This," he had added, "may be realized not long
hence."[23] Although wary by 1830 of the social consequences of a general
emancipation of the slaves, he had remained committed to emancipating individual slaves, whether they immigrated to Liberia or remained in the United
States.

From 1830 to 1835, Stone bought four tracts of land in the vicinity of
Jacksonville, Illinois, amounting to a total of 277 acres. On October 30, 1832,
he bought three lots in Jacksonville, two blocks south of the public square,
which was to become the location of his home. Late in the fall of 1834 Stone
and his family moved to their new home. Four years later Stone had the
satisfaction of confirming that his intention with regard to the Africans who
had been willed to his wife and her children had been accomplished. While
on a trip to Kentucky he paid a visit to the former servants, whom he found
living in Georgetown as a family of free persons. According to a Brother A.
Adams, who accompanied him to their home, Stone made a "full inquiry
concerning their temporal and spiritual welfare" and after much conversation
proposed prayer. Adams reported that all present bowed down before God,
while Stone's "tremulous voice and feeling heart went up to God in devout
supplication," adding that "tears flowed from all eyes."[24]

---

[23] *CM* 4 (September 1830), 276–77; Ware, 296.
[24] Ware, 297; Stone, *Biography*, 294.

17

"The Grand Revolution...
Has Commenced"

Stone had chosen his new home with an eye to his continuing ministry. In the fall of 1834, Jacksonville had a population of eighteen hundred, making it the largest community in Illinois. It was also the location of church-supported Illinois State College. Two years earlier, Stone had spent six weeks in Illinois. With the assistance of Christian preachers Harrison W. Osborne and Josephus Hewitt, both formerly of Kentucky, he had conducted successful meetings in Lawrenceville, Jacksonville, Carrollton, Rushville, Springfield, and other places. He had also effected a union of Christians and Reformers in a well-attended meeting at the recently constructed brick courthouse located in the center of Jacksonville's public square.[1]

As Stone settled into his new home, he was confident that the millennium was near. His confidence was based on his perception of a growing sentiment for Christian union. Not only had Christians and Reformers united, but he believed that Christians "of every name" were recognizing the need for Christian union and overcoming theological differences. In the first issue of the *Christian Messenger* published from Jacksonville, in January 1835, Stone declared that "the present state of christianity, its professors being divided into contending, opposing sects, is in direct opposition to the plan and design of infinite wisdom." Asserting that "Christians of every name" shared his assessment of the present state of Christianity, he admonished, "Be not offended at this plain exposure of error, while the same unhappy fact is acknowledged by you." Instead, he recommended that every Christian take the following steps:

1. Forsake your sectarian establishment—your sectarian name, your sectarian practice.

2. Be established on the foundation of Christ and his Apostles—take his name upon you—be filled with his spirit, and walk in his steps.

He promised that if all Christians would take these steps, "a light would shine upon the world" and "millions would flow to it, drawn by the cords of love, the beauty and excellency of Zion, and the mighty force of truth."[2]

---

[1]Ware, 301–5. See also Don Harrison Doyle, *The Social Order of a Frontier Community: Jacksonville, Illinois, 1825–1870* (Urbana: University of Illinois Press, 1978), 18–38.

[2]*CM* 9 (January 1835), 2–6.

In the same issue of the *Messenger,* Stone began a two-part theological series meant to "pave the way for christians to come to a better understanding of each other," not unlike when he had earlier presented his new theory of atonement in the hope that the millennium was at hand. He aimed to show the fallacy of an "opinion" that had been the point of "endless altercation," the opinion that humanity was created holy but, because of Adam's sin, lost its created holiness, so that all humans are now born sinners. Stone asserted it was accepted by all that holiness in humanity is love of God and humanity, with its corresponding conduct. Stone further stated that a person cannot love or hate anything before knowing that thing; nor can one know anything before one exists. This being the case, he continued, "Adam must have known his God before he loved him, and he must have existed before he could possibly know him." Therefore, he concluded, Adam was "not created a holy spiritual man; but merely a natural man, with physical capacities to know, to will, choose, love and hate." According to Stone, Adam knew and loved God; that is, became spiritual and holy, because "God manifested himself to Adam as his Creator and benefactor." He proposed that Adam also became a sinner by the exercise of his capacities to know, to will, to choose, to love, and to hate.[3]

Stone argued that Adam's descendants inherited from him not sin, but death, referring to Romans 5, the plain meaning of which, he stated, was that "by Adam's one offence all mankind were according to the divine constitution, treated as sinners, by the suffering of death." Stone further argued it was because of death that all of Adam's descendants have sinned. Stone described how death begets sin in the developing human being.

> The soul of the infant, imprisoned in mortal flesh, is continually teased, fretted, and tortured by death in the members of its body. Reason, the helm of self government, is not sufficient, it is too weak, to govern its temper, its conduct and propensities. The child is entirely under the dominion of the flesh, of carnal appetites and passions, and continues so till reason begins to act; at which time the flesh, having had the rule so long, still predominates. He becomes now acquainted with right and wrong. He sees and approves the right, but follows the wrong, greatly influenced by the example of a wicked world. Like a slave he would be free but must do the commands of his master. He is sold under sin, and compelled to obey.[4]

Stone concluded, "As man originally became holy by the exercise of his physical powers on God; as he became unholy by the exercise of the same powers on improper objects; so God has ordained that man should become holy again by the exercise of the same powers on the everlasting gospel."[5]

---

[3]Ibid., 6–7.

[4]Ibid., 8–10.

[5]Ibid. This remained a favorite doctrine of Stone's. See *CM* 12 (November 1841), 8–9; *CM* 10 (May 1843), 12–17; *CM* 14 (June 1844), 42–49.

In this two-part series Stone observed that the notion that humanity was created holy, but due to Adam's sin had lost its created holiness, had led to the corollary that humans "cannot believe, repent, nor obey the gospel, till God by some divine illumination, or powerful operation, extraneous from the word, produce these things in them." This view, though shared by Calvinists and Arminians, had led to interminable disputes between them regarding who would be saved. The alternative view was that "the word of the Lord, with the evidences of its divinity, is so plain that sinners, though fallen and greatly depraved, can, and do...believe that Jesus is the Christ, the Son of God, and through faith...can repent, reform and obey the gospel, and receive salvation, remission, and the Holy Spirit." He noted that for advocating the latter view he had been "driven from the ranks of orthodoxy" thirty years earlier. He was pleased to report, however, that opposition to the latter view was weakening and would soon cease due, he asserted, to the "increasing light, flowing from the book of God."[6]

Stone also reprinted articles in the *Messenger* advocating Christian union by leaders of other churches. In the May issue of the *Messenger* for 1835, Stone reprinted several articles by Cumberland Presbyterians calling for Christian union. In his "Editor's Remark," he rejoiced at the "growing spirit of Christian Union," hailing it as "the dawn of the world's salvation."[7]

Seven months later, in the final issue of the *Messenger* for 1835, he reprinted an article by the prominent Congregationalist Lyman Beecher titled "A Proselyting Spirit Dangerous to the Prosperity of the Church." Beecher argued that the "spirit of proselytism, which regards exclusively the interests of one denomination, and is concerned in bringing men to heaven in one way or not at all, and which disregards the feelings and interests of other churches, is a principle of war" that had exhausted the resources of the church. Beecher concluded with this prayer: "God grant that this generation pass not away, before a delegation from all *Christian denominations* shall assemble, to attend the funeral of bigotry and heresy; and to lay them so deep in the same grave, that they shall not rise till the trumpet of the Archangel shall call them to judgment, to answer for their crimes and to receive the punishment of their deeds."[8]

In his "Remarks" on Beecher's article, Stone exclaimed, "Would to God that all Christians of every name would view this subject in its true merits! and say AMEN, heartily to the Doctor's concluding prayer; and not barely assent, and consent to the petition, but actively engage in sending a delegation at some time and place agreed on, to attend the funeral..." Stone declared that if he could be "heard" by Dr. Beecher (whose son, Edward Beecher, was president of Jacksonville's Illinois College), he would beseech him to designate the time and place of the meeting. He further admonished, "Let all

---

[6] *CM* 9 (March 1835), 52–55.
[7] *CM* 9 (May 1835), 112–15.
[8] *CM* 9 (December 1835), 281–82.

christians, who are in sentiment with the Doctor on this all important subject, speak out, and be not afraid."[9]

Two months later, in February 1836, Stone began a series of articles in the *Messenger* regarding the question, "Why, how, and when should Christians of all names and parties be united in one body?" Stating that "many of all orders are now enlisted in the good cause, and advocate the union of Christians," he indicated that his purpose was "to encourage all the friends of christian union, and to enlist more in the noble cause."[10]

The content of the series was vintage Stone. As to why Christians should unite, Stone argued that Christian union was the will of our Lord and Savior, as expressed in his prayer "that all may be one" reported in John 17:20–21 and in the teachings of the apostles. Stone also argued that it was God's design to "conquer and save the world" by the "union and joint co-operation" of Christians. As to how all Christians could unite, Stone argued that it could never be on the basis of a creed "invented by man," as history showed that such creeds only served to divide Christians. Neither, he continued, could Christians unite on the Bible itself, as long as "opinions of that book are made tests of christian fellowship." Equally impossible, he observed, would be any effort to unite persons without the spirit of Christ. "The attempt to unite righteousness and unrighteousness, piety and impiety, the spirit of Christ and the spirit of the world," he suggested, was "as vain as the attempt to unite fire and water, or light and darkness." Also doomed to failure, he argued, would be any effort to unite while retaining the "different names, by which the different parties are distinguished." "As soon as a man is called a Methodist," he observed, "the Presbyterian looks at him with a jealous eye, and attaches to him all the errors of that sect, which as a dark cloud roll before the view of his mind, and stand in the way of union." Persons who believed that party names had no power to divide, he suggested, "must be ignorant indeed of human nature, as pourtrayed [*sic*] in ancient and modern history, in the political as well as religious circles of the world."[11]

In regard to when Christians should be united, Stone answered "NOW." In response to the demure that in order to "act in concert," each denomination would require time to consider any proposal of union according to its established procedures, Stone advised that individuals unite without waiting for their denominations to act, promising that "if all would act up to their conviction of truth, independently, the great obstacle to christian union would be removed."[12]

In July 1836, Stone published in the *Messenger* a letter signed by eleven missionaries to India calling on the managers of the different missionary societies to send out such missionaries, and such only, as "will unite most cordially with all their missionary brethren of different denominations" and "not

[9]Ibid., 282–83.
[10]*CM* 10 (February 1836), 17.
[11]Ibid., 17–18, 28–30.
[12]*CM* 10 (April 1836), 52–53.

turn aside from the great object of preaching Jesus and the resurrection" to engage in sectarian strife. Pointing to both history and scripture, the missionaries asked where and when God had "ever sent down the special revivings of his grace and Spirit, where real Christians have been at strife about a doctrine or a name?" "On the contrary," they answered, "how soon, even in a revival of religion, has the spirit of disunion extinguished the kindlings of his love and mercy, and buried both Christians and impenitent sinners in moral death." Stone declared that the "deep feeling and solemn earnestness" of the missionaries' appeal would commend it "to every pious heart."[13]

By the fall of 1836, Stone was confident that the union of Christians of every name would soon be achieved. Ironically, one reason for his confidence was the increasing number of Protestants expressing concern over the growth of Roman Catholicism in the United States. Protestants were also increasingly registering concern regarding the growth of "infidelity" and "skepticism" in America.[14] Affirming popular Protestant views of the threats to the United States represented by the growth of those two forces, Stone declared, "Out of this great evil, God will bring good—the union of all christians." "Already," he reported, "they [Protestants] begin to feel the force of this argument." "Partyism," he continued, "must be humbled before it will submit to truth; and that remedy must be powerful that can effect this object, so desirable—so necessary."[15]

A second reason that Stone was confident that the union of Christians of every name would soon be achieved was that Presbyterians were in the throes of the Old School–New School division. The Old School opposed the New School's departure from Presbyterian orthodoxy and its support of missionary societies established by Congregationalists. Baptists were also dividing in the 1830s over the support of missionary societies. Although the divisions of the Presbyterians and Baptists might have been interpreted as indicating that the union of Christians was far from being accomplished, Stone viewed the divisions of the Presbyterians and Baptists as signifying just the opposite. As the Christian Church in the West had emerged out of an earlier Presbyterian division, Stone was confident that the current divisions of the Presbyterians and Baptists would result in fresh recruits to the cause of Christian unity. In the second issue of the *Messenger* published from Jacksonville, in February 1835, Stone reported that a Presbyterian minister "not one hundred miles from Jacksonville" had immersed a person for the remission of sins. He claimed the doctrine preached by the New School Presbyterians and the Christians was "distinguished by only a few light shades of difference." He further stated

[13] *CM* 10 (May 1836), 99–103.

[14] See Ray Allen Billington, *The Protestant Crusade, 1800–1860* (New York: Rinehart, 1938); and Charles I. Foster, *An Errand of Mercy: The Evangelical United Front, 1790–1837* (Chapel Hill, N.C.:University of North Carolina Press, 1960). In January 1836, Stone had printed without comment a Jesuit oath that included the statement "I do renounce and disown any allegiance as due to any heretical king, prince, or state named Protestant, or obedience to any of their inferior magistrates or officers." See *CM* 10 (January 1836), 9.

[15] *CM* 10 (December 1836), 183.

that he "joyfully" anticipated the day when the New School Presbyterians would exchange the name Presbyterian for the name Christian. In November 1836 he boldly announced: "The grand revolution in the Christian World is doubtless commenced. The fire of discord has long been gathering strength in all the sects, and now begins to burst forth in hostile divisions." "The Lord," he declared, "will bring order out of confusion, and that order will be the same established 18 centuries ago."[16]

Stone's confidence that the millennium was at hand was also based on new hope for the abolition of slavery. His disappointment in the nation's response to the colonization scheme had led him to endorse a more radical approach to abolishing slavery. In the April 1835 issue of the *Messenger*, Stone wrote that he had "designed" to give his readers "a few numbers" on the subject of slavery from his "own pen," but had decided, instead, to serialize a tract sent to him by a friend. The tract was an "Address to the People of the United States on Slavery" published by the New England Anti-Slavery Society, organized by William Lloyd Garrison in 1832.[17]

The "Address" called for the immediate abolition of slavery. Noting that it had been said that the slaves were not prepared for liberty, the "Address" asserted that "it is clear that the first step toward civilizing and christianizing the negro is to acknowledge that he is a man, whose confidence we have to gain by confessing that we have wronged him, and endeavoring to repair the injustice by abandoning forever the inhuman principle that man can hold property in man." The "Address" further noted that it had been said that if suddenly emancipated, the slaves would seek revenge against the masters. The "Address" replied that "it would be strange indeed" if the army and militia that had previously "secured the unrighteous authority of the master over the slave, should not be able to uphold the rightful dominion of the law over the freeman." "It seems stranger still," the "Address" further stated, "to suppose, that by an unaccountable perversion of the most natural feelings, the colored man who had no cause for hatred and desire of revenge against the white man, except the fact that he holds him in slavery, should hate, and desire to revenge himself upon him, for restoring him to liberty." The authors of the "Address" buttressed their assertions with the observation that "the history of the past, as well as the experience of our days, does not record one instance in which the immediate abolition of slavery has stirred up the freed man to violence, outrage and war."[18]

The "Address" also warned that the danger of a slave uprising was gaining every year, since the annual increase of the slave population was more than sixty thousand, and every day nearly two hundred children were born into slavery. The "Address" further warned that "as the more northern of the slave states, seeing the advantages of free labor, dispose of their slaves in a more southern market, and by degrees abolish servitude, the whole slave

[16] *CM* 9 (February 1835), 47; 10 (November 1836), 173–74.
[17] *CM* 9 (April 1835), 82.
[18] *CM* 9 (May 1835), 97–98.

population, and with it the danger of a terrible revolution, are crowded together in the more Southern States." Noting that despite these circumstances neither the Southern States nor the Congress had done anything to avert the impending calamity, the writers hailed "the disinterested devotion of the few" who had gone forth to prepare the way for the gospel of universal freedom "by teaching that slavery is a sin of which all the people of this country are more or less guilty, and ought immediately to repent and to reform."[19]

Stone left off printing the "Address" after three installments. In its place, he published in the July 1835 issue of the *Messenger* two articles defending immediate abolition as desirable and not to be feared. The first was an extract of a letter written to the editor of the *Vermont Chronicle* by a resident of the British island possession Barbados, dated March 3, 1835. England had abolished slavery in the British colonies the previous year. "I wish it were possible," the correspondent declared, "to show to all the inhabitants of the United States,–particularly Christians–the demonstration now exhibiting in the West Indies, that *abolition is practicable*–safe, and *immediately* beneficial to all concerned." The writer claimed that "there were in this island, (20 miles by 12) on the first of August last, 80,000 slaves" and of the remaining 40,000 inhabitants, not over 10,000 were white. "I speak what I *know*," he professed, "to be the general view, when I say, that the state of things in town and country is so good–there is such industry, sobriety and order among the whole black population, as to have effected a total revolution in the view of nearly all, who once fought against emancipation step by step...If ever you hear any one speak of the danger of emancipation," the correspondent advised, "point him to all the West India islands, where the blacks are to the whites as ten to one, and where I would as soon sleep with open doors, as I would in any town on the banks of the Connecticut river." [20]

The second article was a report of hopeful prospects of emancipation in the French colonies based on a speech made by the Duc de Broglie in the French Chamber of Peers on February 23, 1835. The Duc de Broglie was reported to have argued that the successful abolition of slavery in the British colonies proved that apprehensions regarding the consequences of abolition were "exaggerated" and that "such a transaction was possible, without causing trouble or disorder; and was compatible with the continuance of the most scrupulous respect for persons of property." This example of the successful abolition of slavery in the British colonies, he was reported to have declared, "had deprived the indefinite continuance of slavery of its last excuse–its last justification."[21]

[19] *CM* 9 (June 1835), 124–26.
[20] *CM* 9 (July 1835), 160–61. The bill to emancipate all slaves in British dominions received the royal assent on August 28, 1833. To ensure the continuing supply of plantation labor, all slaves over six years of age were "apprenticed" to their former masters. Field slaves were to work forty hours a week until 1840. Household slaves were to work full time until 1838. The apprentice system broke down and was abolished for all former slaves August 1, 1838. See Patrick Richardson, *Empire and Slavery* (London: Longmans, Green, 1968), 94–95.
[21] *CM* 9 (July 1835), 161–63.

In the September issue of the *Messenger*, Stone responded to a query from J. V. Himes, the Christian Church pastor in Boston who would later become the foremost promoter of William Miller's predictions of the premillennial return of Christ. Himes asked, "Do the Scriptures justify slavery in any sense?" "If not," Himes continued, "can an American slaveholder justify himself by them, in holding his slaves in perpetual bondage?" Stone answered that the slavery of the Canaanites under the Hebrews was ordained by God as a punishment for the iniquities of the Canaanites. Therefore, he was "disposed" to justify that "species of slavery" that consisted of confining "evil doers" to "labor in a penitentiary or state prison." "But to say that the scriptures approve of and justify the present practice of African slavery in America," he declared, "is to slander that book, and outrage its holy principles." "Slaveholders, as far as my acquaintance extends," he observed, "presume not now to justify the practice on any principle." "They acknowledge the evil," he added, "but plead the difficulties of emancipating them."[22]

In the November issue of the *Messenger*, Stone explained why he had discontinued the "Address of the New England Anti-Slavery Society" after the third installment in June. Not long after he had begun publishing the "Address," he had "heard of the evil effects of the ultra abolitionists in the North" and had "determined to desist from publishing more of the piece, fully persuaded that it would do no good in the present ferment, and might do harm." The evil effects to which he referred were riots and acts of violence against abolitionists. He further noted that "for publishing these few [installments], numbers of my old patrons and friends in the East and South are offended, and have ordered a discontinuance of the Messenger." He declared, "I have in principle and practice been a conscientious opposer of slavery for nearly 40 years; but how to remedy the evil I knew not...I am persuaded it will be done; but I am ignorant of the means by which it shall be accomplished." Meanwhile, he admonished Christians to "beware of being swept from their foundation, the Bible, by temporizing principles and practices."[23]

Stone's confidence that the millennium was near was not based on profits from the *Christian Messenger*. The total number of subscriptions to the *Messenger*, which had reached 2,000 before Stone moved to Jacksonville in the fall of 1834, had dropped to 1,700 by the fall of 1836. Part of the drop in subscribers was a result of his publishing the "Address of the New England Anti-Slavery Society." However, it was not the reduced number of his subscribers, he claimed, but the number of subscribers who had failed to pay their subscriptions, that required him to state in the December issue of the *Messenger* for 1836 that he might not be able to continue publishing the *Messenger*. If he did continue, he added, it would not be until after the winter, as he could not expect to secure paper to print the *Messenger* until spring.[24]

[22] *CM* 9 (September 1835), 203.
[23] *CM* 9 (November 1835), 263.
[24] *CM* 10 (December 1836), 186, 190.

Noting that the December 1836 issue might be the last number of the *Messenger* that he would ever publish, he declared in that issue that he wished to "make a statement of a few doctrines" for which he had been "charged as an errorist from orthodoxy." He prefaced the statement with the observation that he did not pretend "to defend every speculation and opinion" he "may have formerly broached in order to oppose the speculations and opinions of opponents," adding that he wished others would do the same. This was, then, one more attempt to remove doctrinal obstacles to Christian union, offered in confidence that the union of Christians would soon be achieved.[25]

Stone's statement consisted of six items. The first three items related to God the Father, Jesus Christ, and the Holy Spirit. Stone's purpose was to show that to speak of God the Father, Jesus Christ, and the Holy Spirit in the language of scripture alone was sufficient to Christian faith. The fourth and fifth items were the atonement and the way of salvation through faith in the gospel and baptism. The sixth item was salvation itself. Stone testified that by means of faith in the gospel and baptism "we become new creatures, and partakers of the divine nature, without which none will see the kingdom of God." "Let none," he warned, "vainly hope for Heaven, who know not its joys in part on earth–who has not the witnessing Spirit, testifying with his spirit that he is a son of God." "Without this," he added, "religion is but a dream, which will forsake him when he wakes in the morning of the resurrection."[26]

With the beginning in May of the Panic of 1837, which, after a brief economic recovery, was followed by the onslaught of an even more severe depression beginning in 1839, the *Messenger* did not reappear for nearly four years. During those years, Stone, though sixty-four years old on December 24, 1836, worked with other members of his family on his Morgan County farm, four miles southeast of Jacksonville. Stone's daughter Mary (who was also called Polly) had married Lloyd P. Hallack the previous year. On May 12, 1838, Stone sold Hallack three lots in Jacksonville. It is supposed that following this sale Stone moved from Jacksonville to the farm.[27]

Stone also preached in Illinois, Missouri, Kentucky, and Indiana during his hiatus from the *Messenger*.[28] In June 1839 he attended the first state meeting of the Christian churches in Indiana, held at the Kentucky Avenue Christian meetinghouse in Indianapolis. Though Stone's name had not appeared in the notice inviting "able champions of the faith" from neighboring states to attend the Indiana meeting, he delivered five sermons with remarks especially directed to young preachers. The sermons drew such a crowd the Kentucky Avenue building could not accommodate the people, and it was necessary to

---

[25]Ibid., 186.

[26]Ibid., 186–89.

[27]Ware, 306. In a letter dated September 14, 1840, Stone wrote, "I am now almost past labor, yet have to exert my little remaining strength to help on the farm," in Stone, *Biography*, 281.

[28]Stone mentioned having just returned "from Missouri, after an absence from home of five weeks" in a letter dated Jacksonville, Illinois, March 30, 1840. See *CM* 11 (September 1840), 3.

move to the Methodist meetinghouse. Arthur Crihfield, whose name had appeared in the announcement of the Indiana meeting, reported that before returning to Illinois, Stone also "spent some time preaching at Logansport, Bloomington, and other places with considerable success."[29] Despite disappointment over the nation's reaction to the call for immediate abolition of slavery, when in the fall of 1840 Stone resumed publication of the *Messenger*, his confidence that the millennium was near remained undiminished.

[29]Shaw, 93; *Christian Preacher,* August, 1839, 152–53, quoted in Shaw, 93.

18

Christ's Return

Millennialists were divided over whether the coming of Christ to judge the world, which they believed was prophesied in scripture, would be at the beginning or end of the millennium of Christ's earthly rule. Premillennialists believed that Christ would come in judgment at the beginning of the millennium and personally reign on earth with the saints for a thousand years. Postmillennialists believed that Christ would reign spiritually on earth with the saints for the thousand years prior to his coming to judge the world. Stone was a premillennialist, at least from the 1830s onward. In response to a question regarding the coming of Christ, Stone answered in the January 1832 issue of the *Messenger,* "Several events were to take place prior to his coming, which have not yet taken place: as the return and salvation of the Jews, and the fulness of the Gentiles brought in." He added, "Several events will take place *at his coming,* so notorious that it is evident he had not yet come: *as the Millennial Glory;* the resurrection of the dead; and the final judgement, his putting down all the power, rule and authority he had received as Mediator, and delivering up the kingdom to the Father."[1]

Stone's first fully developed statement in the *Messenger* of his view that Christ would return at the beginning of the millennium appeared in October 1833. Just before the beginning of the millennium, he wrote, the "spurious church of Christ" would be judged and destroyed, leaving the "true church of Christ" prepared for the "marriage supper of the Lamb." Immediately after, at the very beginning of the millennium, Christ would come in his glory and destroy all of the "wicked nations of the earth." At that same time, Satan would be bound for one thousand years, during which time he would not have even one subject alive on earth. The saints who had died would rise from the dead, and those who were living would be changed from mortality to immortality, and together they would reign with Christ for the thousand years. There would be no resurrection of the wicked. At the close of the thousand years, Satan would be loosed and the wicked would be raised from the dead. Satan would collect an army composed of the wicked. But just as they

---

[1] *CM* 6 (January 1832), 31. Italics mine.

were gathered, the judgment would set upon them and they would be condemned to suffer the "vengeance of eternal fire."[2]

Key to understanding Stone's millennialism was his view that "the return and salvation of the Jews" and "the fulness of the Gentiles brought in," both of which he believed would precede the return of Christ, depended on the union of Christians. This was a view Stone held in common with many postmillennialists. For Stone, the union of Christians was the hinge on which the millennium turned. Stone was confident the millennium was at hand because he believed God was working in the nineteenth century to unite the church. Convinced God was working to unite the church, Stone's expectation that the "spurious church" would be judged and destroyed just before the return of Christ and the beginning of the millennium, and that Christ would destroy the "wicked nations" at his coming, allowed him to continue to believe the millennium was near even when *other* features of Christ's millennial reign, in particular the abolition of slavery, seemed far from being accomplished. Assured that God was seeking the union of Christians, Stone's expectation that the "spurious church" would be judged and destroyed before the beginning of the millennium also allowed him to exhort the church to reform by threat of God's imminent judgment. Stone's first application of premillenialism in the *Messenger* was in relation to the Christians' practice of slavery. In what turned out to be his last appeal to the Christians to support the American Colonization Society by freeing their slaves and giving them the opportunity to go to Liberia, he advised, "Let not the wares of Babylon, among which are slaves, be found among us at the coming of the Lord. Behold, he comes quickly." Stone applied his premillennial view of Christ's return in the *Messenger* a second time in November 1835, again in relation to slavery. Explaining that he had discontinued the "Address" of the New England Anti-Slavery Society because he believed it "would do not good in the present ferment," Stone advised his fellow Christians, "The day of righteous Judgment is at hand—prepare for it by cleansing yourselves from all filthiness of flesh and spirit that at the coming of the Lord, we may be found without spot and blameless."[3]

Stone declared in March 1841 that he viewed the present time as "the most important age for many centuries past." He offered two reasons for his assessment. First, Protestants had awakened to "the real state of the christian world" and were calling for union. Second, Catholics in Europe and America were "on the alert to subdue the world to their faith," which Stone, like most American Protestants, clearly viewed as a threat to American liberties. "Who,"

---

[2] *CM* 7 (October 1833), 313–14. Stone responded to objections to his views in later issues of the *Messenger*. See 7 (December 1833), 365–66; 8 (April 1834), 119; 8 (May 1834), 145–48. It is not possible to date Stone's adoption of premillennialism with any precision. David Edwin Harrell's statement that Stone was a postmillennialist as late as 1829 is based on his misreading of a statement Stone meant to be a satire of views held by ministers he viewed as his opponents (*Quest for a Christian America*: The Disciples of Christ and American Society to 1866 [Nashville: Disciples of Christ Historical Society, 1966], 39–41).

[3] *CM* 7 (September 1833), 274–75; *CM* 9 (November 1835), 263.

he asked, "can forsee the events just about to astound, and revolutionize the world?" In light of his view of the momentous character of the times, Stone proposed, "Would it not be a good thing to have a convention of the various denominations of Christians to be holden in some central point in America, and there and then consult upon some general points respecting the union of Christians?"[4]

Stone announced in the April issue of the *Messenger* that a "convention of all denominations of Christians" had been called by the Christians in Kentucky and was to be held in Lexington on April 2, 1841. In the May issue of the *Messenger* he published J. T. Johnson's disappointing report of the response of denominational leaders to the Lexington meeting. In June he included in the *Messenger* a report of the meeting by its chief organizer, John Gano, who stated, "It was proved in the Athens of Kentucky, that the leaders of the sects were afraid to meet the truth."[5]

Stone's appeal for a convention of the various denominations of Christians had been made in the midst of growing interest among Baptists and Christians in William Miller's prediction of the imminent return of Christ. Following his conversion in 1816, Miller, a Low Hampton, New York, farmer, had joined the Baptist church and had begun to study the Bible with particular attention to the last times. In 1836 he had published *Evidence from Scripture and History of the Second Coming of Christ, About the Year 1843*. The Panic of 1837 had increased interest in Miller's calculations. However, it was Joshua V. Himes, pastor of a Christian Church in Boston, who had been most responsible for the spread of Miller's views. Himes, who met Miller in 1839, while Miller was on a speaking tour of New England, had equipped Miller with a great chart for displaying his calculations and purchased the biggest tent in the country for Miller's meetings. Himes also edited two journals advocating Miller's predictions, *The Midnight Cry* in New York and *Signs of the Times* in Boston.[6]

In April 1841, Stone published an advertisment for the *Signs of the Times* in the *Messenger* at the "special request" of Himes. In a brief note introducing the advertisement, Stone recommended the journal, stating, "The Signs of the Times affords the best facilities of obtaining a knowledge of the second coming of Christ of any paper now published." A year later, in May 1842, Stone published a summary of Miller's calculations in the *Messenger*. Although Stone stated that "it is a subject worthy of all attention," he indicated that he would "leave the matter [of Miller's calculations] to be determined by the public." Stone noted, however, that Miller argued that the scriptures prophesied that the papacy would lose its dominion in 1798, the very year a French army had entered Rome, established a republican government, and taken the pope as a captive to France. Acknowledging the objection that the papacy still existed, Stone reported that Miller answered that the scriptures did not

---

[4] *CM* 11 (March 1841), 246–47.
[5] *CM* 11 (April 1841), 281; (May 1841), 323; (June 1841), 355.
[6] Jonathan A. Butler and Ronald L. Numbers, *The Disappointed: Miller and Millenarianism in the Nineteenth Century* (Bloomington: Indiana University Press, 1987).

prophesy that the papacy would cease to exist in 1798, but only that it would lose its dominion. Miller's view, according to Stone, was that "Popery, like a person in a consumption, has been ever since consuming, and will continue in this sickly state till it shall be utterly destroyed by the brightness of Christ's coming."[7]

Stone appealed a second time, in May 1843, for a "convention of the churches of all protestant denominations" to consider union. Elaborating on common Protestant views of the threat to civil liberties represented by the growth of Catholicism in America, Stone advised that by their divisions Protestants were "fast paving the way for papal despotism, for papal rule, and for the papal inquisition." He added that their divisions were also "driving thousands to scepticism, and hardening the world of the ungodly to their utter ruin." "Let the churches," he advised, "select their wisest and best men" and let them "come together in the Spirit, and in the spirit of meekness confer on this all important subject [of union]."[8]

Three months later, there having been no response to Stone's appeal, he challenged Miller's view of the sickly status of the papacy, offering an alternative version of an imminent return of Christ. Stone declared that Protestants "have dreamed that the papal power is crippled, consuming and dying, and [that] this monster–the man of sin, the dread of christendom, will soon expire to live no more." The facts, he argued, told a different story: The friends of the papacy were "pouring their thousands of men and money into every land, especially in America, in order to accomplish one great end–the subjugation of the world under her domination and power." Meanwhile, Protestants remained in "hostile bands fighting against one another." "Are we," he asked, "prepared for the contest? for the faggot? for the horrid inquisition?" The "insincere of every party," he observed, would not be able or willing to bear "the fiery trial" and would deny their profession of faith. Thus, persecution, he proposed, might be the means of purifying and uniting the church! "When the infuriated enemies of the real church of God shall be marshalled, and ready to strike the fatal blow," he predicted, "then shall appear the Son of Man in the clouds with power and great glory for the rescue of his people, and for the destruction of his enemies."[9]

The following month, in September 1843, Stone argued in the *Messenger* that the "apostacy" and "man of sin" prophesied in scripture were not limited to the Roman Church. "The apostacy," he argued, "means a departure from the doctrine and Spirit of christianity." The phrase "man of sin," he suggested, "must mean an assumption of powers, and privileges, not granted by the Lord Jesus Christ to any man, or company of men on earth." He declared that "all the christian nations, and churches are partial apostates from the doctrine and Spirit of christianity as taught and practised by Christ and the apostles." He further noted that at the beginning of the century, he had seen "the man of sin

---

[7] *CM* 11 (April 1841), 258; *CM* 12 (May 1842), 218–20.
[8] *CM* 13 (May 1843), 8–9.
[9] *CM* 13 (August 1843), 97–99.

ruling in every sect as viceregent, having assumed the power, and the keys of the kingdom, by which they claim to open and shut the door into the kingdom, and to remit and retain sin at their pleasure." "My settled conviction," he reported, "then was, and yet is, that the disunion of the sects will be the union of christians on the broad foundation laid in Zion, the Bible." Thus, he hailed the divided state of many of the denominations! Stating again his own particular version of millennialism, he declared: "Though the man of sin may prevail over nominal christianity, yet this will drive true christians together," adding triumphantly, "The king himself will soon come to take possession of his own kingdom, and drive off the usurpers from their unlawful seats and reign himself alone over the house of God forever."[10]

Miller had predicted Christ would return sometime between March 21, 1843, and March 21, 1844. In the March issue of the *Messenger* for 1844, Stone began the publication of a series of articles by S. M. McCorkle, who referred to himself as "The Layman." McCorkle was critical of Miller's calculations, believing that it was more likely that Christ would return in 1847 or 1848. He was even more skeptical of the hopes of postmillennialists, such as Alexander Campbell, who taught that Christ would reign on earth spiritually for a thousand years before his return.[11] In their introduction to the series by McCorkle, Stone and D. P. Henderson, a young Illinois preacher with Kentucky roots who had joined Stone as coeditor of the *Messenger* in May 1843, stated that they did not endorse "the correctness of every sentiment advanced" by McCorkle. They noted, "The prophecies of future events to us are very cloudy, and for this reason we have said but little about them." Nevertheless, they added, "The world is sleeping–dreaming about future events of peace, which we fear will never come." "The vials of indignation," they warned, "will be poured out on an unprepared, ungodly world." "Let us," they concluded, "hear the Layman on these points."[12]

In a statement published in November 1844 explaining why he had not and would not publish more on the subject of prophecy, Stone declared: "We have long observed, that when once the mind becomes intensely fixt on this subject, it seems to relax its hold of every other, and is oftener floating in the unexplored regions of fancy, than of truth; and loses the spirit of pure devotion, and contracts a zeal for opinions, and inspires too often an unholy opposition againt those who differ." "Our firm conviction, from observing the signs of the times," he allowed, is "that some mighty revolution is just ahead, and that it behooves all men to be ready to meet it. But, [as to] when, how, or what that revolution may be, we confess our ignorance."[13]

Meanwhile, Stone had acknowledged in the summer of 1844 that the prospects for Christian union appeared "gloomy." He noted, in particular,

[10] *CM* 13 (September 1843), 138–40.
[11] *CM* 14 (March 1844), 348–51, 361–64; (June 1844), 49–53; (July 1844), 68–72; (August 1844), 97–100; (September 1844), 148–53; (October 1844), 175–79.
[12] *CM* 14 (March 1844), 348.
[13] *CM* 14 (November 1844), 216–17.

that ministers were "discordant in their views of truth, and entirely wedded to their systems, from which it seems, they will never move." In March 1844 he had expressed disappointment in the Christian churches. He noted that earlier he had been "greatly cheered" with "the hope that christian union would soon be effected, when so many thousands from the various sects banded together in love, rejecting their party man-made creeds—and taking the Bible alone as the rule by which their faith and lives should be formed—abandoning their party names, and cleaving to the good old name Christian." "Had we only," he continued, "lived and walked in the fear of God, and in the comforts of the Holy Ghost as we commenced, doubtless, the effect anticipated would have been realized; real good men of every sect could not oppose, but would unite in so holy a cause." He lamented that "we have neglected to keep ourselves in the love of God, and in the humility and gentleness of Christ"; that some had "turned aside to vain jangling for opinions, and to provoke to disputation and debate and strife"; and that many were "more intent to proselyte than to covert souls to pure christianity." Three years earlier he had declared, "The secret is this, that want of this spirit, the spirit of Jesus, is the grand cause of division among Christians: consequently, this spirit restored will be the grand cause of union." Promising that "with this spirit, partyism will die," he had warned, "without it antipartyism in profession only, will become as rank partyism as any other, and probably more intolerant."[14]

Nevertheless, he did not relinquish his hope that Christian union *might* soon be accomplished. In June 1844 he noted that he had "sometimes thought that God by some strange, unexpected work in providence, may drive or draw" Christians together. He repeated the notion that "Popery may prevail, and drive the alarmed shepherds together for common safety." "They may unite with their flocks in the truth," he observed, "and spread it through the world." He proposed alternatively that God might unite the church by restoring the miraculous gifts of the Holy Spirit that had ceased since the time of the apostles.[15]

Neither did he give up on the possibility that Christian union might be achieved without papal persecution of the true church or the restoration of the miraculous gifts of the Holy Spirit. In the March 1844 article in which he confessed disappointment in the Christian churches, he nevertheless declared, "Yet there are enough of wise and holy men amongst us to steer the ship by the word and spirit of truth, and the expected good be yet effected." In the introduction to the fourteenth volume of the *Messenger*, published in May 1844, Stone noted that Protestants of every name had formed, or were forming, "antipapal societies, in order to counteract and stop the influence of popery." After expressing his fear that the "reverse" would be the consequence, unless

---

[14] *CM* 14 (June 1844), 41; *CM* 14 (March 1844), 331; *CM* 11 (June 1841), 334.

[15] *CM* 14 (June 1844), 41. The latter idea that God might restore the miraculous gifts of the Spirit as a way of uniting the church was not new to Stone in 1844. He had suggested the same possibility in an article on the Holy Spirit published nearly a decade earlier. See *CM* 9 (August 1835), 178. See also *CM* 9 (December 1835), 281; *CM* 10 (January 1836), 14.

such societies were "managed in the spirit of truth," Stone asserted that if, however,

> all the parties among the protestants would agree to reform their lives, to be holy, humble and obedient to all God's commandments–if they would agree to cease from their unhallowed debates and striving one against the other, and to unite as one to promote godliness and brotherly love in the earth–if they would abandon their human schemes and platforms, exchange them for the Bible and the Bible alone–if they would agree to become active and diligent in their Master's cause, and set an example before their flocks and the world, and exhort them affectionately to follow them as they follow their professed Lord–if they would agree to meet together at the throne of grace in fervent, solemn and faithful prayer, then the spread of popery would cease, and skepticism be confounded and silent if not converted to the Lord.[16]

"Nothing short of this," he vowed, "will save us from the iron grasp of popery–nothing less will save the world."

Less than a year earlier, Stone had expressed his hope for Christian union, on the Bible alone, without persecution of the real church or restoration of miraculous gifts, by an image from the farming world in which he had lived most of his life. Quoting a Catholic priest as having said that "now there were but two great antagonistic powers in christendom…the Roman Catholics who build upon the traditions of the fathers; and…those who rejected all such traditions, and built upon the Bible alone," he wrote, "I have seen sheep pent up in a lean pasture, looking through the crevices of their inclosure at a flock grazing on a rich field at liberty–I have seen their manifestations of anxiety to be with them, in their bleating, and running along the fence to find a place of escape." "At length," he continued, "one made the leap and many followed."[17]

Since Stone believed that Christian unity would precede the "salvation of the world," the judgment of the spurious church, and the return of Christ, he was certain that to work for Christian unity was to hasten Christ's return. Although discouraged in the summer of 1844 by the immediate prospects of Christian union, he repeated his long-standing counsel: "We must be co-workers with God; every one should be engaged; and as large bodies move slowly, let each one begin in himself…"[18]

---

[16] *CM* 14 (May 1844), 4–5.
[17] *CM* 13 (July 1843), 85–86.
[18] *CM* 14 (June 1844), 41. See also *CM* 9 (January 1835); *CM* 11 (June 1841), 333–34.

19

Christ's Kingdom

Beginning in 1842, Stone recommended that Christians not participate in civil government. Behind his adoption of this position were his reactions to two developments. One was his disapproval of the political party system that had emerged since the 1820s.[1] The other was his disappointment with America's failure to abolish slavery.

The drafters of the federal Constitution had not envisioned a party system. The founders believed that parties were formed by self-seeking individuals and were a threat to the order of society and the rights of the citizenry. The first American party, the Jeffersonian Republicans, was organized not as a party, but as a movement to defend the rights of the people against the Federalists, whom Thomas Jefferson charged with having become a party. The Federalists, for their part, accused the Jeffersonians of seeking to form a party. The leaders of the Democratic and Whig parties that emerged in the 1820s after the collapse of the Federalists and the dissolution of the Republicans, accepted parties as inevitable and even constructive. Vigorous contests between Democrats and Whigs developed in all sections of the country, with members of each party predicting that the election of members of the other party would result in disaster for the nation.[2]

Stone maintained the earlier political ideas of harmony and deference enshrined by the Republic's founders. In August 1832 he had allowed in the *Messenger*, "In the present state of society, civil governments are indispensibly necessary." Asserting that "the time is approaching, when the government and laws of Jesus will universally prevail, and all the rest shall pass away, as the fogs of the morning [a reference to the millennium]," he had affirmed that "it is right to support the civil and free government, under which we live, till they exist no more." However, he had observed that he had "long thought that public teachers of christianity should have very little to do with *noisy* politics."

---

[1] Stone's last reference to slavery in the *Messenger* was his publication in May 1841 of a short notice from the *Journal of Christianity* in which the editor of the *Journal*, Christian Church abolitionist Nathaniel Field, praised "the God of JUSTICE" for "simple *justice*" in the case of the *Amistad* captives. The captives were Africans who had been seized in Africa and unlawfully sold as slaves. The Supreme Court had declared them free. *CM* 11 (May 1841), 324; Roos, 129. Field was a medical doctor and editor of a succession of Stone-Campbell journals. See Shaw, 107; Tucker and McAllister, 197.

[2] See Richard Hofstadter, *The Idea of a Party System: The Rise of Legitimate Opposition in the United States, 1780–1840* (Berkeley: University of California Press, 1972).

To see such [a public teacher of Christianity] rise up in the multitude,and make an electioneering speech—with warmth reviling the rulers of the people—speaking reproachfully of prominent men—and extolling their favorites to the skies—to see them very zealous to promote their party—my soul sickens at the sight. See the same preacher in the pulpit—is he equally zealous for religion as for politics! With what face can he teach the people to speak evil of no man?—nor revile the rulers of the people? when just before he had been guilty of these things, and it is yet fresh in the recollection of his audience? Such a preacher must and will sink from that lofty station, which he ought ever to retain in order to be useful to his fellow creatures. He will incur the displeasure of many, and lose the friendship and respect of those, who think politically different from him. In vain, may he expect to do them good by his ministrations. A warm political preacher, or professor of religion, and a warm, devoted and useful preacher of the Gospel, are rarely ever found in the same person.[3]

Stone's instruction to Christians in the election year of 1832 had been to "watch and pray lest you be led away from your duty and your God." Stone was not alone among church leaders in his negative reaction to the emergence of electioneering and political parties. In a letter published in 1819, David Rice, the patriarch of Kentucky Presbyterians, advised his children, "Meddle but little in political matters unless you have a better opportunity for usefulness than seems now to present itself." He added, "Never be a fire-hot republican, nor a fire-hot federalist. As truth ordinarily lies between two extremes, there you are to seek it." Rice stated that candidates who defamed their rivals, boasted of their own intentions or abilities, and bribed the people with spirituous liquors might "imagine" that they were "serving their country," but they were "greatly mistaken." In Rice's view, "the means they use to obtain their election do more injury, by corrupting the morals and political principles of men, than all their services in the legislature do good." In November 1835 Stone published the report of a committee of the Christians in Illinois advising Christians to "cease...to be numbered among the Political aspirants...While we take sides in the Political contests of this evil day, and suffer ourselves to use the common means, by which to advance the interests of any party, we virtually renounce the laws of our King...We cannot counteract the influence of corruption by partaking of its stream." In 1836 the General Conference of the Methodists declared, "It is highly improper for any member of an annual conference to engage in political strife, and to offer for a seat in the legislative councils, or congress hall..."[4]

---

[3] *CM* 6 (August 1832), 251–52.
[4] *The Virginia Evangelical and Literary Magazine* 2 (June 1819), 259–60; *CM* 9 (October 1835), 250; Nathan Bangs, *A History of the Methodist Episcopal Church*, 4 vols. (New York: Phillips and Hunt, 1880), 4:265–66.

Stone proposed that Christians should not participate in civil government in a series of four articles published from 1842 to 1844: a dialogue between two "Christian brethren" regarding "Civil and Military Offices Sought and Held by Christians," "Reflections of Old Age," "Reply to T. P. Ware [a Mississippi lawyer and Christian who wrote to Stone in response to the first article in the series]," and "An Interview Between an Old and Young Preacher." In these four articles, Stone advanced two arguments for why Christians should not seek or hold offices in government. The first argument was that participation in politics had a negative impact on Christian spirituality. In the dialogue, the "brother" representing Stone's view asserted that "it is a stubborn fact, that whenever a Christian seeks for, or holds a civil or military office in the governments of this world, he loses the savor of religion, his zeal, and ardent desire to promote the interest of Zion." The Christian who seeks or holds public office, he continued, "must mingle with the wicked, and conform in some degree with their spirit, and manners. His mind becomes alienated from God and his people, and he loses the spirit of holy contemplation and prayer...Instead of devoting himself to the study of the laws of the king of saints, and of regulating his heart and life by them,...much of his time is necessarily devoted to the study of Caesar's laws, especially that part of them which may particularly pertain to his office."[5]

Stone further argued that the negative impact of politics on spirituality was not limited to Christians who actually sought or held civil and military offices, but extended to all Christians who participated in politics. As early as September 1840, Stone had asserted that "Zion's glory" would not be restored until Christians gave up their "vain attempts to have better laws, and better rulers in the civil government to the neglect of the king and kingdom of peace." He proposed that "had half the zeal been expended in the cause of christianity which of late had been spent by religious professors in state politics, religion would have raised her drooping head, and smiled in hope of better times." In "Reflections of Old Age," he declared he had "never seen a man much engaged in politics and religion at the same time." Must we not conclude, he asked, "that the politics of the day are in opposition to the politics of heaven?" In "An Interview Between an Old and Young Preacher," Stone's young preacher lamented that he could accomplish nothing due to politics, which he declared "appears to be the all absorbing theme, and spring of action among the people of every age, sex, religion, and profession in the land." As an example of the public's infatuation with politics, which the young preacher bemoaned had "banished shame from the heart of the professor, who seems to enjoy the revels of the day" and had even "entered the modest precincts of the women," he described having "accidentally" fallen in with "a large body of men and women, wending their way" to a political meeting. "The young ladies in a separate company," he continued, "rode before in uniform, bearing each a small banner in their hands, following a large flag waving over

---

[5] *CM* 12 (May 1842), 202.

their heads with the names of their candidates written in large letters, and a band of music before them." Remarking that he was "completely astounded at such a novel sight," the young preacher added, "The small still voice of religion cannot be heard in such a turmoil, nor can she have entrance or abode into hearts so heated with politics."[6]

Stone's second argument against Christians' seeking or holding civil or military offices was that the government and laws of Jesus were sufficient to rule the world. In his dialogue, the brother representing Stone's position asked, "Did our Lord ever authorize any uninspired man to legislate for his kingdom?" "To do it," he exclaimed, "is without authority–it is presumption." He further stated that human laws, like their makers, were "ever changing and varying as the wind." They could not, he advised, be made to suit the "cases and interest of all persons, and sections of an empire"; therefore, legislators were "always making and unmaking their laws." The result, he observed, was "continual jars, collision, strife and war. Even our best of human governments, for this very reason, is now tottering and unstable, and must ultimately submit to the divine government, and unchanging laws of our king, before it becomes right." It was wrong, he declared, for Christians to be legislators, or to vote for legislators, as legislators were but representatives of the voters.[7]

In "Reflections of Old Age," Stone related his argument that the government of Christ was sufficient to rule the world to a sweeping view of human history. The first organized government was a theocracy: "God by Moses was the only lawgiver–the judge, and executive." But the Jewish nation insisted that they have a king, and from that day "they never were the same united, devoted people." At length, God changed Israel's government by appointing his Son, Jesus Christ, Lord of all. Jews and Gentiles alike were now "under his government, and bound to obedience to his laws." If all were to submit to Jesus' government, he asserted, "peace, love and harmony would unite, and keep united the now jarring, wretched world." However, in the fourth century the clergy rejected Jesus as king and assumed his government for themselves, finally putting it on "the shoulders of one man, the Pope." Protestants rejected the Pope as king, but substituted themselves in his place, claiming "the right to change the government of the Lord, and to add to his laws, and form governments for the people, and to rule them." The difference between Papists and Protestants was that "the Papists are ruled by one infallible Pope, and the Protestants by many." The lawful king, Christ Jesus, would "shortly put them all down, and reign with his Saints on earth a thousand years, without a rival." Then would "peace be restored to Zion" and "all man made laws and governments be burnt up forever."[8]

In his "Reply to T. P. Ware," Stone contrasted the effect on human behavior of human laws and what he variously referred to as "God's government," "the law of God," "the law of Christ," and "the Gospel." Asserting that the

[6] *CM* 11 (September 1841), 30; *CM* 13 (August 1843), 123; *CM* 14 (December 1844), 225–26.
[7] *CM* 12 (May 1842), 203.
[8] *CM* 13 (August 1843), 124–25.

design of human laws and government was "to make mankind blest and happy in their social relations," Stone proposed: "Let facts answer, let the past history of such laws from their introduction speak.–Since then, the world has been a slaughter-pen of human victims–hatred, strife, war, contention, division and every evil work have followed; and lamentable [as] it is, crime increases under the accumulation of laws." The problem, Stone declared, was that "human laws cannot govern the evil world." "The carnal mind," he continued, "is not subject to them." Indeed, he allowed, "the carnal mind is not subject to the law of God." However, he proclaimed, the gospel "directs to certain duties, in the performance of which, we receive divine power, or the Spirit of God, by which alone we gain the victory over the carnal mind, and are made new creatures in Christ Jesus." As new creatures in Christ Jesus, he argued, "God's law is written on our hearts, and becomes the principle of action, we delight in it, and it is our pleasure to walk in it continually." Social blessing and happiness could not be produced by human laws, but only by the power of the Holy Spirit received through obedience to the Gospel.[9]

What, then, was the Christian's duty to civil government? In the dialogue, the brother representing Stone's views stated that the duty of Christians to civil governments was "to be subject to them, and to all their ordinances, which do not stand opposed to our king's." He indicated, alluding to Acts 4, that in the case of a conflict, Christians were to follow the example of the apostles in obeying God, rather than humanity. He advised that Christians were to "pay tribute to whom tribute is due; custom to whom custom; and honor to whom honor." Christians, he declared, were also to pray for human governments and to "so live and shine" in their own government "as to show its superiority over all human governments, and by this means engage others to receive it and be saved."[10]

In his "Reply to T. P. Ware," Stone stated that Romans 13, which declares that "the powers that be are ordained of God," presented questions of a "serious nature": Are "all the governments of the world ordained of God–the tyranny of the Caesars–the autocracy of Russia–the monarchy of England–the democracy of America–the despotism of the Pope? etc." "Must we," he asked, "be subject to all these powers, never resist them, but always obey them?" In "An Interview between an Old and Young Preacher," the Old Preacher observed,

> If it be the duty of christians under one worldly government to uphold and support that government, then it is the duty of christians living in every worldly government to uphold and support that government; those living in N. America must uphold and support the democracy of *all* the U. States [a reference to laws supporting slavery]; those in Britain, must support the monarchy of England; those in Russia, must

---

[9] *CM* 14 (October 1844), 168. Stone's view of the contrast between the limited power of earthly governments and the rule of Christ may have been influenced by an article by Missouri preacher Jacob Creath, Jr. See *CM* 11 (February 1841), 189–91.

[10] *CM* 12 (May 1842), 202–4.

support the despotism there; those at Rome, must support the government of the pope, the man of sin, the antichrist of our rightful Lord–those in South America must support every petty tyrant that wades through blood to sit in the supreme chair of state.

Referring to Acts 4, Stone indicated that the apostles had obeyed the "higher power" when they "chose to obey God rather than man."[11]

In "An Interview Between an Old and Young Preacher," the young preacher asked how Christians could live on earth in safety without civil government. The Old Preacher answered, "We may imagine a thousand difficulties; but have we not a king in Zion, who is jealous for the glory of his church upon earth? Is he not almighty?" The real issue for the Old Preacher was the church's faith in its king. The way forward might well include suffering. However, "persecution," he proposed, "would add a score to the ranks of Immanuel for [every] one cut off." The church, he continued, would gain conversions from the world by the truth and its suffering for the truth, until "he whose right it is to reign" triumphed over all.[12]

An aspect of the question of the Christian's duty to government was the issue of military service. A peace movement had emerged in the United States after the War of 1812. In the July 1835 *Christian Messenger*, Stone had published portions of a letter by Stephen Thurston refusing a commission from the governor of Maine to be chaplain of a regiment of the Maine militia. Thurston noted that chaplains were expected "to appear on days of regimental reviews, and by solemn prayer, to ask the blessing of God on the labors and service of the occasion." Thurston stated, "As war, in my view, is at variance with the gospel, I cannot consistently *countenance a system of preparation for it.*" Thurston further noted that should the militia be called into active service, he would no doubt be expected to "pray for the success of my nation's cause, and my nation's arms; that the God of armies would give us signal victory and triumph over our enemies."

> And is not this equivalent to praying that God would give us great success in the work of human butchery? that he would enable us to shoot, cut, stab, and destroy our fellow men with great skill, and rapidity; and lay them at our feet, weltering in their gore? Now would this, my duty as a chaplain, comport with my duty as a christian minister? Can prayer for the success of arms, prayer for victory over our enemies, when that victory is to be gained by butchery and blood, be justified in the sight of that God who requires us to love our enemies, and pray for them?[13]

---

[11] *CM* 14 (October 1844), 169–71; (December 1844), 227–28.

[12] *CM* 14 (December 1844), 229–30.

[13] *CM* 9 (July 1835), 157–59. William Ladd, who led in the formation of the American Peace Society in 1828, advocated the formation of a Congress of Nations to interpret international law and a Court of Nations to apply it. In the same July 1835 issue of the *Messenger*, Stone published extracts from a pamphlet calling for adoption of Ladd's plan (ibid., 201–3). Stone was still calling for a Congress of Nations as late as June 1841. See *CM* 11 (June 1841), 358.

Most members of the peace movement distinguished between the use of force in aggression and defense, opposing only the former. However, in 1838 "ultraists" within the movement, led by Henry Clark Wright and William Lloyd Garrison, formed a Non-Resistance Society to oppose the use of force even in self-defense. Wright and Garrison argued that the practice of non-resistance would usher in Christ's reign on earth. Stone had been open, as late as 1827, to arguments in support of Christians defending themselves against aggression. In response to the question, "Is war right or wrong in the king-dom of Christ?" he answered in the *Messenger* that although the gospel "aims a death blow at the very root and principle of war," yet "if an assassin were to enter our houses to kill us, our wives or children, should we not act right in endeavoring to defend ourselves and families? If this be justifiable in a family, it would be equally so in a neighborhood attacked by a band of assassins; and if this be justifiable in a neighborhood, a nation would be justified in repeling by force the aggressions." In his dialogue, published in 1842, Stone addressed the question of whether Christians should go to war. The brother representing Stone's views noted that when Peter "smote a servant of the high priest" in "defence of his master," Jesus said to Peter, "Put up thy sword, for he that taketh up the sword, shall perish by it." Stone further stated, "Nothing ap-pears so repugnant to the kingdom of heaven as war," whether it be Chris-tians "fighting against Christians with deadly hate" or "Christians whose duty and work is to save the world, fighting against the wicked, and hurrying them unprepared into eternal punishment." He seemed to stop short, however, of eschewing war in every situation, stating instead, "As the laws of the kingdom prevail, and have their effect upon the hearts of mankind [*sic*] war precedes. Hence we read of a period in [the] future when the gospel shall triumph, that the nations shall learn war no more." He concluded, "Lord! hasten the happy day!"[14]

By July 1844, Stone had become an advocate of nonresistance. In a lec-ture on Jesus' Sermon on the Mount published in the *Messenger*, Stone noted that nonresistance of "an evil or injurious person" was obviously the meaning of Jesus' teaching in Matthew 5:39: "But I say unto you, that ye resist not evil; but whosoever shall smite thee on thy right cheek, turn to him the other also." Stone advised that by observing this teaching, "you may overcome the injuri-ous person, and bring him to submission to the truth." Christ, he proposed, had "set the example."

> If genuine christianity were to overspread the earth, wars would cease, and the world would be bound together. A nation professing christianity, yet teaching, learning and practicing the arts of war, cannot be the kingdom of Christ, nor do they live in obedience to the laws of Christ—the government is anti-christian, and must reap the fruits of their infidelity at some future day.[15]

---

[14] *CM* 12 (May 1842), 204–5; *CM* 2 (December 1827), 36; Peter Brock, *Pacifism in the United States: From the Colonial Era to the First World War* (1968).

[15] *CM* 14 (July 1844), 65–66.

Stone knew that there would be opposition in the church to his view that Christians should not participate in civil government. In the 1842 dialogue, the character representing Stone's view indicated that he hesitated to speak, knowing his views would be classified as "fanaticism or ultraism." As Stone saw it, however, his views on participation in civil government were only an extension of views long held by the Christians in relation to the church. In his "Reply to T. P. Ware," he stated, "Our brethren have not seen the legitimate issue of what they have been doing, in arguing against human creeds and laws for the government of the church. In doing this they were clearing away the rubbish from the foundation of God's government of the world."[16]

Stone's disapproval of the emerging American political system and his disappointment in the failure of America to abolish slavery did not diminish his belief that the millennium was near. In his 1842 dialogue, one party encouraged the other to speak his mind on whether Christians should seek or hold offices in government by declaring, "The sanctuary, the church of God must be cleansed, and the time draws nigh. Happy the man who shall be instrumental in effecting it." At the conclusion of the dialogue, the same party exclaimed, "If these things be true [that Christians should not participate in government], the Christian world is truly in an awful state of apostacy! It is surely high time to think seriously and reform; for eternity is near." In the conclusion of his "Reflections of Old Age," Stone urged his readers to either show that his opposition to the participation of Christians in the political process was wrong or "labor to promote the great and needed reformation," adding, "If we do not, it will be done by others–the millenium approaches." In "An Interview Between an Old and Young Preacher," the old preacher stated that Israel was never "gathered together from their dispersions, till they returned to the laws and ordinances of God which they had forsaken." This history was written, he continued, "for our example, on whom the ends of the world are come. We must return to the government [the] laws and ordinances of our rightful king, the Lord Jesus, before we shall be ever gathered together and become worthy subjects of his kingdom."[17]

---

[16] *CM* 12 (May 1842), 202; *CM* 14 (October 1844), 167–70.
[17] *CM* 12 (May 1842), 202; *CM* 13 (August 1843), 126; *CM* 14 (December 1844), 227.

Conclusion:
The Spirituality of
Barton Warren Stone

In March 1840, Stone had accepted Alexander Campbell's "friendly invitation" to correspond with him in the *Millennial Harbinger* on a number of points related to the doctrine of atonement. He advised Campbell, however, that the years "have despoiled me of much of that vigor and strength of mind I may have once possessed." He also expressed to Campbell his fear that "though we might discuss those points in a perfect Christian spirit, yet the minds of the people might be withdrawn from humble piety and devotion, to strife, contention, and division."[1]

Although the correspondence continued through several installments, little new light was shed by either party.[2] In the introduction to his third letter to Campbell, Stone remarked: "Hitherto our discussion has proceeded in the mild spirit of the gospel; nor do I fear that we shall depart from it, if truth be our object. If nothing more be effected by this discussion, I hope we shall convince the world of what had been deemed impracticable, if not impossible, that Christians can love one another, and dwell together in unity, and yet differ in sentiment." "One thing is certain," Stone added, "that the Bible student will be more diligently engaged to understand the important things concerning which we write."[3]

Stone's expressed hopes for the correspondence were only partially fulfilled. In May 1841 he replied to Campbell, "I think it is time now to close this discussion, seeing fair debate cannot be had." The following month he wrote, "I am perfectly willing to rest the whole of our discussion with our readers, and if they have received any profit from it, let God have the glory. We have written honestly, I hope; and if we have in any thing erred (and who but his infallibility is exempt from error) we hope it will not be imputed to us for sin." "By long observation, and experience," he added, "I have found that when

---

[1]*CM* 10 (September 1840), 3.
[2]Ibid., 3–28; (October 1840), 37–58; (November 1840), 73–96; (December 1840), 109–18; *CM* 11 (January 1841), 145–54, 157–69; (February 1841), 181–89; (March 1841), 219–32; (April 1841), 261–79; (May 1841), 289–311; (June 1841), 325–30; (August 1841), 397–415.
[3]*CM* 11 (February 1841), 181.

men have exhausted their sum of knowledge in debate, they supply that want with cynical remarks, which produce strife and angry contention. Brother Campbell and myself," he was quick to state, "have not advanced thus far; but we are men, subject to like passions." Moreover, he declared, "My days are nearly numbered, and I wish to spend the remnant of them in preparing myself and others for eternity."[4]

Barton W. Stone's spirituality sprang from the New Light Presbyterian community at Caldwell's Academy, which he joined in January 1790. From his classmates and from James McGready, the Presbyterian preacher who had stirred revival among those students, Stone learned that true and abiding happiness was to be found in knowing and enjoying God. The son of an upper-middle-class Southern family, Stone had arrived at the academy believing happiness was to be found, as in the novels of Fielding and Smollett, through wealth and social status. It was in pursuit of these goals that he had come to the academy. This view of how happiness was to be obtained was discredited for Stone by the authentic happiness he saw in the religious students at the academy and by the preaching of McGready, who proclaimed it was only through relationship with God that human beings could know the happiness they were created to enjoy. Persons who failed to know and enjoy God, McGready warned, stood under God's judgment and wrath and would be cut off forever from the source of all happiness and joy.

Following the instructions of McGready, Stone sought "religion" through the "means of grace," which involved avoiding sin, performing duty, reflecting on the "destitute" human condition apart from Christ, "attending to conscience and the Holy Spirit," seeking God's pardon, praying, meditating upon salvation, and trusting in God to implant the spiritual principle (or the desire for God). At length he caught a view of what McGready called the "saving sight," a view of the excellence of God in having sent his Son to suffer and die for the forgiveness and spiritual renewal of sinners. Finding his heart filled with love for the God so disclosed, Stone had "come to Christ" for the gifts of forgiveness and the Holy Spirit by which he might live a new life to the glory of God.

From both McGready and Caldwell, Stone learned the New Light Presbyterian view that God deals with rational creatures through rational means. The saving sight, according to McGready, was not seen by the eye of the body or by one's imagination, but was beheld by the understanding. God normally called persons to ministry, Caldwell advised, not by performing a miracle but by giving one a "hearty desire to glorify God and save sinners by preaching" and through the encouragement of the ministry.[5]

Stone's theological development was rooted in conflicts between his New Light Presbyterian spirituality and his Enlightenment-influenced view of doctrines and propositions that he found "contrary" to reason. For example, prayer

---

[4] *CM* 11 (May 1841), 311; (June 1841), 329–30.
[5] McGready, "The Saving Sight," 2: 191–92; Stone, *Biography*, 12.

and meditation were critical to his New Light Presbyterian enjoyment of God; hence, doctrine that interfered with prayer could not be accepted. With the doctrine of the Trinity, his efforts to understand propositions that appeared contrary to reason left him so confused that he did not know how to pray. This doctrine also threatened to take away the very subject of his meditation: the excellence of God in sending the Son to die for sinners. Given Stone's understanding of propositions that were contrary to reason, he could not believe that three persons in one God could be real, distinct persons, as that would contradict the teaching that there is but one God. If the Son was not a distinct person who had actually suffered and died, Stone could not see God's moral excellence in his suffering and death for sinners. Neither could Stone believe, given the classical theism of the Westminster Confession that he accepted, that the one true and living God could suffer and die, since it would contradict the teaching that God is "immutable" and without "passions." Hence, Stone adopted Isaac Watts's view that the Son was the soul of Christ, formed before the creation of the world and united to the one God, who in the fullness of time was united with a human body and did suffer and die for sinners. Stone did not require that others adopt his particular "opinions" of the Son of God. Rather, as he stated after the union of the Christians and Reformers, he viewed as Christians all who affirmed that "the Father sent the Son to be the Savior of the world; that the Son of God lived, died and rose again for our justification and salvation; that the Holy Spirit is given to them that obey him."[6]

Stone had suffered a progressive loss of hearing for many years, and in August 1841 he suffered a stroke that paralyzed his left side and impaired his speech.[7] In the 1841–1842 volume of the *Messenger*, which he commenced following his stroke, he included a series on christology. He observed that many people were opposed to discussion of that subject, doubtless because it had been handled "without the guidance of revelation" and had "produced strife, even with blood, and excited angry passions among brethren." However, "If it were wrong to treat this divine subject," he exclaimed, "why should our Lord, and his inspired apostles have mentioned it so often? Surely, they did not think it dangerous, far less unprofitable." His approach was to confine himself "chiefly, if not entirely" to the New Testament in answering the question, "Who is Jesus?" He examined texts from the gospels, Acts, the epistles, and Revelation. He also referred to Isaiah 11 and the Psalms. From his survey of scriptural texts he concluded, "In Jesus we see the perfections of God, not only of power, but of wisdom, love, mercy, truth, faithfulness, all the fullness of Godhead—the very image of God."[8]

A year and a half later, he took up the subject of christology again, employing the same approach. He noted that at the end of Butterworth's

---

[6] *CM* 6 (April 1832), 118–21.
[7] *CM* 11 (November 1841), 2; 4 (August 1830), 209; Stone, *Biography*, 304–5.
[8] *CM* 11 (November 1841), 11–16; (December 1841), 42–44.

Concordance there was an alphabetical listing of the names and titles of Jesus Christ. "It struck my mind forcibly," he wrote, "that we could not engage in a more useful work, than to present our readers with a short dissertation upon each of them; for he who bears these names and titles, is the author and finisher of our faith, and in the knowledge of whom we are commanded to grow."[9] In a dialogue titled "The Knowledge of God," which followed his discussion of the first four names and titles on the list, the character representing Stone's views observed that while "wranglers" used such texts to "support their controversial systems," they had "lost the marrow and fatness of truth." "They know not the truth as it is in Jesus," he asserted, "and therefore it is, that so little of divine life is experienced, and manifested in the hearts and lives of professors of christianity." The world was wrong, he continued, "in speaking of and viewing God and the perfections of God in an abstract manner." The "true way" to view and speak of God was to look to Jesus: "All that love, mercy, grace, faithfulness, truth, power, benevolence, we see in Jesus, in his works, in his words, in his tears, in his sufferings, in his death and resurrection," he proclaimed, "is the true character of God manifested in the flesh."[10]

Stone's difficulties with the Calvinist doctrine of predestination were similar to his difficulties with the Trinity. He had been "enraptured," to use McGready's term, by the excellence of the God who sent his Son to save sinners. Filled with love for this God, he had gone to Christ for the gifts of forgiveness and the Holy Spirit. According to the Calvinist doctrine of predestination, God had determined that some sinners would be saved through faith in the gospel while others would not believe and would be damned. For Stone, this doctrine of predestination contradicted the teaching of God's love for sinners and made it difficult for him to enjoy God or to go to Christ for forgiveness and the Holy Spirit. This problem was resolved for Stone by his belief that God did love all sinners and sought to bring sinners to Christ for forgiveness and the Holy Spirit through the hearing of the gospel. A year and a half after suffering his stroke, Stone wrote his autobiography, "principally," the cover states, "for his children and Christian friends."[11] Describing once again the time shortly after his settlement at Cane Ridge and Concord when "the fires of hell" got hold of him, he declared that Calvinism "is a dark mountain between heaven and earth, and is amongst the most discouraging hindrances to sinners from seeking the kingdom of God, and engenders bondage and gloominess to the saints." Yet, he added, "there are thousands of precious saints in this system."[12]

Stone's problem with the doctrine of substitutionary atonement was an outgrowth of his rejection of the Calvinist doctrine of predestination. According to the doctrine of substitutionary atonement, Christ had died as a substitute for sinners, to pay the penalty for their sins. Having determined that God

---

[9] *CM* 13 (June 1843), 38.
[10] Ibid., 46–47.
[11] Stone, *Biography*, 1.
[12] Ibid., 34.

desired the salvation of all, Stone declared that Christ died for all, which, as his former Presbyterian colleagues were quick to point out, implied–according to the doctrine of substitutionary atonement–that all would be saved. The view that all would be saved contradicted the preaching of the "day of grace," which gave immediacy to the need to come to Christ for salvation. Thus, for Stone, the challenge was to discover from the scriptures how Jesus could have died for all without undermining the urgency of the call to reconciliation with God. His solution was to see Christ's death as a sacrifice for sin that cleanses or frees believers from sin and reconciles them to God. Thus, Christ died for all, but only the sinners who believed in what Stone would eventually call the "designs" or purposes of his death, which showed forth the grace and mercy of God, would be saved.

David Rice noted that the distinguishing mark of the Calvinist doctrines was that they "consider man as totally ruined by his apostasy from God, and make his salvation wholly depend on the free grace of God." It is hard to see how Stone's new doctrines revised this view of humanity. For Stone, as for his New Light Presbyterian forebears, sinners had no power to save themselves, but were saved only by a view of the glory of God in Christ Jesus that made them willing to come to Christ for forgiveness of sin and for the Holy Spirit. In his first published essay on Christian union, Stone defined Christians as persons who trusted in Christ for their present and eternal interests. He added that this implied they were "convinced of their own ignorance and weakness–of their own inability to save themselves." Commenting on the "great good to the Christian Church" that had come as a result of the loss of members to the Shaker mission, Stone observed that by it we are "taught our entire dependence upon the great Head of the Church for all good, and that he only can keep us from falling."[13]

No aspect of Stone's spiritual heritage from New Light Presbyterianism influenced him more than his belief that persons who come to Christ receive the Holy Spirit. For Stone the Holy Spirit was not a person but a power that enabled believers to glorify God. In 1826 Stone stated that all who believed and trusted in Christ had received "the spirit of promise," which he indicated was also referred to as "the spirit of God–the spirit of Christ, or Christ dwelling in us." He defined this spirit as "the spirit of holiness, which when received, hungers and thirsts for righteousness, pants for God and a perfect conformity to his lovely character." He also referred to it as the "spirit of adoption, *whereby we cry Abba, Father.*" The Spirit was not "the form of knowledge," but the "spirituality and power of it." In 1833, he wrote to David Purviance regarding the internal witness of the spirit, stating, "Exclude love, joy, peace, etc. as evidences of our acceptance, and salvation, and there is nothing in religion desirable." Three years later, in what he thought might be his last doctrinal statement, Stone warned, "Let none vainly hope for Heaven, who know not its joys in part on earth–who has not the witnessing Spirit,

---

[13]Rice, "Epistle," in Bishop, 320; *CM* 1 (November 1826), 5–7; Stone, *History*, 46.

testifying with his spirit that he is a son of God." In all of his writings on Christian union, Stone stressed that it is the Spirit that enables Christian union. It was also God's Spirit "by which alone we gain the victory over the carnal mind, and are made new creatures in Christ Jesus" that would make human-kind "blest and happy in their social relations" where human governments and laws had failed.[14]

Stone did not identify the Spirit with any particular human behavior. In his autobiography, he defended the "exercises" associated with the revival, noting, "So low had religion sunk, and such carelessness universally had pre-vailed, that I have thought that nothing common could have arrested the attention of the world; therefore these uncommon agitations were sent for this purpose." In 1834, after the adoption of baptism for remission of sins by many of the Christians, Stone wrote approvingly, "For a number of years back we have neither heard, nor seen" anything like "noise and fuss" among the Christians. In advice to preachers, whom he instructed to "preach in the spirit," he observed that the spirit was not to be confused with a "great vocif-erous zeal and manner," which might be "nothing more than mere animal nature."[15]

The high value that Stone placed on having the Spirit led him to oppose popular amusements, such as dancing, which he believed distracted persons from seeking and enjoying the Spirit. As is evident from his autobiography, Stone also believed that "tea parties" and "social circles" could hinder the spiritual life. Describing a time when social engagements had caused him to nearly make "shipwreck" of faith, he wrote: "Though I still maintained the profession of religion and did not disgrace it by improper conduct, yet my devotion was cold, and communion with God much interrupted."[16]

New Light Presbyterian spirituality was concerned not only with know-ing and enjoying God but also with honoring and glorifying God through the worship of God and the love of neighbor. The influence of Stone's New Light Presbyterian spirituality can be seen in his efforts on behalf of the union of Christians for the salvation of the world and in his opposition to slavery. Al-though in the 1820s Stone supported an approach to ending slavery that did not challenge white racism, he eventually came to see that only by according full respect to the African could the goal of justice for the African slave be achieved. Confident that Jesus Christ would rule the world, he called on Chris-tians in the 1840s to withdraw from civil government and live by God's rule, convinced that America's emerging democratic political order was in conflict with the "politics of heaven."

Late in May 1843, Stone began a three-month tour of Indiana, Ohio, and Kentucky. His son Barton Warren Stone, Jr., who had recently begun preach-ing, and his youngest daughter, Catherine, accompanied him. On Sunday,

---

[14]*CM* 1 (November 1826), 5–7; 7 (January 1833), 18–19; (July 1833), 202–3; (October 1833), 315–16; 10 (December 1836), 186–189; 14 (October 1844), 168.

[15]Stone, *Biography*, 38; *CM* 8 (March 1834), 74; 12 (August 1842), 316–20.

[16]Ibid., 15.

June 10, they arrived in Noblesville, Indiana, where he met with many of the leaders of the Christian churches in Indiana. From Noblesville they traveled to Preble County, Ohio, home of David Purviance. On Sunday afternoon, June 17, Stone surprised many of his "old friends and fellow-laborers" by arriving at New Paris while a meeting was in progress. From New Paris, they traveled to Kentucky, arriving on June 23 at the home of his daughter and son-in-law, Mary Anne and C. C. Moore, in Fayette County, near Lexington.[17]

Stone resided in the Moores' home through August. From the Moores' home, he made visits to several points in Northern Kentucky. When he preached at Carlisle, where the former Concord church then met, several of his old Presbyterian friends attended and greeted him with "demonstrations of affection and good feeling."[18] He was twice at Cane Ridge for meetings extending over a weekend and the following Monday. On the second occasion, embracing the second Sunday in August, Stone preached the closing sermon. Still crippled from the stroke he had suffered two years earlier, he entered the high, boxed-in pulpit of the Cane Ridge meetinghouse with staff in hand. Reading as his text Paul's farewell address to the Ephesian elders, Acts 20:17–36, he related his own ministry and final admonitions to the Cane Ridge congregation to those of the apostle. After the sermon, a parting hymn was sung, and Stone descended from the pulpit and embraced his brethren. As the hymn ended, he knelt among them and prayed for the church and for the world, and especially for the brothers and sisters present, "that they might be faithful unto death, and meet in heaven to part no more."[19]

Stone's return to Kentucky reminded him of his lifelong relationship to African Americans. In an account of the first meeting that Stone attended at Cane Ridge during the summer of 1843, John Gano, pastor of the Cane Ridge church, described Stone's reunion with former associates, declaring, "But while we record the joy of the aged Houston, and Lucky, and Rogers, and others we cannot omit to mention the deep and heartfelt joy of that pious and venerable old servant, brother Charles." It appears from Gano's statement that brother Charles was a slave. In the conclusion of a letter Stone wrote to the Cane Ridge congregation after his 1843 visit, thanking them for their "great love and unbounded kindness" to him when he was last with them and encouraging them to keep the faith, he exclaimed, "May we all–all–old and young–black and white, meet in our Father's house above, and be forever with the Lord!" In advice to a "young preacher," published in January 1844, Stone

---

[17]Ibid., 80–82. Mary Anne was a daughter by his first wife, Eliza. In the April 1842 issue of the *Messenger*, Stone had printed the obituary of her daughter, Eliza C. Clark, who had died just a few weeks short of her nineteenth birthday in Havana, Cuba, where she had been taken by her husband, Robert Clark, in the hope of restoring her health. Stone noted that her remains had been interred in "her father's garden." He also wrote, "Though she was my grand-daughter, I must be permitted to say, she was among the most accomplished literary females of the West, amiable, pious, and a zealous Christian." See *CM* 12 (April 1842), 192.
[18]Stone, *Biography*, 83.
[19]Ibid., 84–92.

added the following item: "Let your charity condescend to men of low estate, and treat them with respect, even the poor African slave. The salvation of their souls is equal to that of the kings of the earth. In death—in heaven, the distinction is lost forever."[20]

Alhough grateful for the expression of love he had received in Kentucky, Stone was not entirely pleased with what he observed of the Kentucky Christians in 1843. Returning to Illinois in September, he began the publication of "A Ramble" in the *Messenger* in which he shared his observations of the Kentucky churches. Religion in Kentucky, he noted, was "onward in its march, but not so triumphant" as he had anticipated to find it, given the large numbers who had recently professed faith in Christ.

"Several things of a serious nature," he asserted, had conspired to check the progress of religion in Kentucky. More attention had been given to making converts than to teaching them how they must live once they had made a profession of faith. In like manner, more recognition was given to evangelists than to pastors. In both cases, this was a serious mistake, as the work of teaching the faith was critical to the life of the church. Moreover, the preachers were almost the only ones engaged "in working in the Lord's vineyard, while the people, and professors are gazing on without employment, without praying, without exhorting one another, without instructing, admonishing and comforting the young converts, and without building them up in the most holy faith." In addition, extravagance in worldly things was siphoning off money needed to support both evangelists and pastors. This was particularly evident, he believed, in the younger Christians, in whom he also observed an alarming lack of "sobriety." "When levity in conversation and manners are exhibited," he asked, "does it not show a light, empty heart—empty of spiritual things?"[21]

Stone was also concerned about what he perceived as a lack of solemnity in worship and in "the house of God." He noted that when the people met for worship, no one prayed or exhorted until the preachers arrived. "True," he allowed, "they sing, but too often with new theatrical, or piano tunes applied to sacred songs without solemnity either in the tune or singer—only a few join, the rest being unacquainted with the tune or song, and before it is learned, another of the same class is introduced." He reported that after the preachers arrived, one long discourse would be delivered after another until the congregation became "wearied and fatigued." The exhaustion of the congregation was evident, he argued, "for as soon as they are dismissed each flies to his hat—puts it on his head in the house of God, and makes a rush to the door, like children dismissed from the disagreeable toil of learning in a school room." Taking off one's hat was a sign of respect. Should we not, he admonished, show "respect for the house of God…and keep our hats off while we remain in it?" He continued, "I never saw a well engaged congregation act thus. They

---

[20]Ibid., 142, 284; *CM* 14 (January 1844), 259.
[21]*CM* 13 (September 1843), 129–32; (October 1843), 166–67; (November 1843), 199–200.

were slow to leave a house, where they had been feasting on heavenly food, or where their minds were solemnly impressed with truth."[22]

Stone drew special attention to what he believed to be a lack of solemnity in observance of the Lord's supper and congregational prayer. He reported that the majority seemed to attend to the Lord's supper "as a duty, or as a custom, and not as a divine privilege—many of them sitting and gazing around on the multitude, and passing events among them, while they were receiving the symbols of the body and blood of Christ!" He noted that at the time of prayer some were kneeling, some sitting, and others standing. "Now," he instructed, "there may be cases in which a congregation cannot kneel, as in a great crowd; but few cases can justify the posture of sitting. It does not shew that reverence which ought to be possessed by every worshipper."[23]

On October 2, 1844, Stone wrote his will. Three hundred and twenty acres of Morgan County land were bequeathed to his youngest sons, Barton and Samuel, who were to maintain their mother and their sister Catherine at the farm homestead as long as their mother and sister remained unmarried and continued to live on the farm. To Catherine he gave one hundred and seven acres of timbered land in Woodford and Marshall Counties. To his wife he gave a house and lots in Jacksonville, along with their carriage and carriage horses. His wife was also to receive half the proceeds from the sale of the press once owned by himself and his last coeditor, D. P. Henderson.[24]

The following day Stone left Jacksonville with Celia and their son Samuel to visit their children and friends in Missouri. An annual district meeting of Missouri Christians was held October 18–21, 1844, at Bear Creek Church in Boone County, three miles north of Columbia. Arriving on Saturday, the nineteenth, Stone was greeted by many brethren and friends whom he had known in Kentucky. However, he was so weak that he soon left the meetinghouse and did not return until Monday, the twenty-first. Though still weak when he returned on Monday, he took the pulpit and preached. T. M. Allen, who had known Stone for many years, wrote the following day, "He can preach well yet. But he looks like time had marked him as a victim for eternity."[25]

Stone spent a day or two with his son Dr. William Bowen Stone before leaving for Illinois. He got no farther than Hannibal, Missouri, where the party stopped at the home of Stone's eldest child, Amanda, and her husband, Captain Samuel A. Bowen. In 1844, Hannibal was a town of twenty-five hundred people. The Bowen home on Front Street was a two-story frame dwelling with a room on each side of a center hall and a porch along the entire front, facing the Mississippi River.[26]

[22] *CM* 13 (September 1843), 132–33.
[23] *CM* 13 (October 1843), 165.
[24] Quoted in Ware, 318–19.
[25] Ibid., 320.
[26] Ibid., 321.

Stone suffered intense pain for several days. In an exposition of Romans 12:7–9 published in the *Messenger* for July 1842, he had declared, "We are bound to glorify God in our death, as well as in life." "Go," he advised, "to the bed of one who has lived for the Lord. No gloom of misdeeds beclouds his face or excites his fears. The smiles of faith and hope sparkle in his face—and praise flows from his feeble tongue. He testifies that God is good and faithful even unto death to those who live for him." Stone declared, "This is loud and successful preaching; and by it, seed is sown which grows up unto eternal life in those who may witness the scene." Stone had written in the letter he sent to the Cane Ridge congregation following his visit in the summer of 1843, "I have shortly to grapple with the fell monster death: O, pray for me, that I may gain the victory."[27]

Tabitha, his second-eldest child, had died four months earlier. Amanda wore mourning clothes. Stone complained and she changed them for a bright garment. Other children and grandchildren came from Illinois and Missouri. He wept only when his son Barton and a daughter arrived at separate times from Jacksonville. On November 8, Stone had a visit from Elder Jacob Creath of Palmyra, Missouri. Creath asked him if he was afraid to die. He replied, "No, my religion has not been the result of mere excitement, nor am I now excited; I know in whom I have believed."[28]

He called his family around him and admonished them individually to fulfill their various responsibilities with honor to themselves and to the glory of God. He urged his daughters Amanda, Polly, and Catherine to bring up their children in the nurture and admonition of the Lord. He admonished his son Barton, who had recently entered the ministry, never to leave the ministry. He asked God's blessings on his son Samuel for Samuel's tenderness to him and urged Samuel to prepare to meet his God.[29]

His physician, D. T. Morton, remarked, "Father Stone, you have been much persecuted on account of the peculiarities of your teaching. Are you willing to die in the faith you have so long taught to others?" Stone answered that he was, that he believed that he had taught the truth, and that he had tried to live what he had preached to others. "But," he added, "it is not by works of righteousness that I have done, but according to his mercy he saved me...It is of grace, it is all of grace."[30]

It was nearly four o'clock in the morning on Saturday, November 9, when Stone asked to be placed in an armchair and requested his pipe. A hymn was sung. Stone repeated the verse that began, "Why should we start, and fear to die?" He called for his son Barton to come to him. After a few moments, leaning his head against his son's shoulder, he died without a struggle or moan.[31]

---

[27] *CM* 12 (July 1842), 273; Stone, "To the Church of Christ at Cane Ridge, Jacksonville, Ill., Oct. 26, 1843," in Stone, *Biography*, 284.

[28] Ware, 322; *CM* 14 (November 1844), 222.

[29] Ibid.

[30] Ibid., 223.

[31] Jacob Creath, Jr., to Bro. Campbell, Palmyra, Nov. 11, 1844, quoted in Stone, *Biography*, 107; *CM* 14 (November 1844), 223.

Stone's family and friends followed a wagon that bore Stone's body back to his Morgan County farm, where he was buried in a locust grove west of the house. Memorial services were conducted first at Concord Church, a few miles south of the farm, on Sunday, December 8, and then at the Jacksonville Church three weeks later. A third service was conducted at Cane Ridge on June 22, 1845. The farm was sold in January 1846, and Stone's body was removed to the cemetery of the Antioch Christian Church, seven miles east of Jacksonville. In 1847 his remains were moved to Cane Ridge.[32] The marble monument provided by the Cane Ridge congregation and other Kentucky friends reads, "Barton W. Stone, Minister of the gospel of Christ and the distinguished reformer of the 19.th Century."

---

[32]Ware, 323.